WITHDRAWN

D0205778

Begging the Question

165
W174b

BEGGING THE QUESTION

Circular Reasoning as a
Tactic of Argumentation

Douglas N. Walton

Contributions in Philosophy, Number 48

GREENWOOD PRESS
New York • Westport, Connecticut • London

Library of Congress Cataloging-in-Publication Data

Walton, Douglas N.
    Begging the question : circular reasoning as a tactic of
argumentation / Douglas N. Walton.
        p. cm.—(Contributions in philosophy, ISSN 0084-926X ; no.
48)
    Includes bibliographical references and index.
    ISBN 0-313-27596-3 (alk. paper)
    1. Reasoning. 2. Fallacies (Logic) I. Title. II. Series.
BC177.W322   1991
165—dc20   90-24984

British Library Cataloguing in Publication Data is available.

Copyright © 1991 by Douglas N. Walton

All rights reserved. No portion of this book may be
reproduced, by any process or technique, without the
express written consent of the publisher.

Library of Congress Catalog Card Number: 90-24984
ISBN: 0-313-27596-3
ISSN: 0084-926X

First published in 1991

Greenwood Press, 88 Post Road West, Westport, CT   06881
An imprint of Greenwood Publishing Group, Inc.

Printed in the United States of America

The paper used in this book complies with the
Permanent Paper Standard issued by the National
Information Standards Organization (Z39.48-1984).

10 9 8 7 6 5 4 3 2 1

In loving memory of my mother,
Olive Helen Walton

6-19-92 MLS 50.70 CATS: 28'92

ALLEGHENY COLLEGE LIBRARY

Contents

Acknowledgments

Research for this work was supported by a Killam Research Fellowship from the Canada Council, a Fellowship from the Netherlands Institute for Advanced Study (NIAS) in the Humanities and Social Sciences, and a Research Grant from the Social Sciences and Humanities Research Council of Canada. The Dean of Arts and Sciences at the University of Winnipeg, Mike McIntyre, should also be acknowledged for his help in making arrangements that enabled the author to spend five months at NIAS in 1987-1988. During this period at NIAS, numerous discussions on the subjects of dialogue theory and fallacies with Erik Krabbe turned out to be helpful when, later, the present project was taken up.

Chapter two is based on the author's previously published article, "Burden of Proof," *Argumentation* 2 (1988): 233-54, revised and supplemented to fit the purposes of this book. Grateful acknowledgment is given to the editors of *Argumentation* for their permission to use this material.

Thanks are due to Frans van Eemeren and Rob Grootendorst, whose conversations and writings on the subject of argumentation have had a powerful and constructive influence on the formation of the ideas developed in this book. Discussions of linked and convergent arguments with John Hoaglund and Michael Schmidt, at the Conference on Critical Thinking at Newport News in April 1988, turned out to provide important motivation and insights for development of the theory of argument reconstruction advanced in chapter three.

Among the many others who have contributed to this book through their conversations or writings, I would especially like to thank Lynn Batten, Charles Harper, John Biro, David Sanford, John Woods, Trudy Govier, Henry W. Johnstone, Jr., Michel Meyer, Jaakko Hintikka, and Nicholas Rescher. Clearly, the work in this book has also been greatly influenced and advanced by the work of the late Charles Hamblin, whom the author remembers with great respect and warmth as a kindly and helpful senior colleague.

My deepest thanks to Amy Merrett for the word processing of this manuscript through its various stages.

Preface

According to a story told by the French comedian Sacha Guitry, three thieves were arguing about how to divide up seven pearls they had just obtained. One of the thieves cut off the discussion by handing two pearls to each of the other two, and announcing, "I will keep three!" The other two thieves were not too happy with this arrangement, and one of them asked, "Why do you get to keep three of the pearls?" The reply: "Because I am the leader." The questioner was still not satisfied by this reply, and asked another question: "Why are you the leader?" To this the man with the three pearls responded, "Because I have more pearls."[1]

According to the story, this argument satisfied the two thieves. It seems that they were both pretty gullible, however, for most of us would agree with Fearnside and Holther's (1959) classification of the argument used to persuade them as an instance of the fallacy of begging the question. We see that the thief's argument is circular. And you have to be pretty dull not to realize that this circular sequence of argumentation is being used as a sophistical tactic to cheat the other two thieves out of their fair share of the pearls.

It has been known at least since the time of the classical Greek philosophers that circular reasoning can be used as a deceptive tactic of argumentation. Logic textbooks since the time of Aristotle have identified begging the question *(petitio principii)* as a fallacy. Curiously, however, there has always been a good deal of confusion and uncertainty regarding the identification of this fallacy. The logic textbooks have never explained very clearly just what is wrong with arguing in a circle, or in determining when an argument is fallaciously circular. More curiously still, there appears even to be very little agreement about the meaning and etymological origins of the phrase "to beg the question." And the texts appear to exhibit very little or no clear agreement on what the expression should properly mean. Indeed, many texts use the phrase in such a broad and sweeping manner that it could be taken to refer critically to virtually any argument that contains an unwarranted presupposition or inadequately supported premise.

Evidently then, we have here a problem worth solving. What is begging the question? And what's wrong with it when it is fallacious or wrong?

In the nineteenth century, Richard Whately, John Stuart Mill, Augustus DeMorgan and Alfred Sidgwick had some insightful, if puzzling things to say about begging the question. Indeed, Aristotle himself had a fair bit to say on the subject, but most of it appears obscure and problematic to the modern reader. And there has been a spate of journal articles on begging the question as a fallacy by twentieth-century authors. But putting all these sources together, along with the accounts given in both traditional and modern logic textbooks, one comes up with many interesting problems and disagreements, but few if any clear answers on what this elusive fallacy amounts to as an error of logical reasoning.

Never before has a book been written on the fallacy of begging the question. Only recently, with the advent of new pragmatic methods and theories of argumentation and informal logic has it become possible to provide a useful analysis of this fallacy. This kind of project has only become feasible through the revival of the Socratic and Aristotelian conception of the art of logical reasoning as a form of interactive conversation or dialogue–"reasoning together by question and reply." Building on this pragmatic concept of reasoned argumentation, the theory is advanced that circular reasoning is not fallacious on the grounds that it is deductively or otherwise invalid, but because it is useless to try to reasonably persuade another party with whom you are engaged in argumentative discussion to accept a conclusion that he doubts by offering him a circular argument where one of the premises presupposes or depends on his acceptance of that same conclusion.

This book offers a new theory of begging the question as an informal fallacy, within a pragmatic framework of reasoned dialogue as a normative theory of critical argumentation. The fallacy of begging the question is analyzed as a systematic tactic to evade fulfillment of a legitimate burden of proof by the proponent of an argument in dialogue by using a circular structure of argument to block the further progress of dialogue and, in particular, the capability of the respondent, to whom the argument was directed, to ask legitimate critical questions in reply to the argument.

To support this analysis of begging the question as a fallacy, there is a chapter on the dialectical contexts of use of an argument, and a chapter on the use of argument diagramming as a technique of argument reconstruction. The current techniques of argument interpretation and evaluation are advanced by the formulation of a set of contexts of dialogue to be used in conjunction with the method of argument diagramming. The powerful method of argument analysis developed in these three chapters is then applied to over one hundred case studies of argumentation where the charge of begging the question is, or has been thought to be an appropriate criticism.

Throughout this work, much-needed light is thrown upon the relation between the problem of circular reasoning and broader issues in the critical analysis of argumentation. Ground-breaking use is made of the pragmatic theory of argument as interactive dialogue where two parties "reason together" to explore a conflict of opinion in a discussion. Normative models of several kinds of dialogue framework of this sort provide standards of "good reasoning" to validate or refute the criticism that a particular argument begs the question.

NOTE

1. This story was related in Fearnside and Holther (1959, p. 167).

Begging the Question

1
Origins, Preconceptions, and Problems

The fallacy of *petitio principii,* or begging the question, also some-times known as circular reasoning or arguing in a circle, is one of the standard, informal fallacies that have traditionally been included for treat-ment in the logic curriculum. This particular fallacy has a long history, going back to Aristotle's discussion of it as a "sophistical refutation," or deceptive tactic of contentious disputation used when two parties "reason together." Due to the neglect of the study of the fallacies in favor of the study of formal logic in the modern period, however, no improvement on Aristotle's analysis of this important fallacy has been made, even in the twentieth century. In fact, in some ways we are worse off, because the Aristotelian context of the fallacy has survived into the modern texts in a garbled and incoherent form that makes the fallacy less comprehensible than it may have appeared to the Greeks.

According to the standard treatment, the basic fallacy is "assuming what is to be proved," but most texts recognize a subcategory of this same error called the fallacy of question-begging epithet. The etymological origin of the term "beg the question" (along with its Latin and Greek counterparts) is problematic, and in fact the term is often misunderstood and misused. Nevertheless, in the nineteenth century three authors of noted logic textbooks, John Stuart Mill, Augustus DeMorgan, and Alfred Sidg-wick, raised some insightful questions about the fallacy of begging the question that merit careful attention. Beginning in 1971, two series of analytical articles appeared that tried to grapple with the problem of begging the question as a logical fallacy. These articles opened up the field for further serious, scholarly investigations, but posed more problems than they solved.

1. THE STANDARD TREATMENT IN LOGIC TEXTS

The standard treatment of the fallacy of begging the question can be found in its barest, quintessential form in the one page of text Copi (1986) devotes to this informal fallacy. Copi called the fallacy that of circular reasoning, or begging the question, and wrote that it occurs "[i]f one assumes as a premise for an argument the very conclusion it is intended to prove" (p. 107). Copi gives two types of examples, both among the most popular examples of this fallacy given by texts.

In the first case, "one and the same proposition occurs both as premise and conclusion," although the two propositions are formulated in a different enough manner to try to obscure their identity. This famous example, repeated in many texts, was originally due to Whately (1836, p. 223):

Case 1.0:   [T]o allow every man an unbounded freedom of speech must always be, on the whole, advantageous to the State; for it is highly conducive to the interests of the Community, that each individual should enjoy a liberty perfectly unlimited, of expressing his sentiments.

This first concept of the fallacy of begging the question (represented by case 1.0) is called the *equivalence conception* in the survey of the standard treatment given in Woods and Walton (1975a, p. 108), said to obtain when the conclusion of an argument is tacitly or explicitly assumed as one of the premises--that is, where the conclusion is equivalent, or even identical to a premise.

The second case given by Copi is an instance of what is called the *dependency conception* of circular argument in Woods and Walton (1975a, p. 108), where some premise depends on the conclusion, in the sense that one needs to accept the conception as a prior requirement of accepting the premise. As Copi notes in presenting his version of the example below (case 1.1), this type of case characteristically involves a chain of arguments.

Case 1.1:   [O]ne may argue that Shakespeare is a greater writer than Krantz because people with good taste in literature prefer Shakespeare. And if asked how one tells who has good taste in literature, one might reply that such persons are to be identified by their preferring Shakespeare to Krantz. Such a circular argument clearly begs the question and is without value as proof.

A similar type of case often used by textbooks has the same general structure of the dependency conception put in the context of a chain of arguments. This case, noted by Hamblin (1970, p. 34), has been used by many textbooks, including Black (1946, p. 236).

Case 1.2:   The context is a dialogue between a man, Smith, and his bank manager, where the manager asks Smith for a credit reference. Smith replies: "My friend Jones will vouch for me." The manager comes back: "How do we know *he* can be trusted?" Smith's reply, "Oh, I assure you he can."

Another favorite example of the same sort has been used by Engel (1976, p. 76), among many other texts.

Case 1.3:   God exists!
How do you know?
The Bible says so.
How do I know what the Bible says is true?
Because the Bible is the word of God!

As Hamblin noted, these three last cases of dependency arguments are also arguments from authority, and therefore involve the equally contentious fallacy of the *argumentum ad verecundiam,* or illicit appeal to authority. Therefore, they are all somewhat problematic as examples of fallacious reasoning, which are supposed to be clear illustrations for textbook use.

Certainly it is not hard to appreciate that some sort of error of circular reasoning is involved in all three cases, however. In the last case, for instance, the ultimate conclusion of the chain seems to be the proposition that God exists. This proposition depends evidentially on the veridicality of the Bible as a source, which in turn is based on the proposition that the Bible is the word of God. However this last proposition in the chain, in turn, is based on the presumption that God exists, which was the initial proposition to be proved by the argument.

Even in this type of case, however, where the fault is simplistic to the point of appearing ridiculous, the precise nature of the error is not too clear. For a committed Christian, the Bible is the word of God, in a sense. At any rate, it is an important part of the testimony through which the Christian learns about, and comes to accept the existence of his or her God. Such testimony is so important to Christian belief, at least in part, because it is supposed to be the record of the words and deeds of the Son of God. However, this circularity in the network of Christian beliefs is, in itself, not necessarily bad, or evidence of some logical error or fallacy inherent in the use of the Bible as a source of religious commitment to theistic beliefs.[1]

More of a good case for a fallacy of circular reasoning emerges if a different sort of background context of dialogue is filled in for this case. The original dialogue, it may be supposed, took place between a religious proponent of the existence of God, and a respondent who doubts, that is, an atheist or agnostic. In this setting, the argument does appear to be fallacious, or at least not very helpful, from the respondent's point of view.

Not being a believer, he is unlikely to accept the Bible as the word of God. In fact, since he even doubts whether God exists, to try to persuade him to change his mind by arguing that the Bible is the word of God, and is therefore a reliable source, is bound to be wholly futile. What is wrong is that the argument is of no useful value, in this context, as an exercise that can have any hope of proving what needs to be proved.

At any rate, the examples above, whatever the final word on them may turn out to be, clearly illustrate the standard sort of case used by the logic textbooks to teach students what is taken to be the fallacy of begging the question (arguing in a circle). This standard approach was already outlined nicely by Whately (1836, p. 220).

Let the name then of "petitio principii" *(begging the question)* be confined to those cases in which one of the Premisses either is manifestly the same in sense with the Conclusion, or is actually proved from it, or is such as the persons you are addressing are not likely to know, or to admit, except as an inference from the Conclusion: as, *e.g.* if any one should infer the authenticity of a certain history, from its recording such and such facts, the reality of which rests on the evidence of that history.

In these words, Whately expressed perspicuously the characteristic dual nature of *petitio principii* that is the standard feature of it in the logic textbook presentations of it as a fallacy, both traditional and current. However, in this very phrasing, a basic problem of the *petitio* as a fallacy is evident. According to Whately's account, the dependency relationship, characteristic of (the one form of) the fallacy, is defined or measured in relation to what the person to whom the argument in question is likely to know or admit. But this immediately presents a problem. For what one person thinks he knows, or is ready to admit in argument, may be, and indeed generally is, quite different from what another person knows or admits. Is the question of whether or not an argument commits the fallacy of begging the question purely subjective? If so, the whole idea of a fallacy of begging the question seems to have been pushed beyond the limits of logic as a discipline.

What then are the equivalence and dependency relations that define the fallacy of question-begging? Here the textbooks are less than helpful, either falling back on metaphors like "An argument cannot pull itself up by its own bootstraps," and "Such an argument spins its wheels," or pointing out that this type of argument does not "prove anything new," or "give us any real *reasons* for believing the conclusion to be true"–see, for example Waller (1988, pp. 188-89). But what kind of failure is this?

If I ask you to prove that Auckland is in New Zealand, and you argue, "Auckland is in New Zealand, therefore Auckland is in New Zealand," your argument is deductively valid–it is logically impossible for the premise to be true and the conclusion false. Indeed, since the premise and the conclusion are the same proposition, the argument could scarcely fail to be valid. To declare otherwise would seem to violate the ancient "law of non-contradiction" to the effect that a proposition cannot be both true and false in the same argument. If circular arguments are deductively valid then, what error or lapse of logic do they commit?

The answer usually given seems to be that if you were to use the argument above to prove to me that Auckland is in New Zealand, I would have the perfectly justifiable right to object that this argument tells me "nothing new"–it gives me no real reason to accept the proposition that Auckland is in New Zealand. But why not, if it is a valid argument? The reason would seem to be that the point of your offering the argument is to convince me or give me some evidence that could lead me to accept, or come to have grounds for accepting the proposition that Auckland is in New Zealand. But the whole point of your offering this kind of argument is that I must have taken up some stance to indicate that there is some possibility for me to doubt this proposition, or at least to seek out evidence or grounds that could be useful in removing such doubts. But the circular argument above, while valid, is not useful for these doubt-removing purposes. There is some sense of *proof* in which it is useless or futile as a proof.

The claim made here, as Hamblin (1970, p. 33) put it, is that what is wrong with inferring something from itself is the presumption of an accompanying "claim to have proved something." But what does such a claim, in general, amount to, over and above a claim of deductive validity of one's argument? The claim, to put it another way, is that begging the question is a failure of proof (in some sense), as contrasted with a failure of (valid) inference. But as Hamblin noted, nobody has made or successfully used a distinction between fallacies of proof and fallacies of inference as a feature of classification or analysis of logical fallacies. Hence we seem to be stuck. Begging the question is a mysterious and unstudied failure of arguments, which, for all we can seem to know, may be a purely subjective failing of an argument. And the textbooks and current state of the art of analyzing this fallacy don't offer any gateway to a theory of fallacious argument that would enable us to understand what kind of error is involved in question-begging arguments, or to verify them as fallacious when in fact they are certifiably erroneous as bad arguments of some sort.

Virtually all logic textbooks that deal with informal fallacies have a section, usually a part of a chapter, on begging the question. Many of the texts also have a separate section on a special type of subfallacy of begging the question called "question-begging epithets," "question-begging terms," or something of the sort. Some of the texts, however, treat this subfallacy under the general heading of the fallacy of begging the question.

2. QUESTION-BEGGING EPITHETS

A special type of question-begging argument, often described as a subcategory of the fallacy of begging the question in logic textbooks, has to do with the meaning of a key term or phrase (epithet) that occurs in the argument. The classical example is the following one, usually attributed to Bentham.[2]

Case 1.4:   This doctrine is heresy.
                Therefore, it should be condemned.

The alleged problem with this type of argument is that the premise, in defining or classifying the doctrine in question by using the negative term "heresy," begs the question by assuming that the doctrine (so described) is one that should be condemned. It is a typical case of begging the question, but the distinctive feature is that the question-begging is due to the meaning, definition, or use of a term or phrase. Hence the fallacy is really a kind of linguistic fallacy, turning on the use of "loaded" terms in argumentation.

A brief sampling of some current textbooks will convey the conventional wisdom on question-begging epithets as a species of fallacy.

According to Engel (1976, p. 79) the *fallacy of question-begging epithets* is the error of using slanted language (epithets) "that reaffirms what we wish to prove but have not yet proved." Since, according to Engel, "to beg the question is to assume the point in dispute," the fallacy of question-begging epithets is to use a word or phrase to beg a question–that is, to suggest that "a point at issue has already been settled when in fact it is still in question." The example given by Engel (p. 80) is the following.

Case 1.5:   This criminal is charged with the most vicious crime
                known to man.

This statement is said to be a case of the fallacy of question-begging epithet because it "attaches prejudicial labels" instead of plainly saying "This man is charged with homicide." Presumably, it begs the question because the man's guilt is assumed when it should be proved. What is supposed to be proved, presumably by the prosecuting attorney, is the proposition that this man is guilty. But to label him a criminal is, presumably again, to antecedently assume that in fact he is guilty. Hence, the argument commits the fallacy of begging the question (assuming the conclusion to be proved).

However, the use of the emotively loaded phrase "the most vicious crime known to man" to describe the crime of murder is not so obviously or clearly objectionable solely because it begs the question. More accurately, the problem with the use of this phrase is one of the deployment of loaded or emotive terminology to suggest by transference that the defendant is a vicious person who deserves to be dealt with severely. To call such a use of language "question-begging," however, may be stretching this category of fallacy more thinly than it can bear.

Two other texts, Copi (1986, p. 103) and Toulmin, Rieke, and Janik (1979, p. 167) cite the use of terms like "screwball radical" and "cowardly pacifist" in argumentation. But in both texts, the main objection appears to be to the complex nature of the expression, which may make a double denial necessary on the part of anyone against whom this epithet is used. We should be careful, however, in this type of case to be aware that the use of a complex expression in an argument (even if the expression is emotionally loaded) does not necessarily amount to committing the fallacy of begging the question.

According to Damer (1980, p. 27), the *fallacy of question-begging expression* "consists in discussing an issue by means of terms that imply a position on the very question at issue." The fault, according to Damer (p. 28), is that the listener is "begged" to infer a particular conclusion instead of being offered evidence to accept that conclusion. This account of the fallacy seems to equate question-begging expression or epithet with lack of adequate evidence being offered for a proposition. For what is wrong, according to Damer, is that the use of a particular term implies a particular position on an issue without giving any good evidence to support that position. The failure is the lack of good evidence offered by the arguer to support his position.

The examples given by Damer support this interpretation of the fallacy. The following case is cited as a questionnaire sent to his constituents by a US congressman.

Case 1.6:   Do you favor the give-away of the Panama Canal?

This case is an instance of question-begging expression, according to Damer, because the inclusion of the expression "give-away" was the congressman's "attempt to lead his constituents to a particular conclusion on the issue of the Panama treaties." But what needs to be questioned here is whether case 1.6 is really an instance of begging the question. From the information given, it is not clear why it is, and in fact it appears to be more reasonable to simply take it as a loaded question that uses a particular term in a way that is not well supported.

Manicas and Kruger (1976, pp. 288-291) distinguish between question-begging expressions and question-begging epithets as two distinct categories of fallacy. An example of what they mean by a question-begging expression is given by the following case.

Case 1.7:   You cannot let this man go free because your sister or
                your wife may be his next victim.

We are told that the fallacy in this case is the assumption "that the man had previous victims and is thus guilty." If the assumption is that the man is guilty, then in a criminal trial, this (unproven) assumption would beg the question by assuming the very conclusion to be proved by the prosecution.

However, the problem in this case is not so much traceable to a single expression like "victim." It seems instead to be a run-of-the-mill case of begging the question more than a distinctively linguistic fallacy of the use of terminology.

By contrast, as Manicas and Kruger define it, fallacy of question-begging epithets is the attempt to persuade by using certain expressions of confidence in argument like "obviously," "certainly," "surely," "it is clearly evident," and the like. But the use of these terms can constitute an assumption of what is supposed to be proved, according to Manicas and Kruger, because "the conclusions dealt with in discourse on controversial subjects ordinarily do not lend themselves to the type of conclusive proof suggested by such terms." So described, however, the fallacy committed in this type of case seems more like that of *argumentum ad ignorantiam* than that of begging the question. This fallacy consists of the unjustified leap of confidence when one argues that a proposition must definitely or certainly be true because (even though there may be only a little evidence in favor of it) nobody has proved it false. The fault here is a kind of "bullying," or pressing ahead too confidently in argument, by using phrases like "certainly," "nobody could deny," and the like. But it is far from obvious that the problem in these types of cases is exclusively, or even distinctively, the fallacy of question-begging epithets.

One of the strongest influences in determining the nature of present-day treatments of the fallacy of question-begging epithets appears to have been Jeremy Bentham's section on question-begging appellatives in his *Book of Fallacies* (Part IV, chapter one). Bentham advocated a very broad definition of the fallacy of begging the question, applying it to the use of emotionally loaded terms that can be used to support one's own side of an argument or to undermine one's opponent's side. He called such terms *question-begging appellatives,* in a way that is very similar to the usage of recent logic textbooks as outlined above.

According to Bentham (1838, 1962, p. 436), the fallacy of *petitio principii* (begging the question) occurs when "[i]n answer to a given question, the party who employs the fallacy contents himself by simply affirming the point in debate." This seems an appropriate definition to the extent that it ties the fallacy to the point to be made (conclusion to be established) in a disputation. However, it appears to be an unfavorable definition in another respect, for Bentham interpreted it very broadly, allowing it to encompass any instance of a proposition asserted but not proven, where that proposition should be proved in the debate. By such a definition, the fallacy of begging the question has become indistinguishable from simple lack of evidence or proof in an argument. This broadness is a real problem in Bentham's account.

According to Bentham's account, appellatives can be divided into three types: (1) neutral, (2) eulogistic or laudatory, and (3) dyslogistic or vituperative. For example, according to Bentham, the term "improvement" is eulogistic, whereas the term "innovation" is dyslogistic because "it means something which is new and bad at the same time" (p. 437). So if your opponent in debate introduces a new measure that he calls an "improvement," you can let your own partisans pass censure on that measure by employing the term "innovation" to refer to it. By secretly or unobtrusively slipping in this dyslogistic appellative, you can make it seem that your opponent's measure deserves general disapprobation.

But why would this use of appellatives in a debate be an instance of the fallacy of begging the question? Bentham's reply (pp. 436-37) is revealing.

> The proposition thus asserted is commonly a proposition that requires to be proved. But in the case where the use of the term thus employed is fallacious, the proposition is one that is not true, and cannot be proved: and where the person by whom the fallacy is employed is conscious of its deceptive tendency, the object in the employment thus given to the appellative is, by means of the artifice, to cause that to be taken for true, which is not so.

Bentham's answer is that there is a conscious awareness of the deceptive tendency by the arguer who engages in this type of use of language–the intention of the arguer is to deceive his audience by causing them to take as true what is not true.

We can certainly appreciate the kind of error Bentham had in mind here, and it does seem to represent an important kind of fallacy or deceptive tactic of argument that is well worth knowing about and guarding against.

But in one way Bentham's classification of the fallacy is too broad, because he equates it with the overly aggressive or unjustified use of loaded language. In another way, it is too narrow, because he links the committing of the fallacy with a specific intent to deceive on the part of the proponent of the argument. Bentham's account is perplexing, and does not seem to get to the heart of the fallacy. But he is clearly on to something, and it is easy to see why his remarks have been such a powerful influence on the current treatment of the fallacy of question-begging epithets in the logic textbooks.

The accounts of question-begging generally, and the special subfallacy of question-begging epithets, given by the current textbooks are in an unsatisfactory state. They are replete with many problems and unanswered questions, and fail to diagnose or explain the precise fallacy or fault of reasoning that is alleged to have been committed.

Moreover, one suspects that the examples treated by the texts are relatively trivial and simplistic cases of kinds of errors that could be quite serious in more complex, longer, and difficult sequences of argumentation on topics of serious controversy.

An initial stumbling block to gaining access to the nature of begging the question as a serious error of reasoning, however, is the very phrase "begging the question" itself, which seems somehow unfamiliar or even incomprehensible as an expression. Most speakers of English are familiar with the expression "circular reasoning" and have some idea of what kind of reasoning this is or could be. But many people do not appear comfortable with the phrase "begging the question." In fact, as we will see, there is evidence that this phrase is often used in a confused and misleading way.

3. Etymology of the Phrase "Beg the Question"

The phrase "begging the question," and the Latin term *petitio principii* from which it was derived (or translated), are obscure and problematic for modern readers. *Petitio principii* could helpfully be translated as "petitioning (or asking) for the principle (or question) that is at issue." As a description of a fallacy or logical error, however, this translation is as baffling as the phrase "begging the question." Why "beg" and what is "the question"? Why "petitioning" and what is the "principle"? In fact, the translation is only helpful to someone who understands the Greek context and the etymology of these terms.

Aristotle, in the *De Sophisticis Elenchis,* (On Sophistical Refutations) presumed a context of disputation, after the Greek pattern, where one party has the task of proving a proposition (the "question" to be proven) to another party.[3] To carry out his task, the first party will have to ask the second party to grant or concede premises that the first party can use in his argument. However, if the first party were to ask (beg for) the very conclusion as a concession, without doing the required work of proving it, then he would be "begging for the question at issue." This would not be allowed in this Greek pattern of disputation, because the prover would be avoiding his task of proving this proposition at issue. He would fail to fulfill his burden of proof. And *proof* is the main point of the game, in this context.

Since this Greek context of argument as a two-person interactive and contestive proving dialogue is now antiquated and obscure, making no sense to the modern reader–or, at any rate, it cannot be presupposed as a known background context to the idea of argument–the phrase "begging the question" appears alien, unfamiliar.

Hamblin's etymological sketch makes the background of these phrases more comprehensible (1970, p. 33).

> In fact "beg the question" is a reasonably accurate translation of Aristotle's original Greek τὸ ἐν ἀρχῇ αἰτεῖσθαι (–in place of αἰτεῖσθαι Aristotle also sometimes uses the word λαμβάνειν "to assume"–) provided we suitably interpret the word "question": the phrase in the original actually means something like "beg for that which is in the question-at-issue." The Latin *principium petere* is the vulgate translation of this, and "beg the question" has been the accepted English one at least since the sixteenth century.

Once this etymology is understood, the term "beg the question" starts to make a little more sense. The "question" is a proposition in dispute, so that one party in the dispute has a "burden" or obligation of proving it to the other. But if this party assumes what is to be proved, that is, begs for it from the other party instead of doing the work of proving it, then a fallacy, or at least a shortcoming of some sort has taken place. Here the entry for *beg the question* in the *Concise Oxford Dictionary* (ed. H. W. Fowler and F. G. Fowler, 4th ed., Oxford, Clarendon Press, 1952, p. 105) is helpful: "assume the truth of matter in dispute." The fault of begging the question is to assume (or ask to be assumed) what is required to be proved.

Even after this etymological enlightenment, however, many problems and uncertainties about what these phrases really mean still remain. Why is begging the question the same fallacy as, or related to, circular reasoning? Or is there a difference between these? Why or how is a failure of burden of proof in a two-person Greek-style disputation a "fallacy"? Since all fallacies could be described as "failures to prove" or inadequate arguments, how is the fallacy of begging the question a distinctive fault, separate from other traditional informal fallacies? All these are good questions, suggesting that although the phrase "beg the question" is widely used, our understanding of the real meaning of it as an identifiable fallacy is at best superficial and at worst lacking, or even erroneous.

Unfortunately, a recent trend is to use the phrase "beg the question" to refer to any failure to answer a question, or reply adequately to it. This usage is not consistent with the logician's proper use of the phrase. Evidence of this trend is given in a recent letter to the editor, "Begging the Question," in the Toronto *Globe and Mail* (Feb. 24, 1987, p. A6). The author, Professor D. D. Todd, of the Department of Philosophy, Simon Fraser University, criticized the *Globe and Mail* for allowing their writers to misuse the phrase "begging the question":

> Will you please inform all your writers, particularly Thomas Walkom (although he is by no means the only offender, just the most recent: see his column Aquino May Pose a Threat to Herself–Feb. 12), that since 1581 the phrase "begging the question" has been English designations for the form of fallacious reasoning known to logicians as *petitio principii*. It is a form of circular reasoning, which consists of taking for granted, tacitly or overtly, in a statement or argument, precisely the matter which is in dispute.

Professor Todd went on to quote Whately's example of case 1.0 as an illustration of a proper instance of an argument that is "uselessly circular" and therefore begs the question, in the correct sense of the term. Continuing, he distinguished between this fallacy and the misidentification of it with the simple failure to reply to a question.

> To beg a question is not, as Walkom *et al.* seem to think, earnestly to request or demand that a certain question be raised and answered, or otherwise dealt with. The persistent abuse of this logician's term lately in the columns of *The Globe and Mail* is an ominous symptom of editorial decadence and, as regards the guilty scriveners, a sure and certain sign of ignorance masquerading as education. Please put a stop to it.

The problem pointed up here is that the phrase "beg the question" appears to have been watered down to the extent that it no longer refers to a logical fallacy or faulty argument, but is broadly taken to refer to any reply to a question considered inadequate, or even to a failure to raise a question or otherwise deal with it. This use of the phrase is broad to the point of vacuity, and clearly inconsistent with the intent of the logician's use of it.

Additional evidence of the confusions and abuses surrounding the current usage of the phrase "beg the question" comes from a recent article in *Newsweek*. An article on the nuclear disaster at Chernobyl (William D. Marbach, Mary Hager, and Vern E. Smith, "The Chernobyl Syndrome,"

Newsweek, May 12, 1986, p. 25) was concerned with the extent of the disaster, and in particular with the question of how many people died. One section of the article accused the Soviets of "begging the question."

Case 1.8:   **Begging a question:** On Tuesday the Soviets released a little more information. They offered four short paragraphs revealing that two people had been killed "during the accident," which begged the question of how many people had been killed by the effects of the disaster–or were likely to die later.

As far as one can tell, the real complaint against the Soviet sources made in this allegation is that they made the wrong claim. The criticism seems to be that instead of addressing the issue of how many people died in the disaster as a whole, the Soviets concentrated on the proposition that two people had been killed "during the accident"–that is, presumably during the actual explosion itself, thus ignoring the question of how many died later. The fallacy complained of here would seem to be more like that of *igno-ratio elenchi*–changing the issue, not that of begging the question. The fault is one of switching to a different issue by answering a question other than the one asked. Such a tactic of evasion, whatever its precise failure as a logical fallacy, is a different fault of argument from the fallacy of begging the question.

This type of misconception about the meaning of the phrase "beg the question" is so common that *Fowler's Modern English Usage* (Oxford, Oxford University Press, 2d ed., 1965, p. 367) cites the following as a common misapprehension: "That to beg a question is to avoid giving a straightforward answer to one." A basic underlying problem is that the term "begging the question," although widely used, is not well understood, and often wrongly used to refer to various faults of argumentation that are broader than, and also different from, what appears to be the proper usage of the term indicating a logical fallacy related to (or perhaps consisting in) circular reasoning.

Whatever the phrase "begging the question" should rightly be taken to mean, as a term of logic–which is ultimately the problem of this book–Hamblin's account of it as to "beg for that which is in the question at issue" (1970, p. 32) begins to make some preanalytical sense of the error as failure to meet a burden of proof in a context of two-person contestive dialogue where the goal of each party is to prove something to the other. This interpretation gives us at least a place to start, an initial grasp of the general idea of begging the question as some sort of violation of a rule or obligation of proof-oriented dialogue.

The etymological remarks of Sparkes (1966) support Hamblin's interpretation of the phrase "begging the question" as a description of a kind of move in dialogue, and argues that this interpretation is "consistent with the importance accorded face-to-face disputation in Aristotle's Athens" (p. 463). The fault referred to, according to Sparkes, is that of asking your opponent in such a dialogue to grant you the truth of a statement, namely your conclusion to be proved, where the truth of that statement has been (or is under) question by your opponent. The exact manner in which this error takes place remains to be seen, but at least, under this explanation of the meaning of the phrase "beg the question," we get some idea what sort of error or shortcoming of argument is involved.

However, as plausible and potentially useful as Hamblin's account seems to be, it should not be taken as the final word on the etymology of "begging the question." DeMorgan (1847, p. 298) also presented what essentially amounts to Hamblin's interpretation, but at the same time argued for another possible interpretation of the Greek phrases used in Aristotle. And DeMorgan strongly suspected that this second interpretation, below, was the true derivation of the phrase. In this second interpretation, the *principium* is the *principle,* a kind of generally acknowledged proposition that could not be subject to dispute by any of the participants of a disputation. DeMorgan describes a "principle" as a kind of indisputable axiom in relation to the philosophy of Aristotle's time.

   The philosophy of the time consisted in a large variety of general propositions (principles) deduced from authority, and supposed to be ultimately derived from intrinsic evidence, self-known, or else by logical derivation from such principles. These were at the command of the disputant, his opponent could not but admit each and all of them: the laws of disputation demanded the assent which the geometer requires for his postulates.

The fallacy of *petitio principii* occurs then, according to DeMorgan's explanation, when a disputant tries to prove a proposition by making it "an example of a principle which was not among those received" (p. 299). According to this interpretation, both disputants must prove from a stock of principles that they both accept non-retractably, and the fallacy of begging the question is committed by any argument that draws a premise that does not fall under one (or more) of these principles.

It is hard to know what to make of DeMorgan's second interpretation since, on it, begging the question does not appear to be the fallacy of circular reasoning that traditional and modern textbook accounts generally take it to be. Nevertheless, at least one recent analyst of begging the question appears to interpret the phrase in something like DeMorgan's second way. Johnson (1967, p. 137) asserted that begging the question occurs when a protagonist, in defending his argument, is forced back to an "ultimate principle" upon which he bases his argument and cannot (or refuses to) argue for that principle, yet still insists on rejecting the opposed argument of his antagonist. Johnson posed the situation of two people engaged in a philosophical dispute, "each one working from a different ultimate principle." In such a case, he claimed, each would "beg the question against the other." Whatever Johnson meant by "begging the question" here, it does seem similar to what DeMorgan describes as his second interpretation of Aristotle's use of that phrase.

4. ARISTOTLE ON BEGGING THE QUESTION

The remarks on begging the question in the *De Sophisticis Elenchis* clearly presuppose a context of two-person disputation where one party has undertaken to prove a particular proposition (his conclusion to be proved), and the other party has taken on the obligation of doubting this proposition, and of resisting the first party's attempts at proof. The fallacy of begging the question can arise in this context if the first party tries to get the other party to grant the first party's conclusion without doing his proper job of proving it.

Aristotle presupposes that the reader understands that there is a context of dialogue wherein two participants are "reasoning together," but where the purpose of the dialogue is at least partly contestive. This is the Greek game of *elenchus* (refutation), where each party has the goal of "reasoning against" the other, by trying to refute the other party's contention (point at issue).[4] In such a framework, when you concede the other party's point (his thesis or conclusion to be proved), you are not granting it as proven, for that would, in effect, concede that you have lost the game. Rather, you are only "conceding" or "granting" it in the sense that you are acknowledging it as the thesis you now propose to argue against. Your opponent must *prove* his point, not merely ask you to grant it without proof.[5] And any proof useful for the purpose of this contestive type of game of dialogue must, as Aristotle put it above, be independent of the original point. In short, it must not depend crucially on the original point, or it would beg the question, and therefore be useless as a proof.

Within its Greek context, this concept of begging the question must have been intuitively meaningful to Greek readers. But in a twentieth-century context, where the game of *elenchus* is not known, Aristotle's concept of begging the question makes no sense, and generations of subsequent commentators have found it obscure or useless, not knowing what to make of it.

In the *Prior Analytics,* Aristotle treats begging the question as a failure of a general requirement of priority in a special type of reasoning which he calls *demonstration.* According to Aristotle, the kind of argument characteristic of demonstration always proceeds from premises that are better established—"more certain" and "prior"—in relation to the conclusion to be demonstrated. He goes on to write that when begging the question is a fault, it is because certain types of arguments violate this requirement of priority in the context of demonstration. (64 b 28-37).

Most interestingly as well, Aristotle does not claim in the *Prior Analytics* that circular arguments always commit the fallacy of begging the question. Instead, he claims that, in some cases, a circular argument can violate the priority requirement of a proper demonstration, and therefore be faulted as erroneously question-begging. This is the famous principle that some things are self-evident while other things are known through something else.

How could it be that any proposition is "self-evident"? Isn't this an old idea that has now been (properly) rejected as "unscientific" or even contrary to principles of good reasoning?[6] And, when begging the question is supposed to be a fallacy, how can we verify this by identifying the case as one of those improper attempts to prove something that violates the priority requirement? No useful analysis of the fallacy of begging the question would appear to be extractable from Aristotle's remarks in this passage of the *Prior Analytics* until these questions can be given acceptable answers.

Hamblin comments (1970, p. 77) that Aristotle has made a distinction between two interpretations of argument. One is the dialectical one of the *De Sophisticis Elenchis*. The other Hamblin calls "epistemological," wherein propositions have a "peck-order." This epistemological idea of the demonstration, Hamblin notes (p. 76), is also described elsewhere in Aristotle *(Posterior Analytics* 86 a 21), where it is again stated that argument proceeds from the more certain to the less certain. Aristotle summarizes his own view in the *Prior Analytics* (65 a 35) by writing that question-begging is a similar fault, but at the same time a distinctively different fault, in a scientific demonstration as opposed to a dialectical argument. Hamblin (1970, p. 74), however, describes this passage (65 a 10-38) as "quite puzzling." A summary and analysis of Aristotle's views on begging the question that considers some of these puzzles is to be found in Woods and Walton (1982a).

The Aristotelian view of begging the question can be found re-expressed in the medieval logic textbooks. Peter of Spain (1220-1277) wrote that this fallacy is a probative failure, or failure of proof, even though it is no impediment to an inferring syllogism—see de Rijk (1972, pp. 144-45), Hamblin (1970, p. 33), and Mackenzie (1984a). The dual nature of the Aristotelian treatment of the fallacy was nicely expressed by William of Sherwood (1210-1271) in his *Logic* (Kretzmann, 1966). William first described the dialectical variant of the fallacy of begging the question (p. 158) as the failure of an inference to produce "belief regarding a doubtful matter." Then he went on to write that this cannot be accomplished without premises that are "prior and better known."

Both Peter and William follow Aristotle, as well, in distinguishing the five ways in which the fallacy of begging the question can take place.

This duality of the two different background contexts of argument in which *petitio principii* is portrayed as a fallacy, or failure of good argument, has persisted throughout the history of informal fallacies. But are these contexts of argument we can make sense of? It seems not, according to the current literature outlined in section eight below. In the twentieth century, deductive logic, in the form of mathematical (formal) logic has dominated the field of logic and argument analysis. But whatever kind of failure *petitio principii* is, it is not a failure of deductive inference.

Indeed, the relationship of circular reasoning to deductive logic is puzzling, perhaps even paradoxical, for another reason. Some critics have even argued that deductive logic is itself circular, and therefore commits the fallacy of begging the question.

ALLEGHENY COLLEGE LIBRARY

5. IS ALL DEDUCTIVE REASONING CIRCULAR?

According to Hamblin (1970, p. 35), the most important controversy surrounding *petitio principii* concerns the claim of John Stuart Mill that all deductively valid argumentation commits this fallacy. Mill's claim centers on the syllogism as the paradigm of the deductively valid argument. His claim is based on the concession, often made by logicians, that there is nothing more in the conclusion of a valid syllogism than was already assumed in the premises. Mill (1843, p. 120) uses this concession to question whether the syllogism can really be called "reasoning" in an important sense of the term.

The gist of Mill's argument can easily be grasped from his own example and subsequent comments:

> It must be granted that in every syllogism, considered as an argument to prove the conclusion, there is a *petitio principii*. When we say,
>
>> All men are mortal,
>> Socrates is a man,
>> therefore
>> Socrates is mortal;
>
> it is unanswerably urged by the adversaries of the syllogistic theory, that the proposition, Socrates is mortal, is presupposed in the more general assumption, All men are mortal: that we cannot be assured of the mortality of all men, unless we are already certain of the mortality of every individual man: that if it be still doubtful whether Socrates, or any other individual we choose to name, be mortal or not, the same degree of uncertainty must hang over the assertion, All men are mortal: that the general principle, instead of being given as evidence of the particular case cannot itself be taken for true without exception, until every shadow of doubt which could affect any case comprised with it, is dispelled by evidence *aliundè;* and then what remains for the syllogism to prove?

Mill concludes that reasoning from the general to the particular can never really *prove* anything, in some important sense. The reason he offers for this highly paradoxical claim is that we can never infer any particulars from a general principle except those which the principle assumes as known.

Mill claims then that in *any* syllogism, like the one about Socrates quoted above, the truth of the general (universal) premise *depends on* the truth of the conclusion.[7] What is meant by the key phrase "depends on" in Mill's argument? According to Mill, as quoted above, "we cannot be assured of" the general premise, "unless we are already certain of the mortality of every individual man." In particular then, we cannot be assured of the truth of this general premise unless we are already certain of the truth of the conclusion "Socrates is mortal." Hence the premise depends on the conclusion. But of course this is a circular mutual dependency. For according to the exponents of the syllogism as a kind of reasoning, the conclusion is supposed to depend on the premises, in order to be proved as a conclusion.

Mill's contention that a general principle can only be established as true by prior knowledge that all the particulars that fall under it are true has often been criticized. Cohen and Nagel (1934) expressly deny this contention, countering that Mill's argument itself rests on a fallacy about reasoning. They propose that Mill's argument rests on a mistaken idea of scientific inquiry because Mill demands absolute certainty in matters of fact. Cohen and Nagel suggest that this is a misconception, that no universal hypothesis in experimental science can ever be known to be *certainly* true. They suggest that to think that the only way a general principle can be supported by scientific reasoning is by enumerating all the particular instances that fall under it is a naive and inaccurate account of scientific method as a kind of reasoning (p. 179).

> Thus one consequence of Newtonian physics is that a pair of double stars will revolve around their common center of gravity in elliptic orbits. But Newtonian physics is established with considerable security without first examining double stars; and the evidence for the theory may be greater than that for the existence of such elliptic orbits even if we try to examine double stars directly. The inference that double stars do move on such orbits is therefore not circular. The conclusion is, indeed, not certain, since the theory is not certainly true. But only a mistaken idea of science, such as Mill's, which demands absolute certitude in matters of fact, would reject it as useless for that reason. Similarly, we infer the mortality of any living man from the premise *All men are mortal* without basing this premise upon an enumeration of dead men. For we know that *All men have organic bodies* and *All organic bodies disintegrate with time* are supported by evidence of a far-reaching character which itself does not rest in turn upon an examination of the mortality of any one human being.

Cohen and Nagel are suggesting that a general principle is mistakenly viewed as a mere compendium of particular cases that all need to be observed before the principle can be proven or established as acceptable by scientific reasoning.

Of course, it may be that if the major premise of Mill's syllogism were simply an enumeration of a finite number of particular instances, then the syllogism would be circular in its reasoning. But Cohen and Nagel are claiming, with a good deal of plausibility, that viewing a general principle in this way would be mistaken and inaccurate in many cases. In many cases, there does indeed seem to be a body of evidence that can be appealed to in support of the general premise of a syllogism that does not absolutely require the prior verification of any particular case falling under the premise.

Mill's argument that deductive reasoning is circular was anticipated by a very similar argument to the same conclusion that appeared in the *Outlines of Pyrrhonism*, written by Sextus Empiricus in the second or third century. In chapter XIV, Sextus attacks the Aristotelian syllogisms on the grounds that they are involved in "the perplexity of the circular fallacy" (OP II 197). Sextus considers the following syllogism, which, like Mill's example, has a universal premise and a particular conclusion (OP II 196).

Case 1.9:   Every man is an animal.
Socrates is a man.
Therefore, Socrates is an animal.

According to Sextus, the advocates of the syllogism as a type of proof propose to deduce the particular conclusion "Socrates is an animal" from the universal premise, "Every man is an animal." But these same advocates, Sextus points out, think that the universal premise is established by induction from particular instances, like "Plato is an animal" or "Dion is an animal." This is circular, according to Sextus, because the universal premise also presupposes the particular instance "Socrates is an animal," yet that is the conclusion to be established by the syllogism. Sextus concludes that the advocates of the syllogism as a type of proof have fallen into the error of circular reasoning.

The passage of the *Outlines of Pyrrhonism* (II 195-97) in which Sextus formulates his principal argument is worth quoting, because the argument is formulated very clearly and cogently. It is clear that the basic thrust of what is generally regarded as Mill's argument had already been presented by Sextus in all of its essential elements.

Well then, the premiss "Every man is an animal" is established by induction from the particular instances; for from the fact that Socrates, who is a man, is also an animal, and Plato likewise, and Dion and each one of the particular instances, they think it possible to assert that every man is an animal; so that if even a single one of the particulars should apparently conflict with the rest the universal premiss is not valid; thus, for example, when most animals move the lower jaw, and only the crocodile the upper, the premiss "Every animal moves the lower jaw" is not true. So whenever they argue "Every man is an animal, and Socrates is a man, therefore Socrates is an animal," proposing to deduce from the universal proposition "Every man is an animal" the particular proposition "Socrates therefore is an animal," which in fact goes (as we have mentioned) to establish by way of induction the universal proposition, they fall into the error of circular reasoning, since they are establishing the universal proposition inductively by means of each of the particulars and deducing the particular proposition from the universal syllogistically.

When Sextus refers to "induction" in this passage, he is evidently indicating Aristotle's notion of logical induction in the *Prior Analytics* (Book II, 23, 68 b and following), where Aristotle writes how a syllogism can "spring out of" induction. What Aristotle appears to have in mind is a kind of logical induction that proceeds to support a general proposition through an enumeration of the particular instances that fall under it. Thus Sextus accuses Aristotle of circularity when he appeals to this kind of induction as a way of supporting the general premise of a syllogism like the one in case 1.9 above. According to Sextus (anticipating Mill), you have to consider each particular instance that falls under the general premise in question. But since one of these particular instances has to be the conclusion of the syllogism, circular reasoning has to be involved (just as Mill claimed).

Interestingly, Sextus even goes on to generalize his criticism to apply to the stoic principles of deductive logic. The particular case that provides his target is an instance of *modus ponens*. Sextus has clearly formulated his criticism of the circularity of deductive logic so that it applies not only to syllogistic logic, but also to what we would nowadays call the propositional calculus. Sextus (OP II 198) asks us to consider the following argument:

Case 1.10:   If it is day, it is light.
It is day.
Therefore, it is light.

According to Sextus, the defenders of this type of argument as a kind of proof claim that the two premises together are capable of proving the conclusion, "It is light." But Sextus adds, the hypothetical premise "If it is day, it is light" would not have been considered to be established unless the constant coexistence of "It is day" with "It is light" had already been observed (199). Hence Sextus sees a fallacy of circular reasoning here too. The coexistence of day and light is supposed to be proved, but it is also assumed by the hypothetical premise of the very argument that is supposed to do the proof.

Once we kick away the basic "inductivist" presumption of the Sextus-Mill argument that a general principle can only be proved or supported by an enumeration of all its instances, the argument loses most of its sting. While some syllogisms may still be circular, it no longer follows that every use of a syllogism to prove a conclusion in argument has to commit a *petitio principii* fallacy.

Even so, the argument still raises some interesting questions about the syllogism and other structures of deductive logic as vehicles of reasoning. The Sextus-Mill argument presumes that we think of a valid syllogism as *reasoning* or *proof* because in some important but unarticulated sense, the conclusion *depends on* the premises. Evidently, this presumption means that in the absence of the premises, the conclusion would be somehow subject to doubt, and that these premises are required, or are instrumental in reasoning that doubt and securing acceptance of the conclusion. Whatever this dependency relationship really amounts to (which is highly obscure), it seems to be at the bottom of the very idea of *petitio principii* as a fallacy. When this relation of dependency goes both ways in an argument–from the conclusion to the premises, as well as from the premises to the conclusion–the *petitio principii* fallacy arises on the scene as a criticism to be reckoned with in that argument.

Augustus DeMorgan (1806-1871), a contemporary of John Stuart Mill (1806-1873), also had some very interesting views on the subject of begging the question. His point of view was diametrically opposed to Mill's, and in some respects his conclusions were as paradoxical as Mill's.

6. DEMORGAN ON BEGGING THE QUESTION

Augustus DeMorgan included several pages of remarks on begging the question in a chapter "On Fallacies" in his *Formal Logic* (1847). His remarks on begging the question are full of innovative probings and profound insights that show an advanced grasp of the subject. His comments are often striking in their originality. But in some instances his conclusions on begging the question appear to run so contrary to the conventional views that they are on the edge of being paradoxes.

DeMorgan begins his treatment of begging the question by reminding the reader of an important distinction (p. 254). While the conclusion of a valid argument is, in some sense "contained in" the premises, nevertheless "the presence of the premises in the mind is not necessarily the presence of the conclusion." Straight after making this distinction, DeMorgan puts forward a straightforward statement of the equivalence conception of the fallacy of begging the question: "[B]y this fallacy is meant the absolute assumption of the single conclusion, or a mere equivalent to it, as a single premise." DeMorgan's intent, at this point, would appear to be to try to make out a case that the *petitio principii* is really a formal fallacy of some sort.

Curiously however, in his subsequent discussion, he explicitly grants that, in several respects, the *petitio principii* is really not a purely formal matter at all. First, he presents a formalistic example to illustrate the point that whether there is really a *petitio principii* in a particular case depends on whether the premises in the case in question can be supposed to be fully agreed on between the disputants. This point (quite insightfully) makes *petitio principii* a pragmatic matter of whether the premises in question have been conceded by the participants in the discussion.

But then in the very next sentence, DeMorgan seems to pull the rug out from under this pragmatic account of the fallacy when he claims: "Strictly speaking, there is no formal *petitio principii* except when the very proposition to be proved, and not a mere synonyme of it, is assumed." But now having emphasized the essentially formal nature of *petitio,* DeMorgan immediately concedes that such a formal *petitio principii* "rarely occurs," adding "the fallacy to be guarded against is the assumption of that which is too nearly the same as the conclusion required." Evidently, a problem for DeMorgan is that the concept of a premise being "too nearly the same" as a conclusion is not a concept of formal logic, or amenable to treatment or analysis by formal logic. At any rate, having now once again emphasized the non-formal or pragmatic nature of the real fallacy to be guarded against, DeMorgan puts this fallacy down as "nothing distinct in itself: but merely amounts to putting forward and claiming to have granted that which should not be granted." DeMorgan seems torn. He wants to recognize the importance of non-formal (pragmatic) elements of the fallacy, which depend on factors of which premises the participants in a dispute have or have not conceded as commitments in the discussion. But on the other hand, this champion of formal methods in logic could not bring himself to accept that these non-formal aspects of argument really amount to anything important when it comes to saying whether the argument is correct or fallacious. He was included to presume that, strictly speaking, the really distinct underlying character of the fallacy is purely formal in nature.

Despite his clear misgivings about *petitio principii* as a clear-cut logical error, DeMorgan made a serious effort to diagnose the fallacy as a practical error of reasoning, and proposed constructive and useful comments for dealing with it. He saw the fallacy as a fault of proof not being offered, when it should be offered by a disputant, but also saw that it is a complex kind of fallacy, which could also be committed by another party who refuses to make reasonable concessions to make the offering of such proof possible (p. 255). DeMorgan also saw that there are cases of reasoning where proof is not required, because the context is one of explanation or elucidation, and that therefore the adjudication of *petitio principii* depends very much on the context of use of an inference.

DeMorgan (pp. 257-60) also had some remarks of theoretical interest to make, stemming from his comments on the Sextus-Mill argument that every valid syllogism begs the question. DeMorgan insisted (p. 257) that, in accord with his earlier account of the fallacy, begging the question refers to what is assumed *in one premise*. From this he inferred that it can never be correct to say that a pair of premises beg the question. From this, of course, it follows that no syllogism could ever beg the question.

It seems then that Mill and DeMorgan are very strongly opposed on this issue. Mill claimed that *all* syllogisms beg the question. DeMorgan claimed that *none* does. Both seem extreme positions, for the common sense view is more likely to be that some do and some don't.

But in Mill's example (1843, p. 120) of the syllogism, is it not the one premise, "All men are mortal," that begs the question? Not according to DeMorgan, who astutely pointed out that this view of the matter is simplistic.

DeMorgan (p. 258) considered a parallel example.

Case 1.11:   All men are mortal.
              Plato is a man.
              Therefore, Plato is mortal.

The Sextus-Mill objection is that in order to know that it is really true that all men are mortal, we first need to know that Plato is mortal. But DeMorgan doubted this. He replied that it may be true that someone has found out that all men are mortal even though he does not even know who or what Plato is. In other words, "The whole objection tacitly assumes the superfluity of the minor [premise]; that is, tacitly assumes we know Plato to be a man, as soon as we know him to be Plato" (p. 259). In Woods and Walton (1977, 1982a) this counter to the Sextus-Mill objection was called *DeMorgan's Deadly Retort* because it correctly points out that the objection overlooks the second premise.

DeMorgan's Deadly Retort has a similar upshot and thrust to the Cohen and Nagel objection, but it introduces some new subtleties as well. DeMorgan is pointing out that a syllogism like case 1.11 above has two separate (independent) premises that are both required to support the conclusion. It has what is now called in informal logic a *linked* argument structure–both premises are necessary, and interlock to support the conclusion. But the same interlocking structure characterizes the alleged dependency relationship cited by the Sextus-Mill objection to hold between the conclusion and the major premise. If such a dependency exists in a particular case, according to DeMorgan, it is a complex relationship involving the conclusion and both premises. But since, according to DeMorgan, only one premise can beg the question, a genuine syllogism like case 1.11, which has two linked premises, can never commit the fallacy of begging the question.

DeMorgan's Deadly Retort makes the dispute between his point of view on *petitio* and the Sextus-Mill point of view a Mexican standoff that raises many puzzling questions about begging the question as a fallacy. DeMorgan evidently seems to have gotten the best of it, but his insistence on some apparently extreme points of view remains puzzling. Why did he only accept the equivalence conception of the *petitio* and reject the dependency conception entirely? Why does he maintain that no syllogism (or any multipremised, linked argument) could ever beg the question in any context of use? Why is the number of premises and the nature of their linkage so critical in judging begging the question, as they rightly seem to be? None of these provocative questions is given an adequate answer.

7. SIDGWICK ON BEGGING THE QUESTION

Alfred Sidgwick (1850-1943) wrote several logic textbooks that stressed informal fallacies and adopted a point of view of informal logic. Indeed, Sidgwick could quite rightly be seen as an important precursor of the recent informal logic movement. However, Sidgwick's work has usually been dismissed as of lesser importance than the better known logical scholars of the previous generation–Whately, Mill, and DeMorgan. For example, Hamblin (1970, p. 176) commented that although Sidgwick is the only person ever known to have tried to develop a theory of logic around the study of fallacies, his work has been "passed over and left behind by modern developments." Hamblin concluded that the result of Sidgwick's effort was not a success.

Sidgwick's best-known work, *Fallacies: A View of Logic from the Practical Side* (1884)–the only work referred to by Hamblin–does not have much to add that is very original or striking on the subject of begging the question. For the most part, his remarks are a summary and commentary on the previous findings, theories, and examples of Bentham, Whately, Mill, and DeMorgan.

In this text, however, Sidgwick did make some interesting remarks about what he felt were the limitations of the formal approach adopted by DeMorgan. Quoting DeMorgan's claim that a formal *petitio* only exists where the exact proposition to be proved (and not a "mere synonyme") is assumed, Sidgwick expresses reservations: "Nothing, however, appears to be really gained by restricting the name to so small a compass as this; and there is no doubt that such a restriction would be very much at variance with the popular acceptation of the term" (p. 194). This remark could serve as the introduction to the much deeper and more original treatment of *petitio* to be found in two of Sidgwick's later textbooks, *The Application of Logic* (1910) and *Elementary Logic* (1914). In these lesser-known works, we find a much more experienced Sidgwick, who has some highly original points of view on begging the question to be expounded.

In these later works, Sidgwick claimed that the fallacy of begging the question has to do with the ways in which assumptions are made in an argument. According to Sidgwick, the right use of assumption in argument is to put an assertion forward openly, and the fault of *petitio* is a wrong way of putting forward an assumption in an argument. More specifically, question-begging is a fallacy when it is the attempt of a disputant to prevent question-raising. The fault is that of attempting to put forward an assumption in a closed or dogmatic manner.

Sidgwick's approach to begging the question shows how much he really is a kindred spirit to the pragmatic, modern orientation of informal logic to the concept of argumentation as a two-person interactive question-reply dialogue where contestive disputation takes place. And his point of view on *petitio* is at once practical and promising. However, when we try to get down to the details of the precise fault of dogmatic argument that *petitio* is supposed to consist of, the details seem to be vague.

According to Sidgwick (1910, p. 205), there is nothing wrong with openly disputing a premise of a syllogism. It is when the proponent of the syllogism tries to suppress this kind of disputative questioning that a fallacy of begging the question has been committed: "Under this conception of the fallacy, then, to beg a question is simply to slur over, in a dispute, any doubts which an opponent may be asking us to consider" (p. 213). Hence the fallacy of *petitio* is not to be found simply in the literal assertions, the propositions that make up the syllogism as an entity of formal logic. It is to be determined by examining how the syllogism is presented by its proponent in a context of disputation. It is the manner of use of the syllogism in the context of question-reply dialogue that determines whether a fallacy of begging the question has occurred or not.

Sidgwick's approach to the fallacy of begging the question as a dialectical failure of openness of presentation of an assumption in argument is a fascinating departure in a practical direction, and shows great promise of potential usefulness as a novel theoretical perspective on the problem. But unfortunately, he doesn't carry his analysis any further than this by showing us how to diagnose the precise error, or how *petitio* is a failure of openness in specific cases that reveal the real nature of the fallacy.

Instead, Sidgwick was content to emphasize the difficulties of substantiating and pinning down an allegation that the fallacy has occurred in a particular case. However, even these general points about the complications of "nailing down" a fallacy are far ahead of their time in sketching out the need for methods of discourse analysis and argument reconstruction now widely recognized as the tools of informal logic.

8. A SERIES OF CONTEMPORARY ARTICLES

A whole chain of articles on begging the question, each replying to previous ones, grew out of a provocative article by Richard Robinson published in *Analysis* in 1971. Robinson's article has the form of a dialogue that skeptically questions whether the idea of begging the question makes sense.

Robinson (1971a, p. 113) characterized begging the question as "assuming what you are to prove," and offered the following example.

Case 1.12:   God has all the virtues.
　　　　　　　Therefore, God is benevolent.

Robinson gave the following context for this argument as a case of begging the question. Suppose you are asked to prove that God is benevolent. You advance the argument of case 1.12. The objection is that the argument begs the question. Why? Because the premise, that God has all the virtues, assumes that God is benevolent (conclusion). But what is wrong with that? Why is it a fault of the argument? Robinson's paper took the form of a dialogue that investigates several possible answers to this question, and comes to the skeptical conclusion that there is really nothing wrong with begging the question. His conclusion was that the accusation of begging the question is not a proper way of condemning an argument.

Robinson's argument against begging the question as a serious fault of arguments has the form of a dilemma. He argued (p. 114) that there are only two proper ways of condemning an argument, to say that the conclusion does not follow from the premises, or to say that you do not accept the premises. Since begging the question does not fit into either of these categories, it is not a proper criticism of arguments.

In a short note, Hoffman (1971, p. 51) replied to Robinson's article. Hoffman postulated that every argument must have at least two premises.[8] He defined begging the question as the case where "the same proposition is asserted twice," both as premise and conclusion. Both of these claims follow DeMorgan (although DeMorgan is not mentioned in Hoffman's article). Hoffman also claimed that in a case of begging the question, the "condition of there being at least two propositions is unsatisfied and there is no argument at all." He added that in any case of begging the question where there are more than two putative premises, the other premises are unnecessary, so in this type of case as well, there is no argument at all.

Robinson concluded that begging the question is not a kind of defective argument, but an error of merely asserting the truth of a proposition while purporting to present an argument.

Sanford (1972) concluded that begging the question is not a purely formal failure, that it is a failure "to increase the degree of reasonable confidence which one has in the truth of the conclusion" (p. 198). According to Sanford, an argument begs the question if the person to whom it was directed "would believe one of the premises only if he already believed the conclusion." This criterion is a version of the dependency conception of begging the question.

In expounding the dependency conception, Sanford brought forward an interesting argument designed to refute Hoffman's version of the equivalence conception. Making the point that some arguments that have the form of the disjunctive syllogism beg the question while others do not, Sanford noted that in this type of argument, neither premise is identical to the conclusion. Hence the DeMorgan-Hoffman proposal of a purely formal analysis of begging the question evidently does not do justice to our ordinary preconceptions about this fallacy. As Sidgwick had already put it (1884, p. 194), nothing has been "gained by restricting the name to so small a compass as this." The question remained open, however, whether some broader interpretation of the equivalence conception could be defined.

Sanford's article had opened up new avenues of inquiry by showing that the fallacy of begging the question was a matter of an arguer's reasonable belief in the premises and conclusion of an argument, rather than a matter of logical form. Several aspects of Sanford's view of the fallacy appeared problematic, however, and this led to further articles on the subject that reacted to Sanford's article, and to Robinson's and Hoffman's as well.

Barker (1976, p. 245) pointed out that Robinson's God and the virtues argument, in the form considered by Sanford, is an enthymeme, because the premise "Benevolence is a virtue" has been presumed, but not explicitly stated. It appeared then that the problem of begging the question also involves the potentially troublesome question of when an unstated premise may be presupposed in an argument.

Barker went on to offer an example of his own that he felt was more clear-cut than Sanford's, because it does not involve the "troublesome phenomenon of presupposition."

Case 1.13:   Suppose that two persons are arguing over whether the statement "God is either male or female" is true. One of the disputants presents the argument: "God is male, therefore God is either male or female."

Barker described this case by commenting that "clearly, the question is begged despite the fact that the conclusion is not identical to the premise or to any part thereof." Barker concluded that Hoffman's analysis fails to withstand this type of Sanfordian counter-example.

Barker also showed how the number of premises and the redundancy of premises are both factors that can significantly influence begging the question in an argument. Barker (p. 249) defined an *efficient* argument as "a valid, multi-premised argument from which no premise could be deleted without producing invalidity." According to Barker, the Hoffman type of analysis entails that no efficient arguments are question-begging.[9] But since Sanford's type of case has shown that efficient arguments of the disjunctive syllogism form do sometimes beg the question, Barker concluded that the Hoffman type of analysis cannot be right.

According to Barker (p. 242), the fallacy of begging the question presupposes a context of disputation, and Barker took this to entail that question-begging by one party in the disputation only occurs where his argument is being used against another party who disbelieves the conclusion. Sanford (1977) at least partially disagreed. According to Sanford, a central purpose of argument is to show that something is worthy of belief. But this purpose can be accomplished, in Sanford's view, even where the conclusion is initially neither believed nor disbelieved, or where the conclusion has been believed all along. This disagreement between Barker and Sanford indicates an underlying problem in the analysis of begging the question as a fallacy. The analysis of the fallacy appears to presuppose some sort of initial controversy or conflict of opinion between two participants in a context of dialogue. But exactly how to describe this initial situation, and how it fits into the analysis of *petitio* as a fallacy, are open questions.

The final article in this series, by John Biro (1984), agreed with Sanford that the fallacy of begging the question related to a failure of a requirement of an arguer's knowledge or belief, but disagreed by phrasing the requirement differently.[10] While Sanford preferred to phrase his version of the requirement in terms of "reasonable belief," Biro thought that the appropriate requirement is one of comparative knowability. According to Biro (p. 239), the problem with question-begging arguments is that they are "epistemically non-serious." An *epistemically serious* argument, in Biro's account, is one where the premises are more knowable than the conclusion.

What matters in an argument designed to be serious, Biro claimed, is "that there should be a way in which we can learn the truth of the premises, so that we can use that knowledge to argue to the truth of the conclusion." An argument that begs the question is fallacious because it fails to meet this requirement of leaving an evidential route to the premises open. In arguing for this type of dependency conception of begging the question, Biro agreed with Sanford about the nature of the fallacy, but he disagreed about the precise wording of the appropriate requirement on argument that begging the question violates.

Biro (p. 241) also raised some interesting questions about how the requirement ought precisely to be phrased, even from his own point of view on it as a comparative knowability condition. Should it require that the premises be more knowable than the conclusion, or only that the premises be no less knowable than the conclusion? This question is open whether one should prefer Biro's comparative knowability type of requirement or Sanford's degree of reasonable confidence type of requirement.

It seems then that the solution to the problem of begging the question lies in some sort of general requirement of an argument, which arises out of the argument's usefulness for a purpose. One primary purpose appears to be that of convincing someone in argument to come to believe, know, or accept the conclusion. Out of this purpose arises a requirement that relates premises to conclusion in such a way that the premises must be more knowable, believable, acceptable, or something of the sort. Begging the question is a fault or fallacy where this requirement is violated because a premise depends on the conclusion (or perhaps is even equivalent to it, in some sense). Such dependency is a fallacy because it blocks an arguer's way of coming to know that such a premise is true, other than through his prior acceptance of the conclusion. Thus a rough and hazy picture of begging the question as a fallacy has emerged, but many essential details are left to be filled in, and problems to be solved.

The dialectical tradition of formulating rules for the conduct of two-person argumentative exchanges as strict rules of formalistic games of dialogue has always had strong ties to the study of fallacies. This tradition was the basis of Aristotle's treatment of the fallacies in the *De Sophisticis Elenchis,* and even more explicitly formulated games of dialogue can be found in the works of the logicians in the Middle Ages. In the medieval game of Obligation, for example, one player tried to draw out contradictions or impossibilities from the concessions of the other, according to rules of inference and procedure agreed upon by both at the outset of the game.

The first attempt to study *petitio principii* in relation to a formalistic structure of dialogue, however, appears to have been undertaken by Hamblin (1970). Hamblin designed a "Why-Because-System-with-Questions," called (H) by Woods and Walton (1978a, p. 74), and then formulated two additional rules for (H) that, he conjectured, banned *petitio.* The technical details can be found in Woods and Walton (1978a).

The conclusion of Woods and Walton (p. 85) is that whether or not problematic sequences of dialogue are fallaciously circular or not depends on how you interpret the context of the dialogue. In particular, one property of dialogue is crucial. A dialogue is *cumulative* (p. 83) where at every move of the dialogue, once a player becomes committed to a particular statement, then he must remain committed to that statement at every succeeding move of the dialogue. In other words, no statement (once made) is ever retractable, by the player who made it, in a cumulative dialogue.

A cumulative dialogue represents a sequence of reasoning that builds up an "increment of knowledge" that never allows you to "change your mind," so to speak. In this context, begging the question appears very strongly to be a fallacy, apparently because a cumulative type of dialogue tends to move in a linear direction, which is not compatible with circling back to a previous point. Woods and Walton (p. 84) show how Kripke's interpretation of intuitionistic logic as a progression of "advancing states of knowledge" is a cumulative context of reasoning where circular argumentation is excluded–see chapter eight, section nine.

Another puzzle about dialogue concerns how we interpret the relationship between the premises and conclusion of an argument in dialogue. An argument in dialogue strongly appears to commit a question-begging fallacy if we presume that one party's conclusion is *grounded on* the premises cited by the other party, meaning that these premises somehow may be taken to represent the evidential basis for the first party's acceptance of the conclusion. But what does groundedness really mean? It could mean that all the premises are necessary in order to prove the conclusion. But what does that mean? Here we seem to be at an impasse. Once we waive the idea of groundedness as a significant factor, the contention that a *petitio principii* fallacy has been committed in the dialogue becomes less convincing. But what the concept of groundedness really means or refers to, when we are trying to interpret or reconstruct an argument, remains an open question, and a puzzling one at that.

A different diagnosis of the problem is given by Mackenzie (1979), who constructs two new systems of dialogue, DC and DD, that are similar to (H) in general outline, but add different rules. DC is not cumulative with respect to statements, but it is cumulative with respect to challenges–in DC a statement is said to be *under challenge* for the one party where the other player is committed to the question "Why A?." Mackenzie's innovation was to introduce the idea that a player can be committed to a question, in addition to being committed to a statement. In the game DC, it would be ruled that Black begged the question at move (4) by replying to a challenge with a statement (A), which is under challenge with respect to him at move (4). Mackenzie concluded (p. 127) that cumulativeness (at least of statements) is not the crucial factor in *petitio*.

Mackenzie (1980) took a similar approach to begging the question in confronting the problem of explaining where there is an informal rule in axiomatic geometry of never using a higher-numbered theorem in order to prove a theorem with a lower number. To explain why, Mackenzie appealed to the same rule he used to ban question-begging in DC in Mackenzie (1979). This rule expressly prohibited an arguer using any statement as a premise that is a statement that is under challenge for him. Thus according to Mackenzie, the lower-numbered theorems cannot use the higher-numbered theorems as premises because the latter type of statement is under challenge at the point where the former is to be proved.

Mackenzie's interesting concerns still did not address the problematic concept of groundedness, which remains the key factor in making the dialogue appear to be an instance of circular reasoning. Also, there is an important distinction to be made between *petitio* and what is called *challenge-busting* in Woods and Walton (1982a, p. 595), the procedure of using a statement that is under challenge as a premise in your argument. Although challenge-busting and begging the question are related as types of sequences of dialogue, they are not identical, as shown by Woods and Walton (p. 596). Some more recent articles that also follow along the concerns of this series–Walton and Batten (1984), Mackenzie (1984a), Mackenzie (1984b), Walton (1985a) and Hintikka (1987)–raise further technical questions on how to model the fallacy of *petitio* in formal dialogues.

9. VICIOUS CIRCLES AND PARADOXES

The standard treatment of the logic textbooks, as noted above, is to equate begging the question with circular reasoning, as two equivalent terms for the same fallacy. But a basic problem with this traditional approach is that there do seem to exist cases of circular arguments that are not fallacious arguments.

Case 1.14:   When asked why the economy in a certain state is in a recession, an economist replies: "A lot of people are leaving the state. Things are very poor in the housing industry, for example, because there is no need for new housing." As the dialogue continues, the economist is asked why people are leaving this state in such large numbers, and he answers, "The condition of the economy in this state is poor. People don't seem to be able to get jobs, because of the recession in this state."

We might notice that the economist's answers have taken us in a circle. The economy in this state, he has claimed, is in a recession because people are leaving. But as we eventually get around to the reason why people are leaving, he replies at the end of the dialogue that the economy in this state is in a recession. Since there is clearly a circle here in the economist's sequence of argumentation, shouldn't we say that here we have an instance of *petitio principii,* the fallacy of arguing in a circle?

But perhaps the circularity in the economist's argument could be due to the inherent circularity of human economic behavior. Feedback loops in human behavior are common in economic contexts. As influential dealers sell a certain stock, the price drops. But as the price drops, other stock-holders sell their shares of the stock. Consequently, the value drops. This process is circular, but it is not necessarily a fallacious argument to describe it as circular.

Another problem with this type of case is that the economist's part in the dialogue should not necessarily be classified as an argument. Perhaps he could defend himself against a charge of *petitio* by replying:

"The relationship of housing, jobs, recessions, and so forth, is a cyclical type of feedback process, and is therefore inherently circular in itself. But my explanation, linking these variables, and drawing attention to their circular relationship is not fallacious. For I was only explaining how the structure of the economy works." The economist might imply, for one thing, that his remarks were not meant to be taken as an *argument,* as such, but more as an explanation of a situation. And since it is arguments that are fallacious, not explanations, the charge of begging the question could be inappropriate in this case.

This kind of defense poses a genuine problem. For how do we know, or can we try to prove (if we wanted to) that the economist's speech act in this case is truly an argument, or was definitely meant to be so taken? And then too a second problem remains, for even if it was meant, in some sense, to be an argument, how can we be sure it is a fallacious argument, given the circular (feedback) aspect of the subject matter? Couldn't a circular (or spiraling) argument be informative if the subject matter itself has a circular structure?

Another problem is that we often speak of *vicious circles* in reasoning in a way that suggests that something is wrong with a vicious circle, but what is wrong is a different kind of error, problem, or fault than a fallacy of begging the question.

Another example of a circular progression is the case of the diabetic who, as he gets more overweight, builds up more insulin in his blood. The more insulin there is in his blood, the more he tends to eat, and the more fat he stores up. This process is circular, but there is not necessarily anything fallacious about it. That is just the way nature works sometimes.

We could say that the circle is vicious in the case of the diabetic, because the diabetic himself gets fatter and fatter. Similarly, in the case of the economist's circular reasoning–the state could get into deeper recession as the cycle progresses. In both cases, the circularity is inherent in the situation. Therefore, when the economist describes the process in a circular way, we might say that his explanation is not fallacious, and in fact that he is describing the situation accurately and correctly. If this is right, then in the case of some circular arguments, we could say that the circle is in some sense vicious, but is not necessarily fallacious, or a case of an argument that begs the question.

Such cases of feedback are common in science, where they have been called "deviation-amplifying mutual causal processes" in cybernetics. The following simple example from Maruyama (1968, p. 305) is illustrative.

Case 1.15:   Take, for example, weathering of rock. A small crack in a rock collects some water. The water freezes and makes the crack larger. A larger crack collects more water, which makes the crack still larger. A sufficient amount of water then makes it possible for some small organisms to live in it. Accumulation of organic matter

then makes it possible for a tree to start growing in the
crack. The roots of the tree will then make the crack
still larger.

If a geologist should explain the weathering of rock by appealing to evidence
of the sort cited in case 1.15 above, which in fact goes in a circle, it would
appear to be inappropriate to accuse him of committing the fallacy of *petitio
principii*. For his exposition of this sequence of mutual causal relationships
is genuinely ampliative and informative. It could fulfill a useful purpose in
showing why and how cracks get larger in rocks over time.

Circular reasoning can also occur in artificial intelligence, where it can
be a problem, but is not necessarily fallacious, or the kind of fault that
would appear to be the same as the fallacy of begging the question. For
example, a rule-based expert system is a kind of knowledge base that
contains a set of facts (simple propositions) and a set of rules (some of
which are in an "if-then" form). The following type of instance of circular
reasoning in an expert system is given by Bramer (1984, p. 10).

Case 1.16:   Consider an expert system containing the following three
rules:
(1)   *if* C *then* A
(2)   *if* A *then* B
(3)   *if* B *then* C
The system is queried "Why C?" and therefore wishes to
verify or falsify C by seeking out propositions from
which C can be deduced. Rule (3) indicates the need to
establish B, which, by Rule (2), requires the establishment of A. But when the system moves to Rule (1) to
do this, the result requires the establishment of C.

According to Bramer, detecting this type of circularity in an expert system
is easy, because the system goes into an infinite loop. So as a method of
searching for information in a knowledge base, circular reasoning is problematic. However, if circular rules are inherent in the body of knowledge
built into the expert system, such circular reasoning is not necessarily fallacious. It would not necessarily be the case that the user, the system, or the
expert who was used as a knowledge source begged the question or reasoned
fallaciously. This type of criticism does not seem to hit the point. The
point is not that the circle is necessarily evidence of someone's bad
reasoning or logical error, but only that it may represent an impracticality
in the program, for some purposes, that may have to be blocked or avoided.

The logic textbooks' standard treatment, however, does not characteristically mention, much less try to deal with these types of cases. So it

remains an open question how they are to be handled in relation to the fallacy of begging the question.

Where vicious circularity has come in for treatment in the logic textbooks is in relation to paradoxes of self-reference. These include the Liar Paradox, embodied in the sentence, "This sentence is false," and mathematical problems like Russell's paradox, involved in the construction of the set of all sets that are not members of themselves. Part of the problem with Russell's paradox is the reflexivity or circularity of sets being members of themselves. But the paradoxicality of such a set is more usually diagnosed by showing that it implies a contradiction–such a set is a member of itself if, and only if, it is not a member of itself. By these lights, the vicious or self-defeating aspect of the paradox is that it contains a self-contradiction (inconsistency).[11] But inconsistency is not necessarily fallacious.[12] Or at any rate, to be inconsistent in one's beliefs or commitments is not, in general, the same kind of fault as committing the fallacy of begging the question. Once again then, a vicious circle is not necessarily a fallacious circle, or a case of the fallacy of begging the question. Thus Bartlett (1987, p. 11) describes many kinds of reflexivity, self-reference, self-justification of theories and inferences, and self-supporting arguments, that are evidently not to be classified as instances of the fallacy of *petitio principii*.

On the other hand, circularity or self-reference in any kind of reasoning often makes us suspicious that some kind of error, viciousness, or funny business of some sort may be lurking. Puzzles like, "Can God create a stone so heavy that he cannot lift it?" put us on our guard, make us wary that we might become ensnared in some trap or contradiction. It seems then that while circularity is not necessarily fallacious as such, it may be worth detecting or knowing about in argument anyway, as a potential problem that could lead to fallaciousness in the right (or wrong) context.

Circular reasoning of another sort can happen when you try to set requirements for the success of an argument within the argument itself. The kind of circularity involved in this type of case has to do with different levels of argument or meta-argument. A case in point is the Paradox of Self-Amendment described by Hofstadter (1982, p. 16).

Case 1.17: My friend Scott Buresh, himself a lawyer, described the following perplexing hypothetical dilemma, which he first heard posed in a class on constitutional law. What if Congress passes a law saying that henceforth all determinations by the Supreme Court shall be made by a 6-3 majority (rather than a simple 5-4 majority, as is currently the case)? Imagine that this law is challenged in a court case that eventually makes its way up to the Supreme Court itself, and that the Supreme Court rules that the law is unconstitutional–and needless to say the ruling is by a 5-4 majority. What happens?

This case involves a problematic instance of self-reference that is definitely circular. And it certainly does pose a practical, as well as a theoretical problem of argumentation generally. But it is not clear that Congress, the Supreme Court, or anyone else in the case has committed the fallacy of begging the question.

Hence it seems that there are circular arguments that are not necessarily fallacious, and even problematic and viciously circular arguments that are not, at any rate clearly, instances of the fallacy of begging the question. The main problem for the analysis of this fallacy then is to provide criteria that would usefully help a critic to arrive correctly at an evaluative classification between those cases of allegedly circular argument where the fallacy of begging the question has occurred, and those cases where it has not. Judging by all the problems, paradoxes, and unanswered questions that have surfaced in this chapter, this will not be an easy job.

NOTES

1. See the distinction between vicious and fallacious circles in section 9 of chapter one. A more extended analysis of the argument in case 1.3 can be found in Colwell (1989).

2. So far, the exact source in Bentham, or other documentation of this attribution, has not been verified by the author's research.

3. See Kapp (1942) and Evans (1977).

4. Ibid.

5. Here arises the burden of proof.

6. See also Basu (1986) on the question of the interpretation of these doctrines of Aristotle.

7. See Woods and Walton (1975b).

8. See also Palmer (1981) on this issue of the number of premises.

9. Ibid.

10. At least it is the final one remarked on here. More recent articles will be dealt with in subsequent chapters.

11. Note Hamblin's comment (1970, p. 33) that a vicious circle is one that involves "self-contradiction or self-defeat," like the Liar Paradox.

12. Despite the title of Nicholas Rescher's paper, "How Serious a Fallacy Is Inconsistency?" *Argumentation* 1 (1987): 303-16.

2

Contexts of Dialogue

Making sense of begging the question as a fallacy presupposes the requirement that an argument has a purpose of proving something. Then the error or shortcoming of the fallacy can be seen as a failure to fulfill this goal of argument. A question-begging argument is one that is not useful for proving what it is supposed to prove. To use the traditional phrase, an argument that begs the question is a fallacy because it fails to fulfill its *burden of proof.* From a pragmatic perspective, an argument can be viewed as a device or instrument that has a purpose or goal that indicates its successful use to fulfill a burden or obligation in dialogue.

The background context against which begging the question begins to make sense as a fallacy, or critical fault of argument, is that of a pragmatic context of the use of an argument. This context is a sequence of dialogue exchanges or interactive speech acts between two or more participants in some sort of organized, purposeful exchange. Evidently, however, there can be different kinds of contexts of dialogues of this sort.

One goal of argument could be to convince or persuade somebody who doubts a particular proposition to come to accept that proposition. Another goal of argument could be to obtain secure knowledge in a process of collaborative inquiry by basing a conclusion only on securely established evidence. In both these contexts of dialogue there is a burden of proof. But, understandably, it might operate quite differently in the two types of cases. The standard of argument required to fulfill the burden of proof might be generally higher in the second kind of context. And in other respects, the way the requirements of burden of proof are to be met might be different, in significant respects, in the two types of dialogue.

This viewpoint of seeing begging the question as a failure of *proof* (in some sense) rather than a failure of inference, however, shifts the focus of the problem from semantics to pragmatics (the study of the uses of arguments).

1. INQUIRY VERSUS PERSUASION DIALOGUE

One normative model of argumentation is the persuasion dialogue, where the goal of one participant is to persuade the other of the truth of a designated proposition, and its best-known subtype, the critical discussion, which starts with a conflict of opinion and has the goal of resolving the conflict. The main instrument used to resolve the conflict in a critical discussion is the probative obligation to fulfill burden of proof. Conflicts of opinion in critical discussions are characteristically issues of values that are inherently subject to controversy, and therefore plausible reasoning is the best standard of proof one can normally hope for in order to resolve such disputes. When two arguments are relatively evenly matched, the stronger prevails, and the device of burden of proof makes it possible to have closure of the persuasion dialogue by setting out in advance what margin of victory in proving is required.

A contrasting normative model of argumentation is the inquiry, which starts with a proposition that is not known to be true and has the goal of proving that it is true. Once the inquiry has run its course, and closure has been reached, if it has not been proven that the proposition in question is true, then the conclusion is that the proposition should be conceded as false. This *ad ignorantiam* principle of burden of proof reflects the assumption that the inquiry has completely exhausted all the relevant knowledge concerning this proposition.[1] If new knowledge turns up, the inquiry may be declared open once again. The goal of the inquiry is to cover all the existing available knowledge on a subject, in order to establish whether or not a proposition is true or false.

Unlike the persuasion dialogue then, the inquiry is not concerned with open questions where controversy is always inherently possible, and can never be entirely closed off; the inquiry seeks to prove something, to establish it as definitely true. Thus the inquiry looks for premises that are definitely known to be true, propositions that can be verified as "facts," or that can be established as items of knowledge.

One basic characteristic of the inquiry is its cumulative nature. The method of operation of an inquiry is to establish certain premises as solid foundations, and then to build from these to establish further premises, on this basis. The intent of the inquiry is to avoid having to come back to these earlier propositions, once established, and later retract them. Retractions may have to be possible in an inquiry, in some instances, but the goal of the inquiry is to minimize the need for retractions, or even to eliminate retractions, if possible. The way this is done is to adopt strict methods of proof and verification. These methods and standards necessarily, however, vary with the subject of the inquiry.

The paradigm of the inquiry is Euclidean geometry, which starts with axioms that were, at one time, supposed to be self-evident, and then uses only deductively valid rules of inference to deduce theorems. The theorems are then numbered, and the general rule of argument is that only the lower-numbered (previously established) theorems can be used to prove the higher-numbered ones. This ordering of the sequence of proofs in Euclidean geometry as a feature of argumentation that excludes circular reasoning has been well described in Mackenzie (1980). And Aristotle's description of a type of argumentation he called a *demonstration* is an excellent description of the basic concept of the inquiry.[2] The basic principle of argument behind the inquiry is that of evidential priority–the premises should always be better known than the conclusion to be established at any particular stage of the inquiry. Hence the inquiry is much more unfriendly to circular argumentation–even more so than the persuasion dialogue.

In persuasion dialogue, circular argumentation is generally subject to suspicion as potentially confusing, and, even worse, as a kind of argument that may be strongly suspected of committing the fallacy of begging the question. But in the inquiry, circular reasoning is absolutely forbidden. It is opposed to the basic principle of the inquiry, which is always going ahead in a linear progress of establishing new knowledge on the basis of what has been previously established. Circling backward, so to speak, is the very kind of argumentation that the inquiry tries to rule out.

It is the inquiry that is the real vehicle for knowledge-based reasoning. The inquiry always works from a set of propositions called a knowledge base, and then derives conclusions from the propositions in that knowledge base by means of logical rules of inference. The counterpart to the knowledge base in persuasion dialogue is the arguer's position, his set of commitments (called a commitment-store by Hamblin) at a given point in the dialogue.

It would be inappropriate to conduct an inquiry into the subject of whether tipping should be maintained as a practice, because the issue is one of values, and it would be immature to think that an inquiry into the facts of the matter could definitely resolve this disputed question by arriving at a well-established conclusion. However, it would be appropriate to have a critical discussion (persuasion dialogue) on the issue. Such a discussion might be an interesting debate, and the winning side might show effective rhetorical techniques in shifting the burden of proof against the weaker side. But winning the dispute might not be the only valid criterion of whether the discussion was successful. A well-contested discussion could be truly revealing if it reveals two opposed positions underlying the two sides of the issue. For each position may represent a point of view that is also implicitly held, even if it has never been clearly articulated, by members of an audience, viewers, or readers who can themselves follow the argument and be influenced by it.

A circular argument might reveal an interesting and previously unknown sequence of connections among several propositions contained in the position of an arguer. By bringing out these connections through a circular series of questions and replies in dialogue, an arguer might be making a genuinely useful and informative contribution to the dialogue.[3]

Therefore, in persuasion dialogue, it cannot be taken for granted that a circular sequence of argumentation must be classified as a case of the *petitio principii* fallacy.

Reasonable dialogue has to do with shifts in the burden of proof according to the rules of dialogue. These rules may include specific rules for deductive argument, plausible argument, and procedural rules of various kinds. There are many special contexts of dialogue, but we still need to ask–is there some deeper, fundamental purpose of critical persuasion dialogue, and if so what is its principal benefit? Why study plausible reasoning if it is so notoriously subject to fallacies, errors, and subtle shifts that can easily lead us astray?

It is a natural presumption that the most significant benefit of argumentative dialogue–where the goal of dialogue is for the one participant to convince or persuade the other by reasonable argument–is the insight, or information increment, produced by the dialogue in the one to whom the argument is directed. And this is the objective of persuasion dialogue that we have emphasized so far. Thus if I become convinced of some proposition I was not previously committed to, by your argument, then the value or benefit of the dialogue has been my increased understanding, awareness, or insight with regard to my own position in the argument. Good dialogue has altered my position, and thereby deepened, refined, or articulated that position in some positive way.

However, it is less often recognized that there may be an important benefit of argumentative dialogue for the one who has advanced the reasoned argument, as well as the benefit gained by the recipient. For by constructing and successfully mounting the reasoned argument, the arguer may have also succeeded in refining and articulating his own position. Sometimes at the outset of argument, an arguer's position may be clear in some respects, but murky and shapeless in others, and through the process of having to defend his position against an opponent's queries and criticisms, that position may be more clearly and broadly defined. This process can give the arguer significant insight into his own position.

This description of critical persuasion dialogue as a process of deepened insight into one's own position on a controversial issue is consistent with the Socratic view of dialogue as a means to attain self-knowledge. For Socrates, the process of learning was an ascent from the depths of the cave toward the clearer light of self-knowledge through the process of reasoned, and primarily verbal, dialogue with another discussant, on controversial issues. What Socrates emphasized as a most important benefit or gain of dialogue was self-knowledge. It was somehow through the process of articulation and testing of one's best arguments against an able opponent in dialogue that real knowledge was to be gained.

This Socratic point of view draws our attention to the more hidden and subtle benefit of good persuasion dialogue. Not only does it enable one to persuade rationally an opponent or co-participant in discussion, but it is also the vehicle that enables one to come to understand better one's own position on important issues, one's own reasoned basis behind one's deeply held convictions. It is the concept of burden of proof that makes such shifts of rational persuasion possible, and thereby enables dialogue to contribute to knowledge.

From this Socratic perspective then, the educational value of dialogue is self-knowledge, the insight offered into the arguer's own convictions gained through argumentative interaction with an able opponent. From this point of view, a circular argument may be a failure as an attempt to persuade the other person in a dialogue to give up his own thesis. But even so, if not meant as a deceptive tactic, it may be more of a blunder, or ineffective strategy of persuasion, than a fallacy. Moreover, it might not be entirely without value in the dialogue. To condemn an argument as a fallacy then, we have to be able to identify the goal of the argument in the type of dialogue in which it occurs.

2. OTHER TYPES OF DIALOGUE

Aside from the persuasion dialogue and the inquiry, many other types of dialogue are important contexts of argumentation. In the study of informal fallacies, the persuasion dialogue (critical discussion) clearly has a central, or even primary, place among the many contexts of dialogue. However, because of dialectical shifting, many other contexts of dialogue are important to study as well.

The basic goal of the persuasion dialogue is for each participant to prove his thesis from the concessions of the other party. However, a secondary goal of the persuasion dialogue, which can be equally important in some cases, is for each participant to come to understand the other participant's position in a better light, and for that matter, his own position as well. It is this knowledge-revealing (maieutic) function of the persuasion dialogue that distinguishes it from more eristic contexts of dialogue like the debate and the quarrel. The persuasion dialogue characteristically combines an adversarial goal with Gricean maxims of collaboration and informativeness.

Burden of proof is defined as an allocation made in reasoned dialogue that sets a strength (weight) of argument required by one side to reasonably persuade the other side. Making this definition useful presupposes prior definition of the concept of persuasive reasoned dialogue. Chapter three will consider other contexts of reasoned dialogue. In persuasion dialogue, a useful argument has the function of proving its conclusion. But what is meant by "proof" here? A clue is to be found in Stoic logic.

Sextus (OP II 135) presented the conventional wisdom of his time (i.e. the Stoic philosophy) concerning what *proof* is by the following quotation: "an argument which, by means of agreed premises, reveals by way of deduction a non-evident inference." In this account, "agreed premises" are "judgments adopted by consent for the establishment of the inference" (OP II 136). "Deduction" refers to what Sextus called "conclusive" arguments, which corresponds to the concept of a deductively valid argument. And "non-evident" was not defined in this passage by Sextus, but it seems to refer to judgments that are not known to be true or accepted as true, at a particular stage of an argument. The basic idea behind the above conception of proof is made clearer in the following passage (OP II 140), where Sextus introduces the idea of a probative argument, a type of argument that "proves something," as we might say.

> Of true arguments, again, some are "probative," some "non-probative"; and the probative are those which deduce something non-evident by means of pre-evident premisses, the non-probative those not of this sort. For example, an argument such as this—"If it is day it is light; but in fact it is day; therefore it is light" is not probative; for its conclusion, that "it is light," is pre-evident. But an argument like this—"If sweat pours through the surface, there are insensible pores; but in fact sweat does pour through the surface; therefore there are insensible pores"—is a probative one, as its conclusion ("there are therefore insensible pores") is non-evident.

A *probative argument,* by this account, is one that deduces a conclusion that is non-evident from premises that are pre-evident. Thus a probative argument effects a kind of change or movement from a prior situation where the conclusion was non-evident, to a new situation where the conclusion becomes evident.

A probative argument is supposed to go from pre-evident premises to a non-evident conclusion. But if the argument begs the question, or is fallaciously circular, it can never do this. Why not? Because one of the premises is somehow too tightly locked into the conclusion, that is, too dependent on, or too closely equivalent to, the conclusion. As a result, if the conclusion is non-evident, then this premise must be non-evident too. Hence the premises, as a set, must be non-evident. This is because in a circular argument, the only way to be secure of the pre-evident status of a particular premise requires the prior assurance of the pre-evident status of the conclusion. If the conclusion is non-evident, then the pre-evident status of the premises cannot be secure when the argument is locked into a circular interdependence of premises and conclusion. If the conclusion is non-evident, the premises can't be pre-evident.

This novel idea that an argument can have a probative use in bringing forward "new" evidence is the precursor of the concept of the probative function of argument (chapter eight, section three), which will be the basis of our theory of begging the question.

According to the theory developed in chapter eight, the basic problem with a fallaciously question-begging argument is that the *only* way to support one of the premises as evident is by a route of argument that includes the conclusion as part of the evidence. Sextus had already given a kind of explanation of this problem, in terms of evidential priority. The pre-evidence of the premises as a set of propositions requires that the conclusion be in evidence as well, thus ruling out the non-evidence of the conclusion. Hence an argument that begs the question can never be a probative argument. Here we already have the beginnings of a nice theory.

The burden of proof for successful argument is to effect a shift so that the conclusion, which was formerly non-evident, has become evident (due to the pre-evident premises used). Begging the question is a fallacy because a question-begging argument can never fulfill this burden of proof. Many details of how this fallacy is a failure need to be worked out, however.

In examining any particular text of argumentative discourse, the question may (and should) be asked: What strength of evidence is required to prove? In most cases of argumentative discourse on controversial issues in natural language, absolutely incontrovertible evidence is not required to establish a claim. In some cases, no evidence at all need be required–for example if a proposition is already accepted by all participants, and is not subject to doubt or challenge. In other cases, a tiny amount of evidence can reasonably swing the outcome to one side–for example, if arguments on both sides are equally balanced. Thus to understand the concept of burden of proof in reasoned argumentation, we must come to understand how the initial plausibility of a proposition can come to be altered–either raised or lowered–through the dynamic of objection and reply in reasoned dialogue.

Recognition and use of burden of proof in argumentation can be a powerful factor in reasoned persuasion, and yet it is a subtlety, in many cases, that is overlooked. Consider the following parliamentary question-reply exchange.

Case 2.0:   **Q:** Why are my constituents the targets of such savage and unacceptable cutbacks?

A: The Government is doing the best it can to retrain employees and proceed in a humane manner.

This answer may be a reasonable reply to the question, as far as it goes. But where the respondent may have significantly failed is through not having questioned the presupposition that the cutbacks were "savage and unacceptable." Because this presupposition of the question, in effect, makes a positive assertion of a contentious proposition, there is a burden of proof on the questioner to back it up if challenged. By not raising this challenge in his response, the respondent concedes too much to the side of the opposition. In effect, the response makes the government seem guilty of the unacceptable offenses argumentatively advanced in the question. By failing to shift the burden of proof back onto the questioner, the respondent overlooks his strongest argument on the issue of contention.

Whately (1846, 1963, p. 113) warned against this type of strategic failure in argumentation when he compared it to the case of an army occupying a fort that it is perfectly capable of defending. By sallying forth into the open field, they are defeated. Similarly, in argument, if you forget to insist that there is a burden of proof on your opponent's side that you can show has not been met, and instead use positive arguments that may be weak to try to defend your own side, you may be succumbing to a feeble defense by overlooking your strongest arguments. Whately (p. 114) quotes the French proverb "Qui s'excuse, s'accuse" to illustrate the unfortunate instance of a respondent who unnecessarily makes himself appear guilty in the face of an accusation by taking on the burden of trying to prove his own innocence, when what he should be doing is defying his accuser to prove his charge.

Whately's excellent advice reveals that mounting a persuasive argument in reasoned question-reply dialogue requires a fine tuning and awareness of matters of burden of proof. Further evidence from Hamblin (1970) and Walton (1985a) suggests that in fact many of the so-called informal fallacies are important kinds of persuasive strategies in argumentation precisely because they reflect subtle shifts in the burden of proof that can be powerfully effective, yet often go unnoticed in the heat of a dispute.

One special type of persuasion dialogue is the *dispute,* where the thesis of the one party is the opposite of the other's thesis. Another way of classifying different subclasses of the persuasion dialogue is by the degree of articulation of reasoned rules or procedures, and consequently by the level of rationality of the participants in enunciating and sticking to these rules. The *quarrel* is characterized by anarchy and uncritical personal attack. The *debate* is characterized by better articulated rules than the quarrel, but still retains a strong propensity for personal attack and appeal to popularity. The *persuasion dialogue* is characterized by an adherence to logical rules of inference and procedural rules of questioning and answering that have been spelled out in greater detail. Logical proof is a very important and central part of reasoned persuasion dialogue, as noted in chapter two.

Persuasion dialogue is generally based on an initial position based on plausible presumption. Then the sequence of dialogue modifies each participant's commitments to tilt the burden of proof to one side or the other by increasing or decreasing the plausibility of each initial position. Retraction of commitment is a characteristic of persuasion dialogue, and criticism based on inconsistency of position is also very important.

The parliamentary or congressional debate is a good example of the *debate,* especially on occasions where free questioning on a controversial issue or topic is allowed. The institution of Question Period is a segment of the parliamentary debates in Commonwealth countries where open questioning on a controversial issue is allotted a period of time for discussion. The speaker of the house moderates the debate, but the range of questioning and answering allowed is very broad, and there are few restrictions. A member cannot call another member of parliament an outright liar or otherwise make very severe personal attacks, but the latitude allowed is very broad. So in any particular case, an argument that scores well in a debate may not be a justifiable or reasonable argument from a logical point of view.

TEN BASIC TYPES OF DIALOGUE

	TYPE OF DIALOGUE	INITIAL SITUATION	GOAL	BENEFITS
1.	PERSUASION (CRITICAL DISCUSSION)	CONFLICT OF OPINION	TO PERSUADE OTHER PARTY	UNDERSTAND POSITIONS
2.	DEBATE	ADVERSARIAL CONTEST	PERSUADE THIRD PARTY	DISPLAY OF RHETORICAL SKILLS
3.	INQUIRY	NEED TO ESTABLISH A FINDING	PROVE OR DISPROVE CONJECTURE	OBTAIN KNOWLEDGE
4.	NEGOTIATION	CONFLICT OF INTEREST	MINIMIZE GAINS (SELF-INTEREST)	SETTLEMENT AND CONSENSUS
5.	PLANNING COMMITTEE	COLLECTIVE ACTION REQUIRED	JOINT PLAN OR DECISION	AIRING OF OBJECTIONS
6.	PEDAGOGICAL	IGNORANCE OF ONE PARTY	TEACHING AND LEARNING	REVERSE TRANSFER
7.	DELIBERATION	PRACTICAL PROBLEM OF ACTION	SOLUTION TO PROBLEM	GOALS ARE ARTICULATED
8.	QUARREL	PERSONAL CONFLICT	TO DEFEAT OPPONENT	VENTING OF EMOTIONS
9.	INTERVIEW	CURIOSITY ABOUT POSITION	DEVELOP SUBJECT'S POSITION	SPREAD OF INFORMATION
10.	EXPERT CONSULTATION	NEED FOR EXPERT ADVICE	DECISION FOR ACTION	SECOND-HAND KNOWLEDGE

Table 2.0

In short then, the debate can be a friend of reason, but something of a fair-weather friend. We cannot count on an argument in debate to be exempt from reasonable criticism, or free from logical fallacy. Once again, the basic purpose of debate is to win out over your adversary, whether it is by logical proof or not.

The *negotiation* type of dialogue is very different from the debate or the persuasion dialogue. For that matter, it is also very different from the inquiry. The whole point of the negotiation dialogue is not to prove anything, to seek the truth, or to uncover knowledge. Instead, to put it bluntly, the purpose is to "make a deal." Concern with the truth of a matter is, generally, highly secondary to the aims of a negotiation. Moore (1986, p. 74) described negotiation dialogue accurately when he characterized interest-based conflict as a process of competitive collaboration where the participants collaborate to compete for a set of goods where there is a real or perceived scarcity.

In North America, the *planning committee* dialogue usually resolves its differences of opinion by a vote, reflecting the majority opinion. In Japan, the norm appears to be more of a teamwork process of arriving at a unanimous consensus. In neither instance does the outcome necessarily indicate a process of logical reasoning as the means of concluding the argument. The outcome may be based on self-interest, or corporate interest. However, the committee meeting can, in some cases, involve persuasion dialogue as part of the process. Committee meetings can have well-organized rules, like those proposed in books that outline rules of order for conducting a successful meeting. Often these rules are highly institutionalized by traditions or regulations of a particular body or group.

In negotiation, each party starts with a particular goal in mind, and the specific items in the goal comprise that party's *agenda*. The conflict arises because there are differences between the goals of the two parties. The function of negotiation dialogue is for the two parties to move toward, and ultimately agree upon, some middle point that partly meets both goals at the cost of losses on both sides. Thus the dialogue proceeds by each party making offers of concessions to the other. A *concession* is an offer agreed to by one party that sacrifices some agenda items of that party while fulfilling some agenda items of the other party. Concessions in negotiation dialogue are the counterparts of commitments in persuasion dialogue.

The ordering of items to be discussed on an agenda in negotiation is often very important. A party's priorities in its own agenda are also very important–some goals may be "bottom-line" goals that a party must hang onto at all costs. Other goals can be more easily conceded or sacrificed.

Often in negotiation, one party is the defender of the status quo, and the other is the attacker. For example, in union contract negotiating, often the company is trying to hang onto the existing arrangement without giving in to demands for change, while the union is trying to extract some new benefits, not previously conceded. In this respect, something parallel to burden of proof is operative. But in negotiation, proof is not the goal of the dialogue, and therefore burden of proof does not have the central place it has in persuasion dialogue.

3. SAMPLE DIALOGUE ON TIPPING

The following sample persuasion dialogue is a dispute on the topic of tipping. The issue concerns the practice or custom of tipping as it presently exists for certain services–for example, tipping taxi drivers or waiters and waitresses in restaurants. There are two arguers in the dispute, and each has a thesis to be argued for. Bob is to argue for the thesis that tipping should be maintained as it presently is in North America. Helen is to argue for the thesis that tipping should be eliminated. Each takes turns to present arguments.

The rules of conduct of arguments that govern persuasion dialogue will be discussed and developed throughout subsequent chapters. However, even in advance of identifying specific rules and guidelines, it is well to learn, by looking at a realistic case of fairly well-reasoned persuasion dialogue, what the main components of this kind of dialogue are.

Bob: Well, I think that tipping is good because it rewards excellence of service. If a service is performed courteously, efficiently, and with excellence, then that excellence can be rewarded. This rewards a better effort, and leads to better work.

Helen: Well, the problem with that is that tipping becomes expected, after a while, as a customary practice. Then a tip is expected for even mediocre service. If you don't tip, you are penalized. Also, this can lead to many misunderstandings. One time my husband failed to leave a tip for the coat check service because he did not remember whether it was the custom to pay this tip before or after the meal. He did not pay it before the meal, thinking it should be paid afterward. During the meal, the waiter intentionally spilled soup on my husband's suit. We are sure he did it because of the failure to tip. So you see, what happens is that the tip becomes an expected practice, whether the service is any good or not. Then you may be penalized with worse service if you fail to tip. Also, many misunderstandings are possible, because customers may not be sure when a tip is expected.

Bob: If you could convince me that these bad consequences of tipping–the misunderstandings and abuses that arise out of the practice of tipping–outweigh the good effects of tipping, then I would concede that tipping ought to be discontinued. But you have not convinced me of that, and indeed, I think that the beneficial effects of tipping are greater than the bad side-effects. There are always going to be abuses or misunderstandings of any practice or custom, no matter what this custom is. If someone comes to expect a tip for mediocre or poor service, then the client should correct this expectation by making it clear that he is not tipping in that case. Customers should have an obligation to use their consumer skills, and only tip for value received in above-average service. Also, a lot of people would never get jobs if it weren't for tipping, because their employers could never afford to pay the salary that they would need without the income from tips.

Helen: One thing that really bothers me is that tipping is so undignified. It is as if the customer is saying that the service person is some type of low "peasant" or "servant" who is supposed to be lucky to get some small change thrown their way by a big spender. In fact, I think that one reason that tipping appeals to people who have a snobbish inclination is that they feel that, by tipping, they can show they are better than somebody else. They can show they are a "big wheel" who can toss some "chicken feed" to the underlings. The practice of tipping encourages and legitimates this indignity and snobbery.

Bob: Well, here again you are talking about excesses and abuses. People who are snobbish, phony, or elitist, are always going to find ways to feel superior. They may drive an expensive car, belong to a country club, or look down on others whom they believe to be their social inferiors. Tipping or not tipping is not going to change that. If people who accept tips feel undignified, that is their problem. They shouldn't, because they may be making good money, and tipping can be a good source of revenue for them. If they are doing a good job, they should be paid well for it. And tips can help them to earn a good income. Earning a good income is the most important thing in making them feel secure and dignified.

Helen: If a person is doing a good job they should get a regular pay for that job that reflects the value of the work. If the job is worthy and productive, the person who does it should get a regular salary, and not have to depend on the whims of customers for a living. Pay should be based on comparable worth of the job, as decided by a government evaluation of what is fair and equitable.

Bob: I don't think any government committee can or should decide the worth of someone's work. What your service or skills should be worth should be settled by what your clients or customers are willing to pay for it. The whole idea of comparable worth is a socialistic nightmare, based on an impractical and misguided idealism.

Helen: Comparable worth is simply a matter of fair guidelines to assure human dignity and equality. The market forces of capitalism are not the best means of assuring guidelines that give people fairness and dignity. Tipping just is not dignified or fair. It is degrading.

Bob: Tipping is fair and dignified because it rewards excellence. It is well known that under any government system of bureaucratic regulations, excellence is discouraged and frustrated. Under such a system, there is no real dignity or fairness–just patronage and special privileges bestowed on those who are in favor with the government or who climb to bureaucratic positions of power.

In this dialogue, both parties respond to the points made by the other party's previous move. There is a good interchange of viewpoints, and both sides of the argument are well represented on many points of contention. This interchange is maintained throughout the dialogue because each participant, at each move, either replies to a previous argument of the other party, or introduces a new argument that is relevant to the issue.

Bob's thesis to be proved is that tipping should be maintained. At his very first move in the dialogue, he brings forward an argument that is relevant to his thesis, namely the proposition that tipping is good because it rewards excellence of service, which leads to better work. Then at her move, Helen makes an objection to Bob's argument. She argues that tipping becomes a customary practice, expected even for mediocre service. What she is pointing out then, is that tipping doesn't necessarily reward excellence of service. In short, her objection applies to Bob's previous argument. Then she goes on to add some other points about misunderstandings that can arise from tipping. Then at his next move, Bob, in turn replies to Helen's objection by arguing that there are abuses of any practice, and that it is up to the consumer to make tipping a reward for excellent service only. Overall then, the argument is an interlocking network of moves (Figure 2.1).

BACK-AND-FORTH EXCHANGE IN DIALOGUE

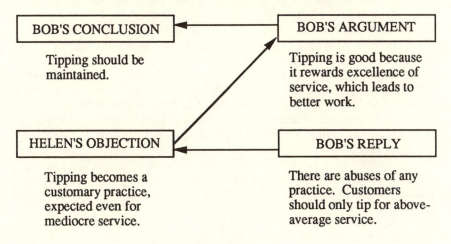

Figure 2.1

Then at this point in the dialogue, Bob introduces a new argument that tipping leads to more jobs. And Helen, at her next move, also introduces a new line of argument. She argues that tipping is undignified. However, both these arguments are highly relevant to the issue of the dialogue. And later in the dialogue, Helen replies to Bob's argument that tipping leads to more jobs by arguing that the government should take over and regulate the economy.

The overall pattern of the dialogue, we can see, is made up of linkages between groups of moves of the participants. A given group of moves, we have seen, exhibits the pattern shown in figure 2.2.

OVERALL PATTERN OF REASONABLE DIALOGUE

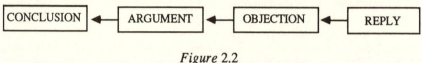

Figure 2.2

We can judge then that the dialogue between Helen and Bob is fairly reasonable because each step is connected to other steps in the overall argument. Each step follows the last one, for a while at least, but then at many junctures new arguments are introduced.

The new argument between Helen and Bob could be more regulated. If we wanted to make the dialogue more precisely regulated, we could require that only one argument or reply be introduced at each move. We did notice, for example, that in some cases each participant would introduce several arguments at his or her move. But on the whole, each participant is fairly polite and reasonable. Both arguers restrain themselves very well, and neither of them tries to block the other from replying. The argument could be more regulated. But as it goes, the pattern of objections and replies seems fairly reasonable.

Perhaps the most interesting observation is that although the issue does not seem to be conclusively decided—neither party decisively wins the argument in that sense—still the argument is not a waste of time. It is an informative argument because the reasoning behind each side of the argument is brought out. That is, the position of each arguer is more fully revealed as a reasonable stance that someone might take. Although you may not agree with Helen's thesis, having followed through the dialogue, you are probably in a better position to appreciate why she, or anyone else, might reasonably be inclined to adopt her position. The same could be said for Bob's point of view.

Here then is the most valuable function of reasonable dialogue. It may resolve the issue by making apparent which is the stronger and which is the weaker argument, or it may not. In either event, it is good dialogue if it more fully reveals the reasons behind each side of the argument. Dialogue is good, or informative, to the extent that through the course of the dialogue, the position of each arguer becomes more fully articulated or revealed, both to that arguer, the other arguer, and anyone else who may follow the course of the argument. This articulation of an arguer's previously hidden or implicit commitments can be called the *maieutic function* of dialogue.

In a game of reasonable dialogue then, there are really two objectives or purposes. The ostensible and primary purpose of each arguer is to prove or argue for his thesis and to refute or criticize the opponent party's thesis. This is the probative function of dialogue that Sextus described as an argument that deduces a non-evident conclusion from pre-evident premises. It is also a contestive or adversarial aspect of dialogue. To perform this function, according to the rules of reasonable dialogue, an arguer must ask probing questions, challenge the opponent's arguments, produce sound and compelling arguments for his own position, and level justifiable criticisms at the opponent's arguments. But if all this is done successfully throughout the dialogue, the maieutic function of reasonable dialogue will also be fulfilled. The maieutic function is to explore and reveal the reasons behind one's own position on the issue, and by challenging the opponent's position to uncover the logical basis of that position as well. This is the information increment that can be achieved by good dialogue, and the reason why reasonable dialogue has educational benefits.

Good dialogue can have a cumulative effect of revealing the contours of a controversial issue if each reply is relevant to the previous argument in the series. For example, Bob starts out by making the point that tipping rewards excellence of service. Helen replies to that point by making the objection that expectations lead to tipping for mediocre service. She makes the additional point that these expectations can lead to unfortunate misunderstandings. But then Bob replies to that objection by pointing out that any accepted practice can lead to abuses or misunderstandings. Then he adds the new point that some people would not have jobs if it weren't for tipping.

The pattern of the dialogue between Helen and Bob always continues along similar lines. As each one makes a point, the other replies to that point by making an objection or criticism, then also adding a new relevant point to support his or her own thesis. Thus each of the arguments is relevant within the dialogue as a whole. Each point is either a reply to a previous argument or objection, or it raises a new point that furnishes an additional argument to support the arguer's thesis. Thus the dialogue, as a whole, has a certain continuity. It holds together. Each move is linked to previous moves, and together the moves have direction and unfold the development of the issue. This continuity or relevance is the mark of good dialogue. It enables the dialogue to make progress.

This holding together of a dialogue is called *dialogue coherence,* meaning that each speech act in the dialogue is linked to adjacent speech acts so that the whole sequence has a continuity, and fits together with the other speech acts like the pieces of a jigsaw puzzle. Each speech act has felicity conditions and each related speech act has matching conditions. For example, in order to be a good or reasonable (happy) speech act in a dialogue, a question has to fulfill certain conditions. But to be an adequate reply to a question, the next move after the question in a dialogue also has to fulfill certain conditions. A whole sequence of questions and replies in a dialogue are coherent if they match each other and move in a sequence toward the goal of the dialogue.

To make an argument explicitly coherent, it must be reconstructed from the text *(corpus)* of discourse. But to accomplish this, a specific argument, with premises and a conclusion, must be fitted into a coherent context of dialogue.

4. COMPONENTS OF AN ARGUMENT IN PERSUASION DIALOGUE

Our objective will be the study of arguments, to evaluate arguments and classify them as correct or incorrect, justifiable or open to criticism, strong or weak. However, before you can fairly evaluate an argument, you must determine what the purpose of that argument is supposed to be in the context of dialogue in which it was advanced. If advanced in a persuasion dialogue, the probative function of the argument is to convince the other party to accept a conclusion. Arguments in persuasion dialogue have ten basic characteristics or components, and it will be helpful to keep these in mind in locating and studying the particular arguments of the case studies in chapters four and five.

The first characteristic is that an argument is basically a claim put forward or advanced by an arguer, directed to some audience or recipient. Therefore, every argument has two sides. Or, as we might say, every argument is really a *dialogue*. Although argument often takes place between or among large groups of arguers, all argument as dialogue ultimately reduces to two sides, a *pro* and a *con*. Every argument is advanced by a *proponent,* and aimed at or directed toward a *recipient,* most often an *opponent.* Any argument, therefore, is fundamentally a form of dialogue interaction between two participants in the argument.

In the argument on tipping, the two participants are Bob and Helen. We do not know much about Bob and Helen, who they are or what they stand for. But as the argument unfolds, we begin to get a better idea of who they are.

So an argument is an interaction. But what sort of interaction? The second component of an argument is that each side takes turns making its claims or counter-claims, its questions, answers, replies, and objections. At each juncture or move, each arguer advances a speech act. This speech act contains certain statements or propositions. In a reasonable argument, each participant takes turns, or in other words, allows the other arguer "equal time." In real life, equal time is not always practically possible. But where it is not, one must remember in evaluating the argument that one side may not have been fairly or equally represented.

A question is a request for information or a request that the person questioned supply certain propositions as directed by the request. There are many kinds of questions. For example, a yes-no question poses two alternatives, each one the opposite of the other. In our example, Bob and Helen do ask questions. But they often make assertions and advance arguments as well. Assertions and arguments bring with them a burden of proof.

The third basic component of an argument is that there must be an *issue,* a proposition to be decided or resolved by the outcome of the argument. In our sample study, the issue is tipping. More precisely, the issue is whether the practice of tipping should be maintained or eliminated. Each arguer takes one side of the issue. Bob defends the thesis that tipping should be maintained, and Helen argues for the thesis that tipping should be eliminated. Thus the issue is defined by the determination of the *thesis* or *final conclusion* to be proven by each participant, and by how it is to be proven. The issue of any argument should be clearly stated at the outset. The issue defines the scope, limits, and general direction of the argument as a sequence of individual moves or interactions. The issue defines the goal of each arguer and provides the ultimate criterion against which the successes or failure of the argument should be evaluated.

As we look over the argument between Helen and Bob, we see that the argument is made up of many single or local moves or arguments (subarguments) that, taken all together, form the one big argument. For example, Bob starts out by saying that tipping is good because it rewards excellence. Here Bob is advocating a conclusion, namely the proposition "tipping is good." And he is advancing a premise, another proposition, "tipping rewards excellence of service," meant to back up, or provide a reason for Helen to accept his conclusion. But then Bob's local conclusion is in turn meant as a premise to provide a reason for Bob's ultimate conclusion that tipping should be maintained. This linking of local arguments into a global sequence of dialogue is the fourth characteristic of argument.

That is how arguments are put together. Each argument is linked with other arguments so that, in a good argument, there is an overall coherent movement or direction toward the ultimate conclusion. As Bob goes on, he advances many other local arguments that also help to support his ultimate contention.

But notice that, at each local level, there is an interaction between Bob's arguments and Helen's replies. At her first move, Helen criticizes Bob's previous argument. She argues that tipping becomes expected or customary, even if the service is mediocre. In other words, Helen is criticizing Bob's contention that tipping rewards excellence. She goes on to add other criticisms and objections. For example, she argues that tipping leads to unfortunate misunderstandings.

This back-and-forth movement is a fourth characteristic of good argument. If one arguer proposes an argument, then it is very good if the other arguer makes a challenge, question, or criticism that is relevant to the first argument. That way, there is real interaction, both sides can be represented, and the argument can be very revealing, and make progress toward resolving or exploring the issue. A good argument does not always decide or close the issue, but it should reveal the best arguments for and against.

As Helen and Bob go along, each offers particular arguments. Helen argues that tipping is undignified. Bob argues that without tipping, many people would not have jobs that they now have. But as the argument goes on, each of them comes back to certain basic points they seem to feel strongly about. Bob feels that rewarding excellence is important. Helen feels that a working person should get a decent salary that reflects the value of that type of work. Bob feels that the consumer marketplace should decide how excellence is to be rewarded. Through the whole argument, the general overall position of each arguer emerges. The arguer's position is the fifth component of argument as reasonable dialogue. Bob is committed to tipping as an acceptable practice because it is a free-market economy exchange. Helen is against tipping because leaving such decisions to the vicissitudes of the free-market economy is not necessarily fair or equitable, in her view. She favors government regulation to assure every working person a steady income based on the comparable worth of his or her job.

Once we have followed through the whole course of the argument then, we get a picture of which propositions each arguer is committed to. According to the conception of argument modeled in Hamblin (1970), the most fundamental aspect of argument as reasoned dialogue is that each participant in the dialogue must have a set of commitments called a *commitment-store*. Physically speaking, a commitment-store can be visualized as a set of statements written out in a list on a blackboard. Or it could be visualized as a set of propositions recorded in the memory of a computer. The point is, in any event, that a commitment-store must be a definite set of propositions. It can be an empty set, unless the thesis of each participant must be counted as an initial, given commitment of that participant.

What Hamblin calls a commitment-store of a player we here call, collectively, the position of that participant in reasonable dialogue. Hamblin thinks of the commitment-store as being visible to all the participants. However, it does not necessarily need to be visible to all or any players at all or any times. All that is required is that it be a definite set of propositions.

The idea is that as the game of dialogue proceeds, propositions are added to, or deleted from, the commitment-stores of each of the players, according to the rules of the game and the moves made by the players during the course of the game. And from this, we get a general appreciation of the position of each of the arguers on the issue. From our knowledge of their positions, we could plausibly predict which side each of them might be likely to accept on other propositions that might arise as questions on this or related issues. Each arguer has a position, and that is the fifth characteristic of argument.

In a good argument, each party learns a good deal about the position of the other. A good arguer must have empathy, the ability to understand the other party's position, and the reasons found acceptable by the other party for taking a particular stand on the issue. A good arguer must be sensitive to what the other arguer accepts as plausible or implausible. In addition, however, a good argument may also teach a person more about his or her own position on the issue. By testing one's commitments on an issue in argument, one may find through dialogue that one comes to a better understanding of one's own position.

The sixth component of an argument is the *corpus* or *text* of that argument. Once an argument is run through, it leaves certain traces or records of the moves that were made during the argument. An argument may be videotaped, or minutes may be taken. In some legal cases, a court stenographer may take a transcription of the argument. Where the argument is printed, in a book or newspaper for example, the writing on the page is the corpus. A corpus provides the evidence of what was said during the argument.

In evaluating an argument afterward, one has to go by the evidence of what was said or what took place. Interpretations of what was said, or how it was said, may differ widely according to the account given by each side. Therefore, the corpus is the evidence of what the argument was, or is.

In any argument, if a participant advances a proposition as a conclusion or assertion, then he should be taken to be committed to that proposition, except where he may subsequently be allowed to reasonably retract it. The collective commitments of an arguer define his position in the argument. If an argument is to be fairly evaluated, some record of each arguer's log of commitments should be available. However, in practical terms of realistic argumentation, these things may be forgotten or later questioned. Consequently, the arguer's position must be defined in relation to the existing corpus given to the argument evaluator. This means that if you plan to criticize some argument, you had better start by clearly stating what the argument may be taken to consist of. At the very least, you must have some text or corpus that can be clearly identified.

A seventh component of argument is the *burden of proof,* which states what each participant in the argument must prove in order to win the argument. For example, to review from chapter two, in criminal law, the burden of proof is normally on the prosecution to prove, beyond a reasonable doubt, that the person charged committed a crime. The defendant only has to prove that there is a reasonable doubt. That is, all the defense attorney has to prove is that the prosecutor's argument is weak, that it does not prove guilt beyond reasonable doubt. In this type of argument, the burden of proof is not equal–it weighs much more heavily on the prosecution than on the defense.

However, in our argument between Bob and Helen on tipping, the burden of proof is roughly equal. Bob has to prove that the practice of tipping should be maintained. Helen must prove that tipping should be eliminated. These two propositions are roughly equal in plausibility, so we could say that the burden of proof is equally distributed in this argument.[4] But if Helen had to prove that tipping is never acceptable and Bob only had to prove that tipping is sometimes acceptable, then Bob would have a much easier job of proving his thesis. In that case, we would say that the burden of proof is not even approximately equal, and that the burden of proof on Helen's side is much heavier.

The burden of proof generally determines how strong an argument must be in order to build a successful case to prove its proponent's thesis. In this dialogue, the burden of proof is *symmetrical,* meaning that each party must produce an equally strong argument to prove his or her thesis. In other dialogues, the burden of proof is not equally distributed. In such a dialogue, we say (following chapter two) that the burden of proof is *asymmetrical,* meaning that one party has a heavier burden of proof than the other. For example, in some dialogues, the role of one party is simply to question or criticize the arguments of the other party, while the other party must positively prove his thesis in order to be successful. In this type of dialogue, one arguer is more of a defender while the other is more of an attacker or critic.

An eighth component of argument are the criticisms used by an arguer to attack the other participant's arguments. A person's argument can be criticized in many ways, and the study of reasonable dialogue is largely composed of the study of many different types of criticisms in order to evaluate when a criticism is reasonable or unreasonable. An argument may sometimes be criticized as weak if it is not a valid argument. Or an arguer's position may sometimes be criticized on the grounds that it contains a logical inconsistency.

A *refutation* is an overwhelming criticism that, if successful, destroys or negates the argument that it is directed against. A *fallacy* is (primarily) a sophistical refutation, that is, a tactic or strategy of argument that is not a successful refutation or even a reasonable criticism even though it is the kind of argument that may seem plausible and may be taken to be a reasonable criticism, or even a successful refutation by an uncritical audience or arguer, and is aggressively portrayed by its proponent as an argument that should overwhelm a respondent.[5] In other words, a fallacy is a type of powerfully deceptive tactic of argumentation that often looks good. As we go on however, we will see (somewhat paradoxically) that traditional so-called fallacies are not fallacies at all, in every instance. Sometimes they turn out to be criticisms, or weak arguments that are open to criticism, but are not totally refuted as worthless—more blunders than fallacies. We will also see (in chapter six) that some fallacies are not sophistical refutations but are lesser faults called errors of reasoning, which do not require a context of dialogue.

The ninth characteristic of argument is that most really significant issues are argued in the medium of natural language. That is, arguments take place in a natural language, like English, rather than an artificial language, a formal language or computer type of language where all the terms are exactly defined. The terms in natural language are often vague and ambiguous. This means that we must expect that many of the arguments we will have in particular cases will be on issues like how a term can be fairly defined, or whether a term used in argument is misleadingly ambiguous.

Because the arguments we are primarily concerned with are expressed in natural language, the logical regimentation of arguments is limited. Rarely is an argument fairly judged to be either altogether perfect or altogether worthless. Instead, we have models of reasonable dialogue, and a good argument is one that conforms closely enough to the model in important respects, whereby the argument may be judged to be reasonable or defensible. That doesn't necessarily mean that the argument is perfectly correct in every respect, only that it can be defended against certain criticisms alleged against it.

The function of an argument in a persuasion dialogue should be to shift the burden of proof. Many of the types of argument criticisms we will subsequently study are good criticisms to the extent that they successfully serve to shift the burden of proof onto an opponent's side of the argument. Begging the question is a fallacy because it puts forward an argument in dialogue in such a way that it can never fulfill this probative function.

Now that we at least have an example of an argument and an itemization of its main components, we can go on to study all the particular points to be considered in evaluating arguments, based on the general perspective or orientation of argument as reasonable dialogue. The considerations of this introduction have not given us a theory of argument yet. But we at least have an initial idea of what an argument is, or should be. As we go on to examine the finer points of many particular arguments in each chapter, we will learn more about what a successful argument is.

5. BEGGING THE QUESTION IN DIALOGUE

Every single argument is normally just a small part of a larger chain of arguments that are linked together in a reasoned discussion of an issue under dispute. Thus more generally, to understand an argument, a critic needs to ask what the overall issue is, and what burden of proof this issue reveals on both sides. These questions are part of the analysis of an argument at the global level.

As we looked over the dialogue on tipping, we saw that it had an overall direction and unity, a macrostructure as a reasoned dialogue. However, the argument as a whole was made up of subarguments, individual steps, replies, or advancements of premises and conclusions.

We now turn to three small segments of dialogue that are kinds of cases where a criticism of begging the question might be likely to arise. First, we will consider each case by itself, as a separate argument with no further context of dialogue given. Then we will consider the same case as if it occurred as a continuation of the sample dialogue on tipping. This experiment may begin to give us an idea of how important pragmatic context is to evaluating question-begging.

Case 2.1:   **Bob:**   Why is tipping a bad practice?

   Helen: If a practice should not be maintained, because of its bad effects, then that practice is bad. Now tipping has bad effects, as I showed by indicating many of these specific bad consequences that are results of tipping. Therefore, tipping is a bad practice.

When we consider case 2.1 as a segment of dialogue on its own, with no further or prior context of dialogue surrounding it, the argument appears to be a reasonable one. At any rate, it does not appear to be a case where the fallacy of begging the question has been committed.

However, the argument put forward by Helen does appear to be an enthymeme–it appears to presume that the reason that the practice of tipping should not be maintained is that it has bad effects. A sketch of a reconstruction of Helen's argument could be given as figure 2.3.

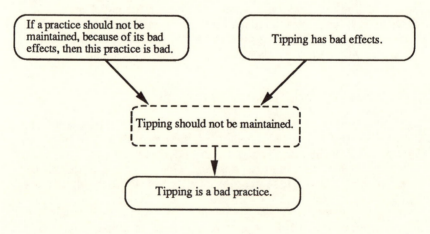

Figure 2.3

The top two premises in Helen's argument function together as a linked argument that enables the listener of the argument to draw the enthymematic conclusion (drawn in figure 2.3 with a broken boundary) that tipping should not be maintained.

It is a question of interpretation whether Helen is utilizing the interim conclusion as an unexpressed step to draw her ultimate conclusion that tipping is a bad practice. But even if she is, the argument does not appear to commit any fallacy. By itself, it appears to be a reasonable kind of argument to advance in a controversy about whether tipping is a good or bad practice.

However, try the experiment of putting case 2.1 in the context of the prior sequence of larger dialogue between Helen and Bob on the issue of whether tipping should be maintained as a practice. Tacked onto the end of that larger dialogue, case 2.1 does exhibit strong evidence of a fallacy of begging the question. For the proposition "Tipping should not be maintained," which is an interim premise for Helen's conclusion that tipping is a bad practice (as shown in figure 2.3), is the very (ultimate) conclusion that Helen is supposed to prove in the larger dialogue. In case 2.1, this proposition serves as both premise and conclusion, by linking together the initial premises with the secondary conclusion, as shown in figure 2.3. Helen's conclusion to be proven is assumed by her as a premise–even if it was derived from other premises–and so, in context, she can be accused of begging the question, with some *prima facie* reasonable justification.

Now consider a second case, first imagining that it does not necessarily bear any connection to the sample dialogue on tipping.

Case 2.2:   **Bob:**   Why should the person who does the better job get more money?

              Helen: She should get more money because she deserves it.

              Bob: But why would she deserve it?

              Helen: Because she is more competent.

              Bob: But how can you tell on good evidence that she is more competent?

              Helen: Because she does the better job.

What would be open to criticism about this sequence of argument? Bob might reasonably want to point out that Helen's argument has gone in a circle. Bob might object as follows: "Look here, Helen. You were supposed to answer my original question by giving me a reason why someone who does a better job should get more money. But in the end, all you are telling me is that such a person should get more money because she does a better job. What I want is some reason why she should get more money in addition to, or independent of, your assumption that she has done a better job. What is it about doing a better job that makes it worth more money? You still haven't answered my question." Here Bob could criticize Helen's argument for committing the fallacy of begging the question. He might feel that, instead of giving a helpful answer to the question, she has simply avoided or "begged" the question. But calling Helen's argument a fallacy does not tell us exactly what is supposed to be objectionable about it.

The so-called fallacy of begging the question, as noted in chapter one, is often related to the claim that an argument is circular. But even if an argument is somehow circular, that doesn't necessarily show why or how the argument can be fairly refuted or criticized, or what exactly is wrong with it. Moreover, although an argument does appear to be somehow closed in upon itself in a way that is less than helpful in the dialogue, it may not be exactly circular. The overall sequence of Helen's argument can be exhibited as shown in figure 2.4.

This pattern of argument may not be exactly circular, because the arrows are not all going in the same direction. But it certainly is a closed pattern of argument. It started at the lower right corner, and then, by a different route, came back to that very same point. Hence our feeling that the argument is somehow circular. But what is wrong, or open to criticism about Helen's argument? Bob's complaint is that the argument does not really, or usefully, answer his question.

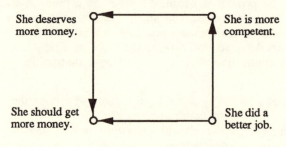

Figure 2.4

The whole problem of what is wrong about circular arguments, when they are wrong, is yet to be solved. For the present, however, Bob's objection may be that a circular series of responses, like those given by Helen represents a less than ideal path for the argument of the dialogue to embark upon. The circle may serve to delay or confuse Bob, and it doesn't appear to take him (or us) anywhere. Also, it doesn't appear to contribute to an increase in information, or to reveal anything especially significant about Helen's position and deeper reasons for her stance on the issue. It would be so much better, from the point of view of reasonable dialogue, if the discussion of tipping were to proceed in a linear sequence that fulfills a maieutic function, rather than in this circular pattern. So one thing that can be wrong with circular reasoning is that it does not contribute very well to the maieutic function of good dialogue. It could even serve to disrupt good dialogue, or distract the participants from more relevant considerations they should be discussing.

A basic problem with circular arguments is that you come back to the same point you started from. So you could say that circular arguments don't go anywhere. However, when reasonable dialogue is informative and revealing, it is so because it has an aspect of going in a certain direction as the sequence of argument unfolds. Hence a circular argument like the one in case 2.2 appears to frustrate the aims of dialogue by diverting the line of argument along a path of inquiry that is uninformative, in the sense that it performs no probative or maieutic function.

Not all circles in arguments are vicious, however (as noted in chapter one), and consequently, not all circular arguments are fallacious. Sometimes circular arguments are harmless. If they don't take us anywhere, at least they don't take us from a true premise to a false conclusion. It could be then that Helen's circular argument is not so much a fallacy, as simply a kind of blunder, or bad strategy of persuasion. Such an argument will not be effective to persuade Bob, and it is so transparently circular that it is more harmless or inept than it is fallacious. This difference remains to be clarified.

Another comment on case 2.2 is that Bob already accepts the conclusion that the person who does the better job should get more money. At least, he accepts it if we take the sample dialogue on tipping into account. Where Bob and Helen disagree is on the question of how it should be judged when a person is doing a better job. If this is so, we could ask why Bob is asking the question in the first place. Perhaps it is just to probe Helen's positions further, in the hope of extracting some potentially useful concessions.

From this angle, Helen's sequence of replies may not be totally worthless. At least Bob now knows that Helen links salary to what a person deserves, and that in turn to a person's competence on the job. Bob, and perhaps Helen too, have found out something.

On the other hand, when Helen closes the circle at the end of the dialogue, she destroys any transference of evidential priority that the chain might have built up to persuade Bob that the person who does the better job should get more money. But who is at fault in this regard? Bob is asking the questions, and perhaps Helen is not really trying to persuade him at all, in this case, but only trying to avoid falling into a trap of making potentially dangerous commitments.

The lesson here is that not every subsequence of argumentation in a persuasion dialogue may be designed to persuade. While the context of dialogue is important, there may also be subgoals and substrategies of argument operative at the local level. An argument that fails to fulfill evidential priority might therefore be too harshly judged as "fallacious." Helen could possibly continue her argument by adding new lines of evidence that could eventually lead toward a fulfillment of evidential priority. This subtle point will come out as highly significant for the analysis of begging the question in chapters four, five, and six.

Another interesting aspect of case 2.2 is that it doesn't really seem to matter whether you consider it by itself, or as a part of the larger sample dialogue on tipping in section three. Either way, it is circular. And either way, it seems about equally bad as an argument. Both ways, it is a circular argument that appears to be not very helpful, but it falls short of being an argument that could be decisively rejected or criticized as fallacious. So here there is a marked contrast with the previous case, where the context made much more of a difference.

Finally, let's turn to a third case that is even more problematic than the previous two.

Case 2.3: **Helen:** So you see, Bob, tipping has so many bad consequences on the daily working lives of so many people that, clearly, it ought to be discontinued. There can really be no room for doubt about it.

Bob: Now wait a minute, Helen. You are begging the question. What you need to prove, as we agreed before, is that these bad effects of tipping outweigh all the good effects of it. If so, then as I said, it follows that tipping ought to be discontinued. But you haven't shown that the bad effects outweigh the good. You are merely assuming, or taking for granted, what you need to prove. You are begging the question to be proved.

Helen: That's not true, because I have shown you so many bad consequences that the practice of tipping brings with it. I showed that it leads to personal misunderstandings, that it is undignified, that it is an inadequate substitute for regular pay, that things are better in countries where tipping is not the custom, and that it leads to tax evasion. I have shown why tipping preserves inequality, and causes repression, along with other forms of mental trauma, to the oppressed. I am not begging the question, because I have given many strong arguments citing bad effects of tipping.

Bob: Yes, I agree that you have presented arguments that these effects of tipping are bad. But what you need to show is that these bad effects outweigh the good effects of tipping. This you haven't done, because I have replied effectively to each one of your arguments. For every bad effect you cited, I showed that either there are

good effects that balance it off, or that the
bad effect is not as great as you seem to think.
You still haven't shown that the bad effects
outweigh the good. By presuming this conclusion, however, you have begged the question.

Here we have a disagreement between Helen and Bob. Has Helen begged
the question or not?

One observation is that Helen has not (nor has Bob accused her of
having) begged her main thesis to be proved in the dialogue–namely that
tipping should not be maintained as a practice. But it may be that she has
pushed ahead too strongly to try to get Bob to accept the premise that the
bad effects of tipping outweigh the good effects.

Bob has said earlier in the dialogue–at the beginning of his second
speech in section four–that he would concede Helen's main thesis to be
proved if Helen could prove her premise that the bad effects of tipping
outweigh the good. So if Helen did prove this premise, she would win
the whole argument of the persuasion dialogue, by proving her point.
So although Helen is not assuming the main thesis to be proved, she is
assuming, or asking Bob to grant a proposition that is pretty close to it in
just the following respect–if Bob accepts this premise, then Helen's thesis
follows immediately from it by Bob's own concessions at a previous point
in the dialogue.

But is that begging the question? Well, certainly it could be begging
a question, because the controversy has now centered around the subissue of
whether the bad effects of tipping outweigh the good effects, or vice versa.
And Helen could be begging *this* question. So Helen could be said to be
begging the question in a kind of derived or localized sense.

Another point to be observed in this case is that the question of whether
Helen has begged a question depends on whether she has adequately proved
that the bad effects outweigh the good or not. Has she met the burden of
proof required for the dialogue? If so, she cannot be accused of begging the
question. So the evaluation of the criticism that she has begged the question,
in this instance, requires the critic to look back over the previous context of
the dialogue and evaluate the critical questions that Bob raised, in relation to
each of Helen's arguments that cited a bad effect of tipping. If Bob did not
reply to a particular argument advanced by Helen to support her contention,
then we may be able to judge, in that case, looking at the speech acts of the
exchange, that Bob conceded the point and accepted that premise. On the
other hand, if Bob raised critical questions, objections, or counter-argumen-
tation, it may be clear that he did not accept Helen's argument on that
particular point. Whether or not Helen may be rightly said to have begged
the question, therefore, depends on an assessment of Helen and Bob's
interactions at the various moves of the prior sequence of dialogue.

Another point to be discussed is the question of whether there is a
dependency relation between Helen's conclusion and one of her premises

that would justify Bob's allegation that she has begged the question. Even if Helen has not sufficiently backed up her premise that the bad effects outweigh the good, it need not follow that she has committed the fallacy of begging the question. It could simply be a case of inadequate argumentation (weak premises). A weak argument need not be circular. If so, Helen could be criticized for some fault, but not necessarily that of begging the question.

The burden of proof should be on Bob to show that there is a circle, or some form of dependency or equivalence relation in Helen's argument, to justify his allegation of *petitio*. Bob would have to do this, presumably, by appealing to the evidence from the text of discourse of the previous dialogue to show the circular sequence of argumentation. And Bob did not do this.

Yet another point is the inevitability of the circle, if there is one. Helen did say that there can "really be no room for doubt" about her conclusion, and this suggests a certain aggressiveness, or foreclosure of further critical questioning, that might be significant evidence of a fallacy if her argument had other properties as well. But by itself, this strong form of putting a conclusion is not necessarily proof that a fallacy of begging the question has occurred.

In this third case, if we consider it apart from the main dialogue on tipping in section four, there has been no fallacy of begging the question committed by Helen. Bob was not justified in advancing this criticism. Instead, he should have criticized Helen for the fault of not adequately supporting her premise that the bad effects of tipping outweigh the good.

However, if we consider case 2.3 as an extension of the sample dialogue on tipping, a much stronger (though by no means conclusive) case can be made out to support Bob's contention that Helen has begged the question. Judging the question of Helen's *petitio* from this perspective entails looking carefully at the text of the whole dialogue to take into account the various factors considered earlier. From this point of view, it could be said that Helen has assumed a proposition in the argument of case 2.3 that she was supposed to prove as a subconclusion in the sample dialogue on tipping. There is textual evidence then that she has begged a question, or illicitly assumed a conclusion that she was supposed to prove. The reason is that Bob singled out this proposition–that the bad consequences of tipping outweigh the good–as a conclusion that would settle the whole argument if Helen could prove it (Bob's second speech in the sample dialogue on tipping). In her next speech in the dialogue, Helen did not question or dispute Bob's way of putting this. Given this exchange then, the proposition at issue is one that Helen should not be allowed to assume as a premise to be freely granted in the subsequent context of dialogue. If she were then to try to use it as a premise, without proving it, or showing how she has proved it, in her opinion, then Bob would appear to have good justification for accusing her of committing a question-begging fallacy.

Whatever the final word on these three interesting cases, it has become quite clear that the larger context of dialogue plays a vital role in a reasoned evaluation of whether an argument can be said to commit the fallacy of begging the question. In light of the above cases, the conclusion that begging the question is a dialectical fallacy that requires essential reference to a context of dialogue does not seem remarkable. But it should be highly unsettling when we consider that in most of the examples of *petitio principii* given in the logic textbooks, short arguments with little context are the norm, and the reader is left to try to reconstruct or conjecture possible profiles of context that might bear on the question of the alleged fallaciousness of the example argument. Too often, there is not enough evidence to settle the question, one way or the other.

6. NORMATIVE MODELS OF DIALOGUE

Deciding whether an argument commits the fallacy of begging the question requires placing that argument in a larger context of dialogue. Moreover, such a decision is highly dependent on identifying the type of dialogue involved. Can such a criticism ever be fully justified or refuted then, given that the context of dialogue may often be unclear, unstated, or even impossible to determine? It would seem that a criticism of begging the question must be judged in relation to the information given on the context. Fortunately, in some cases, like the sample dialogue on tipping, what is going on is fairly clear.

From the point of view of the logic of dialogue, it is important to recognize that there may be different levels of argument. During the middle phases of dialogue, participants are likely to be spending a lot of time engaging in argument. But at the opening and closing phases of a discussion, much of the dialogue may concern second-level arguments about these other arguments. For example, at the opening phases of dialogue, characteristically the discussion is about the rules and procedures of the dialogue. Questions may be asked like "How shall we proceed?" or "Do you agree that this argument should be first on the agenda?" These questions are about the argument. They are about the format of the subsequent argument. And hence they are *meta-arguments,* or arguments about arguments.

Meta-arguments are more common in some contexts than in others. In some contexts of dialogue, the format and rules of procedure may be clearly established, in many respects, well in advance of a particular discussion. An example would be legal rules of evidence, procedure, and burden of proof for a particular type of trial. However, in less structured contexts, there may be considerable argument about procedural questions.

It is most important to realize that, in many cases, criticisms of arguments take place at a level of meta-argument. In effect, the critic who purports to be objective is attempting to rise above the dispute to some extent, and adopt a neutral stance of looking at both sides of the argument. Of course, it is difficult to be objective, and critics can perhaps never, or rarely, entirely extricate themselves from being a participant in an argument rather than a critic of it.

What makes criticism reasoned is that evidence can be collected and interpreted from the corpus and context of dialogue. In the midst of an argument, especially when one is an active participant in the argument, it is hard to be an objective critic. And perhaps the extent to which anyone can be a neutral critic, on issues that are important to anyone, is a matter of degree. But once an argument is completed, a critic can look over the transcript or other record of the argument and evaluate criticisms of parts of the argument on the basis of the given discourse.

The process of argument reconstruction is a matter of interpretation of discourse in natural language that can only be understood by the critic because he and the participant share common knowledge and understanding of the context. This argument reconstruction is inevitably based on implicit presumptions. This is the question of enthymemes, which presumes that the arguer and his critic share "scripts" or broad background story-line themes and common-sense connections among events described in the discourse.[6] Because these background themes are not explicitly articulated as sets of propositions in the given text of argument, all criticism involves plausible reconstruction.

The evaluation of a criticism of an argument takes the step to meta-argument considerations, and to questions of rules of procedure and inference appropriate for the context of dialogue. In some cases of argument, for example in criminal law where the argument is set as a trial, the rules of procedure and evidence are stated very carefully and elaborately in advance of the trial. However, in many familiar contexts of discussion, no agenda, procedures, or rules of inference have been set. In these cases, the criticism can only be objectively evaluated or resolved if the participants can be brought, through a meta-argument discussion, to agree on the agenda, the procedures, and the form of dialogue.

Hence the question of whether criticisms can be evaluated objectively is not a simple black-and-white question. The answer depends on the context of dialogue, and in particular, on how well procedural and logical rules to facilitate discussion have been articulated, or can be agreed upon by the participants. If the rules themselves are subject to dispute, then the possibility of any criticism being evaluated objectively will tend to decrease or even vanish.

It is especially during the initial phase of an argument that there is a good possibility of reaching agreement on the rules and procedures of discussion. But in ordinary argumentative conversations, such ground rules may not be laid down before the discussion begins. In such cases, there may be little evidence to draw on, in order to evaluate a criticism of fallaciousness, without further questioning of the disputants.

Throughout the case studies so far discussed, various guidelines for ruling on criticisms in reasoned dialogue have been discussed and advocated. The basic philosophy is that argument guidelines can be collected together into a dialogue structure appropriate for a particular discussion. The suggestion now brought forward is that each type of dialogue has certain basic goals and also rules of inference and procedural rules that enable these goals to be carried out in a systematic manner. And from chapter one onward, the persuasion type of dialogue was the structure most often appealed to and stressed as the underlying model of reasoned dialogue.

But the reader may well question the extent to which abstract structures or games of dialogue are relevant to real-life argumentation. The problem is that people seldom seem to change their minds by virtue of rules of argument. More often people seem to be influenced by their emotional reaction to an argument.

Indeed, according to Perelman (1982, p. 17), persuasive discourse is addressed to a person's unthinking reactions, as opposed to convincing discourse, which appeals to reason. Could persuading be based more on emotional reaction?

Such doubts point to the lesson that the type of dialogue appealed to throughout chapter two, and now called *persuasion dialogue*, entails an elevated degree of rationality on the part of the participants that makes it, to some degree, an abstraction from many real-life situations of argumentation. In fact the persuasive dialogue is best seen as an abstract, *normative model of dialogue*, meaning that it prescribes how participants in argument ought to conduct themselves if they are reasonable, rather than purely describing how participants in argument do conduct themselves in any particular, real situation. Therefore, Perelman is right to suggest that this type of dialogue is more like "convincing" in some ways, rather than simply "persuading." And Johnstone may be right too that in real situations, people being who they are, winning an argument by changing someone's mind may sometimes not entail that the change of mind took place by virtue of any rules of reasonable argument.

Accordingly, the persuasion model of dialogue is best seen as an ideal that is partly based on common practices of argumentation, but that by no means necessarily describes the real thinking or actual belief modification of any real person or group of persons. The persuasion model of dialogue has to do with reasoned incurring and retraction of commitments according to the rules thought to be appropriate for a particular context of discussion. Commitments are not necessarily the actual beliefs of the participants. And the rules do not necessarily correspond to the way a participant's beliefs come to be changed. Perelman was right, therefore, that the term "conviction" is appropriate. But the term "reasoned persuasion" is also appropriate provided it is accepted that it is the reasoned shift of commitment, and not the modification of belief of any actual person, that is the central concept of persuasive dialogue as a normative model of reasoned argument.

There are two primary dialectical levels of reasonable dialogue. At the abstract (formal) level, a game of dialogue is a normative model—a precisely stated set of rules forming an abstract structure that may or may not correspond in greater or lesser degrees to realistic contexts of argumentation. At the practical (realistic) level, a game of dialogue is a speech event—a regulated sequence of questions and answers that does represent some sequence of verbal exchanges on a controversial or disputed issue.

7. THE PRAGMATIC PERSPECTIVE ON ARGUMENTATION

A traditional informal fallacy where understanding the mechanism of what is fallacious is importantly linked to the concept of burden of proof is the *petitio principii*. First, a careful distinction should be considered between begging the question and arguing in a circle. It has been indicated in chapter one (section nine) why arguing in a circle is not necessarily erroneous or subject to reasonable refutation in every instance, and why care should be taken to distinguish between circular argument and the fallacy of begging the question in argument.

The fallacy of begging the question is best construed as a move or tactic that should be open to serious criticism whenever it occurs in an argument. The reason for this thesis is that the very idea of begging the question is linked to a pragmatic context of dialogue where there is an obligation or burden to prove. Begging the question is inappropriate precisely because the thesis to be argued for is "begged for" instead of being proved.[7] The basic idea behind this failure is that an arguer, to do his job, must prove or give evidence for his conclusion. He cannot just ask for it, in this context, as an assumption to be freely granted by his opponent in the argument, at no cost. By this conception, begging the question is an improper move whenever it occurs in reasoned proof-directed dialogue. An argument that begs the question could be formally valid, but it is not useful to persuade a rational opponent in dialogue precisely because it fails to meet the requirement of burden of proof. So it is the failure to fulfill the burden of proof that makes begging the question a species of fallacious conduct in an argument.

Thinking of begging the question as a failure to meet a burden of proof in argument puts a whole new perspective on the concept of what a good argument is. No longer exclusively concerned with the semantic question of whether an argument is deductively valid, or whether, in general, it has the right sort of formal link between the premises and the conclusion, we are now also concerned with the question of how the premises came to be known or accepted as true, and the grounding paths between the premises and the conclusion.

These concerns require a shift to an entirely different point of view, on what constitutes reasoning, from the traditional viewpoint of reasoning as valid deduction, to a newer conception of the use of reasoning in dialogue. Probative reasoning in dialogue uses rules of inference to extrapolate paths of argument from given premises in order to reach a conclusion, as a goal to be established. The base of initial commitments for one party is a set of propositions from which premises can be drawn by the other party. The conclusion is a particular proposition that is in question and that is required to be proved from these given premises. Such a use of reasoning starts by exploring different ways of attempting to reach the desired conclusion. Each step of reasoning is linked to a next step, and therefore a chain of inferences takes the form of a path of argument. However, generally there can be more than one path diverging from the same point. Hence there can be different lines of argument all leading toward the same conclusion.

Generally, strategic use of reasoning will try to explore different possible paths that seem to lead toward the goal. But in some cases, there may be an overabundance of different paths available, and in these cases, part of the reasoning is the job of cutting down the options by selecting more promising lines of argument.

The concept of fallacy is considerably broadened once the idea of the use of reasoning as argument in dialogue is introduced. For a fallacy is no longer only a failure of a one-step argument to be formally valid. One has to look at the evidential routes, or chains of possible arguments, from a given set of premises to a conclusion. In the case of *petitio principii,* in addition, many possible evidential routes leading from the conclusion to the premises have to be considered. Generally, one has to look at a particular local argument in question by placing it in relation to a global perspective of the context of dialogue.

In this perspective on the use of reasoning, many of the traditional informal fallacies can now be made sense of as failures or faults of good reasoning.

A burden of proof, by its very nature, attaches to one side of an argument. When such a burden is incurred, the weight of evidence required to support the other side of the argument is thereby lightened. Therefore, burden of proof only makes sense in relation to a concept of argument as reasoned dialogue, where there are two sides to the argument.

The idea of a two-sided argument involves an ever-further step away from the traditional semantic concept of good reasoning as the deductively valid argument. This new conception of reasoning is one of *interactive reasoning,* where two participants reason together by exchanging speech acts in the form of a dialogue. The concept of argument as interactive reasoning, therefore, takes us to a radical new point of view on reasoning. Of course, this "radical" idea was familiar to the Greeks, as noted in chapter one. But it is novel in relation to the theories and preconceptions of modern logic.

There can be different types of interactive reasoning, but primarily, in the study of fallacies, we are concerned with the types of interactive reasoning where the goal of the interactive sequence is to succeed in proving a conclusion. A primary context is where one participant has the goal of proving something to the other.

The concept of burden of proof only makes sense in relation to a concept of argument as a balance, with weights on each side. As more weight is placed on one side, the other side becomes relatively lighter. And as more weight is removed from the one side, the other side may be viewed as having relatively more weight. The corresponding shift is indicated by the raising of the balance on one side and the lowering of the balance on the other.

But in order for adjustments of burden of proof in an argument to be reasoned, the two-sided dialogue must have procedural rules that are reasonable or that somehow represent, or are related to, rules of logic. The concept of reasoned dialogue required to support such a conception must have the following components.[8]

1.   *Two Sides.* There must be two participants in the dialogue, each of whom represents one side. Normally, they are called the Proponent and the Respondent.

2.   *Moves.* Each participant must take his turn making a move, in a sequence of pairs of moves. Normally, each move is either a question or a reply to a question, which can take the form of an assertion.

3.   *Commitments.* Attached to each side is a set of propositions called a *commitment-set.* At each move, propositions may be inserted into or removed from a participant's commitment-set.

4.   *Rules of Procedure.* The function of the rules is to define the conditions under which specific propositions are to be inserted into or deleted from a participant's commitment-set at each characteristic type of move.

5.   *Goal of Dialogue.* The dialogue must have some specific goal or criterion of success, so that a particular type of sequence of moves, according to the rules, counts as a successful culmination or resolution of the dialogue.

One of the most common types of dialogue is that where the goal of each side is to persuade the other side. In this type of dialogue, each participant has a specific proposition designated or declared as his *thesis,* to be proved or argued for. The thesis for each side must be proved exclusively from the premises (commitments) *of the other side,* by means of moves of inference allowed by the rules. This type of dialogue is called a *persuasion dialogue* (or *critical discussion*).

The concept of argument as persuasion dialogue is implicit in Aristotle's remarks on contestive argument in the *Topics* and *De Sophisticis Elenchis.* Some components of this type of dialogue are implicit in the games of dialogue studied in Hamblin (1970). But the explicit use of the concept of persuasion dialogue as a tool of argument analysis appeared independently in Walton (1984) and van Eemeren and Grootendorst (1984). The family of formal games, CB(+) and its successors constructed in Walton (1984), are all built on the idea of a persuasion dialogue where the obligation or goal of each player (what he must do to win the game) is to prove his thesis from the concessions of the other player (figure 2.5). This basic idea of the persuasion dialogue is also characteristic of many of the games of dialogue constructed in Barth and Krabbe (1982). And the same idea characterizes the context of dialogue called a *critical discussion* by van Eemeren and Grootendorst (1984).

GOALS OF PERSUASION DIALOGUE

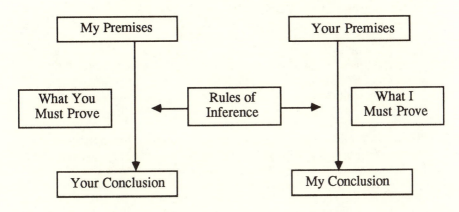

Figure 2.5

The concept of a critical discussion is used by van Eemeren and Grootendorst as a normative tool for the analysis of argumentative discourse. A critical discussion has two participants, and each one has a standpoint. The standpoint of the one participant, the protagonist, is to prove a particular proposition, his thesis or expressed opinion. The standpoint of the other participant, the antagonist, is to question the protagonist's defense of his thesis. According to van Eemeren and Grootendorst (p. 17), "the purpose of the [critical] discussion [is] to establish whether the protagonist's standpoint is defensible against the critical reactions of the antagonist."

In a particular type of persuasion dialogue (critical discussion) called a *dispute,* the thesis of the one participant is the opposite (negation) of the thesis of the other participant. Not all reasoned dialogues are persuasion dialogues. And not all persuasion dialogues are disputes. In some dialogues, like the critical discussion, as defined by van Eemeren and Grootendorst, the goal of one side is to prove a particular thesis while the goal of the other side is merely to throw doubt on the first side's attempted proofs. This is an asymmetrical type of dialogue that is not, strictly speaking, a dispute in the sense above, and it could also be called a *weakly opposed difference of opinion.* According to another usage, both these kinds of dialogue could be called disputes, and we could distinguish between strongly opposed disputes and weakly opposed disputes.

A reasoned dialogue is essentially an ordered sequence of pairs of moves that begins at an initial move or *opening stage,* and proceeds towards a final move, or *closing stage.* Van Eemeren and Grootendorst distinguish an initial phase of reasoned dialogue they identify with the initial confrontation, where the participants articulate the goals of the dialogue and clarify or agree on some of the procedural rules. These agreements or clarifications, to the extent that they are known in a particular case, according to an interpretation of the given text of discourse, serve to define the purpose and scope of the dialogue in an overall way. These matters define the context of dialogue in a global manner. Thus *global* conventions, rules, or agreements pertain to the whole dialogue as a collective sequence of moves. By contrast, *local* considerations in dialogue pertain to a specific move in the sequence.

For example, the setting of the thesis of a participant at the outset of dialogue is a global consideration, for this designation, once set, affects every subsequent move. By contrast, a local consideration could be whether a specific reply, at some particular point in the dialogue, is an acceptable response to the preceding question posed by the other side. In general, evaluations of particular features of a dialogue can be assessed in a more global or more local perspective. This will particularly be appropriate in the case of burden of proof.

What makes reasoned dialogue *reasoned* is the use of logical rules of inference in both directions on the two sides of question-reply argumentation. First, a participant uses *forward-chaining* sequences of argument in proving conclusions from the other participant's premises.[9] For example, if the Respondent has conceded propositions A and "If A then B," the Proponent may then prove B by the following forward-chaining use of *modus ponens:* If A then B, A; therefore B. Assuming that *modus ponens* is a logical rule of this particular context of dialogue, we may say that the Proponent has *proved* B. Depending on the commitment rules, the Respondent may then be required to accept B, and B becomes inserted into his commitment-set.

However, logical inferences can also be used in a *backward-chaining* manner, meaning that a participant may reason backward from his conclusion to pick out the premises in his commitment-set that were used (or could be used) to derive that conclusion. For example, suppose the Proponent has committed himself to proposition B. At a proper juncture in the dialogue, the Respondent may challenge the Proponent with a why-question, "Why B?" A *why-question* directs a request for explanation or proof of a proposition to the participant who is committed to that proposition. The rules of dialogue will determine when a respondent is required to give a direct answer to a why-question.[10] If the Proponent accepts the challenge, he might respond with the backward-chaining *modus ponens* reply: If A then B, A; therefore B. In this event, the Proponent will have shown how B can be inferred, according to the logical rules of the dialogue, from a set of premises.

It is generally important to recognize that the concept of reasoned dialogue is an idealization, an abstract, theoretical device that provides a normative profile against which any particular text of realistic dialogue can be measured or evaluated in various respects. On the other hand, this theoretical device is useful because it can be applied to commonplace reasoning.

According to Hamblin (1970, p. 256), the study of dialogue can be pursued formally (abstractly) or descriptively (practically), where actual texts of discourse can be studied. The concept of burden of proof is so useful and interesting precisely because of its practical ties with actual argumentation.

8. BURDEN OF PROOF

Presumptions are legal devices that can be used to alter a burden of proof. A presumption is a rule that allows one proposition to be inferred from another. It is a kind of rule of plausible inference that states what can normally or customarily be deduced from a particular fact in an argument. For example, if it can be shown as a fact that someone has disappeared without explanation or being heard of for more than seven years, it may be presumed that this person is dead. This presumption holds, however, only so far as it goes uncontradicted by further evidence of the person's being alive.[11]

Presumptions in law usually occur where a proposition at issue would be difficult to prove. A presumption can lighten the burden of proof. Presumptions come into play in a recurring type of situation where normal expectations about an expected type of outcome in this situation can be defined or codified according to a pre-established standard.

The concept of a presumption in law is closely tied to the concept of burden of proof. Both of these factors can be set by the rules of evidence before a specific case is actually tried. Both factors can be important in determining, in a particular case, what is to count as a successful realization of the goal of dialogue by either side of the dispute.

But how does burden of proof work in less strictly organized types of argumentation? Is it similar to the way it works in the law? It does seem to be similar in certain important respects because burden of proof is an important requirement in all persuasive reasoned dialogue. Yet many contexts are different. The goal of criminal law is to determine guilt or innocence (responsibility). Other contexts of dialogue may not share this goal. Even so, certain general patterns stand out as common to all persuasive reasoned dialogue.

The burden of proof gets set, ideally, in reasoned dialogue, at the outset of the round of exchanges between the two participants. Each participant sets out his thesis, which is a proposition. By declaring a proposition as his thesis, a participant thereby incurs a burden or obligation of proof— meaning that he is obliged to offer proof, or at least evidence or backing, for this thesis, if challenged by the other participant in the argument. The ideal point in reasoned dialogue to set the burden of proof for both participants is at the beginning of the dialogue, at the initial stage of discussion.

Van Eemeren and Grootendorst (1984, p. 85) call this first stage that of *identifying the dispute,* where one participant advances a point of view, and another participant advances a different point of view, or casts doubt on the first point of view. Then the second stage of dialogue may be an attempt to resolve the dispute posed by the two different points of view, by subsequent discussion.

Rescher (1977, p. 27) also writes of a probative burden, set at the initiating stage of a dialectical situation, which then remains constant throughout the subsequent dialogue. Rescher calls this type of burden the *initiating* or I-burden, which is characteristically "static, and rests with the inaugurating side constantly and throughout" the dialogue. In Rescher's analysis of reasoned dialogue, the burden of proof, once set for a proposition A in an argument, establishes a presumption that not-A stands, until the burden of proving A has been discharged (p. 32).

Generalizing on these insights from Rescher, van Eemeren and Grootendorst, and legal rules of evidence, some basic principles can be set down. In reasoned dialogue generally, there are two ways in which burden of proof can be set. First, burden of proof is set *externally* by the rules of procedure and goals of dialogue set by the participants, or agreed to by them. The first item to be noted here is that each participant is required to have a thesis to be proved, and once this thesis is set, that participant has a burden of proof (obligation). His goal or obligation is simply to prove that thesis. However, particular types of dialogue, once identified, will also serve to sharpen formulation of the burden of proof for both sides. In a dispute, the burden of proof is equally distributed. In a weakly opposed difference of opinion, the burden of proof falls exclusively on one side.

External burden of proof is set at the global level of reasoned dialogue. External conventions affect arguments over the whole course of the dialogue, from beginning to end. From this perspective, the commitment rules of dialogue can be viewed as part of the external burden of proof requirement. For the commitment rules define, over the whole sequence of dialogue, whether an arguer is committed to a specific proposition, and whether, as a consequence, he is obliged to prove it if challenged.

In general, there are four factors that influence how burden of proof is set externally in reasoned dialogue: (1) the theses to be proved by the participants; (2) the rules of dialogue, especially the commitment rules; (3) the initial plausibility of the theses to be proved; and (4) presumptions required by special contexts of dialogue, for example, safety. The fourth factor refers to special kinds of issues where there may be reason to set the burden of proof higher against one side. For example, a physician, in an emergency situation where the patient's life may be in danger, is expected to "err on the side of life" by acting to presume that there is a danger if the situation is not clear and the costs of acting to preserve life are acceptable. The general principle at work here is that of *tutiorism,* or taking the safer, known way for the purpose of safety where there is both risk and uncertainty.

Burden of proof is set *internally,* at the local level of dialogue, where requirements of proof or argument are set relative to one specific move, or pair of moves, in a sequence of dialogue. For example, the maxim "he who asserts must prove" may dictate that a participant who actively assents to a specific proposition may be called upon or challenged by another participant to prove or support that proposition. Or an asker of a question may be called upon to give evidence for presuppositions of the question. Of course, these are external commitment rules, but they can apply at the local level of one specific question-reply interchange. When they do, specific burdens of proof are set internally, and can be altered or shifted internally, at specific moves in the sequence of dialogue.

There can be different methods of setting the burden of proof externally in reasoned dialogue, and there is room for controversy on the subject of which is the best general method from a theoretical point of view on dialogue. Generally the goal of persuasive dialogue is to shift the burden of proof so that one's own side of the argument has become predominant. And in a dispute one participant's thesis is proved if, and only if, the other participant's thesis is refuted.

In an evenly matched dispute, the plausibility of each participant's thesis is roughly equal to the other. Hence any plausible argument newly advanced during the course of dialogue will tilt the burden of proof against one side by raising the plausibility of the other. Therefore, it might be proposed that whichever side has the higher plausibility at the end of the dialogue should be declared to have the winning (stronger) argument.

However, in dialogue on some controversial issues, the initial plausibility of the thesis on one side of the issue to be disputed may be much greater than that of the other. Thus the burden of proof is much heavier on one side than the other. Here a different procedure for evaluating the respective merits of the arguments on both sides needs to be followed.

Several years ago there was a program shown on Canadian television called "The Great Debate." At the beginning of the program, a controversial issue was stated, and two speakers were introduced, each of whom was slated to argue for one side of the issue. But before any debating began, the audience was asked to vote for whichever side of the issue each person presently accepted. This count was recorded, and then after the debate had taken place, another count was taken of each member of the audience's new position on the issue. Whichever direction the count had gone from the first voting to the second indicated the winner of the debate.

This suggests a different approach. It might be proposed that whichever side has increased the plausibility of its thesis at the end of the dialogue, from the level of plausibility set at the beginning of the dialogue, should be declared to have the winning (stronger) argument. Here the external burden of proof, set for the course of the game, is equal, even if the initial, apparent burden of proof set by the plausibility of each thesis at the outset of play was unequal. The inequality of the relative plausibility of each disputant's thesis is offset by the rule that sets the goal of the dialogue.

In this type of persuasive dialogue, which could be called a *Pierre Berton dispute,* the disputant wins who has the greater positive difference between the initial plausibility value or given weight of presumption (at the first move) and the final plausibility value or final weight of presumption (at the last move) of the sequence of dialogue.

In a Pierre Berton dispute, each participant has two goals. One is to persuade the audience to accept his thesis as more plausible than they thought it to be at the outset of dialogue. The other is to induce a plausibility increase greater than that effected by the opponent's arguments.

One problem in formulating the requirement for burden of proof in a Pierre Berton dialogue is to deal with the cases where neither participant induces a net increase of plausibility, over the course of the dialogue, for his thesis. This could happen where both arguments are ineffective, and the plausibility value of each thesis remains the same at the final move as it was at the initial move. Or it could happen where one or both arguments are counter-productive and there is a drop in plausibility over the course of the argument.

The best way to deal with these cases is to rule that in each of them, the burden of proof requirement fails to be met. The reason behind this way of proceeding lies in the first goal of dialogue in a Pierre Berton dispute. The first goal is to persuade the audience to accept one's thesis as more plausible. And if this fails, the argument as a whole fails, and the burden of proof requirement should not be regarded as having been met.

Moving on to the cases where there is some increase in plausibility value for a thesis over the course of the dialogue, the burden of proof requirement is met by the disputant who induces the greater net increase in plausibility. This requirement stems from the second goal of dialogue in a Pierre Berton dispute.

PIERRE BERTON DISPUTE

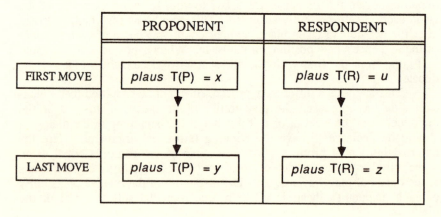

Figure 2.6

Two technical conventions of burden of proof can make these rulings easier to carry out. One is to rule that if a participant either induces a decrease in plausibility for his thesis over the course of the argument, or induces no net increase, then the differential plausibility of his argument is given a value of zero. Then if one arguer is assigned a value of zero, for either of these reasons, any positive gain at all by the other will win the dispute. Here even a very weak argument could swing the burden to one side. A second useful rule is to declare the dispute a tie if the two differential plausibility values for each side are equal.

The burden of proof requirements for a Pierre Berton dispute can be represented as in figure 2.6, where $T(P)$ is the Proponent's thesis, and $T(R)$ is the Respondent's thesis. Generally, we are assuming that $x \geq 0$ and $y \geq 0$ to begin with. The arrows and dotted lines represent the sequence of moves during the course of the dialogue.

Generally, it is a requirement that for any arguer to meet the burden of proof requirement, at least one of them must have a net plausibility increase of greater than zero. Given this is so, then whoever has the greater increase (if one does) wins the dispute. Thus the burden of proof requirement for each participant can be expressed as follows.

Proponent: $(y - x) > (z - u)$

Respondent: $(y - x) < (z - u)$

The direct opposition of these win-requirements makes it clearly evident that a Pierre Berton dialogue is indeed a dispute. For although both conditions can fail in the event of a tie, if either requirement is met the other cannot be.

Burden of proof is important in reasoned dialogue because various strengths can be required in argument to persuade a reasonable arguer to change his opinion. And in the study of the so-called informal fallacies, it has too often been overlooked that plausible reasoning can be a legitimate basis for an argument where the evidence is not sufficient or appropriate to support deductive or inductive arguments.

Arguments based on expert testimony have been classified as informal fallacies–the *argumentum ad verecundiam* has traditionally been thought of as the fallacy of appeal to authority–when often, in fact, such arguments can be plausible arguments that may carry enough weight to reasonably shift a burden of proof in one direction in argument.[12] Of course, the reasonableness of such arguments is subject to an array of reservations. They may be inconsistent, out of date, inappropriate to the topic, or suffer from various faults. But in some cases, they can be reasonable arguments when they are reasonably supported, and correctly classified as plausible arguments that can shift a burden of proof in dialogue.

To cite another instance, the circumstantial *ad hominem* argument can in some cases be a reasonable type of criticism of an arguer's position. If Alice declares that nobody should smoke because it is unhealthy, while at the same time puffing on a cigarette, a criticism that she does not practice what she preaches should rightly shift the burden of proof onto her side of the argument to justify her position. That does not mean that her denunciation of smoking as a general practice is strongly refuted or proved false. But it should indicate, in the proper context of dialogue, that the burden of proof is on Alice to justify her position if she can. If she can't meet the burden, it doesn't follow that the proposition "Nobody should smoke because it is unhealthy" is false. But it should be taken to follow that Alice's advocacy of her argument, taken to include the personal commitment to smoking indicated by her actions–is not reasonably persuasive.[13]

The *argumentum ad ignorantiam* is, of all the traditional informal fallacies, the one most intimately connected to burden of proof. It was John Locke who first noted this connection when he described *ad ignorantiam* as the strategy of requiring an adversary to admit what has been alleged as a proof or "assign a better." The typical sequence of question-reply dialogue corresponding to this strategy is the following:

Case 2.4: **Black:** Why A?
               White: Why not A?

The fault of reasoned dialogue in such a reply is to be found in the backward-chaining burden of a why-question that requires, in this case, proof of A. Where the rules of dialogue indicate that an answer is required, the pattern of replying to one question by asking another is not to be tolerated.

But then, in other cases, replying to a question with another question is not only reasonable, it may be the only kind of reply that is reasonable. For, a respondent should in some cases shift the burden back onto the questioner by challenging the question. And indeed, one of the most important lessons of burden of proof is that this questioning form of reply may be necessary and correct in reasoned dialogue.

One of the most trenchant and fundamental criticisms of reasoned dialogue as a method of arriving at a conclusion is that argument on a controversial issue can go on and on, back and forth, without a decisive conclusion ever being determined by the argument. The only defense against this criticism lies in the use of the concept of the burden of proof within reasoned dialogue. Once a burden of proof is set externally, then it can be determined, after a finite number of moves in the dialogue, whether the burden has been met or not. Only by this device can we forestall an argument from going on indefinitely, and thereby arrive at a definite conclusion for or against the thesis at issue.

Admittedly this way of arriving at a conclusion could be viewed as a form of *argumentum ad ignorantiam,* but of course it does not follow that all argumentation by the method of reasoned dialogue is fallacious or erroneous. It does show that such argumentation is very often, and typically, a species of plausible reasoning.

Having put the fallacy of *petitio principii* in a pragmatic framework of persuasion dialogue, we can see that as a fallacy, it is essentially a failure of a participant in this type of dialogue to fulfill his burden of proof. What has emerged is a framework in which a question-begging argument is not acceptable because it fails to produce "belief regarding a doubtful matter," as expressed by William of Sherwood (Kretzmann, 1966, p. 158). It falls short of the requirement of persuasion dialogue that stipulates that the premises of an argument designed to prove its conclusion to a respondent must be "prior and better known" than the conclusion to be proved.

This account is by no means the end of the story of *petitio* as a fallacy, however, for several reasons. First, although the fallaciousness of an argument that begs the question can be subsumed under the general heading of a failure of evidential priority, it is a certain specific (and very special) kind of failure of this type. Not all failures of evidential priority, in other words, commit the fallacy of begging the question. For as we saw in chapter one (section nine) there is a difference between bereftness of evidence (challenge-busting) and the fallacy of begging the question.

Second, there can be other contexts of argumentative dialogue than persuasion dialogue (critical discussion). The treatment of question-begging by Aristotle, as outlined in chapter one, clearly pointed to the very lively possibility that, as well as a dialectical kind of question-begging, there is also a parallel context of this fallacy in a kind of argument Aristotle called demonstration.

Nevertheless, pinpointing the fallacy of *petitio* as a kind of failure to meet a burden of proof in a persuasion dialogue is a step forward. This pragmatic conception of the fallacy has been concisely presented by van Eemeren and Grootendorst (1984, p. 170): The fallacy is the attempt by a protagonist, whose point of view has been called into question by an antagonist, to try to use this point of view itself as a premise acceptable to the other party, a premise that he claims can be backed up by evidence that is not in question (subject to doubt). This is an error, because if this point of view could be included in these premises, there would be no dispute to be resolved (p. 190). Hence the fallacy is, essentially, to ask to be taken as granted something that cannot be granted, or the discussion immediately collapses.

This description, while it is highly accurate and goes to the heart of the fallacy, is by no means the end of the error of *petitio principii* either. Although the fallacy is essentially a failure to prove a conclusion because that conclusion is included in, or presupposed by, the selected premises of one's argument, the conclusion to be proved at any particular stage of an argumentative dialogue can change, as the dialogue proceeds toward its ultimate outcome. A burden of proof cannot be fulfilled in one step, and an argumentative discussion is typically a complex sequence or chain of arguments that move in a general direction that (one hopes) will fulfill the ultimate burden of proof successfully.

Peter Suber (1987, p. 57) has drawn a parallel legal distinction that brings out this practical dimension of argumentation very perspicuously.

> Anglo-American law distinguishes the *burden of proof* from the *burden of going forward.* The burden of proof is a tie-breaker rule; when the evidence and arguments on each side seem balanced, then the party with the burden of proof loses. The burden of going forward is the obligation to respond after the opponent has made a preliminary case.

Begging the question is objectionable in a context of argument where the point is to prove something because the question-begging argument leaves no way open for going forward to establish the conclusion to be proved. No matter which way the argument could try to proceed, it is blocked by the need to presume the conclusion, with the result that no advance can be made. To model this kind of fallacy then, a dynamic conception of argument, with interlinked chains of proof, is needed.

Finally, there is one other subtlety in the way in which *petitio principii* is related to burden of proof. There should be a burden of proof not only on the proponent of the allegedly circular argument, but also on the critic of such an allegation.

If circular argumentation is not always fallacious, there should be a burden of proof on a critic who alleges that an argument commits the fallacy of *petitio principii* to show (1) what the circle is in the argument, and (2) why the circle violates some requirement of reasoned argument in the particular context of dialogue at issue. The way to prove (1) is to give evidence that there is a requirement of evidential priority in the argument that has not been met. The requirement of *evidential priority* is the condition that the premises be more plausible (or better known) than the conclusion that has been challenged or questioned. So here too, the key to understanding and proving why circular argumentation is fallacious, when it is objectionable, lies in an appreciation of how the burden of proof functions in reasoned dialogue.

But to prove that a circular argument is fallacious, a third requirement may be relevant as well. For in some cases, even though a premise and the conclusion of an argument are on a circle, so that part of the evidential route to the premise contains the conclusion, there may be an additional non-circular evidential route to the conclusion. The possibility here is that, in more complex arguments, there may be more than one way of using the premises to prove the conclusion.

9. GRAPHS OF ARGUMENTS

It has been recognized by Hamblin (1970) that informal arguments and fallacies often require consideration of a chain of argument-stages instead of a single set of premises and conclusion. To be sure, circular arguments are more significant, as potential fallacies, where an argument is more complex, in the sense of being a longer sequence of steps. Shoesmith and Smiley (1978) adopt a logical framework in which an argument can have several conclusions at different stages. Developments in linguistics have also studied the pragmatics of argumentation as an extended discourse. We will use a method of Walton and Batten (1984) that models a sequence of argumentation as a directed graph.

A *formal system* is a triple $F = (P, \Delta, R)$ where P is a set of atoms, Δ a set of n_i -ary operations and R a set of arguments called *rules*. An *argument* is a non-empty finite set of wffs with one distinguished from the others. Notation: $A = \{A_1, A_2, \ldots ; A_{n+1}\}$, where A_{n+1} is the wff distinguished from the others, called the conclusion. The basic idea of the system is that you start out with a set of wffs designated as "initial premises," and the rules determine all the possible ways of deriving the conclusion from those premises. This process generates the "argument" which is associated with a graph.

A graph is a set of pairs of points called *vertices*. Each pair of vertices is called an *arc*. In a digraph (directed graph), each pair of vertices is an ordered pair. The following terminology will be useful. A *digraph* is a triple $D = (V, \mathcal{A})$ where V is a non-empty set of elements called *vertices* and $\mathcal{A}$ a family of ordered pairs of elements of V, called *arcs*. A *diwalk* of a digraph from vertex v to vertex w is a finite sequence of distinct arcs $(v_0, v_1), (v_1, v_2), \ldots (v_n, v_{n+1})$ where $v_0 - v$ and $v_{n+1} = w$. A *dipath* from v to w is a diwalk in which $v_i \neq v_j$ if $i \neq j$. A *dicycle* from v to w is a dipath except that $v = w$.

The basic idea here is that the vertices represent wffs in an argument, the arcs (drawn as arrows) represent an application of a single rule to one or more wffs (labeled with a number that represents that rule), and consequently the graph can represent an overall network of complex argumentation. For example, if *modus ponens* is a rule (Rule 1), then the graph in figure 2.7 could represent an argument with the following initial premises: $A_1 =$ If Socrates is a man, Socrates is mortal; $A_2 =$ Socrates is a man; $A_3 =$ If Socrates is mortal, Socrates will die. An implicit premise is also "produced" by the argument: $A_4 =$ Socrates is mortal. The conclusion is $A_5 =$ Socrates will die.

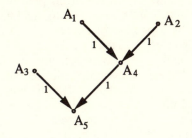

The usefulness of this method of representing argument will no doubt be apparent to those interested in informal logic as a field of study, but one feature of it bears remarking upon here.

If a conclusion happens to be on a dicycle, the argument may be said to be circular. But two cases need to be distinguished. If every available evidential route to a conclusion lies on a dicycle, the argument is called *inevitably circular* in Walton and Batten (p. 150). For example, in the argument on the left in figure 2.8, no matter which way an argument for A is given, it falls on a dicycle also including A. Whereas in the argument on the right, there is an argument for A that is not on a dicycle. The argument on the right is not inevitably circular, even if it is circular. Here, for simplicity, the numbers representing rules are omitted.

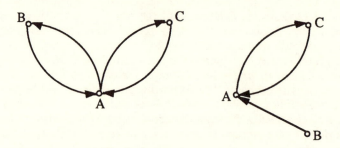

Figure 2.8

So we need to take some care in suggesting, in a particular case, that a circular argument must be "fallacious" or "vicious." In a case like the graph in figure 2.8 on the right, it could be that there is indeed a circle in the argument for the conclusion A. But that might not necessarily indicate a fallacious argument. For the arguer has available an evidential route for his conclusion A that does not contain a cycle. In such a case, the circle could be harmless.

This insight could suggest a reply to the Sextus-Mill argument that all deductively valid arguments are circular. Could there be alternative routes of verification for the major premise of the syllogism mentioned earlier in this connection? It would seem possible that the answer is "yes" because the proposition "All men are mortal" need not be verified or justified exclusively by a process of checking each one of its instances– including "Socrates is mortal." There could be general genetic or physiological justification of this generalization, not necessarily including the specific statement "Socrates is mortal." Similar insight might apply to some of the other cases we looked at. Dialogue with the proponent of an argument could reveal that the argument is not inevitably circular. In such a case, the criticism that an argument is circular may be not so much a knock-down refutation or fallacy as a kind of attack or challenge that can be met or rebutted in some cases.

Whatever the answer to the Sextus-Mill problem turns out to be, the method of graphs appears to be a helpful tool in putting the problem in a form where its nature is more apparent. This is also true for some of the more recent problems posed by the formal study of dialogue games.

According to Mackenzie (1984a, p. 174), the earlier dialogue systems of Mackenzie (1979) and (1980) had wrongly classified the following sort of dialogue as an instance of fallacious question-begging.

Case 2.5:   **White:**   Why is it to be supposed that A?
              Black: Because B.
              White: Why is it to be supposed that C?
              Black: Because A.

This dialogue does appear to be a circular sequence of speech acts, which starts at A and ends at A. But eventually, Mackenzie (1984b, p. 174) was led to concede that dialogues of this form did not commit any fallacy of begging the question, and Mackenzie proposed two new systems of dialogue to reflect this point of view on *petitio*.

However, applying the method of graphs to the argument in case 2.5, the structure of the argument makes the nature of the problem more apparent.

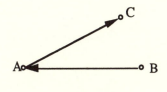

Figure 2.9

We can see in figure 2.9 that there is no circle in the digraph of the argument. The proposition A appears twice, but does so because it is a premise for A, and then a conclusion for C. There is no circle, and therefore no real question of whether the argument commits a fallacious *petitio principii,* the initial appearances of the dialogue notwithstanding.

Another interesting case is the following dialogue, given by Mackenzie (1984b, p. 180).

Case 2.6:   **White:**   How do you know that Johnny is home?
              Black: Because his match was cancelled.
              White: If there are muddy footprints in the hall, does that mean that Johnny's home?
              Black: Yes, it does.

White:	And *are* there muddy footprints in the hall?
Black:	Yes, all over the carpet.
White:	Now, how do you know Johnny's match was cancelled?
Black:	Because he's home.

According to Mackenzie, this sequence of dialogue "comes close to question-begging . . . without committing it." In fact, as Mackenzie points out, case 2.6 is a problematic type of case that relates to many of the problems and puzzles surrounding the Woods-Walton fragment discussed in chapter one. Mackenzie argued that the dialogue in case 2.6 is not fallacious, because the intervening questions and answers between the first move and the last have the effect of making Black's final move acceptable to White. But whatever the solution to the problems posed by case 2.6 turns out to be, the dialogue does pose genuine puzzles for interpretation.

Once again, the nature of the problem of question-begging posed by this type of case emerges much more clearly once we get a more perspicuous grasp of its overall structure as an argument, using a digraph representation.

As Mackenzie has shown (p. 180), the general dialogue form of the argument of case 2.6 is the following sequence.

Case 2.7:	White:	Why A?
	Black:	Because B.
	White:	Is it the case that if C then A?
	Black:	If C then A.
	White:	Is it the case that C?
	Black:	C.
	White:	Why B?
	Black:	Because A.

This dialogue certainly appears to be circular, but according to Mackenzie, it does not commit the fallacy of begging the question. But it is not easy to see clearly and persuasively why it should be held not to commit the fallacy of begging the question.

To see the explanation in a more perspicuous form, however, consider the digraph of case 2.7 in figure 2.10. Looking at the digraph in figure 2.10, we can reconstruct the evidential situation of the argument much more clearly. The ultimate conclusion of the argument is evidently A, because the dialogue started with White's query, "Why A?" And, as figure 2.10 clearly shows, A and B are connected by a circular dicycle. But the argument with A as conclusion is not inevitably circular, because there is another evidential route available to A. The remaining two points in the graph provide a deductively valid argument for the conclusion A, and neither premise is on a circle that includes A. What is clearly shown then is that although the argument is circular, it is not an inevitable circle, and therefore a way is open to defending it against a charge of committing the fallacy of begging the question.

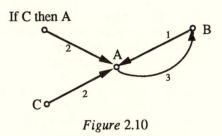

Figure 2.10

The uses to which graphs can be put in analyzing discourse where *petitio* is a serious charge remain to be seen. And in fact, chapter four will show that their use poses some quite general problems of method for informal logic as a field of study. But already we can see that the study of *petitio principii* as a fallacy cannot go much further without the aid of some method of argument reconstruction that uses a heuristic device like the method of graphs.

Moreover, the concept of inevitable circularity turns out to be essential in its own right to any understanding of begging the question as a logical fallacy, as we must now turn to see.

10. SELF-SEALING ARGUMENTS

Begging the question in argument could be described as merely a failure to meet a burden of proof, by offering premises that are begged (not evidentially prior) instead of being proved. But the *fallacy* of begging the question is more than this. It is the more subtle and serious failure of using a circular argument in an attempt to make it look as though proof has been given, when it really hasn't even been offered. Moreover, as a fallacy, or systematic tactic of deception in argumentation, the ploy of begging the question is an attempt to thwart critical questioning by not leaving open any real avenues of potential evidential support for a conclusion. In this regard, Sidgwick's analysis was on the track by proposing that the characteristic of begging the question that most deeply makes it a serious fallacy is the systematic attempt in a question-begging argument to seal off the possibility of further critical questioning by the participant to whom the argument was directed.

This self-sealing aspect of the most subtle and misleading types of question-begging arguments has been remarked on by Waller (1988, p. 193), who cited the following example. This sort of argument is one that has been used to support the practice of allowing children, in child-abuse cases in the courts, to give their testimony without the defendant being present in the courtroom. Waller's version of the argument is quoted directly in case 2.8.

Case 2.8:   It is doubly wrong to allow defendants in child abuse cases to be present when the abused children give their testimony. These child abusers often use terrible threats to keep the abused children from telling anyone about the abuse. To allow such vicious people to continue their intimidation of the children by being present when the children testify–and thus to perhaps avoid conviction–compounds their abuse of the children and extends that abuse into the courtroom.

The context of argument in case 2.8 is that of the criminal trial, where the prosecution has the burden of proving "beyond reasonable doubt" that the defendant committed the crime of child abuse. However, given the terrible stigma attached to this type of crime, it may be extremely difficult for anyone to resist a presumption of guilt, once such an accusation has been made in public. And on the other hand, there are many questions about the reliability of children as witnesses, and questions about whether children understand the seriousness of this type of allegation. The unfortunate tendency in such a case is to fall into the *ad ignorantiam* pitfall of concluding that if the evidence is indecisive, or doesn't go strongly either one way or the other, that given the seriousness of the accusation, there must be something in it.[14]

Hence the argument in case 2.8 presumes that a defendant in a child abuse trial is guilty, and is a "vicious" person who has made threats against the child. The argument begs the question by assuming what it was supposed to prove. But the particularly serious aspect of this circular tactic of argumentation is that, by already assuming guilt, it would prevent a defendant from ever being in a position to prove his innocence. If he cannot confront and question his accuser, he is not in a position to raise critical questions, face-to-face, in response to the testimony of his accuser.

Thus a serious case of begging the question, like case 2.8, is the characteristic type of fallacy that it is not only because it is a circular argument that fails to meet a proper burden of proof in its context, but also because these two factors combine in such a way that the argument tries to seal off further critical questioning in the dialogue. Hence there is an element of inevitability about the most serious case of the fallacy of begging the question.

At the meta-level of argumentation, it is a serious criticism of a circular argument if it can be shown to have failed to meet a burden of proof that is required by the context of dialogue in which the argument occurs. But it is an even more serious criticism if it can be shown that such an argument has tried to close off all further dialogue by sealing up the whole process of seeking out further evidence that could be brought to bear on resolving the issue.

These questions of burden of proof at the meta-level relating to different degrees of severity of criticisms that an argument has begged the question remain a central problem for the analysis of this fallacy.

NOTES

1. Walton (1987a, p. 105).
2. See chapter one, section four.
3. See Walton (1984, p. 291).
4. Some argument theorists would disagree with this interpretation, claiming that the burden of proof always falls on the person who would change an existing practice or custom. See Whately (1836) and (1846).

5. See Walton (1986) on the concept of fallacy.

6. Schank and Abelson (1977), and Schank (1982).

7. See Walton, (1985b).

8. Barth and Krabbe (1982), Rescher (1977), and van Eemeren and Grootendorst (1984) for elaboration of the various components of reasoned dialogue.
9. See Forsyth (1984).
10. See Bratko (1986).
11. *Encyclopaedia Britannica* (1973).

12. For supporting arguments, see Brown (1970) and Sproule (1976).
13. This case is also discussed in Walton (1985a).
14. This tendency is the result of a curious reversal of the burden of proof, which leads to a presumption of guilt as opposed to innocence.

3

Argument Diagramming

The method of argument diagramming originated as a technique of simply using arrows to link up the premises and conclusions of a sequence of argumentation, reconstructed from a passage where an argument is said to have occurred. The resulting diagrammatic representation of the argument is a very handy tool, useful in the reconstruction, analysis, and evaluation of arguments. This technique has become widely adopted, and has been used very effectively, in a fairly standard form, by many informal logic textbooks currently in use.

The first extensive use of this technique that incorporated most of the basic concepts of it in use today is to be found in the pioneering text *Practical Logic* (1950), written by Monroe C. Beardsley. The current state of the art of diagramming has added some new basic concepts and techniques that are fundamental, but the basic ideas and applications are all there in Beardsley's text.

In Walton (1980), and more carefully in Walton and Batten (1984), the basic technique of diagramming was represented within the theory of directed graphs as a model of argumentation analysis, and then applied to the study of the *petitio principii* fallacy.

The diagramming technique should be seen as a model of the reasoning in an argument–that is, the premises and conclusions along with the linkages that join them into a sequence. This technique should be seen as one part of a much broader technique (or group of techniques) of argument reconstruction which processes and interprets the argumentation before it is diagrammed, and then later evaluates the "meaning" of the diagram, using it as part of a process of argument evaluation. Thus the use of the diagramming technique requires subtleties and skills of argumentation interpretation to be executed properly. Chapter three will outline the basic technique and study some of these subtleties of its proper application.

1.   BASIC STRUCTURES STANDARDLY USED IN DIAGRAMMING

The technique of diagramming argumentation, in its present widely used form, familiar in the current informal logic texts–appears to have been originated by Monroe Beardsley in his textbook, *Practical Logic*. In this book, Beardsley used a technique of arrows and circled numbers to trace out the structure of an argument, which he called a "skeletal pattern" that displays the interconnected parts of an argument that lead up to its final conclusion.   According to Beardsley (p. 18), in some cases it is not too easy to see what the structure of an argument is, because the logical indicators are left out, for example, in the "semi-random ravings of white-hot orators, overwrought poets, and worried neurotics."   However most arguments, Beardsley suggested, "fall somewhere between perfect order and chaos," and therefore can be helpfully organized by the technique of diagramming their structure.

The first structure mentioned by Beardsley (p. 19) is what he called the "simplest structure," where a "single reason is given for a single conclusion."   In a diagram, Beardsley added, an arrow indicates the logical relation.   The second structure mentioned is that of the *convergent argument*, where "several independent reasons support the same conclusion."   The illustration shown in figure 3.0 was presented by Beardsley.

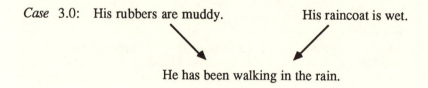

Case 3.0:   His rubbers are muddy.   His raincoat is wet.

He has been walking in the rain.

Figure 3.0

In a *divergent argument*, according to Beardsley, "the same reason supports several conclusions," as in figure 3.1.

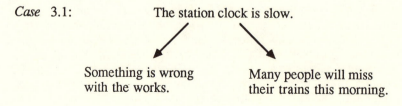

Case 3.1:   The station clock is slow.

Something is wrong   Many people will miss
with the works.   their trains this morning.

Figure 3.1

Beardsley added that an argument may be both convergent and divergent, and then went on to define a *serial argument* as one that "contains a statement that is *both* a conclusion *and* a reason for a further conclusion." He offered the illustration shown in figure 3.2.

Case 3.2: The room was sealed, and
empty when we entered.

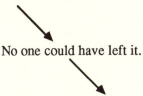

No one could have left it.

The murderer was never in the room.

Figure 3.2

Noting that a serial argument may be both convergent and divergent, Beardsley went on to give numerous examples of complex arguments that combine these three structures in various ways. In executing his technique, Beardsley put each single proposition (statement) in an argument within square brackets, numbering each distinct proposition with a circled numeral, starting at 1. Also, he drew an elliptically shaped type of circumference around each indicator word–like "therefore" or "because"–in the argument.

Essentially, the basic diagramming technique in use today follows Beardsley's basic categories, notations, and methods fairly closely. However, there is one major exception. The current textbooks virtually all make a basic distinction between convergent and so-called linked arguments. In a *linked argument,* both (or all) premises are linked so that each is required in order to support the conclusion. In a *convergent argument,* each line of evidence is separate from that of the other premises, so that neither (or no) premise is required to support the other (or another) premise in order for the conclusion to be derived. The convergent argument represents the concept of a new and independent line of reasoning, or "new knowledge," which is found to support a conclusion previously based on a different line of argument.

The following example, with the accompanying diagrammatic representation as shown in figure 3.3, is found in Acock (1985, p. 248).

Case 3.3: ① : The average American is consuming too much salt.
② : Only one gram of sodium a day is enough to sustain the human body in health, say researchers at the University of Massachusetts in Amherst.

③ :   The average American consumes between five and
        fifteen grams of sodium in table salt each day.

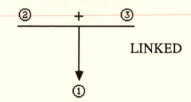

LINKED

Figure 3.3

Copi (1986) followed the standard pattern of adopting Beardsley's basic techniques along with the addition of the convergent-linked distinction, except for several significant exceptions to this standard pattern.

According to Copi (p. 41), "the number of conclusions in a passage determines the number of arguments it contains," and therefore Copi, in contrast to Beardsley (and many others) thinks of a complex network of argumentations as many intertwined arguments rather than as one big argument. Perhaps for this reason, Copi does not use the language of linked convergent, and so on, but speaks of arguments that are "indepen-dent of each other" or not (p. 43). Some examples used by Copi will illustrate how he uses the method of diagramming.

The first example is a passage from an article, "Family," by Carol Steinberg, *Venture* (April 1983): 68.

Case 3.4:   You can read about a country's history and culture, you
              can pore over travel brochures . . . but you can't get
              a true feeling for the people and the culture without
              witnessing both first hand. That's why there is no sub-
              stitute for sending your children abroad to study, and
              why hosting a foreign student yourself can be a valuable
              experience for your family.

According to Copi's analysis, there is one premise in this argument and two conclusions. The premise is ① below, and the two conclusions are ② and ③.

① :   You can't get a feeling for the people and the culture without
       witnessing both first hand.

② :   There is no substitute for sending your children abroad to study.

③ :   Hosting a foreign student yourself can be a valuable experience for
       your family.

According to Copi (p. 42), this passage contains two arguments, diagrammed as in figure 3.4.

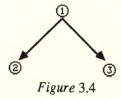

Figure 3.4

For Beardsley (and many others), this is a divergent argument. For Copi, it is two arguments, where two conclusions are inferred from the same premise.

What is standardly called a linked argument is described by Copi as an argument where a conclusion is inferred from a pair (or group of premises). However, Copi did use a diagram (figure 3.5) similar to the standard type of diagram like that of Acock (figure 3.4) for linked arguments.

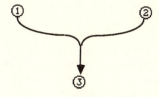

Figure 3.5

Although Copi did not use the term "serial" argument either, he went on to recognize this type of argument (p. 44) and use the type of diagram shown in figure 3.6 for it.

Figure 3.6

To sum up, Copi used the standard type of diagramming technique now widely in use in informal logic texts, but he did not use the standard language for describing the four basic types of argument structures (in addition to single arguments): convergent, linked, divergent, and serial. But the majority of current texts in informal logic use both the standard language and diagramming techniques.

2. THEORETICAL REFINEMENTS OF THE DIAGRAMMING TECHNIQUE

As it is used in logic texts, the diagramming technique has proved to be effective and helpful as a tool for the practical needs of identifying and clarifying arguments in passages of discourse. But it lacks theoretical structure as a coherent method that can be applied systematically to argumentation. Recent developments in the theory of argumentation have begun to suggest ways of organizing the method as part of the larger theory of analysis of argumentative discourse.

A work on formal logic, Shoesmith and Smiley (1978) used directed graphs in conjunction with formal calculi to model arguments with more than one conclusion (essentially what are called divergent and serial arguments above). Independently, two papers in informal logic used directed graphs to diagram arguments. Walton (1980) proposed using graph theory as a theoretical model of argument diagramming. In a more mathematically refined treatment, Walton and Batten (1984) set out a theoretical structure of argument analysis that defined argument structures as directed graphs. Again independently, van Eemeren and Grootendorst (1984) proposed guidelines for analysis of argumentation structures that incorporate the standard diagramming techniques, proposing a parallel but different language from the standard language.

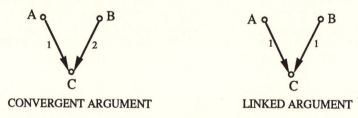

CONVERGENT ARGUMENT   LINKED ARGUMENT

Figure 3.7

Using the directed graph theory method of argument reconstruction given in Walton and Batten (1984), the distinction between the linked and convergent argument types can be represented as in figure 3.7. The number on the arc of the graph indicates the use of a particular rule of inference, like *modus ponens*. In the linked argument, the use of a single rule of inference links the premises A and B together. In the convergent argument, the separate use of two rules indicates two separate lines of (independent) argumentation.

The convergent argument has the characteristic that each of the premises is individually sufficient to meet the burden of proof required to convince the respondent that the argument is plausible. This type of argument is called *multiple argumentation* by van Eemeren and Grootendorst (1984, p. 91), which they define as a "series of separate and independent single argumentations" for the same conclusion. The example they give has three separate premises (figure 3.8).

CONVERGENT (or MULTIPLE) ARGUMENT

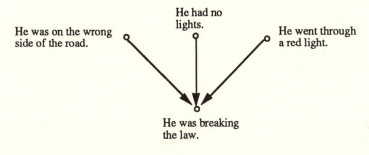

Figure 3.8

Each of the three premises is individually sufficient for the conclusion, "He was breaking the law." And none of them is necessary to prove the conclusion, in this example. Therefore, there are three separate lines of evidence, characteristic of the convergent (multiple) argument.

The linked argument is called a *co-ordinative compound argumentation* by van Eemeren and Grootendorst, defined by them as an argumentative composite where each premise is individually necessary, and the group of premises are only sufficient for the conclusion if taken together. They give the example shown in figure 3.9.

LINKED (or CO-ORDINATIVE COMPOUND) ARGUMENT

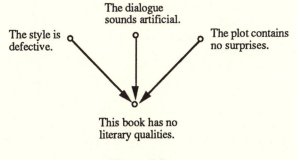

Figure 3.9

According to van Eemeren and Grootendorst, the crucial difference between convergent (multiple) argumentation and linked (co-ordinative compound) argumentation is that the respondent's calling the argument into question has different consequences. In the traffic case, it is not necessary for the proponent to back up all three premises to make his case: "If he succeeds in removing the antagonist's doubts about only *one* of his arguments, that will be enough to resolve the dispute." However, in the case of the book in figure 3.9, this is not so. To convince the respondent, the proponent in this case must support all his premises; "removing the doubts about only one of his statements will not be enough." The distinction between the convergent (multiple) type of argumentation and the linked (co-ordinative compound) type, for van Eemeren and Grootendorst, has to do with the sufficiency and necessity of the premise to discharge the burden of proof in persuading the respondent of the argument that the conclusion is true. If an argument has only one premise, they call it a *single argument,* where that one premise is sufficient, and no other premise is necessary.

The distinction between linked and convergent argumentation is basically pragmatic, because it has to do with how arguments can or should be supported (defended) by a proponent, and attacked (criticized) by a respondent, in reasonable dialogue. The kind of context of reasonable dialogue most often providing the setting for argumentation analyzed by the method of diagramming is persuasion dialogue (critical discussion), where the proponent has the goal of advancing a particular point of view (thesis), and the respondent has the goal of critically questioning the proponent's point of view.

In the case of a linked argument, the proponent has to defend each premise, or line of argument, because if one premise is weak (unpersuasive), the whole argument is unpersuasive, that is, the conclusion is not supported adequately. However, in the case of the convergent type of argument, each premise, or line of argument, is independent of the others. Here *independent* means that even if the respondent successfully attacks one premise, the other premise (or premises, if there are several) can still function as an argument to persuade the respondent to accept the conclusion.

Thus the distinction between linked and convergent argument is pragmatic, because it refers to the structures whereby the proponent of an argument can reasonably defend it, and the critic of the argument can reasonably attack it. The pragmatic nature of these structures was recognized by Windes and Hastings (1965, p. 215).

Consider case 3.3, a linked argument. In order to produce an argument that will have any hope of successfully proving its conclusion and persuading a respondent audience or readership that its conclusion is true, the proponent of this argument must prove that both of his premises are true. Suppose, for example, he successfully proves premise ② by citing a study carried out by researchers at the University of Massachusetts in Amherst, and this appeal to expert opinion is plausible and strong. This, in itself, is not enough, if it turns out that premise ① is weakly supported, and is open to serious questioning. Suppose a critic points out that there is recent evidence that sodium intake by Americans has recently decreased, and that the figure of between five and fifteen grams may be an exaggerated estimate. Given this critical response, the conclusion ③ becomes open to doubt. Even though ② remains well supported, that is not enough (by itself) to sustain ③.

By contrast, in the example of the convergent argument in case 3.0, suppose a critic attacks the premise that his rubbers are muddy. Perhaps they only appear to be muddy. Even so, the proponent can work on the other premise, pointing out that his raincoat is definitely wet, and that this is a good sign that he has been in the rain before coming in. Unless the critic can attack both premises, the argument can still perform its function of convincing its intended audience that the conclusion is acceptable.

SERIAL (or SUBORDINATIVE COMPOUND) ARGUMENT

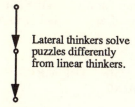

Lateral thinkers start at several places at once, whereas linear thinkers start in one place.

Lateral thinkers solve puzzles differently from linear thinkers.

Lateral thinkers have a logic of their own.

Figure 3.10

A third type of argument, called a *serial argument,* occurs where the conclusion of one (single, linked, or convergent) argument is used as a premise in another argument. Thus serial arguments are multiple-conclusion arguments, and may comprise an extended chain or sequence of argumentation. Van Eemeren and Grootendorst call the serial type of argument *subordinative compound argumentation,* where subordinate argumentation is added to support a main argument. They give the kind of example shown in figure 3.10 (1984, p. 92).

The characteristic of the serial (subordinative compound) argument is that when an argument is challenged by a respondent, the proponent may produce a back-up subargument. Thus in figure 3.10, the premise "Lateral thinkers solve puzzles differently from linear thinkers" becomes a conclusion supported by a new premise. This intermediate premise (conclusion) then "drops out," and the controversy begins to focus on the new premise (at the top, in the figure).

Thus linked arguments and convergent arguments can be combined together by serial arguments, which connect two subarguments by making the conclusion of one subargument function as the premise of the other. The simplest case of a serial argument would be the case where one argument, "A, therefore B" has its conclusion B appear as a premise in another argument, "B, therefore C" (as in the example in figure 3.11.

SERIAL ARGUMENT

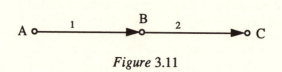

Figure 3.11

And then, of course, complex sequences of argument can be generated by serially combining linked and convergent arguments. Such complex configurations take the form of digraphs that represent the structure of an extended sequence of argumentation in an extended text of argument discourse.

3.   PROBLEMS IN USING THE METHOD OF DIAGRAMMING

The diagrammatic reconstruction of an argument from the passage given in discourse in a particular case is more than a purely descriptive job. It typically involves adding in parts of the argument that were not explicitly stated in the passage. This is required because typically, both the proponent of an argument and the reader, audience, or evaluator to whom the argument is directed share a common understanding of information not stated in the argument, but required in order to make sense of it. In the field of artificial intelligence studies, such unstated items of information present in a discourse text are called *scripts*. Scripts are based on stereotypical expectations or situations known to readers of a text.[1]

Suppose we are confronted with the following text:

Case 3.5:   Bob and Ted sat in the boat behind the duck blind. Several ducks flew past. There were several loud reports, and then Bob and Ted put down their shotguns and called the dogs to fetch the fallen ducks.

When you and I read the text in case 3.5, we know that Bob and Ted fired their shotguns. Note that we are not explicitly told this in the text, and of course it might conceivably be false. But it certainly is a reasonable or plausible presumption that fits the story. For as soon as we are told that Bob and Ted are in a duck blind, we know that their purpose is to hunt ducks. And we all understand the usual goals, practices, and procedures of duck hunting.[2]

Now it could be that Bob and Ted are really actors, spies, or something of the sort, and that all is not what it seems. But barring any information of this sort, it is reasonable to presume that they have pulled the triggers of their guns in the usual way and that they are in the boat for the purpose of hunting ducks.

What this example illustrates is that when we approach a particular corpus (given text) of dialogue in order to evaluate the argument expressed in it as reasonable critics of the argument, we may need to add in some premises or conclusions that were not explicitly stated in the corpus. Indeed, we may need to reinterpret and rearrange the actual wording of the argument considerably, in order for the given information to make sense at all as a persuasive or reasonable argument with premises and a conclusion.

The skills of argument reconstruction cannot be mechanically conveyed in every way, because these skills already presuppose a basic grasp of scripts in familiar situations, and an understanding of the subtleties and nuances of persuasive discourse in natural language (in this case, English). Even so, there are certain basic tools and components of argument reconstruction that can be explicitly defined and taught. And that is the purpose of chapters seven and eight. By applying these tools, you can enhance your already existing abilities to clarify and analyze a corpus of argumentation prior to the job of evaluating the uncovered argument in it.

According to van Eemeren (1986), the first step in reconstructing any given corpus of argumentative discourse is to identify the two sides of the dispute at issue, the *pro* and the *con*.[3] This does not mean in every case that the argument is a dispute in the sense of chapter one, meaning that the thesis of one arguer is the direct opposite of the thesis of the other. For in some cases, one arguer may be only doubting the thesis of the other, not declaring it false or attempting to refute it. Nevertheless, the first step of analysis involves the identification of the context of the dialogue, as outlined in chapter one.

But even beyond this first point, the corpus may have to be clarified and refined considerably, before it can be understood as an argument. According to van Eemeren (p. 10), this task may involve both *completion,* the making explicit of information required to fill gaps in the dialogue, and *addition,* the insertion of propositions that may not have been explicitly stated, but are required to bring out the full force of the argument.

The first job of analysis in the evaluation of any argument is the identification of the premises and conclusion. Once the proper conclusion of an argument is clearly identified, an argument evaluator is at least in the position to begin the job of assessing whether the information given in the premises can be reasonably judged as relevant or irrelevant to that conclusion. The conclusion is an anchor point.

In practical terms, however, one complicating factor is that some arguments, fairly assessed, are very long, composed of long chains of reasoning. Indeed, some arguments are so long that it may take a whole book or more to present the entire argument. In such a case, we are presented with a long argument or discourse, composed of many smaller subarguments linked together. Instead of having just one conclusion, the argument may have multiple conclusions, at different stages along the way, all leading toward one ultimate or final conclusion of the whole argument. These stepping-stone conclusions are called *interim conclusions,* which lead the way toward the final conclusion. Of cardinal importance is the job of identifying this master (final) conclusion. All other premises and conclusions must be evaluated in relation to the master conclusion, which is the arguer's main thesis or contention at issue.

Longer, extended arguments pose certain special problems. The actual given discourse or corpus, the message that is printed on the page, or the words actually delivered in a speech for example, may be only the tip of the iceberg. Many tacit premises may not be specifically or clearly stated. In realistic argumentation, some of the interim conclusions, or even the ultimate conclusion, may not be specifically stated. And the network of linkages between the premises and conclusions of different stages of the argument may be connected up in different ways. Hence the job of one who is to fairly judge the worth of the overall argument, or to evaluate criticisms of it, is a lot like the job of an archaeologist who must try to assemble a picture of the whole structure of a skeleton from the bits of bone that remain as his visible evidence of that structure.

In logical theory, we can judge whether or not an argument is valid, given a set of premises and a conclusion. However, in practical logic, when we try to evaluate a real argument in a realistic context or situation, the prior problem of identifying the argument is non-trivial. In practical terms, we may have to make reasonable conjectures, based on the actual given evidence in a corpus, whether a certain proposition can reasonably be taken to be part of the argument, and where it fits in.

Properly, in reasonable dialogue, the burden of proof should be on the critic to show why a given argument is open to criticism for alleged omissions or shortcomings. Hence the *principle of charity* states that where there is doubt whether an argument is correct or incorrect, the burden of proof is on the critic to show that the argument is incorrect, if that is what he alleges.[4] Of course, if the proponent of the original argument is available to defend or clarify his argument, then the dialogue can be continued, and charity is not necessary. However, if the proponent is not available for reply, then it is only fair to interpret his argument, if there is room for doubt, in such a way that he could have meant it to be correct. Every argument is really a dialogue, even if one participant may not be present to continue his side of the argument, for the moment.

An example would be where you are evaluating or criticizing an argument taken from a book or magazine, and where the author of the article will not have the opportunity, at least for the moment, of replying to your criticism. In this type of situation, you should reconstruct the argument on the basis of the principle of charity.

In applying the principle of charity in argumentation analysis, the first step is to identify the ultimate conclusion of the argument. Then the method is to work backward, finding the premises that are offered in support of this conclusion. In some cases (as in case 3.11), the conclusion may be in the middle of the argument, and it may be identified by an indicator-word, like "therefore." But wherever it is, once the main conclusion is identified, we can work outward to identify the rest of the argument.

The indicator-words identifying conclusions and premises are one main source of textual evidence in reconstructing argumentation. But argument reconstruction is also a process of interpretation. You have to look at the content of each of the propositions in an argument, and decide which premises provide the best support for a particular conclusion in the argument you have identified. This judgment is one of plausibility–you should be trying to reconstruct the argument in order to make it make sense–giving competing possible interpretations and choosing the strongest reconstruction, the one that makes the argument most plausible. Case 3.14 will illustrate how you have to see how given premises most naturally and plausibly fit together to support a conclusion, if the indicator-words leave you free to decide which propositions are supposed to support others.

It is best to begin the study of the use of the technique of diagramming for the analysis of extended arguments by examining some simple cases of the different kinds of structural relationships linking premises to conclusions at each single stage of an argument.

4. SOME SIMPLE CASES OF DIAGRAMMING

The use of the diagramming technique in practice will henceforth adopt the usual conventions of using circled numerals to stand for distinct propositions in a case, and arrows (directed arcs, directed edges) to join up the circled numerals in a graph. However, instead of using the cumbersome technique of joining circled numerals by a line or bracket to indicate a linked argument (a technique not amenable to graph theory), numbers on the arrows will be used for this purpose.

We begin with a type of argument configuration that is already familiar from section two.

Case 3.6:   Every responsible, up-to-date dentist these days uses a lead apron for his patient during x-rays. Dentist Smith is not currently using a lead apron to protect his patients during x-rays. I must conclude that Smith is not a responsible, up-to-date dentist.

In this case, there are two premises and one conclusion, which could be labeled as follows, where ① and ② are the premises, and ③ is the conclusion.

①   Every responsible dentist these days uses a lead apron for his patient during x-rays.

②   Dentist Smith is not currently using a lead apron to protect his patients during x-rays.

③   Smith is not a responsible, up-to-date dentist.

Each of the premises ① and ② is needed to support the conclusion ③. We could say that ① and ② are linked together to lead jointly to the conclusion ③. This already familiar pattern of argument, pictured in figure 3.12, is called a *linked argument*, where the same number on each arc (arrow) indicates the two steps of argument that belong together.[5] The fact that the same number appears on both arrows means that ① and ② are linked together as premises in the same single argument. The basic characteristic of a linked argument, it will be recalled, is that the premises are both required to support the conclusion–each one is dependent on the other(s).

LINKED ARGUMENT

Figure 3.12

By contrast, we now turn to a *convergent argument,* where each of several premises supports the conclusion independently.

Case 3.7:   ① [The Custom Turbo is a good choice for a buyer in today's car market.] ② [It has excellent performance for comparable gas mileage.] ③ [Its frequency of repair record is outstandingly excellent.] ④ [The price is much better than other comparable models.]

In this argument, the conclusion is the first proposition. The remaining three premises each provides support for that conclusion independently of the others (figure 3.13). Here there are different numbers marked on the arrows, indicating that each premise represents a different (independent) step of argument.

CONVERGENT ARGUMENT

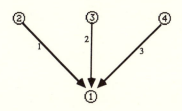

Figure 3.13

We could say (following Copi) in case 3.7 that there are three different arguments for the same conclusion. But since there is a single conclusion, a usual approach, also acceptable, is to say that there is one (single, convergent) argument. The terminological distinction here may not be too critical since, as we will see, in many cases where arguments are complex structures, we do often speak of an overall (complex) argument as one large entity. The important thing is that if there is any danger of confusion whether an argument is linked or convergent, the arrows must be clearly marked. If there is no danger of ambiguity in a particular case, marking the arrows is optional.

Convergent arguments and linked arguments are often combined in more complex argument structures, as the following case (taken from Copi, 1986, p. 22) will illustrate.

Case 3.8:   ① [Desert mountaintops make good sites for astronomy.]
② [Being high, they sit above a portion of the atmosphere, enabling a star's light to reach a telescope without having to swim through the entire depth of the atmosphere.]
③ [Being dry, the desert is also relatively cloud-free.]
④ [The merest veil of haze or cloud can render a sky useless for many astronomical measures.] (Blanchard Hiatt, *University of Michigan Research News*, Vol. 30, No. 8-9, Aug.-Sept. 1979, p. 5).

In this argument, clearly ① is the conclusion. But the remaining propositions go together in different ways to support the conclusion. By itself ② offers support for ①. However, ③ and ④ go together, each requiring the support of the other to provide evidence for ① that is additional to ②.

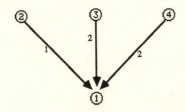

Figure 3.14

Hence the structure of 3.8, represented in figure 3.14, combines the linked and convergent structures. Premises ③ and ④ are linked, indicated by their sharing of the number 2 on their arrows, whereas ② is a separate and independent premise, indicated by the fact that it has a different number on its line of argument (1). A different number on an arrow represents a different step of argument.

Sometimes an argument may have more than one conclusion, and this factor makes two other simple kinds of argument structures possible. One type of structure is the *divergent argument,* where the same premise supports several conclusions.

Case 3.9:　① [The custom turbo has a dual carburetor.]
　　　　② [That means that you will find it gets better per-
　　　　　formance.]
　　　　③ [It also means that you will find that it uses more
　　　　　gas.]

In this case, the arguer draws two conclusions from the same premise, ①. Here we don't need any numbers on the arrows, because there is no possibility of confusion (figure 3.15).

DIVERGENT ARGUMENT

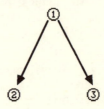

Figure 3.15

You could perhaps say that case 3.9 really consists of two arguments that use the same premise. And indeed, in reasonable dialogue, from the global point of view, an argument should really only have one conclusion, one ultimate thesis to be established or argued for. However, since longer extended arguments can be made up of interlocking smaller arguments, along the way there can be many interim conclusions. These conclusions are, as it were, temporary stages in the unfolding of the argument as it leads toward its ultimate conclusion in a controversy.

This complex interlocking of single arguments, then, does allow an argument to have several conclusions. In fact, sometimes a conclusion of one argument can function as a premise in another argument. When this happens we get a *serial argument* where one proposition is a conclusion of a premise and also a premise of a conclusion.

Case 3.10: ① [You observed the grease stains on the poker, Watson.] ② [One can infer that only Parker could have left grease stains on the poker.] ③ [Consequently, Parker is the murderer].

In this case, ③ is the final conclusion, based on ② as premise. However, ② is also a conclusion, based on premise ① (figure 3.16).

SERIAL ARGUMENT

Figure 3.16

The serial argument is really two single arguments linked together by a common proposition. It is characteristic of extended argumentation that convergent, linked, divergent, and serial structures combine single arguments together in a sequential network.

Case 3.11: ① [North Americans are still having coronary problems.] ② [Jogging is a healthy form of therapy for coronary problems.] ③ [Jogging is an economical form of exercise.] ④ [It does not require expensive equipment.] ⑤ [Therefore, jogging will continue to be popular in North America.] ⑥ [Consequently, levels of fitness will not tend to go below their present levels.] ⑦ [Moreover, the incidence of coronary disease may tend not to get worse.]

The proposition ⑤ is the first conclusion, based on premises ①, ②, and ③. But then, the further conclusions ⑥ and ⑦ are inferred from ⑤.

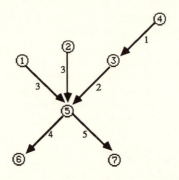

Figure 3.17

Premises ① and ② appear to go together to support ⑤. But ③ appears to be an independent premise for ⑤. And ④ backs up ③, independently of ① and ②. This interpretation suggests the description of the structure of case 3.11 shown in figure 3.17. Since ① and ② are linked, but ③ is not linked to either ① or ②, it is important to put numbers on the arrows to make the structure of the argument clear.

This example includes all four types of single arguments in the complex of the whole argument. Realistic arguments are very often at least this complex in their structure. Consequently, it is easy to see how the method of argument diagramming is a useful way to gain a comprehensive viewpoint of the overall archaeology of an argument.

5. ENTHYMEMES AND OTHER SUBTLETIES OF ARGUMENT RECONSTRUCTION

The main practical problem with diagramming the structure of realistic arguments from a given corpus or text of discourse is that many essential parts of an argument may be left unstated by the speaker or writer. The job of the argument archaeologist is to use good judgment and justified conjecture in filling in the missing bits.

An *enthymeme* is an argument that has one or more missing premises, tacitly but not explicitly stated by the arguer. The job of the argument evaluator is to fill in these missing propositions in a fair and reasonable way, so that the argument can be precisely stated, and then evaluated. To determine whether a proposition is really an enthymematic premise in an argument, one must judge by the context of the argument. In such a judgment, the two foremost factors appealed to are (1) the arguer's position, and (2) the validity of the argument.

The classic example of the enthymeme is the following argument.

Case 3.12:   All men are mortal.
                      Therefore, Socrates is mortal.

The missing premise in this argument, all of us would agree, is the proposition "Socrates is a man." This proposition is needed to make the argument valid. And it is uncontroversially taken as part of the arguer's position because the proposition "Socrates is a man" is a part of common knowledge and is, or would be, accepted by virtually anyone who would advance 3.12, or by a person to whom 3.12 would normally be directed.

Enthymemes are useful for the purpose of persuasive presentation of an argument precisely because the exact formulation of an argument may contain many propositions that are so uncontroversially acceptable to virtually anyone that they would be tedious to include. The argument is more pungent and persuasive if you leave them out, for your audience will not be inclined to dispute them anyway. At any rate, whatever the rhetorical reasons, when we encounter arguments presented in realistic contexts of persuasion and advocacy, typically many logically essential propositions will be omitted, and taken for granted.

Sometimes it is the conclusion of an argument that is left unstated. In the example below, the two propositions stated both appear to be premises.

Case 3.13:   If Bob were a true philosopher, he would never lose his
                      temper.
                      But Bob does lose his temper.

The suggested conclusion here would seem to be the proposition "Bob is not a true philosopher." The context seems to suggest that this is the conclusion any arguer who stated 3.13 would have us draw. Moreover, the construal makes the argument valid. So construed, the form of the argument is that of *modus tollens,* a valid argument form.

Judging from this type of example then, we should expand our definition of *enthymeme* to include the possibility that the missing proposition in an argument could be a conclusion, as well as a premise. An *enthymeme,* in other words, is an argument with one or more missing premises or conclusions, tacitly but not explicitly stated by the arguer.

The problem with enthymemes is that in realistic argumentation it is often not exactly clear what an arguer means to say. While it may be clear that there are some missing premises in his argument, exactly what the missing propositions are may be subject to interpretation. However, while it would be unfair to attribute to an arguer premises or conclusions he does not really accept, it would be equally unfair to omit from consideration premises that he has meant to include and that he needs for his argument, even if he has not explicitly stated them. For if one could not take some things for granted in arguing, one could never condense any argument into a form that would be reasonably brief, and presentable to an audience you need to convince or persuade.

The more context of an argument we have available, the better job we can do of evaluating what the enthymematic propositions in it should be taken to be. As we approach the job of reconstructing longer argument texts, a useful method is to mark each of the individual propositions and then go over the argument to find junctures where a conclusion is derived. Each of these interim arguments can be structured as a linked, convergent, divergent, or series argument. Of course, at the outset, one must decide what the final or ultimate conclusion of the text is. Then one can link up each of the single structures together to display the overall argument structure that leads to the final conclusion.

As the argument structure is revealed, very often there is enough context to yield some enthymematic premises along the way. The following example illustrates this process of argument reconstruction.

Case 3.14:   ① [Teenagers should not be given the idea that their role models consume products that are unhealthy.] ② [Cigarette commercials have rightly been banned from television.] ③ [For cigarette commercials portrayed role models, like the Marlboro man, smoking cigarettes.] ④ [And cigarettes are unhealthy.] ⑤ [The surgeon general has warned that smoking cigarettes is a danger to health.] ⑥ [On beer commercials, role models like sports personalities consume beer, and it looks like a lot of fun to the teenagers who watch these commercials.] ⑦ [Therefore, beer commercials should be banned from television.]

Examining this argument, we see that ⑦ is the final conclusion, but prior to that point in the argument, ② is also a conclusion, based on the linked premises ①, ③, and ④. And ⑤ backs up ④ (figure 3.18).

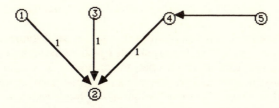

Figure 3.18

But where does the argument go from there?   Well ⑥ backs up ⑦. But if you look at ⑥ and ⑦ together, it is clear that ⑥ is linked to the premise ① in order to support ⑦. But that is not all that is needed. We also need the enthymematic premise ⑧ below.

⑧: Beer is unhealthy.

So the premises ⑥, ①, and ⑧ provide a linked argument for the conclusion ⑦. The total structure of the argument to this point can then be outlined as in figure 3.19.

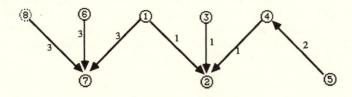

Figure 3.19

However, that does not seem to be the whole story. It does seem that the interim conclusion ② is also meant to make us conclude to ⑦ as well. The idea seems to be that cigarette commercials have rightly been banned, and since the case of cigarette smoking has been shown to be parallel to that of beer drinking, then beer commercials should be banned for the same reasons. To take this aspect of the argument into account, we could draw an arrow from ② to ⑦ in figure 3.19. This would complete the reconstruction of case 3.14.

In this case, the overall structure and context of the argument revealed clearly that ⑧, the proposition that beer is unhealthy, was an enthymematic premise. A critic of case 3.14 could even use this finding as the basis for a criticism of the argument. The critic might reply that beer is not unhealthy, and that a surgeon general has given no warning that drinking beer is a danger to health parallel to his warning about cigarette smoking.

The discovery of enthymematic premises in an argument is often a valuable basis for criticism of the argument by challenging hidden assumptions that, once revealed, may be open to question. Thus the method of argument reconstruction couples the use of argument structures with the analysis of enthymemes. The two techniques come together to enable the evaluator of an argument to gain an overall grasp of what the argument is, and where it goes. And these are always the first steps in reasonably evaluating whether an argument is open to criticism or reply.

In the real world, however, arguments can be very subtle and sometimes very unclear. Often arguers simply are not perspicuous or helpful in expressing what they mean to say. It will therefore be a useful exercise for us to tackle a longer and more complex sequence of argumentation where there is more room for interpretation and judgment. In the sequel, we will adopt the convention (now widely adopted) of writing an enthymematic proposition as a number with a dotted circle around it.

6. AN EXTENDED CASE STUDY

The following argument is a discussion of whether compulsory medical treatment should be given to anyone who attempts suicide. One arguer adopts the position that the suicidal person is a free agent, and therefore has the right to commit suicide without interference, provided he does not harm anyone else in the process. The other arguer takes the opposite point of view, that treatment should be compulsory.

Case 3.15:   ① [Any suicide attempt should lead to a diagnosis of psychosis, or at least lead to compulsory hospital admission.] ② [The reason is that all suicides are strong evidence of a person who is mentally ill or at least seriously disturbed.] ③ [Nobody who is mentally ill or seriously disturbed can be capable of reasonable decision-making.] ④ [It is notorious that suicidal persons are under the influence of drugs or alcohol, and are beset with irrational anxieties or severely disturbing mental conflicts.] ⑤ [The fact that such anxieties and disturbances often indicate more of a wish to reduce their anxieties rather than a wish to die is additional evidence of the severe mental conflicts and irrational motivations that beset suicidal persons.] ⑥ [Therefore, it is the business of medicine or behavioral therapy to cure the suicidal patient's illness.]

As we look over the text of this argument, our initial impression may be that ⑥ is the conclusion. That proposition occurs last in the argument, and is prefaced by the word "therefore." However, some critical reflection may suggest that it is more plausible that ① is the ultimate conclusion, which is based on ⑥. The linkage between ⑥ and ① that seems most plausible is this: the arguer is reasoning that it is proper for suicide to lead to medical diagnosis or hospitalization because it is the business of medicine or allied therapies to cure the suicidal person, for the suicidal person is a patient, someone who is ill. However ⑥ does not by itself enable us to deduce ① as a conclusion by valid deduction, even though the connection between ⑥ and ① is not difficult to perceive, ⑥ seems to require an enthymematic premise to generate ①, namely ⑩ :

⑩ : Diagnosis of psychosis or compulsory hospital admission is the appropriate way to go about getting medical treatment or behavioral therapy for a person who has made a suicide attempt.

By this account, ⑥ and ⑩ are linked premises that lead to ① (figure 3.20).

Figure 3.20

Having established this much of the structure of the argument, next we note that ② seems also to back up ① as a reason. However, evidence of mental illness or serious disturbance, as cited in ②, does not necessarily lead to a diagnosis of psychosis or to a conclusive argument for hospital admission, as stated by ①. Perhaps there are additional links filled in by the rest of the argument.

As we look over the rest of the text to try to sort out the order of the argument, however, we can see clearly that ④ seems best suited to backing up ②. Also, ⑤ is added as "additional evidence" to ④. This suggests that ④ and ⑤ are convergent premises, each providing an independent line of evidence for ② (figure 3.21).

Figure 3.21

This much established, how can we link these two single arguments in the overall sequence?

The connection seems to be that ② leads to ⑥. If the suicidal person is mentally ill or seriously disturbed, therefore it would seem logical that it is the business of medicine or behavioral therapy to cure that suicidal person. Why? Well, generally speaking, as we all know, it is the business of medicine or behavioral therapy to cure people who are mentally ill or seriously disturbed. That then is the required enthymematic premise. Let us call it ⑨.

⑨ :   It is the business of medicine or behavioral therapy to cure people who are mentally ill or seriously disturbed.

By this account ② and ⑨ are linked premises for ⑥ (figure 3.22).

Figure 3.22

So now we have the total structure as shown in figure 3.23.

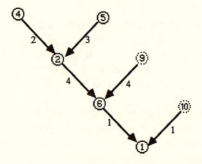

Figure 3.23

The only remaining premise we have not accounted for is ③. How does it fit in?

If you look at ② and ③ side by side, they seem to go together. It seems to flow naturally that if you put the two of them together, you can derive an interim conclusion, ⑧.

⑧ : With all suicides, there is strong evidence of a person who cannot be capable of reasonable decisionmaking.

What does capability for reasonable decisionmaking have to do with the argument? Or is ⑧ a conclusion that leads nowhere in the overall argument? What seems likely as the link is that ⑧ helps to back up ①, because if a person is not capable of reasonable decisionmaking then that is usually the best reason or justification for giving them compulsory treatment or hospital admission, whether they consent or not. Accordingly, ⑧ could be used as a premise for ① if we add an enthymematic premise to provide the link.

⑦ : For anyone who is not capable of rational decision-making, compulsory treatment or hospital admission is acceptable.

This means we have the linked argument shown in figure 3.24.

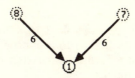

Figure 3.24

If ⑧ and ⑦ go together to lead to ①, then our last conjecture, that ② and ③ together produce ⑧, seems reasonable. So we also require the linked argument in figure 3.25.

Figure 3.25

Putting all these structures together yields the reconstruction in figure 3.26.

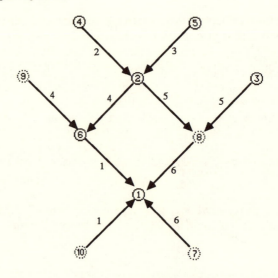

Figure 3.26

This concludes our analysis of example 3.15. We have seen in this case that careful judgment was needed to root out the plausible enthymematic premises. We turn now to a further discussion of the kind of judgment needed for evaluating enthymemes.

7. JUDGMENT AND ENTHYMEMES

Fundamentally, the only really fair and justifiable way to reconstruct an enthymeme is to be very sensitive to the context of dialogue behind a particular argument. Consider the following fragment of an argument that occurs in the context of a discussion on capital punishment.

Case 3.16:   I don't care what you say. If it's wrong for someone
to kill, then it's just as wrong when the state does it.

It is clear how this argument should be taken. The arguer is attempting to refute his opponent's argument. That is, the arguer's ultimate conclusion is the proposition "Capital punishment is not justifiable." The argument is a dispute, and consequently, in order to prove his thesis, the arguer needs to refute his opponent's thesis, "Capital punishment is justifiable."

What case 3.16 suggests is that it must be part of the opponent's position that it is wrong for someone to kill. Presumably, the opponent must be committed to that proposition because his position is based on the proposition that capital punishment is the justifiable form of punishment for the crime of killing, when killing is wrong. In effect then, the arguer who presents 3.16 is advocating the following subargument, where both premises are tacitly expressed but not explicitly stated. This argument is really a portrayal of his opponent's argument:

Case 3.17:   If [as you say] capital punishment is the justifiable form of punishment for the crime of killing, then killing is wrong.
[As you say] capital punishment is the justifiable form of punishment for the crime of killing.
Therefore [you must be committed to the conclusion], it is wrong for someone to kill.

But then, the argument continues, if it's wrong for someone (anyone) to kill, it's wrong for the state to kill. However, clearly the following proposition is also suggested: If it's wrong for the state to kill, then capital punishment is not justifiable. Hence, two other enthymematic premises need to be added, and the final conclusion.

Case 3.18:   If it's wrong for someone to kill, then it's wrong for the state to kill.
If it's wrong for the state to kill, then capital punishment is not justifiable.
Therefore, capital punishment is not justifiable.

How does this final conclusion follow? The conclusion of subargument 3.17 is that it is wrong for someone to kill. Taken with the first premise of 3.18, by *modus ponens* we may conclude that it is wrong for the state to kill. Then taking this conclusion along with the second premise of 3.18, we can infer, once again by *modus tollens,* that capital punishment is not justifiable. When you fill in all the missing links, the argument starts exclusively from premises alleged by the arguer to be commitments of his opponent, and concludes by deducing the negation of the opponent's thesis. In short then, the full argument, once exposed by reconstruction, is an attempted refutation of the opponent's thesis by the arguer.

The analysis of this example shows that we must be very careful in putting in enthymematic premises. Normally, in reconstructing an argument from a given text, we must be careful to show that every proposition inserted into the reconstructed argument as an enthymematic premise is really an acceptable commitment of the arguer who proposed the argument. Otherwise, it may be too easy to build our own preconceptions and assumptions, possibly without reasonable justification, into the argument. However, in this case, the argument proposed is clearly meant to be a refutation of an opponent's argument. Therefore, in filling in the missing assumptions, they are to be found among propositions that the opponent is committed to. For it is the opponent's argument that the proponent of 3.16 is alluding to, in drawing his conclusion.

Therefore, in inserting enthymematic premises in the reconstruction of an argument, the context of dialogue is all-important. You have to study carefully the context of the argument and try to determine whether a particular proposition truly is justifiable to put in as an enthymematic premise or not. This determination is only certain if the original arguer is present to confirm it. Otherwise, it is a question of judgment, and justification must be given.

In cases where missing premises could be controversial, we must be extremely careful in plugging in enthymematic propositions. Suppose a pro-choice advocate in an abortion dispute argues as follows.

Case 3.19: The fetus is not a person. Therefore, a woman always has the right to choose to have an abortion.

What missing premises should be filled in here? Possibly the argument should be filled out as follows.

Case 3.20: The fetus is not a person.
Anything that is not a person has no rights.
Therefore, if a woman chooses to have an abortion, she does not contravene anyone's rights.

But how can we be sure that this reconstruction truly represents the position of the arguer who presented 3.19? Perhaps she meant to argue that the rights of the woman override the rights of the fetus in the case of the woman's choice for abortion. Although she may mean to concede that the fetus may have some limited rights, nevertheless, she could be arguing that the woman's right to choose is a stronger right than those due to the fetus.

Consequently, we must be careful in many cases. Simply plugging in a sequence of missing propositions that would make the argument valid is not good enough. For that may not fairly represent the real position of the arguer who originally put that incomplete argument forward. In such cases, it is better to leave the gap open. The gap could then be questioned or challenged, and the original proposer of the argument has an obligation to fill it.

In some cases, like case 3.12, the required missing premise may be uncontroversial because it is accepted as highly plausible by virtually everyone, including the person who proposed the enthymeme and the persons to whom it is directed.   But if there is a real possibility of controversy or dispute, then the argument evaluator must be justified in his presumption that the appropriate arguer would in fact accept the proposed enthymematic premise as part of his position.   If not, the proposed argument reconstruction may be unfair and prejudicial.   Such a proposed reconstruction could even be a case of the *straw man misrepresentation,* the fault of unfairly or unreasonably attributing a certain position to one's opponent in an argument when that is not really his position at all. The principle of charity requires that when there is room for doubt, a proposition must not be attributed to an arguer's position unless there is good reason to presume that he does or would in fact accept that proposition.

We must be careful then, in reconstructing an argument from a given discourse, to remember that the burden of argument is on the critic to prove that an alleged missing premise can be justified as a legitimate part of the argument being criticized.

8. *REDUCTIO AD ABSURDUM* ARGUMENTS

In reconstructing arguments from a corpus, in some cases it is not enough simply to number the propositions and connect them together by arcs into a sequence, going from premises to a conclusion.   In most cases, it is necessary to understand the context of dialogue, to see the purpose of the argument as an attempt to counter an opposition argument in dialogue. This is especially true in cases where an arguer is trying to establish his thesis by refuting the opposite thesis of the issue of the dialogue.   This type of argument is a widely used and very effective kind of reasoning, especially in a dispute.

Consider the problem of how to reconstruct the following sequence of argumentation.

Case 3.21:   We must accept the thesis that arguments can be plausible. But how could we ever prove this claim, in general? Well, assume the opposite point of view, namely that arguments can never be plausible. This is the point of view of the skeptic who argues that no argument can be plausible, because any argument can be misleading and unreliable. What can we say about this point of view? Well, what does it say? It argues that no argument can be plausible, because it could be misleading and unreliable. But if this argument is right, then it can be applied to itself. In other words, it follows that the argument claiming that no argument can be plausible must itself be an argument that can't be plausible. But that is an absurd result; the argument destroys itself. Therefore, we must in general accept the thesis that arguments can be plausible.

The form of argument illustrated by case 3.21 is that of the *reductio ad absurdum* argument, which works as follows. Suppose an arguer wants to show that a particular proposition A is true. One way he can do this is to begin by making the assumption that the opposite of A is false. Then if he can show that the negation of A leads to an absurdity, to a proposition that is known to be false, or even to one that is inconsistent, then he has proved, indirectly, that A must be true.

The general form of the *reductio ad absurdum* proof is the following.

1.   *Required to prove:* A is true.

2.   *Assume:* Not A is true.

3.   *Prove* (by a sequence of deduction): An absurdity (proposition that is clearly false) follows from 2.

4.   *Conclusion:* A is true.

The reason why *reductio ad absurdum* is a valid form of argument stems from the validity of *modus tollens* (M.T.) and the Double Negation Rule, proved in chapter two. For if step 3 follows by deductively valid argument from step 2 above, in the general form of *reductio ad absurdum* reasoning, then the following conditional must be true: If not A then a false proposition. But since we know that the consequent of this conditional is false, its negation must be true. Therefore, by *modus tollens,* not not A must be true. But then, by the Double Negation Rule, it follows that A is true.

Hence according to deductively valid rules of logic, we can see that *reductio ad absurdum* is generally a valid form of argument.

② No argument can be plausible.

③ This argument itself cannot be plausible.

① Arguments can be plausible.

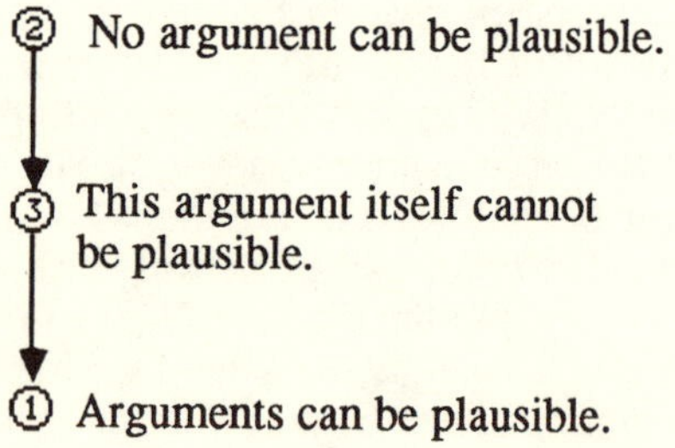

Figure 3.27

Once we understand the strategy of *reductio ad absurdum* as a kind of argument, it is possible to fill in the argument reconstruction of case 3.21.[6] Looking at the basic structure of case 3.21 as a sequence of argument (figure 3.27), it is evident that there is an argument from ② to ③, and that somehow, there is a line of argument from ③ to the initial thesis ①.

The step of argument from ② to ③ is fairly clear; ③ comes from ② by applying ② to itself, a step of argument that is deductively valid, provided only that this argument is an argument, a proposition that is necessarily true.   But how does the argument get from ③ to ①?   To fill this gap, an understanding of *reductio ad absurdum* as a form of argument is necessary.

The sequence from ③ to ① can be filled in as shown in figure 3.28.

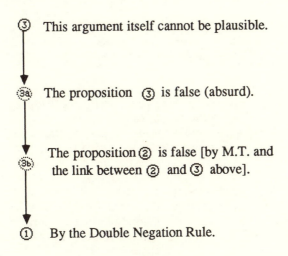

③   This argument itself cannot be plausible.

③ª   The proposition ③ is false (absurd).

③ᵇ   The proposition ② is false [by M.T. and the link between ② and ③ above].

①   By the Double Negation Rule.

Figure 3.28

Hence we can see that the argument is a serial argument that goes from ② to ③, and then from ③ to ③ª to ③ᵇ to ①.

But we are able to put in these enthymematic premises and thereby reconstruct the thrust of the argument because we can understand the underlying strategy of dialogue in it.   The arguer is trying to prove his thesis by assuming the opposite and then showing how this assumption leads to an absurdity.

This *reductio* of his argument could lead the skeptic to reformulate his point of view. He might reply: "When I claimed that no arguments can be plausible, I wasn't trying to *argue* for this point of view. For after all, arguments are futile anyway. I was rejecting the whole concept of an argument as a way of arriving at the truth of a matter." So reformulated, the skeptic's point of view is more difficult, perhaps even impossible, for his critic to refute. Any argument that a critic tries to bring to bear can simply be waved aside by the skeptic as just another untrustworthy and implausible argument.

Taking this stance, the skeptic is claiming that he is not really arguing. Or, if he is, he is discarding the argument once he has used it to achieve the insight that all argumentation is futile and unreliable.

This position is reminiscent of the reply of Sextus Empiricus–cited by Hamblin (1970, p. 94)–to the criticism that any proof of the non-existence of proof would have to be self-defeating. Sextus replied *(Against the Logicians,* II, §481) that some purgatives, after driving the fluids out of the body, can expel themselves as well. Sextus also used another compelling analogy to make the same point (quoted by Hamblin, 1970, p. 95):

> And again, just as it is not impossible for the man who has ascended to a high place by a ladder to overturn the ladder with his foot after his ascent, so also it is not unlikely that the Sceptic after he has arrived at the demonstration of his thesis by means of the argument proving the non-existence of proof, as it were by a step-ladder, should then abolish this very argument.

As Hamblin notes, this passage may be the source of Wittgenstein's famous use of the same analogy in the *Tractatus* (6.54).

But by taking such a radical stance, it may be that the skeptic is begging the question against any person who tries to attack or criticize his point of view. It seems that the skeptic and his would-be critic would always lack any common ground for discussion. The critic wants to use arguments to find weaknesses or contradictions in the skeptic's point of view. But the skeptic has already advocated a wholesale rejection of argument as a process that can never convince him that anything is true or false. There doesn't seem to be enough common ground for each party to communicate with the other.

The problem here is what we will call one of criteria of evidence circularity in chapter six, section four. Neither the critic's *reductio ad absurdum,* nor any of his arguments, can be brought to bear against the skeptic. For any putative evidence of this sort (being in the form of an argument) is presupposed to be spurious by the skeptic. For argument to work then, at very least the skeptic must admit that he is engaging in it.

Generally *reductio ad absurdum* works by deducing a proposition that is known to be false from the assumption of the opposite of the thesis to be proved. But there are various reasons why this proposition can be known to be false. It can be:

(1)   a proposition that is inconsistent with the original assumption, or

(2)   a logical inconsistency, of the form "A and not A," or

(3)   a proposition that is accepted as false (implausible) by all participants in the argument.

An example of case (3) is the following Platonic dialogue between Socrates and Cephalus.[7] Cephalus accepts the definition of justice as speaking the truth and paying one's debts, but Socrates shows that accepting this definition leads to a consequence that all participants in the dialogue accept as absurd.

Case 3.22:   Well said, Cephalus, I replied; but as concerning justice, what is it?–to speak the truth and pay your debts– no more than this? And even to this are there not exceptions? Suppose that a friend when in his right mind has deposited arms with me and he asks for them when he is not in his right mind, ought I to give them back to him? No one would say that I ought or that I should be right in doing so, any more than they would say that I ought always to speak the truth to one who is in his condition.
You are quite right, he replied.
But then, I said, speaking the truth and paying your debts is not a correct definition of justice (B. Jowett, trans., *The Dialogues of Plato, The Republic,* Book I, III, 6, New York: Macmillan, 1892).

In this dialogue, Socrates wants to prove the thesis that speaking the truth and paying debts is not a correct definition of justice. So he proceeds by the *reductio ad absurdum* strategy of assuming that it is a correct definition. However, when applied to a particular case, it follows that it is just to give dangerous weapons to a mentally disturbed person. Everyone in the dialogue agrees that this proposition is absurd and unacceptable. Hence the definition Cephalus accepted must be rejected, and Socrates' original thesis has been proved by the argument.

Many readers will be familiar with the use of *reductio ad absurdum* as a method of proof in mathematics, where it is usually called *indirect proof,* often used in Euclidean geometry. Another famous case is Pythagoras' indirect proof that the square root of two is an irrational number.

9. SUMMARY OF THE ARGUMENT DIAGRAMMING METHOD

Argument reconstructions are made up of four kinds of basic structures. In the *linked argument* each premise depends on the other premise or premises to support the conclusion. In the *convergent argument* each premise supports the conclusion independently of the other premises. Let us say you have a conclusion with two premises, for example. How do you tell whether its structure is that of a linked argument or a convergent argument? The test is whether each premise can stand on its own and yield support to the conclusion, or whether each premise requires the other premise so that the two premises function together to support the conclusion. Van Eemeren and Grootendorst showed that "functioning together" is to be defined in terms of the consequences of the respondent's calling the argument into question.

A third type of structure is the *divergent argument*, where a premise supports two distinctly separate conclusions. We need to recognize this type of argument because, in some cases of extended argument, a further part of the argument may be related to one conclusion of a previous premise, but not the other conclusion.

This brings us to the fourth type of structure called the *serial argument*, where two local arguments are linked together. In this type of structure, the conclusion of one argument also serves as a premise for the next argument. In this type of case, the same proposition serves a dual role in the two subarguments it links together. Sometimes a serial argument is also called a chain argument.

Discussions of enthymemes are often included in textbooks, but deployment of the technique of argument diagramming requires careful attention to the subtleties of enthymemes. Enthymemes become crucially important in reconstructing the parts of an argument that are not explicitly stated, but are definitely important, in a given corpus of argument. In practical terms, we must often deal with a given corpus that is only partially stated in explicit terms and that requires careful judgment and interpretation if the evaluator is to reconstruct it fairly and charitably. The reason for this incompleteness of existing passages of discourse is that the argument proponent and respondent characteristically share many common presumptions that do not need to be explicitly stated. Indeed, if the proponent were to state explicitly all these presumptions, his argument would be less persuasive because it would become too long and detailed to keep the respondent's active attention and interest. In practical terms then, enthymemes can be reasonable arguments, even if many of the significant propositions in them are not stated in the given corpus.

However, the problem from the point of view of one who must evaluate a given corpus of argument is to know how to justify attributing a tacit proposition to an arguer even if he has not explicitly stated it, and thereby made his commitment to it a matter of record.

It has already been noted in Walton (1987a) that the two foremost factors to appeal to in attributing an enthymematic proposition to an arguer are: (1) the arguer's position, and (2) the validity of the argument. This means that generally, a proposition A may be said to be an enthymematic proposition in a proponent's argument if the proponent is clearly committed to A in the context of the dialogue and A is needed in order to make the argument valid.[8] However, that is not the whole story. Sometimes enthymemes are more subtle to reconstruct.

The reason for this additional subtlety is that it is an important function of many arguments to persuade the respondent–the person to whom the argument is directed–to accept the conclusion of the argument by accepting the premises. As we noted in chapter two, a main function of argument in persuasion dialogue on a contestive issue is for one participant to argue on the basis of premises that are commitments of the other party, or parties, to the argument. This means that generally speaking, in an enthymematic argument the missing or unstated premises should be commitments of the respondent, if the argument is to succeed in being persuasive. So there is more to enthymemes than initially meets the eye.

Moreover, as we saw in case 3.16, if the argument is designed to refute a respondent's argument, then the crucial factor is whether the tacitly stated premises are commitments of the respondent rather than the proponent of the argument.

In many cases, however, not only should the unstated premises be commitments of the arguer, but they should also be commitments of the respondent to whom the argument is directed. This in turn means that the evaluator of the argument depends on the knowledge that he shares common cultural and background presumptions with both the original arguer and the respondent or audience to whom the argument is supposed to be directed. Then using this common understanding of what is uncontroversially acceptable to both parties in the context of the dialogue, the evaluator must fill in the unstated parts of the argument, in his argument reconstruction, in a way that is fair and reasonable in relation to both participants in the original dialogue. In making this judgment, the evaluator must abide by the principle of charity, and must justify every attribution of an enthymematic premise by a close and careful reading of the given corpus and a sympathetic understanding of the context of dialogue.

Dealing with enthymemes is therefore a subtle art, in some cases, requiring careful judgment and sympathetic interpretation of an argument. Consequently, whenever a proposition is attributed to an argument as an enthymematic reconstruction, careful justification of that attribution must always be given. The skill of dealing with enthymemes is an important part of practical logic. It would be nice if we could go strictly by what an arguer actually states in the corpus, but as case 3.15 showed, an argument is often most effective as a swift refutation, a "zinger," because it leaves the opponent no time to reflect on a reasoned reply. This swiftness is possible because of what is left unstated in the argument. Yet what is left unstated is a vital part of the argument, and has its effect on the audience, as intended by the arguer. Hence in practical logic, we cannot escape dealing with enthymemes if our goal is to analyze significant arguments that occur in real-life controversies.

The *reductio ad absurdum* is a kind of argument where one participant in a dispute refutes his opponent's thesis by deducing an absurdity from it. By refuting the opposite of his own thesis, the arguer who advances a *reductio ad absurdum* argument thereby proves his own thesis. The absurdity in a *reductio ad absurdum* argument is a logical contradiction in some cases. But in other cases it is simply a proposition that is highly implausible to all parties in the dialogue.

10. ARGUMENT DIAGRAMMING AND CIRCULARITY

It is a curious situation that argument diagramming and the fallacy of begging the question are almost always treated in separate compartments in logic textbooks. The one topic, as traditionally treated, appears to have no bearing on the other. But in fact, the two topics have to be intimately related, as chapters six and seven will show in detail.

To see this relationship, ask yourself the question—what would happen if the argument diagram of a case of argumentation revealed circular structure, like that of figure 3.29. Here, i and j could be any finite numbers greater than 4, so the circle could be as (finitely) large as you like.

What would the analyst of the argument do if such a circular structure became apparent in an argument diagram? So far, at least in the logic textbooks, this question has been rarely, if ever, raised.

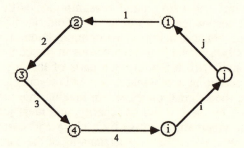

Figure 3.29

Moreover, the kind of circle in the diagram could be more complicated than the one in figure 3.29. It could have other arrows going into the various points on the circle. Or to make a case even more problematic, the arguments going into the circle, and the arguments on the circle, could be a mixture of linked arguments and convergent arguments. When we come to the case studies in chapters six and seven, plenty of cases of exactly these sorts of arguments will be encountered. How could one critically analyze such arguments, and what would the circles depicting them mean?

These are impressively difficult and unexplored questions. To make them less difficult, we have to revert to the idea that circularity is not, in itself, inherently harmful in all reasoning. When circularity is harmful or fallacious, it is because it interferes with legitimate goals of argument in a context of dialogue. In persuasion dialogue, the kind of argumentation our cases cited have usually been embedded in, the fault of a circular argument is that it may be useless to persuade the person(s) to whom it is directed to accept the conclusion of the argument (given the initial doubt of this person, or persons, about the truth of that conclusion). This uselessness to persuade derives, in the circular argument, from the fact that a premise is dependent upon, or equivalent to, the conclusion. And in a persuasion dialogue, the whole purpose of presenting an argument is to persuade the person to whom the argument is directed by presenting him with premises that are more plausible than the conclusion. That way, a respondent who does not initially accept the conclusion can be persuaded to do so by his seeing that it follows from premises that he *does* accept as plausible propositions.

What this tells us is that if a circle like that in figure 3.29 were to occur in an argument—as revealed by its argument diagram—to judge whether it is a case of begging the question or not, we need to know more about the context of the dialogue in which the argument occurs. In particular, we need to know whether it is a reasonable and appropriate requirement that the premises should be more plausible than the conclusion of the argument. But knowing this means knowing something about how plausibility values should be assigned or distributed over premises and conclusion in argument that is intended to reasonably persuade the one to whom it is directed to accept the conclusion.

What are the principles of plausible reasoning? Chapter five will take up this question. The coming into use of the method of argument diagramming has greatly affected this question, however. The rules of plausible reasoning will be distinctively different, depending on whether the argument has a linked or convergent structure.

We can be in a position to evaluate circular argumentation as question-begging or not only when we have at least a preliminary grasp of two areas of argumentation study: (1) the method of argument diagramming, and (2) the rules of plausible reasoning. Only through a conjunction of these two fields of argument analysis can a mature theory of begging the question begin to arise.

NOTES

1. Schank and Abelson (1977).
2. See Walton (1988).
3. See also van Eemeren and Grootendorst (1984).
4. Gough and Tindale (1985, p. 102).
5. The use of the theory of directed graphs to model argumentation is elaborated in Walton (1987a).
6. A useful account of using techniques of argument reconstruction to model *reductio ad absurdum* arguments is given in Freeman (1985, p. 158).
7. This case was cited by Salmon (1984, p. 32), along with other examples of *reductio ad absurdum* arguments. Salmon's explanation of *reductio ad absurdum* arguments is very clear, and is a good source to consult.
8. Walton (1987a, pp. 133-36). See also Govier (1987, chapter 5).

4

Shorter Case Studies

The next two chapters will cover a varied collection of case studies where begging the question is an issue. The more straightforward case studies will be presented in chapter four, and the more complex and difficult ones are reserved for treatment in chapter five. Trying to evaluate these case studies, to see whether the arguments in them can justifiably be said to beg the question or not, will enable us to start to use the tools of argument reconstruction and analysis developed in the previous chapter. At the same time, it will introduce new problems and difficulties that pose the need for refining these tools and methods.

As well as introducing many new examples of circular arguments, chapter four will deal once again with some of the case studies from the previous chapters. Without yet being in a position to deliver the final word on any of these cases, we can now throw more light on them, using the concepts and findings of the previous chapters.

The characteristic problem with the case studies of chapter four is that not enough context of dialogue is given to make complete evidence that would determine, beyond all question, that a fallacy of begging the question has been committed by the argument, or not. This is a very common problem with the examples currently cited in logic texts, and it is quite a general problem that must be contended with by any theory of argument reconstruction that can usefully be applied to adjudicating criticisms that an argument commits the fallacy of begging the question.

1. GOD AND THE VIRTUES REVISITED

When he originally posed the case of God and the virtues (case 1.12), Robinson diagnosed it as faulty, on grounds of question-begging, because the premise that God has all the virtues assumes the conclusion that God is benevolent. Sanford's comment (1972, pp. 198-99) was that this argument could be fallacious in some contexts, but non-fallacious in others. In

Sanford's remarks quoted in chapter one, section eight, the God and the virtues argument is described as fallacious where it "cannot increase the degree of reasonable confidence" that the person to whom the argument is directed "has in the truth of the conclusion." This could occur, according to Sanford, because such a person "would believe that God has all the virtues only if he believed that God is benevolent." Barker (1976) agreed on the importance of context in judging whether or not there is a fallacy in case 1.12, and also noted the importance of the argument's being an enthymeme.

In order to be more precise about what the fault of begging the question could amount to in this type of case, let us take the advice of Sanford and Barker seriously, and develop a more fully worked-out context of dialogue for case 1.12 in which an allegation of question-begging would plausibly arise as a point of contention.

It turns out that even in a specific, but quite standard, profile of dialogue for case 1.12, there is more than one basis for a reasonable criticism of circularity. To see this, begin by recalling from chapter one, section one, that according to the dependency conception of circularity, an argument is circular where some premise depends on the conclusion, in the sense that one needs to accept the conclusion as a requirement of accepting the premise. Such an argument is thought to beg the question, because the only way you could establish this premise as true or acceptable would be to make the prior presumption that the conclusion must be true or acceptable. Suppose Sue, an atheist, and Penny, a fervent Christian, are arguing about the existence of God. Suppose Sue has challenged Penny's claim that God is benevolent, and Penny advances the following argument.

Case 4.0:   God has all the virtues.
               Benevolence is a virtue.
               Therefore, God is benevolent.

Sue might reasonably criticize Penny's argument in case 4.0 as circular. Penny is supposed to be trying to prove, or argue for, the existence of God. Sue does not accept that thesis. Since the first premise of case 4.0 presumes the existence of God, Sue might well criticize the argument by saying that it has to presuppose Penny's ultimate conclusion, and that therefore the argument is circular (dependency conception).

Moreover, Sue might well feel that case 4.0 is a case of dependency circularity in yet another respect. The first premise, "God has all the virtues," surely must presuppose the truth or acceptability of the conclusion, "God is benevolent." For if, as the second premise alleges, benevolence is a virtue, then surely God could not have all the virtues unless God is benevolent.

So there are two ways in which Sue might argue that case 4.0 is an instance of the dependency conception of circular argument. Or Sue might also have posed her criticism by using the phrase "begging the question." Indeed, the original Greek expression, translated into Latin as *petitio principii,* means to petition for the thesis at issue or to beg for the question that is to be proved, according to Hamblin's account.[1] These terms suggest that what is supposed to be fallacious about begging the question in reasonable dialogue is that an arguer should present premises that the person to whom the argument is directed can accept independently of his acceptance of the conclusion. If acceptance of the premises is locked in too tightly to the conclusion, as it may seem to Sue to be in case 4.0, then anyone who doubts the conclusion is also going to doubt the premises. In other words, there is an obligation on an arguer to prove his conclusion by independent evidence–independent of the conclusion, that is–and not just "beg for" acceptance of the conclusion, without a useful and potentially effective argument that could convince one's opponent on a disputed question, and thereby meet the burden of proof for that dialogue.[2]

Although the phrase "arguing in a circle" is probably more familiar and easy to understand, we can also appreciate how Sue might use the term "begging the question" to refer to the same type of fault in argument, in ways that cover both of Sue's objections. In case 4.0, the argument was about the existence of God. So Penny's principal thesis to be proved is the proposition that God exists. However, at the particular point in the dialogue where the argument in case 4.0 comes in, Penny's conclusion to be proved is that God is benevolent. So we may say that Penny's use of the premise "God has all the virtues" in her argument in case 4.0 "begs for" the thesis that is at issue, from a global point of view, meaning that it presupposes her principal thesis that God exists. But it also begs the particular (local) conclusion she is supposed to be proving, that God is benevolent, because it presumes the prior acceptance of the conclusion that God is benevolent, as a prior part of the evidence that would be required in order for the premise "God has all the virtues" to be true. This "local" type of begging corresponds to Sue's second objection.

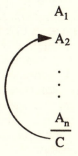

Figure 4.0

Thus the pattern of the dependency conception can be seen to be at the bottom of both of Sue's objections, even though one is at the global, and the other at the local, level of argumentation in the dialogue. One premise depends on the conclusion. Where A_1, A_2, . . . , A_n is the set of premises, then a dependency circularity occurs where one premise, for example A_2 in figure 4.0, depends on the conclusion C.

But we say that the argument begs the question because the premise A_2 depends on, or requires the prior acceptance of, the conclusion, C. What is wrong is that C is not proved on the basis of an independent set of premises A_1, A_2, . . . , A_n. Instead C is begged for or smuggled into the premise set as a prior presumption on which A_2 rests.

Generally speaking, we can see how the idea of circularity as a fault of argument goes back to the basic idea that in all persuasion dialogue, each arguer has a thesis to be proved to the other arguer to whom the argument is directed. The fallacy of begging the question is a species of failure to carry out the burden of proving one's thesis by utilizing premises that the other arguer can accept, independently of one's own conclusion to be proved. For it is in the nature of persuasion dialogue that the other arguer will reasonably be disinclined to accept that conclusion without proof or argument.

Sanford's diagnosis, then, was accurate, but can now be expressed more fully and explicitly. It is right that the argument begs the question for Sue because she would believe that God has all the virtues only if she believed that God is benevolent. But more than this, because of the context of the persuasion dialogue, Sue is not inclined to accept the proposition that God is benevolent, or even the prior presumption that God exists. And unless Penny has some other way of proving that God has all the virtues, by presenting premises that are more plausible to Sue than the conclusion she rejects, her argument could never convince Sue to change her mind.

According to the global interpretation, the objectionable feature of the argument in case 4.0 was that the first premise presumes the existence of God, yet the person to whom the argument is directed, Sue, is bound not to accept the existence of God, without proof. The proposition "God exists," from Sue's point of view, however, appears to be an enthymematic premise in Penny's argument. In other words, from Sue's point of view, the argument in case 4.0 really amounts to a case where argument reconstruction can show that there is a required enthymematic premise that is identical to the very conclusion that Penny has the burden of proving in the persuasion dialogue. For Sue to concede this premise would be for her to concede defeat in the persuasion dialogue. This is shown in figure 4.1.

In the dialogue, the issue of the whole argument is whether God exists. Sue's position is that of doubting whether God exists. But figure 4.1 reveals that Penny's argument evidently does rest on the premise that God exists. But for Sue, the proposition "God exists" is at least as dubious as the proposition "God is benevolent." Therefore the premises of the argument fail to be evidentially prior to the conclusion, from Sue's point of view. For her, the premises are not more acceptable as evidence than the conclusion to be proved. For her, the argument "begs the question at issue." It is fallaciously circular and, for that reason, objectionable. In other words, in the context of this dialogue, if Penny wants to convince Sue that God is benevolent, she will have to find premises that Sue accepts as a potential evidential basis for that conclusion.

RECONSTRUCTION OF CASE 4.0

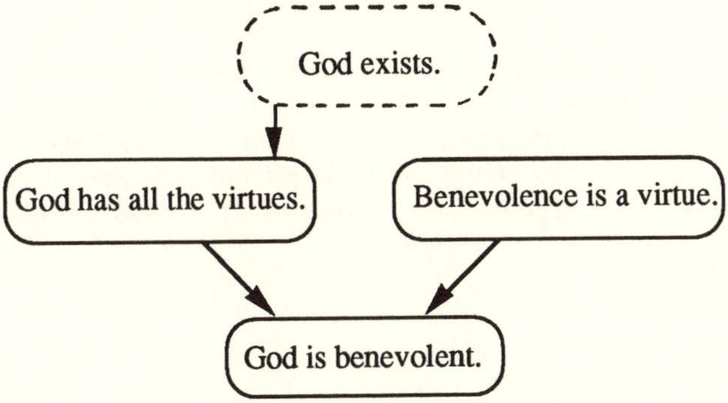

Figure 4.1

Also, there was another circle to be found in case 4.0. It seemed that the first premise "God has all the virtues" must presuppose the conclusion 'God is benevolent.' For if, as the second premise states, benevolence is a virtue, then surely God could not have all the virtues unless he is benevolent. The first premise depends on the conclusion, it seems. Or at least this dependency is what we found objectionable about the argument, and what made it circular.

The problem here too can be seen as a failure of evidential priority. The premise "God has all the virtues" is supposed to be prior to the conclusion "God is benevolent" if Sue is to be convinced of this conclusion. But, asks the critic, how can it be evidentially prior, since it would seem that the only way you could prove this premise would be to presume the prior conclusion that God is benevolent. But only one proposition can be prior to the other. Penny can't have it both ways, so the fact the argument is circular is, in this context, a reasonable ground for objection.

However, in relation to this second interpretation of Sue's objection, we should not be too quick to condemn Penny's argument as hopelessly circular and therefore fallaciously question-begging, beyond all redemption. Her premise is "God has all the virtues." How could she prove this premise? Does she absolutely need to presume, as a further required premise, that God has the virtue of benevolence? Here the burden of

argument is cast back onto Penny's side, by the criticism of circularity. Considerations of meta-argument burden of proof enter the picture.
   Perhaps Penny could continue her argument as follows.

Case 4.1:   God has all the virtues. Why? Because if God failed to have any virtue, he would be less than perfect. But that is impossible. Hence, God must have all the virtues.

Does this argument necessarily presuppose or require the premise that God is benevolent? Perhaps it does not need to, since it refers to any virtue you care to choose, and you do not necessarily need to choose benevolence. If this interpretation is reasonable, we could picture the relevant part of the structure of Penny's argument as shown in figure 4.2, numbering the propositions in the argument as follows.

① :   God is benevolent.
② :   God has all the virtues.
③ :   If God failed to have any virtue, he would be less than perfect.
④ :   It is impossible for God to be less than perfect.

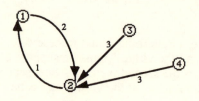

Figure 4.2

The previous part of the argument indicated that ① and ② are locked into a circle. But the two new premises ③ and ④ provide a new and independent line of argument for ②.
   What is critical here is that the linked argument from ③ and ④ to ② is independent of the argument from ① to ②. In other words, the argument from ③ and ④ to ② is a convergent argument—it is not linked to the other two arguments. In other words, Penny's new line of argument is independent of the previous circle.
   If case 4.1 provides a possible extension of the context of dialogue that could carry on from the argument of case 4.0, then Penny could have a way out of Sue's second objection. At least, it would now seem that Penny's argument is no longer inevitably circular.
   The diagram in figure 4.2 shows that the conclusion that God has all the virtues can be supported without having to presume prior acceptance of

the proposition that God is benevolent, so far as has been shown by Sue. So although there is a circle in the argument for ②, there is also additional support for ② that is not on the circle.

In short, Penny could possibly succeed in breaking out of the circle. Although there remains a circle in her argument, and she may well concede this, nevertheless her new line of argument can now potentially meet the requirement of burden of proof. She now has a way of replying to the criticism that the circle in her argument shows that the argument is fallacious because it inevitably violates the more plausible premises rule. She has shown that the argument, now expanded, is a convergent argument where one independent line of argument can offer plausible premises without being locked into a circle.

One important lesson here is that sometimes it may be reasonable to make an allegation of circularity, yet in some cases the criticism that the circular argument commits the fallacy of begging the question can be defended against. Penny might argue in this case that even though there is a circle in her argument, the circle can be defended against as a conclusive indication of fallacious argument. The reason she can make this defense is that she can claim that even though there is a circle between ① and ②, still there is an independent line of argument for ②, namely ③ and ④, that is not on a circle. Therefore, Penny can claim that her argument potentially satisfies the requirement of evidential priority, at its present state of development in the dialogue.

So this particular example illustrates, once again, that an argument can have a circle in it, yet it need not follow that the argument is fallacious. This suggests that even if a critic has identified a circle in someone's argument, the burden of proof should be on the critic to prove his contention that the circle shows that the argument is an instance of the fallacy of begging the question, if that is what the critic contends.

Another interesting and distinctive feature of this example is that Penny added a new line of argument at case 4.1, where she continued on from her original argument at case 4.2. So sometimes, a response to a criticism of circularity may proceed by continuing the dialogue, by introducing a new argument. In such a case the critic's allegation could be judged reasonable on the basis of the given evidence at the time, but the defender's response to the criticism could also be reasonable, by virtue of the new evidence it introduces. So as the dialogue proceeds, and new arguments are introduced, any criticism or reply must be reasonably evaluated relative to a particular point in the sequence of dialogue. If the dialogue is not finished, and the evidence is not totally in, the strength of a *petitio* criticism may have to be evaluated on a basis of burden of proof. This means that, in such a case, the criticism that an argument begs the question is more like a point of order in the dialogue than it is like a refutation.

The bottom line in any dispute about the worth of a circular argument turns on whether the requirement of evidential priority (1) is appropriate to the context of dialogue, and (2) has been met at that point in the dialogue, or can be met by the defender against the criticism of circularity.

The very first question is whether the argument is circular. But if that is settled, and the argument is circular, there remains the question of whether the circular argument is open to criticism on the basis that it commits the fallacy of begging the question. At that point, the key factors (1) and (2) must be evaluated, relative to the context of the particular dialogue. When approaching any argument where an allegation of the fallacy of begging the question has been made, the first important question to ask is whether the context of dialogue requires that the premises be evidentially prior to the conclusion, and the second is whether the argument has closed off all the lines of access to premises that the respondent could reasonably accept as evidence for the conclusion at issue so that the argument really, and not just apparently, violates the requirement of evidential priority. It is precisely for these reasons that when we come to construct a theory of the fallacy of begging the question in chapter eight, circular argument will be only one requirement for question-begging, and not the whole fallacy.

Sanford rested the issue of whether the God and the virtues argument is circular on the question of whether the one to whom this argument has been directed would believe that God has all the virtues only if he believed that God is benevolent. This criterion, however, being based on what the recipient "would believe," led to the Whately-Biro criticism that begging the question depends on the subjective beliefs of a particular arguer. To defend against that criticism, Sanford (1981, p. 50)–see chapter one, section eight–contended that this other-directed feature of argument relates to the degree of reasonable confidence in a conclusion when the purpose of the argument is to convince another person.

In light of what we have learned about the context of persuasion dialogue, we can see how Sanford's type of criterion can be explicated in such a way that it is not just the actual beliefs (the psychology) of the person to whom the argument is directed that should be the criterion of whether the argument begs the question. What is important is whether the respondent in the persuasion dialogue still has an option of finding a line of argument for the premise that God has all the virtues that does not require "God is benevolent" (or "God exists") as a premise. To see in fact whether there does exist such a line of argument, we have to reconstruct the whole argument in its proper context of persuasion dialogue, and see what premises and lines of reasoning have been made available. This depends on the commitments of the participant to whom the argument was directed, but the determination of these commitments is not a question of psychology. It is a question of reconstructing the argument to determine what this arguer's commitments may fairly be taken to be, judging from the text of discourse and the context of the argument (to the extent this information is known).

Case 4.1 is actually a version of the ontological argument, a kind of theistic argument that has historically been criticized on grounds of suspicion of circularity. The apparently simple case of God and the virtues has turned out not to be so simple after all, as an example of the fallacy of begging the question. We return to the ontological argument as an extended case study of the objection of begging the question in chapter seven.

Cases 4.0 and 4.1 have important implications for understanding how the term "fallacy" should be conceived in order to understand begging the question as a fallacy. Whether a circular argument may rightly be said to commit the fallacy of begging the question depends on how the premises of the argument can be supported by a proponent as the argument continues to unfold in the continuity sequence of dialogue. One might say that an argument like that in case 4.0 is circular, and that it is open to objection on the grounds that it appears to be going in a direction of question-begging rather than a direction of meeting its burden of proof. Such a criticism could be a valid point of order, and a criticism that is reasonable and helpful to guide the argument into more constructive channels. But it is quite another thing to criticize such an argument by claiming that it commits the *fallacy* of begging the question. The notion of fallacy is evidently in need of further clarification.

2. HOW TO REPRESENT EQUIVALENCE?

Case 1.0, the standard example of the simple equivalence *petitio*, raises another issue in the methodology of argument reconstruction. Are the two sentences in the argument that represent its premise and conclusion really both sentences that express the same proposition? Or are they distinct propositions, separate assertions that are nevertheless, in some sense, equivalent to each other in a manner that makes the argument circular?

If it is a case of the same proposition being asserted twice in the argument, then the graph of the argument (figure 4.3) is an arc that takes a point back onto itself (a *loop*).

A LOOP OF ARGUMENT

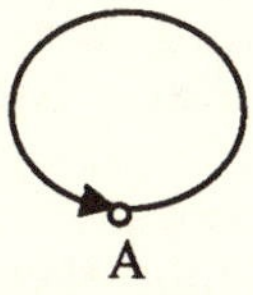

A

Figure 4.3

If, however, it is a case of two distinct propositions that are nevertheless, from a point of view of argument, closely equivalent, then the situation is different. But what does "equivalence" mean here? What it could mean is that not only does the premise directly imply the conclusion, without requiring any additional premises in a linked or convergent argument, but the conclusion also directly implies the premise in the same manner. In other words, the conclusion is so closely linked to the premise that one really has no choice, in reconstructing the argumentation, but to draw a direct inference from the conclusion to the premise. An appropriate way to draw the graph of the argument in reconstructing this type of case would be to draw an arc from the premise to the conclusion, and an arc going the other way, from the conclusion to the premise. This type of digraph is called a case of *multiple arcs* (figure 4.4).[3]

MULTIPLE ARCS IN ARGUMENT

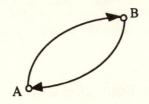

Figure 4.4

These two figures represent different types of argument. In the case of multiple arcs, there are two distinct propositions, A and B, even though they are equivalent in the sense that there is an arc from A to B and an arc from B to A.

But what should equivalence mean here? Should it mean that there is a directed path of argument from A to B, and also a directed path from B to A? If this is what it means, then the case of multiple arcs in figure 4.4 is certainly an instance of equivalence between two points, A and B. But perhaps equivalence should mean that every directed path through A also passes through B, and every directed path through B also passes through A. These choices are open. It remains to be decided how the method of argument reconstruction is to be applied to cases of equivalence circularity like case 1.0, and other similar examples of begging the question of this sort so often cited as illustrations of this fallacy by logic textbooks.

However this issue is decided, one underlying theoretical problem should also be addressed. When it is said that the premise and conclusion of a case like case 1.0 are "equivalent" or "identical," should this be interpreted in an argument reconstruction to mean that the premise and conclusion express the same *proposition,* or should it be taken to mean that they express the same *assertion* by a participant in a context of dialogue? Equivalence of propositions is a semantical notion, whereas equivalence of assertions is a pragmatic notion.

The range of cases may suggest there is room for both interpretations of equivalence in judging the fallacy of begging the question. In case 1.0, the premise and conclusion would appear to be semantically equivalent for any native speaker of English who would respond to this argument. However, in other cases, cited by the text, a looser kind of equivalence seems to be involved. The following example is from Damer (1980, p. 27).

Case 4.2:   Reading is fun, because it brings me lots of enjoyment.

The problem with this case of circular reasoning, according to Damer, is that "in an argument one's personal beliefs or convictions concerning the truth of a claim cannot be evidence for the truth of the same claim." But is this true?   It seems to depend on the claim and the type of argument involved.   Suppose both participants in a persuasion dialogue on whether reading is fun agree on the general principle that whatever brings lots of enjoyment to a person qualifies as "fun" for that person.   In the context of this discussion, if a proponent were to advance the speech act of case 4.2 as an argument, it could well be that the argument does not beg the question. The reason is that the assertions "Reading is fun" and "Reading brings me lots of enjoyment" are not pragmatically equivalent, in the context of dialogue.

Yet in another context of dialogue, it could well be that these two assertions are equivalent.   In this context, unlike the one cited above, it could well be that there is a real problem of circularity.   The problem is that, in this context, as an assertion of the arguer's commitment to a proposition, the premise is equivalent to the conclusion.   In offering the premise "Reading brings me lots of enjoyment," the arguer is doing nothing more than asserting his personal commitment to his conclusion that reading is fun.   Although there may be a semantical difference between the meaning of the proposition in the premise and that of the proposition in the conclusion, this difference by itself is not enough to make the argument non-circular.   It still remains open to the criticism that it begs the question because, in the context of the dialogue, what the premise asserts is no different from what the conclusion asserts.   The two assertions are pragmatically equivalent in this context of dialogue.

From a practical point of view, the use of graph techniques of argument reconstruction are scarcely needed in simple cases of equivalence circularity like the ones above.   But where such cases do arise in an argument reconstruction, perhaps the best way to treat them is to use freely notions of semantic or pragmatic equivalence (with appropriate explanations and justifications), and use the same point on the graph to represent both premise and conclusion.   The main problem is to place the argument in a more specific context of dialogue.

A problem inherent in the equivalence conception is that it can be very much subject to dispute whether two propositions are equivalent, in a context of discussion.   Thus many supposedly simple cases of equivalence circularity that are cited by the textbooks as "obviously" cases of fallacious question-begging arguments may not be so simple. Consider the following case.

Case 4.3:   You ought to give alms because it is a duty to be charitable.

This case was cited by Latta and MacBeath (1956, p. 380) as an instance of the fallacy of begging the question, because "the reason we give for the conclusion is obviously just a reassertion of the proposition to be proved." But is it so obvious?

Suppose Alphonse and Ernest are both religious fundamentalists in a certain sect that explicitly sets out several duties, including the duty to "be charitable." Suppose both Alphonse and Ernest agree that this is one of their acknowledged duties, and, as members of this religious group, are both very conscious that this is clearly one of their duties. Suppose additionally that they both know that there are several ways of fulfilling this duty. They could work for charitable causes, or perhaps they could hand out warm winter coats to "street people" in the winter, or perhaps they could support social welfare agencies that help the poor. However, another way to meet this duty would be to "give alms," that is, to give money to beggars, or people who solicit money on the streets.

Now suppose that in this context, Ernest proposes the argument expressed in case 4.3 to Alphonse, and Alphonse replies: "Well, you know, a problem with "giving alms" to people on the street is that it tends to perpetuate their precarious existence and activities as street beggars when, if they didn't have this source of subsistence, they would go to the proper social agencies and receive the help they need, both for financial support, and for counseling and retraining. So maybe giving alms is not the best way to fulfill our duty to be charitable, because it is not really the way to help these poor unfortunates to improve their situation."

Now Alphonse is objecting to Ernest's use of the argument of case 4.3, but not because it commits the fallacy of begging the question. And indeed, in the context of dialogue sketched out above, it is not true that the conclusion is equivalent to (just a reassertion of) the premise. The two propositions are, in fact, quite distinct (non-equivalent) assertions in the argument. One is quite properly a reason for the recommendation expressed by the other, and is independent of it, as a reason.

We should reconsider this case then. Is it really an obvious instance of the fallacy of begging the question? Or would it be better described, in general, as an argument that is open to a procedural objection of being potentially question-begging because the terms used in it are undefined, in the absence of any further details of context, as the case is cited in Latta and MacBeath? Surely case 4.3 is only open to interpretation as a circular argument because the terms used in it are vague. For all we know, "you ought to" is equivalent to "you have a duty to," and "to give alms" is equivalent to the phrase, "to be charitable," because all four terms are vague and undefined, as far as the given context of argument goes.

Semantically, this pair could be two pairs of equivalent terms, and this opens the argument of case 4.3 to the potential of circularity. But the real test of whether they are being used equivalently is pragmatic. It depends on the context of the dialogue in which the argument of case 4.3 is supposed to occur. Only when this context is filled in can we properly say whether the argument commits the fallacy of begging the question or not.

Hence the concept of equivalence required to support the criticism that an argument commits the fallacy of begging the question is pragmatic rather than purely semantic in nature. Of course, this point of view presupposes that there is a difference between the claim that an argument is potentially circular and the stronger claim that it commits the fallacy of begging the question.

The current logic textbooks are ambiguous when they ask students to identify whether a one-sentence example, given with no further context of discussion, is supposed to be a fallacious *petitio principii* argument or not. Such examples often seem, superficially, as though they ought to be simple cases of the *equivalence petitio*. But in fact, because of the vague terms in these arguments, the argument could often be interpreted as circular or non-circular, depending on the context of the dialogue. What you should really conclude in this type of case is that you don't know whether the argument is circular or not, until more of the context of the discussion is made explicit.

Consider three cases of this type set out as exercises by Fogelin (1978, p. 96). The student is directed to explain why each of these arguments involves either circular reasoning or begging the question.

Case 4.4:   Intoxicating beverages should be banned because they can make people drunk.

Case 4.5:   Capitalism is the only correct economic system because without it, free enterprise is impossible.

Case 4.6:   Gun control laws are wrong because they violate the citizen's right to bear arms.

Of these three cases, the first one is the most likely to be a circular argument, because "intoxicating beverage" just means (exactly) "a beverage that can make people drunk." The third case is the least likely to be circular, in most contexts of discussion in which it would be likely to occur, for reasons essentially similar to those given in the analysis of case 4.3 above. The middle case could be more likely to go either way. If the proponent of the argument takes "capitalism" to mean exactly the same thing as "free enterprise," then his argument is circular. But it is quite possible that he might mean something quite different by these two terms, in the context of the discussion that is under way.

For example, the dispute in case 4.5 might be, let's say, about the issue of whether capitalism or socialism is the better economic system. One party might argue that socialism is often underestimated because its critics fail to realize that it is possible to have a certain degree of free enterprise within a socialistic system, as long as this free enterprise does not get out of hand, and begin to interfere with equality in an intolerable way. The other party might reply: "What you are calling 'free enterprise' is not really free, nor is it enterprise, within a socialistic system. Free enterprise cannot flourish meaningfully and effectively in that kind of climate of state control." This party may then go on to enunciate the wording of case 4.5 as part of his argument against socialism.

In this context, the argument in case 4.5 might be non-circular, and not a case of the fallacy of begging the question. The reason is that it appears to be a reasonable presumption from the context of the discussion that neither party is using "capitalism" and "free enterprise" as such closely equivalent terms in the argument that they have any grounds for objecting to the argument of case 4.5 as fallaciously circular.

3. CRITERIA OF EVIDENCE CIRCULARITY

Cases 1.1, 1.2, and 1.3 are all related to the *argumentum ad verecundiam* type of argumentation, where an appeal to an authoritative source (usually that of expert opinion) is made to obtain advice or assurance. The type of dialogue, in these cases, is therefore closely related to the expert consultation dialogue.[4] However, none of these three cases is a straightforward use of the appeal to expert opinion in argument.

A second factor involved in all three of these cases is burden of proof. In each case, the circle involves an offering of a criterion for good evidence in a context of dialogue, which then tries to support the criterion by appealing to that very "good evidence" itself. What is involved is therefore a kind of argumentation-meta-argumentation circle of the kind more often associated with the logical paradox type of vicious circle discussed in chapter one, section ten. In these cases, the argument for the criterion for what constitutes an adequate argument in a particular context appears to have become entangled with the argument itself, which is supposedly based on that criterion. The problem here is that the meta-task of determining burden of proof for a class of arguments in a context of dialogue needs to be separated from the task or obligation to support an argument internally to meet the burden of proof in that context. Otherwise, a circular argument results.

Consider case 1.1. The criterion for the argument that Shakespeare is a greater writer than Krantz rests on a kind of meta-pronouncement about appeals to authority in judging literary works–those with "good taste" are the best judges. Here then, a criterion, although it is a very vague and general one, is being proposed. But then the question arises–how do we implement this criterion? How do we appeal to some more specific guidelines that would enable us to pick out the particular literary critics who have good taste? By coming back to those who prefer Shakespeare to Krantz, the argument of case 1.1 closes the circle. It appeals to the good evidence it initially cited to support the criterion that supposedly establishes that evidence as good evidence.

The general structure of argumentation for this type of circular reasoning is portrayed in figure 4.5.

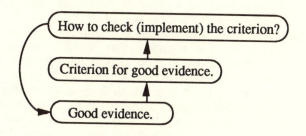

Figure 4.5

This type of argument starts out, at the bottom level, with an argument supported by some kind of putative evidence. Then to back up this kind of evidence as valid evidence in the context, an appeal is made, at the second level, to some general criterion that specifies a criterion for good evidence (burden of proof). Then at the third level, the question arises of how to validate or support the criterion as applicable in this particular case. The problem of circularity then emerges at the fourth step, when an appeal is made to that very evidence itself (from the first level) to support or validate the criterion.

This pattern of circular burden of proof placement is clearly evident in case 1.3, where inclusion in scripture is cited as the criterion for good evidence. But then the question arises–how can this criterion be validated as a reliable source of evidence? The circle is closed when the Bible is cited as a good source of evidence because it is the word of God.

As already noted in the discussion in chapter one, however, case 1.3 is problematic in other respects, because the context of dialogue has not been clearly or unambiguously specified. If we presume that the context is that of a persuasion dialogue where the appeal to authority is brought in by a theist to persuade a skeptic or atheist of the existence of God, then the meta-circularity of the case, as noted in chapter one, can be analyzed as a case of begging the question.

Another example of this type of case was also cited in the quotation from Whately in chapter one, section one, where "any one should infer the authenticity of a certain history, from its recording such and such facts, the reality of which rests on the evidence of that history." (Whately, 1836, p. 220). The problem is that a history text itself presents certain arguments, which can be verified or criticized by appealing to testimony or sources of evidence external to the text. But how can we verify the authenticity of that text? Whatever criteria are proposed, the sources of evidence should be free from bias, at least to the extent that they should be external to the text being judged. Hence to appeal to the internal testimony of "facts" recorded by that history itself would beg the question in the way sketched out by the structure of figure 4.5.

Case 1.1 concerned the seeking of advice on matters of literary taste, case 1.3 concerned theological argumentation, and Whately's case concerned argumentation in historiography. But all three cases share a general pattern of structure of argumentation. In each case, a criterion of good evidence is advanced that is backed up by the very sort of evidence included in or certified by the criterion.

It is also interesting to observe that all three of these cases (but especially case 1.2) are embedded in a context of dialogue where a non-biased recommendation for a conclusion is being sought. Case 1.2 is an especially interesting type of advice-seeking dialogue where a personal recommendation of financial trustworthiness is being sought in connection with a business transaction. Smith is being asked for a credit reference. The presumption is that the bank manager does not just ask Smith to support his own loan request, but asks for a third party, who, it is hoped, will give a non-biased estimate of Smith's reliability. Whether in fact this third party's reference can be taken to be good evidence depends on the extent that it is non-biased. For example, if the third party has an established reputation in financial circles, and if he has no known, direct business connections with Smith that would entail a conflict of interest, his recommendation would tend to carry greater weight, because these criteria would normally be taken to lessen the chances or tendencies for bias. But if, among the criteria for the plausibility or acceptability of the testimony of this third party, we include Smith's recommendation that this party is a good source, we have once again completed the kind of circle similar to the ones inherent in the other cases above. Smith's very use of his own word to validate the reliability of this third party reference brings into question the objectivity of this party. If Smith has to resort to the expedient of *himself* supporting this third party as a non-biased reference, it may suggest that this man really may be biased, or that other evidence for the objectivity and reliability of his advance may be lacking.

Much depends on the words "friend" and "I assure you" in case 1.2, however. If Smith vouched for this third party on the grounds that he has an excellent reputation in the business community, and has no direct business ties with Smith personally, the case would be quite different. In this type of case, Smith could even invite his bank manager to check out these things for himself, thus opening up independent lines of evidence, which would carry weight against the contention that Smith's argument begs the question.

It might also be noted that there is more than just a passing resemblance between Whately's historical evidence case and the case of the Liar Paradox. In Whately's case, a history test asserts its own veridicality as a reliable historical source of its claimed account, within the very test it uses to make these claims. This type of self-referential assertion is similar to that of the Liar Paradox, where a sentence asserts itself as false within the very same sentence used to make the claim that what it asserts may be taken as true. However, in the Liar case, a contradiction is involved. In Whately's case, the problem is a failure related to bias and failure of evidential priority, because of the requirement that the criterion for the reliability of a text as a source must be external to the text itself as a source. The problem here is not one of inconsistency, but a failure of evidential priority related to bias.

On the other hand, there need be no fallacy of begging the question inherent in using internal evidence in a historical text as part of a line of argumentation to support the validation of that text. For example, suppose text A describes a particular event, but text A is a questionable source. And suppose that text B, a more highly reliable and well-supported source, also describes the same event with similar details. Then it could be that this total evidence supports the reliability of text A, and increases its claim as an accurate source of events of the time.

It seems there is nothing wrong with appealing to internal evidence to support an account *per se*. Only in certain cases does the use of internal evidence in conjunction with criteria of evidence constitute a fallacious begging of the question.

Because not much context is given for these cases, the possibility of a dialectical shift is open. For example, in case 1.2, the possibility is open that Smith and his "friend" are in collusion, or even that Smith may be paying this person for his recommendation. This hidden agenda may make the dialogue a negotiation, from the point of view of Smith and his friend, whereas the bank manager sees the dialogue as a kind of advice-seeking whereby he hopes to get a financial rating of an unknown person from someone whose reputation is better known. Thus there is a principle of evidential priority at work, from the bank manager's point of view, but the possible bias or hidden interests of the one whose advice is sought may systematically defeat any recommendation from a source of advice that could have any useful degree of evidential priority. Hence in this case there is at least some evidence, from both the text and context of dialogue, that the circular argument does come very close to committing the fallacy of begging the question. Other sources of evidence are not quite closed off, but Smith's use of the words "friend" and "assure" are indicators that the question is close to being begged.

Generally speaking, there are two kinds of evidence that are relevant to an evaluation of question-begging. The external evidence of the context of dialogue, supplied by adjacent texts and other sources of information, is very important. But second, there can also be evidence supplied through the use of key indicator-words in the speech acts that make up the specific argument accused of question-begging.

The following case, cited by Chase (1956, p. 119), concerned a review of several books on the subject of flying saucers in the *Saturday Review* (1955), where the reviewer identified a "pendulum type of reasoning." This could be called the *flying saucers case.*

Case 4.7:   One way for a reader to test the degree of nonsense contained in a typical book is to examine the bibliography carefully. There he will find a mutual admiration society among flying-saucer writers who cross-reference one another for substantiation. If we ask Author X: "What proof have you that the little men landed in Fresno, California?" he replies: "Author Y confirms it!" And when we ask Author Y for his proof, he declares: "X confirms it!"

This case, like cases 1.1, 1.2, and 1.3, is once again particularly interesting for the student of fallacies because it exhibits an overlap between the *petitio principii* and the *argumentum ad verecundiam.* The argument seems to involve a fallacious appeal to expert opinion in argumentation. Yet, at the same time, it is the circularity of the appeal that seems to lie at the heart of the fallacy.

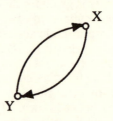

Figure 4.6

In fact the flying saucers case (4.7) bears some especially interesting resemblances to case 1.2, the bank manager case, which involved a similar kind of circular appeal to authority (though not the appeal to the authority of expertise). The flying saucers case is also similar to cases 1.1 and 1.3, which also involved circular appeals to authority (and specifically expert opinion, of a sort, in case 1.1). What is common to all these cases is that one individual X is used as a reference or source of substantiation for the credibility or reliability of another individual Y. But then, in the same argument, Y is also used as a source of substantiation for the credibility of X. The result is a simple case of circular argumentation (figure 4.6).

But is such a case of a circular appeal to authority fallacious? And if so, why?

One thing to note straightaway is that circular appeals to the authority of expert opinion do not tend to be automatically fallacious, simply because they are circular, where both sources cited are genuine experts in a legitimate domain of knowledge. If scholar X cites scholar Y in his bibliography, and Y also cites X in his bibliography, this cross-reference to one another for substantiation is not inherently fallacious.

On the other hand, if both sources cited are "experts" in a dubious area like phrenology, astrology, or flying saucers, their mutual support is not going to substantiate the credibility of their views to skeptical outsiders. For the presumption is that neither is accepted as a credible source by the audience or readership who is supposed to be persuaded of their conclusion. Given such an evident lack of prior credibility of both sources, a circular appeal to authority or testimony is unconvincing.

The problem in this type of case is the lack of external support for either X or Y by some third source, Z, who would be recognized as a credible expert or reliable reference, independently of any presumptions about whether X or Y is reliable. The circularity becomes a problem, in a case like the flying saucers case, because it is conjoined with the initial presumption that the credentials of both X and Y are in question. Certainly then, the circularity is a problem, because neither X nor Y is an antecedently credible source.

But does this mean that there is a fallacy of begging the question in the argument of the flying saucers case? It does seem that there is an element of fallaciousness in this case, because the would-be flying saucer expert who cites another flying saucer expert (who also cites him), would seem to be making an attempt to convince his readers that he is an expert, and that his conclusions should be taken as supported by the say-so and support of this other "expert." If the imputation here is that there is no need to include the writings of legitimate scientists, or even worse, if there is an attempt made to exclude them, then the evidence for an allegation that the argument has begged the question (fallaciously) is there.

But in case 4.7 we cannot justifiably say that the text of the argument contains such evidence. Therefore, while this argument fails to be successful or convincing because of its circularity and is objectionable for that reason, it is premature to conclude that the argument, as it stands, commits the fallacy of begging the question.

Chase (p. 120) does not, in fact, claim that the argument of the flying saucers case commits the fallacy of begging the question, even though he does include this case under the general topic heading of the fallacy of *circulus in probando*, which he translates as "arguing in circles." Chase diagnoses the problem as one of a "mutual defense society" where two propositions, "neither of which has been proved true," are used to "prove" each other. Chase's objection, it seems, is that there has been a failure of lack of proof. However, a failure to meet the requirement of burden of proof in an argument is not necessarily identical to the fallacy of begging the question, perhaps even if the argument in question is circular. And in fact Chase's practical advice on how to deal with an argument like the flying saucers case is to break up the *circulus* by displaying the interdependence of the two propositions. This suggestion could be interpreted as recommending that the way to deal with this type of case is to ask critical questions about the support of the two propositions involved. In other words, to prove either X or Y, you have to find some independent line of argumentation, outside of the circle on which they both lie. So construed then, the real objection should be that the argument needs further support if it is to be convincing. Unless the "mutual defense society" digs in and resists moves toward this external line of argumentation in further discussions, we cannot conclude that a fallacy of *petitio principii* has been committed.

The flying saucers case is similar to another case where faulty circular reasoning is alleged.

Case 4.8: The man who forged the *Hitler Diaries* scoffed at the experts who had initially pronounced the *Diaries* to be genuine writings of Hitler, calling these academics incompetent: "To prove the validity of the *Diaries,* they were comparing these writings to other writings I had forged."

The criticism put forward by the forger is that the academic experts were reasoning in a circle. They were allegedly attempting to verify the *Diaries* by comparing them to other documents they thought were genuine writings of Hitler. Their presumption was that these other works were genuine. According to the forger, however, he knew that this presumption was incorrect, because he had authored these other works himself.

Note, however, that although the forger is accusing the academics of circular reasoning, and a kind of circular reasoning that is erroneous, he is not necessarily accusing them of committing the fallacy of begging the question. For although they may have been begging the question, in some sense, their error was more of a blunder or error of reasoning. The error was one they were making against themselves. For presumably they were not trying to use a deceptive tactic of argumentation to convince others that the *Diaries* were genuine, when they themselves knew that the *Diaries* were not genuine. In that case, they would not be incompetent, but rather dishonest. The forger's criticism of them presumes, instead, that they were honestly trying to test the *Diaries,* but their mistake was the ill-considered presumption that the writings they were testing the *Diaries* against were authentic writings of Hitler.

The problem here, somewhat like that of the flying saucers case, is that if you are comparing two documents X and Y, you have to have independent reasons to think that one of them is genuine. Otherwise, concluding that the other document is genuine, exclusively on the basis of the comparison, is going nowhere. In the flying saucers case, if you have no evidence that at least one of the would-be experts is genuine, your argument back and forth goes nowhere. Similarly, in the *Diaries* case, if you have no good evidence that either the *Diaries* or the other writings used to compare them against are genuine, your argument back and forth goes nowhere. In both cases, the circular argument is useless to rationally persuade the skeptics it is supposed to convince.

In neither case, however, does the fault have to be that the individuals concerned have committed the fallacy of begging the question. And this can be so, even though in both cases the fault is an error of circular reasoning that is open to criticism. This pair of cases therefore resembles cases 4.0 and 4.1 in this respect, even though the two pairs of cases are quite different in other respects. It begins to appear that circularity and begging the question may be two quite different, even though related, things.

4. The Outstanding Team Case

In the following case, no context of dialogue is given. However, this case is based on a similar example used as an exercise in Irving M. Copi, *Introduction to Logic* (7th ed., New York, Macmillan, 1986, p. 112) on identification of informal fallacies.[5] The context that might be conjectured is a discussion of the chances of a team's winning the conference title. However, the ultimate conclusion of the discussion is not given, and the example is self-contained.

Case 4.9:   Our team is the outstanding team in the conference, because it has the best players and the best coach. We know it has the best players and the best coach because it will continue to win games and will win the conference title. It will continue to win games and will win the conference title because the players have a justifiable confidence in their ability to win. Of course the players have a justifiable confidence in their ability to win, for our team is the outstanding team in the conference.

This argument is circular, for it starts out with a proposition and then at the end of the argument comes back to that same proposition. But is the circle evidence of a fallacy, or could it be benign, like the circle in case

1.21? To investigate the question, let us reconstruct the sequence of the argument.

To begin, we number each individual proposition in the argument as follows.

    ① :   Our team is the outstanding team in the conference.
    ② :   Our team has the best players.
    ③ :   Our team has the best coach.
    ④ :   Our team will continue to win games.
    ⑤ :   Our team will win the conference title.
    ⑥ :   The players have a justifiable confidence in their ability to win.

Now we set out to reconstruct each of the single argument steps as follows. First, ② and ③ are meant to be linked premises for the conclusion ① (figure 4.7).

Figure 4.7

The next stage of the argument is subject to some interpretation. One reasonable interpretation is the reconstruction shown in figure 4.8.

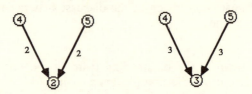

Figure 4.8

Figure 4.8 indicates that there are two separate conclusions reached: ②, our team has the best players and ③, our team has the best coach. Now consider the structure on the left. One interpretation is that we know our team has the best players because of the linked premises that ④, it will continue to win games and ⑤, it will win the conference title. These two premises could possibly be linked, or separate premises in a convergent argument. But since they seem to go together to support the conclusion that our team has the best players, it is reasonable to interpret the argument as linked. Similarly with the structure on the right for conclusion ③.

At this point, the argument of case 4.9 carries on as follows: ⑥ is used as a divergent premise for conclusions ④ and ⑤; and then ⑥ is concluded on the basis of ① (figure 4.9).

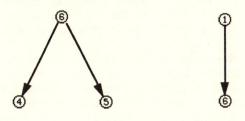

Figure 4.9

Putting all these single arguments together yields the total reconstruction shown in figure 4.10.

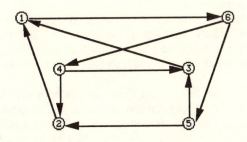

Figure 4.10

If you look over this argument structure, you can pick out several circles in it. For example, you can trace out the following circles: start at ①, then go to ⑥, then to ④, then to ③, then back to ①. Another circle is the following sequence: ①, ⑥, ⑤, ③, ①. Yet another is: ①, ⑥, ④, ②, ①. In each case, you can start at the conclusion ①, and then arrive back at that very same proposition by following a sequence of steps in the argument.[6]

But does this mean that the argument is a fallacious *petitio principii* or that it is full of vicious circles? How could a defender of the argument reply to such a criticism? Perhaps the following defense might be made: "A team can only be outstanding if it has a justifiable confidence in its ability to win. But it can have such a justifiable confidence only if it is an outstanding team. This feedback relationship between the team's confidence and its performance is circular. But it is by no means fallacious. For in fact the team must itself reason this way if it is to be successful and win the title." How should one respond to this defense?

The defense does seem to make a good point. And we can see the similarity of this case to the previous case 1.21, which we judged to be circular but not fallacious. What we should say is that although case 4.9 is circular, it is not an unreasonable argument. Provided there is no confusion about the circularity in the argument, it can be reasonably defended against the charge that the circular argument is evidence of a fallacy.

The reason this defense is possible is the lack of information on the context of the argument. It does appear to be a somewhat plausible conjecture that the context of case 4.9 is that of a persuasion dialogue where two commentators are arguing about which team is likely to win the conference title. According to this reconstruction of context, the speaker is trying to persuade the hearer that his (the speaker's) team will win the conference title. But this must remain mere conjecture. For all we know, the argument might not be about which team will win, but, for example, about whose team is the best team in the conference. In the absence of precise information, the questions of what is the ultimate thesis to be proven, and what type of dialogue is being engaged in by the speaker, cannot be given definite answers.

A critic would be strongly tempted, no doubt, to classify this case an instance of the fallacy of begging the question. But restraint should be called for, upon a more careful evaluation, because the context of dialogue is not given definitely enough to support decisively such a strong criticism.

What this case reveals is that there should be a burden of proof on the critic who would bring forward the criticism that an argument commits the fallacy of begging the question to mount sufficient evidence from the text and context to support this criticism. Not every circular argument definitely or provably commits the fallacy of begging the question, even if suspicion is warranted by given indicators of hypothetical or possible contexts.

Case 4.9 does not admit enough evidence of a requirement of evidential priority to be fairly classified as an instance of the fallacy of begging the question. It fails to meet the requirements of burden of proof that should be reasonably laid upon a critic who alleges that the argument commits the fallacy of begging the question.

5. THE POOR BUS SERVICE AND RUSSIAN JUVENILE DELINQUENCY CASES

In other cases, even though no external sequence of dialogue is given, other than a short sequence of questions and replies, enough internal evidence is given in the text to make it reasonably firm whether a fallacy of begging the question has been committed.

In case 4.10 no information is given aside from the following sequence of dialogue.

Case 4.10: **City Hall:** Why should the bus services to this suburb be improved?

Citizens Committee: Because the bus service is poor. Also, the suburb is well populated by city workers who commute, and many signatories are in favor of improved services. Both these things are true, and if they are true, the bus services to this suburb ought to be improved.

City Hall: Why is the bus service to this suburb so poor? Isn't it because not enough people take the bus?

Citizens Committee: Yes, in a way it is because not enough people take the bus. If not enough people take the bus there is no incentive to improve the services. If there is no incentive to improve the services, the service remains poor.

City Hall: Perhaps, but why is it that not enough people take the bus?

Citizens Committee: Because the service is so poor. If the service is so poor, fewer people are inclined to use it. Instead, they take their cars.

In case 4.10 City Hall is interrogating the Citizens Committee about the bus services. The questions and the replies do have an argumentative flavor, but the context is not clearly given. It could be an inquiry into the bus services. It could be a debate or persuasion dialogue on whether more money should be spent on bus services, for example. Or it could be that the Citizens Committee is merely trying to explain some things about the bus services, in order to supply information to City Hall, so the latter can arrive at a decision. The language of the dialogue appears to be fairly neutral, and none of these contexts is singled out or specified as a leading candidate.

Here then we really lack enough internal or external evidence to say whether a requirement of evidential priority is present. According to the requirements for burden of proof, then, it is best to favor the provisional conclusion that no fallacy of begging the question has been committed, as far as can be fairly determined.

In this case, the argument goes in a circle. But the proponent of the argument could defend the circularity as non-fallacious on the grounds that there is a circular feedback relationship between poor service and few people taking the bus. The case here is similar to case 4.9 in this respect.

Where the overall structure of the argument of case 4.10 is reconstructed as in figure 4.11, there is a circle between ② and ⑥. A critic must show that ② is prior to ⑥, or ⑥ is prior to ②, to justify a criticism that the circle in the argument indicates a fallacy.

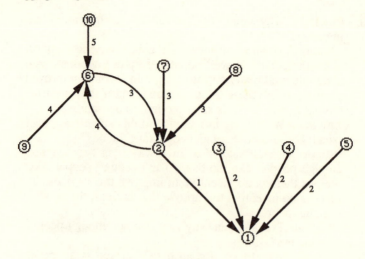

Figure 4.11

① :   The bus services to this suburb should be improved.
② :   The bus service is so poor.
③ :   The suburb is well populated by city workers who commute.
④ :   Many signatories are in favor of improved services.
⑤ :   Both ③ and ④ are true, and if so, ① is true.
⑥ :   Not enough people take the bus.
⑦ :   If ⑥ then there is no incentive to improve the services.
⑧ :   If there is no incentive to improve the services, the service remains poor.
⑨ :   If the service is so poor, fewer people are inclined to use it.
⑩ :   Instead of using the bus, people take their cars.

In this case, there is no good evidence that the context of argument requires that ② must be evidentially prior to ⑥, or that ⑥ must be prior to ②. Consequently, it is fair to conclude that the argument can be defended as non-fallacious, despite its circularity, as shown by figure 4.11.

   In the following case, as well, there is no context supplied other than the sequence of dialogue given below.

Case 4.11   **Black:** How can you determine that juvenile delinquency is widespread in the USSR?
White: Well, we know that there has been loss of social control recently in the USSR. because of difficult economic problems. And if there's loss of social control, there must be delinquency on a large scale.

Black: Yes, perhaps, but how can you really be sure that there has been the extent of loss of social control you speak of? After all, we don't have much access to data.
White: Well, we know that there has been a breakdown in state and political organization in the cities. If so, there must be loss of social control to a wide degree.
Black: I hate to be so persistent, but how on earth can you be sure that there has been such a breakdown in state and political organization in the cities?
White: Well there is widespread juvenile delinquency, and where that is present, there is always breakdown of state and political organization in the cities.

In this case, too, there is a circle in the argument at the local level, within the given sequence of dialogue. The circular structure can be seen in the argument reconstruction in figure 4.12.

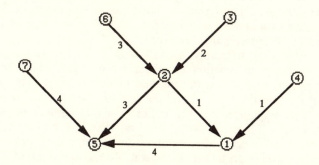

Figure 4.12

① : Juvenile delinquency is widespread in the USSR.
② : There has been a loss of social control in the USSR.
③ : There are difficult economic problems in the USSR.
④ : If there's a loss of social control, there is widespread juvenile delinquency.
⑤ : There has been a breakdown in state and political organization in the cities.
⑥ : If there has been a breakdown in state and political organization in the cities, there must be loss of social control.
⑦ : If there is widespread juvenile delinquency then there is always breakdown of state and political organization in the cities.

The circle in the argument is amongst ①, ②, and ⑤. If you look over the whole argument, it starts at ① and ends at ①. But is the circle open to criticism as a *petitio principii?* To evaluate this, we look to the phrases used by Black at each question.

First Question: "How can you determine that . . . ?"

Second Question: "[H]ow can you really be sure that . . . ?"

Third Question: "[H]ow on earth can you be sure that . . . ?"

Does each of these questions ask for evidence that is better established or more plausible than the proposition queried? Yes, each of them does, and therefore there should be a requirement of evidential priority on the arguments presented by White in answer to these questions. Therefore, the fact that White's argument goes in a circle can be fairly criticized as a fallacious *petitio principii* by Black.

In this case we are given no separate information about the issue of the dialogue. So we have to go by what internal evidence we have in the given text. Here we have to go by the questions asked by Black at each stage of the dialogue. This example shows that in evaluating criticisms of *petitio,* we must look at the questions asked, as well as the sequence of steps of argument in the answers that are given.

It is interesting to compare cases 4.10 and 4.11 because, in both cases, the judgment of whether the argument may justifiably be said to beg the question depends on the internal evidence to be extracted from interpreting the questions posed and the replies given, in the sequence of dialogue. This sequence strongly indicates a requirement of evidential priority in case 4.11, even using wording that is characteristic of an inquiry. But there is no similar evidence to be extracted from case 4.10, and certainly not enough to satisfy reasonable requirements of burden of proof on a critic who alleges question-begging as a fallacy.

These two cases will turn out to be important in setting the proper requirements of allocation of burden of proof on a critic in chapter seven, section four.

6. THE ADVERTISEMENT FOR MOTORISTS CASE

The next two cases bring out new subtleties in judging the interpretation and critical implications of the factor of inevitable circularity, in assessing begging the question, especially in light of the principles and methods of argument reconstruction in chapter three.

The context of the following dialogue is an advertisement for Rolls-Royce automobiles that appeared in a popular magazine. The issue of the discussion is whether the ad was thoroughly read by many motorists. The writer of the ad is particularly proud of one catchy sentence that occurred near the end of the ad: "People who feel diffident about driving a Rolls-

Royce can buy a Bentley." The editor of the magazine admits to the writer that he liked the ad, but still questions whether the ad was thoroughly read by many motorists. The writer argues that many motorists bandied about the word "diffident" in conversation, indicating that they did read the ad.

Case 4.12:   **Editor:** Do you think that the ad was thoroughly read by many motorists? I mean how can we know for sure?

Writer: Well, I think I can establish it by some careful reasoning from known facts. First, research shows that readership of ads falls off sharply up to fifty words of copy, but then drops very little up to five hundred words. Now my ad was five hundred words long. Therefore, we can conclude that many readers of my ad must have still been paying attention by the end of the ad. Now, the word "diffident" occurred near the end of my ad. Therefore, many readers of my ad must have been paying attention when they read the word "diffident" and bandied it about. I conclude that my ad was thoroughly read by many motorists.

Editor: Yes, this is all very well. But how can you be sure that these motorists were influenced to use the word "diffident" by reading the ad?

Writer: Well, we have already established that many readers of the ad must have been paying attention when they read the word "diffident." And we know that the ad was thoroughly read by many motorists. Clearly, therefore, these must be the reasons why such a large number of motorists picked up the word and bandied it about.

In this case, the context of dialogue is clearly given in its basic outline. It is a persuasion dialogue between the writer and the editor. The writer is trying to persuade the editor that the ad in question was read by many motorists.

In the editor's opening question, he asks how we can "know for sure" that the writer's contention is true. This indicates that a heavy burden of proof will have to be fulfilled by the writer's argument before the editor will be convinced. Indeed, the wording of the editor's question even suggests that the context of dialogue could be that of the inquiry. This impression is reinforced by the subsequent wording of the exchange. The writer uses the term "establish" in his reply, and the editor uses the phrase "how can you be sure" in his next question.

What should be said here is that whether the dialogue is taken to be a persuasion dialogue, with a high burden of proof, or an inquiry, the principle of evidential priority will be applicable.

The final conclusion of the writer's argument is the proposition ① below. That ① is the conclusion is indicated by the context of dialogue, which states that the issue is whether the ad was thoroughly read by many motorists. The editor is questioning whether ① is plausible, and the writer's argument is directed to showing that his contention, ①, is plausible. The remaining propositions in the author's argument are numbered as below.

Editor: Do you think that ① [the ad was thoroughly read by many motorists]? I mean how can we know for sure?

Writer: Well, I think I can establish it by some careful reasoning from known facts. First, ② [research shows that readership of ads falls off sharply up to fifty words of copy, but then drops very little up to five hundred words]. Now ③ [my ad was five hundred words long]. Therefore, we can conclude that ④ [many readers of my ad must have still been paying attention by the end of the ad]. Now ⑤ [the word "diffident" occurred near the end of my ad]. Therefore, ⑥ [many readers of my ad must have been paying attention when they read the word "diffident"]. Now put this together with what we observed. We observed that ⑦ [large numbers of motorists picked up the word "diffident" and bandied it about]. I conclude that ① [my ad was thoroughly read by many motorists].

Editor: Yes, this is all very well. But how can you be sure that these motorists were influenced to use the word "diffident" by reading the ad?

Writer: Well, we have already established that ⑥ [many readers of the ad must have been paying attention when they read the word "diffident"]. And we know that ① [the ad was thoroughly read by many motorists]. Clearly, therefore, these must be the reasons why ⑦ [a large number of motorists picked up the word and bandied it about].

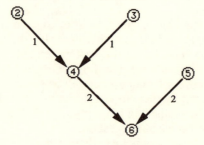

Figure 4.13

The first stage of the argument is that ② and ③ are used as linked premises for the conclusion ④. Then ⑤ is used as an additional premise that is linked to ④. So ⑤ and ④ serve as linked premises for the conclusion ⑥. Since ④ appears first as a conclusion, and then as a premise in the next step of the argument, there is a serial argument involved in linking the two subarguments together. This much of the argument reconstruction is diagrammed in figure 4.13.

The next stage in the argument follows the same pattern. We are directed to put the previous conclusion, ⑥, together with ⑦, and conclude that ① follows from these two premises. This yields the total recon-struction as shown in figure 4.14.

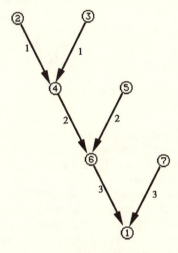

Figure 4.14

Now we turn to the writer's last segment of argument in the dialogue. What the writer now proceeds to argue is that ⑥ and ①, as already estab-lished in the argument, can serve as linked premises for the conclusion ⑦ (figure 4.15).

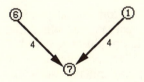

Figure 4.15

Putting this bit together with the previous argument reconstruction yields the complete diagram as shown in figure 4.16.

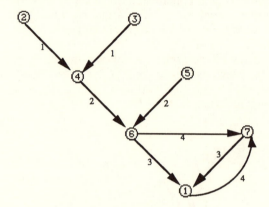

Figure 4.16

Now the circle in the argument is clearly displayed in the reconstruction. The propositions ① and ⑦ are on a circle, and ⑥ and ⑦ are used as premises for ①. But then ⑥ and ① are used as premises for ⑦. It is a clear case of circular argument.

Is this circle in the argument a fallacious case of *petitio principii?* To evaluate this, we need to look at the internal evidence given in the editor's answers in the dialogue. In the editor's first question, he asks, "how can we know for sure?" The writer, in his answer, uses the word "establish." In his second question, the editor uses the same language, asking, "how can you be sure . . . ?" In his answer, the writer uses the terms "already established" and "we know that," referring to previous premises in the argument. All this evidence strongly indicates that a requirement of evidential priority is reasonable to apply to the context of the writer's argument. This evidence indicates that it would be reasonable to criticize the circle in the writer's argument as a case of the fallacy of begging the question. The argument does not prove, on a basis of evidential priority as required by the context of dialogue, what it is supposed to prove.

It would also appear, from the argument reconstruction in figure 4.16, that the ultimate conclusion ① is locked into a network of inevitably circular argumentation. This might appear to be additional evidence that the argument commits the fallacy of begging the question. But the situation is more complicated than it may initially appear to be, in this respect.

The first thing to notice is that the subgraph ①, ⑥, ⑦ is not a dicycle, because it is not true that the arrows on the arcs all go in the same direction. It is true that ① and ⑦ form a dicycle. But, on the other hand, this circle does not appear to be an inevitable one, because an arc goes from ⑥ to ① and another arc goes from ⑥ to ⑦. And other arcs, as well, lead into ⑥. This leaves an evidential route leading into ①, and another route leading into ⑦. The circle, then, is not inevitable. It would appear to be similar to the circle in case 2.4, reconstructed in figure 2.6.   And in that case, the circle was judged not to be an inevitable circle.

However, there is even a further dimension in case 4.12. Both of the arcs from ⑥ to ① and ⑦ are parts of linked arguments. The arc from ⑥ to ① is linked with the arc from ⑦ to ①, and the arc from ⑦ to ① is linked with the arc from ⑥ to ①. In other words, you could argue that ⑥ is not much use as an evidentiary base for either ① or ⑦, because in either case it is linked to another premise that is on a dicycle. From this point of view, we could say that some circularity, at least, is inevitable.

This case is a critical one. Although ① is not on an inevitable circle, and neither is ⑦, it is the nature of the argumentation leading into ① (and also ⑦) that is the critical factor. Both arguments are linked. The critical factor is that there is no line of evidence going into ① or ⑦ that does not link up with the circle between ① and ⑦. Hence the argument is open to the criticism that it is question-begging.

The problem with case 4.12 is essentially the following disagreement. The writer feels that he has established his conclusion that the ad was thoroughly read by many motorists, because that is the conclusion he reached at the end of his first speech. And the editor even conceded the establishment of this conclusion, saying, "Yes, this is all very well." Therefore, the writer feels that he can already rely on this conclusion in any succeeding argumentation. For it has now been established, as a kind of lemma, or provisional conclusion, at this stage of the argument. So when, in his final speech, the writer uses this conclusion as a premise to support his final argument, in response to the editor's question just preceding it, he feels the argument is reasonable.

The editor may see it differently, however. He has asked the question, "But how can you be sure that these motorists were influenced to use the word "diffident" by reading the ad?" just before the writer's last speech. His asking this question appears to indicate that he does not yet accept the writer's conclusion that the ad was read thoroughly by many motorists. For by asking the question quoted just above, in effect, the editor is raising the possibility that the motorists who bandied about the word "diffident" may have been led to do this by encountering the word in some other source than the ad. Possibly, for example, "diffident" is a trendy word that many people are tending to use these days, whether they have read it in an ad or not. The doubt that the editor is raising in asking this question suggests that he is not yet convinced that adequate evidence has been presented to secure the conclusion that the ad was read by many motorists.

From this point of view, the writer's reliance on the conclusion that many motorists must have read the ad, in the argument of his final speech, is not a presumption that can be taken for granted. From the editor's point of view, the writer's use of this (questionable) premise begs the question that remains to be established.

The writer and the editor, then, appear to have grounds for disagreement on whether the writer's argument begs the question or not.

In this case, there is a circle in the argument, as figure 4.16 shows. But it remains subject to dispute whether the circle, in the context of dialogue in which it occurs, is sufficient evidence to say that the argument commits the fallacy of begging the question. Certainly however, from the editor's point of view in the dialogue, it is legitimate to say that the argument is open to criticism on the grounds that it begs the question, unless better evidence can be introduced by the writer to support his conclusion.

It is useful to compare this case with another one that appears to be similar but calls for a significantly different kind of evaluation.

7. THE CASE OF EQUALITY OF OPPORTUNITY AT THE UNIVERSITIES

George and Karl are engaged in a discussion. Karl is trying to convince George to accept the conclusion that the universities are institutions of class rule, and not institutions of equal opportunity. George is skeptical about this point of view, and is not inclined to accept it.

Case 4.13: **Karl:**   My thesis is that the universities are institutions of class rule, and not institutions of equal opportunity.

George: Why do you think that, Karl?

Karl: Right of entry may be formally guaranteed at universities, but there are social and economic impediments to the exercise of this right.

George: What makes you think that?

Karl: Well, this may come as a shock to you George, but the majority of university students come from the wealthier and more educated sections of society.

George: You may say that, Karl, but how can you prove it? Such statistical claims depend on how you define your terms, and so forth. I can't really accept this claim without proof.

Karl: Well, it's true, for several reasons. Financial constraints, including low bursaries and reduced opportunities for summer jobs, are one reason. Another reason has to do with aspirations and perceptions. Most secondary school students from lower socioeconomic groups do not see university education as being for them.

George:	Why not? How can you support this claim?
Karl:	There is always an emphasis on education that is congenial to the social values of the pupil. And the universities reflect the values of the more affluent middle and professional classes, these pupils having come from a better-educated home environment that makes them comfortable with these values. Consequently, university education has tended to move further away from those whose home and social backgrounds do not predispose them toward placing a high value on academic achievement.
George:	Well, you have certainly sketched out a large picture of the way you see things, Karl, but for some reason I can't quite put my finger on, I am still not convinced that you have proved your point.[7]

Here the dialogue closes. George senses that something more needs to be said about Karl's argument, however. Could it be a case of begging the question? To investigate this possibility, we number the assertions made in Karl's argumentation, and produce an argument diagram that recapitulates the overall flow and direction of his argument.

①: The universities are institutions of class rule, and not institutions of equal opportunity.

②: Right of entry may be formally guaranteed at universities, but there are social and economic impediments to the exercise of this right.

③: The majority of university students come from the wealthier and more educated sections of society.

④: Financial constraints, including low bursaries and reduced opportunities for summer jobs, are one reason.

⑤: Most secondary school students from lower socioeconomic groups do not see university education as being for them.

⑥: There is always an emphasis on education that is congenial to the social values of the pupil.

⑦: The universities reflect the values of the more affluent middle and professional classes, these pupils having come from a better-educated home environment that makes them comfortable with these values.

⑧: University education has tended to move further away from those whose home and social background does not predispose them toward placing a high value on academic achievement.

In basic outline, the simplest reconstruction of the stages of Karl's sequence of argumentation takes the form of the diagram in figure 4.17.

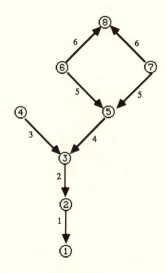

Figure 4.17

Starting from the bottom of figure 4.17, Karl's argument can be straight-forwardly diagrammed. The only very questionable part is the last asser-tion, where Karl begins with the word "consequently," and then makes assertion ⑧. Where, in Karl's view, is ⑧ supposed to come from? This is not too clear, but in figure 4.17 we have pictured ⑧ as coming from ⑥ and ⑦ in a linked structure of argument.

This much of the reconstruction completed, however, there has been no suspicious circle revealed in the argument. It's true that ⑤, ⑥, ⑦, and ⑧ are locked into a cyclical structure. But the arrows are not all going in the same direction. Therefore, the structure is not a dicycle. It is not a circle in the argument that would give a critic grounds for establishing a criticism that the argument commits the fallacy of begging the question. It seems that George needs to go further, if this is the criticism he suspects to be appropriate.

To go further, let us reflect a little more on ⑦. This premise may seem open to suspicion. In fact, if you think about it, ⑦ could hardly be proved without already presuming the acceptance of ③. Let us picture this link on the argument diagram in figure 4.18.

To represent the idea that ⑦ depends on ③ in the argument, we put in a dotted (broken) arrow between ③ and ⑦, going from ③ to ⑦. But now, looking at the resulting diagram, figure 4.18, there is a circle, ⑦, ⑤, ③, ⑦, and all the arrows go in the same direction. The argument, so conceived, is an instance of the dependency conception of circular argumentation.

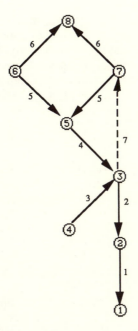

Figure 4.18

Is this interpretation justified? To evaluate this question, reflect for a bit on Karl's premise ⑦. This premise certainly seems to presume that the majority of university students come from the wealthier and more educated sections of society.

Does the circle in the argument diagram of case 4.13 represent an instance of the fallacy of *petitio principii?* There are several factors to be taken into account in judging this question. One factor is that the circle ③, ⑦, ⑤, ③ is not an inevitable circle. An independent line of argument goes in from ④ to ③, and it is not linked with any of the premises on the circle. Note, however, that there are no such independent lines of argument going in to either ⑤ or ⑦. It is true that ⑥ goes in to ⑤, but ⑥ is linked to the premise ⑦, in order to support ⑤.

Another factor is that the dialogue is a persuasion dialogue, and the indicator-words of the text of the dialogue given in case 4.13 support the hypothesis of the existence of an evidential priority requirement. George asks questions like, "Why do you think that, Karl?" and "You may say that Karl, but how can you prove it?" Clearly George is requesting that Karl provide arguments with premises that he (George) can accept, independently of his doubts about the conclusion at issue, ①.

But ① is not on the circle ③, ⑦, ⑤, ③. This circle is what will later be called a *mid-argument circle*.

Another factor is that the argument in case 4.13 might naturally be expected to contain feedback and circular argumentation, because it is concerned with aspirations and perceptions, and how these affect human behavior and its consequences. Even so, however, the presence of the evidential priority requirement could make such circularity useless or unacceptable in the task of persuading George to accept Karl's conclusion.

The motorists case and the equality of opportunity case are somewhat similar, but there are significant differences. The equality of opportunity case seems more severe, or there seems to be a stronger claim that a fallacy of begging the question has occurred in this case. One reason is that in the equality of opportunity case, premise ⑦ very definitely seems to include premise ③. It seems very hard to imagine how anyone could prove ⑦ without already presuming ③. Here the circle seems tight.

In the motorists case, however, there is more room for maneuvering. Perhaps the writer could come up with some way of proving that the motorists had to have bandied about the word "diffident" precisely because they read his advertisement attentively.

Another difference is that the circle in the motorists case included the ultimate conclusion, ①. In the equality of opportunity case, by contrast, the circle, ⑤, ③, ⑦, ⑤, does not contain the ultimate conclusion of the argument, namely ①.

In both cases, there is good textual evidence of a requirement of evidential priority. So in both cases, the criticism that the argument begs the question has bite.

Note also that both the motorists case and the equality of opportunity case share a notable feature with both of the two previous cases of the poor bus service and juvenile delinquency in the USSR. In all four cases, perception is intertwined with reality in a characteristic situation of feedback. This might make these cases less susceptible to the criticism of begging the question, were it not for the evidence of the requirement of evidential priority.

8. THE JUSTIFICATION OF INDUCTION CASE

One form of the problem of justifying induction as a reliable type of argumentation takes the form of questioning what grounds we have for forming reasonable expectations about the future. The sun has risen regularly every day, so far in our experience. But what reliable grounds could we have for expecting that it will continue to do so? Why should one have such expectations? Isn't it possible that you might wake up tomorrow and find that, like the man in Kafka's *Metamorphosis,* you have turned into a giant cockroach?

This line of questioning has led some to try to justify the reasonableness of inductive reasoning by a kind of pragmatic reasoning–our expectations about the future are reasonable because they work. Commonplace expectations about the future are regularly confirmed by experience, and this seems justification enough.

Russell (1959, pp. 64-65) felt that such a pragmatic attempt to justify induction was open to the criticism that it begs the question.

> It has been argued that we have reason to know that the future will resemble the past, because what was the future has constantly become the past, so that we really have experience of the future, namely of times which were formerly future, which we may call past futures. But such an argument really begs the very question at issue. We have experience of past futures, but not of future futures, and the question is: Will future futures resemble past futures? This question is not to be answered by an argument which starts from past futures alone.

Elaborating on the dialectic of Russell's criticism of the pragmatic justification of induction, Rosenberg (1978, p. 44) put this criticism in a particularly clear and pointed manner. According to Rosenberg's interpretation, the pragmatic justifier of induction claims that our expectations about the future are shown to be reasonable because they work, that is, they have regularly been confirmed by our experience. But the question is—will these expectations continue to be confirmed by our experiences in the future? To assume an affirmative answer to this question appears to be circular.

Case 4.14:   In our initial response, the claim is that our expectations about the future are shown to be reasonable by the fact that they work. They are regularly confirmed by experience. But are they? Well, we might grant that they always *have been*. But will they continue to be? We *expect* them to be, of course, but that is an expectation about the future. The response simply assumes that it is a reasonable expectation. The issue in dispute, however, is whether *any* expectations about the future are reasonable. And so the response begs the question (Rosenberg, 1978, pp. 44-45).

Rosenberg's criticism of the pragmatic justification argument seems to be similar to Russell's criticism in outline. But questions remain. Exactly where is the circle in the argument? And why is the circle evidence that the fallacy of begging the question has been committed?

Rosenberg's re-expression of the argument of case 4.14 helps further to make the criticism clear.

> The question is whether any of our expectations are reasonable. The response points out that any expectation which works is reasonable and that our past expectations have worked. Will our future expectations also work? We can't say for sure, of course, but the response takes it for granted that it is, in any case, reasonable to *expect* our future expectations to work. But that is supposing at least one expectation to be reasonable (p. 45).

Rosenberg's basis for criticizing the argument under consideration as question-begging is that it uses its own conclusion as a premise. Rosenberg's way of phrasing this criticism is particularly clear and plausible, making it a good example for further analysis. Let us see whether we can use the method of argument diagramming to help document the basis behind this criticism.

The issue in dispute is whether any of our expectations about the future is reasonable. In other words, the ultimate conclusion to be proved is:

①: Any of our expectations about the future is reasonable.

The goal of the project is to "justify induction," meaning that some basis for validating induction as a trustworthy process must be given. Presumably, this basis must be independent of any assumption that induction is already presumed to be a reliable process.

To do the job, the argument under consideration begins by advancing the following three-step inference.

②: Any expectation that works is reasonable.
③: Our past expectations about the future have worked.
④: Our past expectations are reasonable.

The third proposition, ④, is a conclusion, based on the premises ② and ③. This is a linked argument, and it is deductively valid.

According to Rosenberg, what is "taken for granted" by this argument is the following proposition.

⑤: It is reasonable to expect our future expectations to work.

But why is ⑤ taken for granted by the linked argument from ② and ③ to ④? Rosenberg doesn't appear to tell us exactly why. He does say, "that is supposing at least one expectation to be reasonable." And the conclusion to be proved, ①, says that *any* of our expectations about the future is reasonable. But contrary to what Rosenberg says, it is not the case that this premise or supposition that *some* of our expectations about the future are reasonable is the same as the conclusion that any (i.e., all) of our expectations about the future is reasonable. The argument does not, at least literally, use its own conclusion as premise, as claimed by Rosenberg (p. 45). Where then is the circle?

The problem is that if you have to prove that *all* of our expectations about the future are reasonable, is it OK to presume as a premise that *some* of them are reasonable? The answer is: not unless you can prove it. Otherwise you may be begging the question. But an even worse problem is that if you try to prove it, to avoid that objection, you would seem to be arguing inductively. So you would be begging the question anyway, by presuming that induction is a reliable method of argumentation. In short, there does seem to be a fallacy of begging the question to be discovered in the argument under consideration. It will take a little more work to bring out exactly where the circle is, in the sequence of argumentation.

Generally, there need be nothing inherently wrong or fallacious about arguing from "some" to "all," although such an argument is not, by itself, deductively valid. But it could be a reasonable argument, if it is supplemented with further premises, or if it is an inductive argument, or some type of argument other than, or weaker than, a deductive argument. Surely if I want to show that all our expectations are reasonable, I could argue about some area, and then try to move from there to establishing that all (like these some) are reasonable. To try to pre-empt or choke off this line of argument too prematurely as question-begging should not generally be admissible.

On the other hand, we can see that there is further evidence that the argument under consideration has a tendency to be question-begging. The issue in dispute is whether *any* of our expectations about the future is reasonable, that is, justifying induction as a reliable method of reasoning. According to the argument under consideration, what shows our expectations about the future to be reasonable is that they "work," that is, they have turned out to be reasonable in the past.

But this begs the question of whether they will continue to work. Will our future expectations about the future continue to be reasonable in the same way our past expectations about the future have been? The assumption of continuity seems to be based on inductive reasoning of some sort. Or, at any rate, it seems hard to see how it could escape being so based.

The circle can be brought out by considering the following sequence of question-reply reasoning.

1.   Do any expectations about the future work?
2.   The past ones did.
3.   Will the future ones be like the past ones?
4.   How can an affirmative answer to 3 be proved without assuming some form of induction?

Once we get to step 4 in the chain of reasoning, it seems we can't get any further without circling back to 1 by assuming that induction is a reliable process of argumentation that can be used to prove a conclusion.

The implicit circular reasoning in this process of reasoning can be made more explicit by the method of argument diagramming, following the general outline of an analysis of a somewhat similar case given by Walton and Batten (1984, pp. 143-47). This analysis postulates that in order to support ①, the attempt to justify induction that is under consideration proceeds by advancing a counterpart argument to supplement the already existing linked argument from premises ② and ③ to the conclusion ④. This counterpart argument, analogous to the argument from ② and ③ to ④, uses the same premise over again, ②, but links it with a new premise about future expectations about the future, ⑤. This new premise is the proposition that Rosenberg cited as somehow being "taken for granted" in the argument. The two premises ② and ⑤ are linked together to support a new conclusion, ⑥.

② :   Any expectation that works is reasonable.
⑤ :   It is reasonable to expect our future expectations to work.
⑥ :   It is reasonable to expect our future expectations to be reasonable.

Filling in the gaps by reconstructing the argument, we can see how the new argument ②, ⑤, ∴ ⑥ above enables the reasoning to leapfrog from the earlier subargument ②, ③, ∴ ④ to the ultimate conclusion ①.

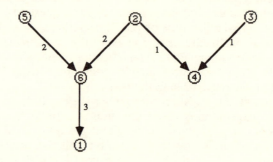

Figure 4.19

The final step is the leap from ⑥ to ① (figure 4.19).

But much remains unexplained. Premise ② seems to be a matter of defining a term in the argument, and it does not seem to be a very contentious or problematic premise. A more serious question is–how could ⑤ be supported? For ⑤ seems like it should be a serious bone of contention in the dispute about the justification of induction.

If you reflect on the argument, the most natural interpretation of its sequence of reasoning is that ⑤ could only be backed up by presuming some further linked premises. Suppose you ask the justifier of induction why ⑤ should be accepted as true–why is it reasonable to expect our future expectations to work? Presumably, his answer is that this assumption has to be based on the knowledge that they have always worked before. In other words, his answer is this: Our past expectations about the future have worked, therefore it is reasonable for them to keep on working, that is, it is reasonable to expect our future expectations to work. But how has he made this transition? Presumably, the only way he can make it is by assuming that the future will continue to be like the past. But this assumption really amounts to presuming the following proposition, ⑦.

⑦ :   Our expectation that the future will resemble the past is reasonable.

Evidently then, according to this reconstruction, the basis for supporting ⑤ is a linked argument that has ⑦ and ③ as its premises (figure 4.20).

Figure 4.20

Now ③ is not a problem to support. Evidently, it is an empirical proposition. But how could ⑦ be supported? The root of the problem is that ⑦, in effect, expresses the very principle of the justifiability of induction.
　　What ① really means is not that literally *all* of our expectations about the future have to be confirmed, once the future becomes the past, and is definitely known to us. What ① means is that *most* of our expectations have to turn out right, or at least enough of them so that we can say that induction is reliable. But ⑦ is so close to making the same claim that there would seem to be no way open to proving ⑦ other than already presuming the truth of ①. This is where the circle comes in then. The difference between ⑦ and ① is not clear enough for us to disassociate proving one of them from proving the other. How could you prove ⑦ without already presupposing ①?

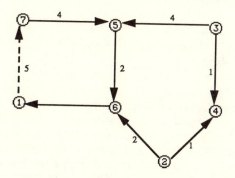

Figure 4.21

At first, the lack of sufficient difference between ⑦ and ① might incline us to think that these two assertions should be declared to be equivalent. But, in fact, it is not clear that they are precisely equivalent, in the context of

in fact, it is not clear that they are precisely equivalent, in the context of the discussion about the justification of induction. Let us conclude that, at any rate, there appears to be no way open, in the discussion, for proving ⑦ other than by using premises that would have to rely on ① as an assumption. Interpreting the argument in this way, let us represent it by saying that ⑦ depends on ①. Or even stronger, we could say that ⑦ has to depend on ①, no matter how the proponent of the justification of induction might try to justify ①. In figure 4.21, the argument diagram for all the argumentation revealed to this point, a dotted (broken) arc appears from ① to ⑦.

As figure 4.21 shows, the only circle in the argument is ①, ⑦, ⑤, ⑥. There are other bounded areas in the diagram, but none of them is a dicycle.

The justification of induction case is especially interesting for two reasons. It falls under the heading of criteria of evidence circularity, and it incorporates an interesting variant of the requirement of evidential priority.

The whole project of trying to justify a type of argumentation like induction is inherently tricky, because you have to use argumentation to do the job. Hence the danger of circularity. If you intend to justify induction, you had better be careful lest you use induction in the process. It is easy to mix up your evidence with your criteria of evidence.

Second, the whole process of *justification* seems to imply a need for evidential priority. If you plan to *justify* induction, it seems you need to do it by appealing to some process that is more reliable than induction. Hence you had better not presuppose induction.

9. SOME BORDERLINE CASES

The following case was cited by Chase (1956, p. 117) as an example of the logical fallacy of *circulus probandi,* or arguing in a circle.[8] Chase calls it the *case of the moral bees.*

Case 4.15: A traveller is visiting a fetish priest in the African Congo. Somewhat to his surprise he finds a box of live bees in his room. He asks the reason and the priest says: "If you had been an enemy those bees would have buzzed you out of there. Only last week a man came here with evil intentions. Those bees drove him out, he ran away screaming."
"What did the man say to you?"
"Nothing. He didn't have a chance."
"Then how do you know that he had evil intentions?"
"Because the bees attacked him!"

The circle inherent in this dialogue can be reconstructed as follows. First, the traveller asks the reason that the priest has the box of bees in his room. The priest's reply is: "The bees guard me from individuals who have evil intentions." The security provided by these reliable bees can be expressed in the following conditional statement that is being made by the priest.

(C1) If X (some person) has evil intentions, the bees attack X.

But then the dialogue continues. The traveller asks the priest, in effect, "How do you know who has evil intentions?" More specifically, the traveller is putting the following question to the priest: "How do you identify X as a person who has evil intentions?" The traveller is asking the priest to state his criterion for identifying evil persons. The criterion, according to the priest's last statement in case 4.15, is whether or not X is attacked by the bees. In other words, the priest has replied by advocating the following conditional statement.

(C2) If the bees attack X, then X has evil intentions.

But now if you put the reasoning in the whole dialogue together, you can see that (C1) and (C2) together make up a circle (figure 4.22).

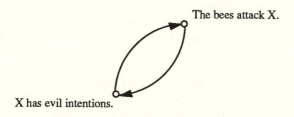

Figure 4.22

But is the circle fallacious? What we should say here is that the circular sequence of dialogue is certainly objectionable or problematic, as it stands. What is needed to make the circle non-fallacious, to secure it against the objection of having begged the question, is some *other* proof that X has evil intentions. By "other" we mean some way of identifying X as a person of evil intentions other than the exclusive criterion of X's being attacked by the bees. Some independent line of proof is needed (figure 4.23).

This case is an instance of criteria of evidence circularity. For the only criterion used to identify X as a person of evil intentions is X's being attacked by the bees. The problem is that this *presumes,* instead of proving, that anyone in fact attacked by the bees must be a person who had evil intentions. As Chase commented, the priest assumes a moral sense in the bees: "Presumably a man with good intentions could hit the hive with a hammer without arousing it." Such a presumption is highly implausible, however. To be convinced that the bees are reliable identifiers of persons with evil intentions, we need to have some basis for correlating their attacks with prior identification of the person attacked as an individual who can be shown to have had evil intentions.

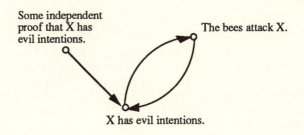

Some independent
proof that X has
evil intentions.

The bees attack X.

X has evil intentions.

Figure 4.23

The additional dimension of potential fallaciousness present here is provided by the vagueness of the phrase "person who has evil intentions" and the inherent difficulty of identifying such persons by clear and well-established, objective criteria. Given this difficulty, an opening is created for the priest always to retreat back to his criterion of being attacked by the bees as an overriding criterion. The danger here is one of inevitable circularity.

So should we say that the priest commits the fallacy of begging the question? Or is he only open to the weaker criticism that his circular argument is useless to persuade the traveller (or the rest of us) of its conclusion unless he can provide independent, further evidence that the bees attack only those individuals who have evil intentions? On balance, the more cautious and collaborative approach would be to opt for the weaker criticism, in the absence of any indication of how the priest would react to further questioning. This approach would imply that Chase was not justified in labelling the case of the moral bees (precisely as stated above) as an instance of the fallacy of arguing in a circle. Only if the priest were to resist giving, or opening up, an independent line of evidence for identifying individuals with evil intentions could we classify his argument as an instance of the fallacy of begging the question. As things stand, we should say that the priest's argument is open to objection on the grounds that it has not provided such a non-circular criterion. By this approach, it should be concluded that the priest's argument is circular, and is open to criticism for that reason. But, according to this judgment, the priest's argument has not–at any rate, not quite, or not yet–committed the fallacy of begging the question.

However, it should be noted that the case of the moral bees is an interesting kind of borderline case, because, as noted above, it verges toward begging the question to some extent, given the vagueness of the phrase "person who has evil intentions." There is a kind of suggestion or implication in this case that the priest may well be inclined, in subsequent dialogue, to cleave to bee attack as his sole and exclusive criterion for identifying such persons. However, the conservative and cautious approach to argumentation interpretation (following the principle of charity) would advocate not convicting an arguer of committing a fallacy on the basis of how he might likely be inclined to argue at some future point in a discussion.

This much said, however, it should also be observed that there is some textual evidence in the dialogue that gives an indication of an inevitable circle. When the priest replies, "Nothing. He didn't have a chance," this reply could be interpreted as a sign that his argument is meant to be self-sealing. It could be an indication, in other words, of the presence of the tactic of trying to close off further investigation of the evidential basis or criteria behind the finding that a particular person has evil intentions. The priest could be interpreted as showing some indication here, in other words, that this man's being attacked by the bees is the only criterion of his having evil intentions that is worth considering. This exclusivity of stance could be interpreted as evidence that the priest's circular argument is a case of an inevitable circle, and therefore should be judged as an argument that commits the fallacy of begging the question.

The problem, however, is that while the priest's remark does show some indication or sign of inevitable circularity, it is not clear that the indication is strong enough to meet reasonable requirements of burden of proof, according to a fair and judicious interpretation of the textual evidence. While it is true that the priest doesn't appear to be very open to the possibility that the man attacked by the bees could have been innocent of evil intentions, on the other hand it is not clear that he is undertaking a systematic argumentation tactic of trying to exclude this possibility. If so, his argument could be objectionably circular without being fallacious.

The following argument is claimed to be an instance of the fallacy of begging the question by Cederblom and Paulsen (1982, p. 94), but there are problems in interpreting the argument.

Case 4.16:   **Realtor:**   If you're choosing between the house our competitors have listed and this one, you ought to buy this one. You'd make more money on it.

Customer: Why would I make more money on it?

Realtor: Well, you said you planned to sell in five years. You have to consider real appreciation, not just how many dollars you pay, and how much you sell for. That means figuring in the rate of inflation. I would estimate that at the rate houses like this appreciate, taking account of fees, taxes, and so on, in five years you'd come out with a greater net profit on this house than on the other one.

Two possible interpretations of this argument are open.

Interpretation I: Is the realtor just repeating his conclusion, after having advanced a set of premises that provide only weak and incomplete support for it? The realtor is supposed to prove his stated conclusion that his customer would make more money on house A rather than house B. But all he does is give a sales pitch, a series of generalities about interest rates and so forth, that proves nothing in relation to the specific question of whether the customer would make more money from house A or house B. So construed, the argument is weak and incomplete. It is a failure of burden of proof. But it is not an instance of the fallacy of begging the question. For merely repeating a conclusion does not make an argument circular or fallacious. A conclusion could be repeated for emphasis. Or, as in this case (possibly), it could be repeated to clarify that it is the conclusion of the foregoing premises.

Interpretation II. Is it a linked argument where the last proposition has been put in as a premise? In this case, the argument is circular, presuming that the premise "You would make a greater net profit on this house than on the other one" is equivalent to the conclusion "You would make more money on this house than on the other one." According to this interpretation, the realtor gives his (unpersuasive) spiel, and then, to back it up in order to try to clinch the argument, he slips in a rewording of the conclusion.

According to this second interpretation, there is some evidence for classifying the argument as a case of begging the question by the realtor. However, there is not very strong evidence that the circle in the argument is an inevitable circle. The realtor is presenting all these weak and incomplete premises, and then, as a final push, he puts in the conclusion itself. It is evidently a way of pushing for the concession of the conclusion, even though the argument given is not even remotely adequate to secure rational acceptance of the conclusion by the customer. Thus it is an overly aggressive argument, so interpreted. But there is not enough textual evidence to indicate clearly that it is an instance of an inevitable circle.

Both interpretations I and II seem to be possible, given what we know from the textual evidence available in case 4.16. But since the burden of proof should be on the critic to show that an argument is circular, if it is to be refuted on the ground that it begs the question, we should conclude that, in this case, this argument should not be so criticized. In response to such a criticism, the salesman could reply, quite consistently with what he has said, that he was merely repeating his conclusion for emphasis.

Cederblom and Paulsen comment, quite rightly, that if a premise is merely a restatement of the conclusion of an argument, it doesn't make any progress in the job of supporting the conclusion by adducing premises that are more plausible or better established than this conclusion. But a more careful look at case 4.16 illustrates three negative lessons. One lesson is that an argument can fail to make progress in the job of supporting its conclusion without being an instance of the fallacy of begging the question. Another lesson is that an assertion in an argument could be a restatement of the conclusion without necessarily having to be interpreted as advancing a premise. A third lesson is that textual evidence that shows a circle to be inevitable is necessary if the very strong claim is made that an arguer is guilty of the fallacy of begging the question.

Both the moral bees case and the realtor case were cited in logic textbooks as instances of the fallacy of begging the question. While it is evident, in both cases, that circular reasoning is involved, it has been shown that the move from this step to declaring that the argument commits the fallacy of begging the question is non-trivial. Making this charge stick presupposes a careful interpretation and reconstruction of the argument in a well-specified context of dialogue.

In December 1988, Yasser Arafat made a speech at the UN. Speaking on behalf of the PLO (Palestine Liberation Organization), Arafat renounced all forms of terrorism. The relevant part of his speech was quoted by *Newsweek* (Dec. 26, 1988, p. 19), in the following words: "As for terrorism . . . I repeat for the record that we totally and absolutely renounce all forms of terrorism, including individual, group and state terrorism." This speech created pressure for several countries that had previously refused to talk to the PLO to enter into negotiations with them on peaceful settlement of problems in the Middle East. This situation is the context of the following case, where a response to Arafat's offer to negotiate was solicited.

Case 4.17:   Reporter: Will you enter into dialogue with the PLO?
Israeli government spokesman: We don't believe in encouraging terrorist organizations, because encouraging terrorist organizations means encouraging terrorism.[9]

The question is whether this reply could be criticized for committing the fallacy of begging the question. The grounds for such a criticism are the following. The reply to the question presumes that the PLO is in fact a terrorist organization. But it is precisely the denial of this presumption that prompted the question in the first place.

One can certainly appreciate the logic of the reply, in general terms. If you have a policy against terrorism, then it follows that generally, you should be against encouraging terrorist organizations. And if entering into dialogue with an organization would be to encourage it, then presuming the PLO is a terrorist organization, you should not enter into dialogue with it. This much represents a logical line of reasoning.

But should the respondent be making the presumption that the PLO is a terrorist organization, in view of the known fact that its leader just went on record as denying it? If the respondent doesn't believe or accept this denial, and is of the opinion that the PLO should still be called a terrorist organization, isn't that what he should say, giving his reasons for this opinion, instead of offering a circumlocution of argument that presumes this opinion tacitly?

It could be said that the spokesman's circumlocutory reply presumes the truth of a proposition that is, or should be, an issue, namely whether the PLO is truly a terrorist organization or not. It is as if the Israeli spokesman is taking the defensive stance: "We have always presumed that the PLO is a terrorist organization, and we are not going to change that now." But this seems a hard and dogmatic stance. In view of Arafat's renunciation of terrorism, shouldn't the Israeli spokesperson at least consider reasons for and against changing their policy, even if they think the reasons for not changing it remain much stronger than this new argument for changing it?

This case is a curious one, because it is one where an answer to a question seems to beg a question. But the question apparently begged (whether the PLO is a terrorist organization) is not the question that was asked. The answer given is a straightforward "No." But in giving the reasoning behind his answer, the respondent seems to beg or presume one side of a subissue that, it would seem, he should not be taking for granted, in view of the prior context of dialogue.

But is this case really an instance of circular argumentation, or is it just one where the respondent is refusing to budge from an entrenched, official position? In the latter event, the fallacy might not be begging the question. Indeed, the respondent might not be committing a fallacy at all, but simply sticking to a presupposition that represents his (or his government's) position on the issue. This stance could be called inflexible, dogmatic, or hardline. But that does not necessarily make it a circular argument, or a fallacy of begging the question.

A number of open questions remain to be discussed concerning the relationship of the fallacy of begging the question to associated faults of argumentation, including the fallacy of many questions, the use of loaded terms in argumentation, and aggressive answers to questions. Evidently then it remains open to further analysis whether case 4.17 represents an instance of question-begging or not. In any event, it is an interesting case that is on the borderline of being an instance of the fallacy of begging the question. This kind of problem is taken up further in chapter six.

The following case is an exercise from Copi (1982, p. 135), where it is supposed to be an instance of the fallacy of begging the question.

Case 4.18:   She says that she loves me and she must be telling the truth, because she certainly wouldn't lie to someone that she loves.

Now this argument does seem to be circular, at least if we interpret the conclusion as "She loves me." For the premise, "She wouldn't lie to someone that she loves," presupposes the truth of that conclusion.

But is the argument an instance of the fallacy of begging the question? The "must" and "certainly" provide textual evidence to support this criticism of the argument. But there are some interesting questions to be raised about the context of dialogue.

What, we may ask, is the purpose of this argument? Is the proponent trying to convince some third party that the second party (the "she" of the argument) loves him? Or is he only trying to convince himself? If the first hypothesis is correct, then the argument could be a fallacy, on the grounds that it involves a calculated tactic of deceptive persuasion. But if the second hypothesis is correct, the argument seems more like a blunder or error than a calculated tactic of deceptive persuasion to defeat an opponent. For so interpreted, it seems that the poor soul is pathetically deceiving himself.

If the second interpretation is right, then, the interesting question is raised–can you commit a fallacy against yourself? This question tests what is meant by the term "fallacy." In one sense, a fallacy is a sophistical tactic, used by one party in a dialogue to trick or deceive his dialogue partner. In another sense, a fallacy can be an error of reasoning, a kind of mistaken inference where a reasoner is led to blunder in a way that is not necessarily being used to fool anyone else as a clever tactic.

If the second hypothesis is correct, with respect to the interpretation of case 4.18, the circular argument could still perhaps be a fallacy, but only a fallacy of the error of reasoning type. The poor soul could be deluding himself by failing to see the obvious flaw in his reasoning, and thereby committing a fallacy of a sort.

At any rate, case 4.18 raises generally interesting questions about the concept of fallacy that will be taken up systematically in chapter six.

10. The Ingredients of a Case of Begging the Question

What is well brought out by all the case studies in this chapter is the lesson that whether a given argument may properly be said to commit the fallacy of begging the question depends on various factors extractable from the text and context of dialogue in a particular case. In other words, both the equivalence and dependency *petitio* are based on pragmatic criticisms of argumentation that are highly dependent on the specific context of dialogue of an argument. Even in the relatively simple cases 4.0 and 4.1, for example, a correct understanding of whether the argument begged the question depended heavily on the context of dialogue. This was a dependency circularity, but cases 4.2 to 4.6 made the same point for the equivalence conception. The remaining cases brought out the lesson even more deeply and emphatically.

According to the traditional *equivalence conception,* an argument is circular if one of the premises is identical or equivalent to the conclusion. According to the traditional *dependency conception,* an argument is circular if the only way you could establish this premise requires the prior assumption that the conclusion is true or acceptable. But circularity is only one of the requirements that an argument must meet in order to qualify as a bona fide case of the fallacy of begging the question. Hence the question arises of whether the equivalence and dependency conceptions are really conceptions of circularity or question-begging.

It depends on what you mean by "equivalence" and "dependency." The traditional way of interpreting these concepts would appear to be somewhat vague, leaving them in a twilight zone between circularity of argument and question-begging as fallaciousness of argument. We noted in section three that equivalence can be interpreted semantically or pragmatically. When interpreted pragmatically, it seems to incorporate the notion of inevitability, to some extent, and this seems to make it appear more like a concept of question-begging. The concept of dependency, as characterized in the paragraph above, incorporates the notion of the "only way" of establishing a premise. And this too makes it seem more like a concept of question-begging than just a concept of circularity of argument. However, circularity is not always conclusive evidence that an argument is fallacious, and consequently the traditional account of circular argument as a fallacy is inherently misleading.

In case 4.9 there was enough textual evidence to give some reasonable basis for an allegation that the argument begs the question. The argument is circular (something that always looks suspicious), and it seemed a plausible conjecture that its context is that of a persuasion dialogue. But is that enough to convict the argument of having committed the fallacy of begging the question? Applying requirements of burden of proof yields a negative answer, and properly so.

This answer is the right way to go, because the claim that an argument commits a fallacy should be regarded as a serious accusation. But there is an unfortunate tendency in textbooks in informal logic to leap ahead to identify a fallacy as soon as *some* evidence of a recognizable type of inadequacy of argument is spotted. But it is one thing to challenge an argument on the ground that it may be in danger of committing a fallacy, and quite another thing to claim that it has committed a fallacy. The term "fallacy" is generally taken to refer to an underlying, systematic error of reasoning or sophistical tactic, which means that the argument that commits it is wrong, and should be rejected. Such a strong form of refutation is often more difficult to substantiate properly than it seems, however.

Basically, there are three components involved in pinning down a criticism that an argument commits the fallacy of begging the question. The first requirement is that the argument be shown to be circular, according to a well-laid-out argument reconstruction. The second requirement is that the "circle" in the argument should be shown to be on the right dicycle to be part of the evidence that the argument begs the question. Very often, this means showing that the circle in the argument reconstruction is an inevitable circle. Or, at least, it involves checking over the text and context of the argument to see which avenues of evidential support for the premises are still being left open to subsequent dialogue. The third component is the requirement of evidential priority.

Evidential priority is easier to demonstrate in some contexts of dialogue than others. It may be pretty well taken for granted as a universal requirement in any inquiry. But in other contexts of dialogue, like negotiation, it may be generally presumed that it is not applicable. But in persuasion dialogue, probably the most important context of dialogue for the occurrence of question-begging argumentation, evidential priority is generally applicable, but is not necessarily a requirement of every speech act.

Basically, an argument is a claim advanced that the conclusion is true or acceptable, based on the reasons given by the premises. Therefore, in many, but not all, contexts of argument, the premises should be more acceptable, or more plausible, for the one to whom the argument is directed, than the conclusion is. Why? Because in many cases, the purpose of argument is to convince someone who is doubtful of the conclusion. If this person is equally doubtful of the premises, the argument will not serve its purpose. Therefore, in such a context of argument, the premises must be less doubtful. They must be more plausible than the conclusion. Otherwise the argument will not be useful to fulfill its purpose in dialogue.

But a useful argument designed to convince a respondent in dialogue must have premises that are more acceptable to that respondent than the conclusion. If one premise in an argument is too closely equivalent, or even identical to the conclusion, it can scarcely be more plausible–or at any rate, its superior plausibility may be thrown into question–and the argument will not serve the purpose of convincing the respondent who doubts that premise that the conclusion is acceptable. Similarly with the dependency type of relationship. If the only way to come to accept a premise of the argument is by prior acceptance of the conclusion, yet the person to whom the argument is directed finds the conclusion dubious or unacceptable, then that premise surely cannot be acceptable either. Hence a circular argument showing dependency also fails to serve its purpose in argument, where the context of the argument requires premises evidently prior to the conclusion.

In short then, there is one special context of argument where circularity is objectionable. That is where the premises of a good argument must be more acceptable as evidence, or better established than the conclusion. In this context, a circular argument is open to justifiable criticism.

However, generally, the burden of proof should be on the critic who claims that a circular argument is fallacious to show that the context of argument is this special context. These requirements of burden of proof on a critic will be further analyzed in chapter six.

How is an evaluator of an argument supposed to determine whether, in a particular case, a requirement of evidential priority should be mandatory? The answer is that the evaluator must judge by the evidence that is offered by the context of dialogue. There are two kinds of evidence: external evidence and internal evidence.

External evidence is given by information we may have about the basic purpose of the argument, the point or program required to be carried out or fulfilled by argument in that context. For example, suppose the context is a geometry examination where a student is asked to prove the theorem of Pythagoras. The program required to be carried out in geometry is to prove a theorem from given premises, namely certain axioms or prior propositions already proved from the original axioms.[10] Therefore, when your professor asks you to prove the Pythagorean theorem, he is asking you to prove it from prior, previously proven, or accepted propositions. That is the program, and the students and the professor clearly understand the nature of the program to be carried out in the context of the study of Euclidean geometry.

Now if a student were to write on his exam booklet, "The Pythagorean theorem is true, therefore the Pythagorean theorem is true," he would correctly receive a grade of zero. Both his classmates and his professor would rightly reject this answer as worthless, except for its humorous value, because they understand the basic purpose of argument in Euclidean geometry is to prove a proposition by deducing it by valid arguments from prior propositions already proven or accepted as axioms. The context of argument in this case makes it quite clear that the basic purpose of argument requires evidential priority.

However, in another case, the context may not clearly demand evidential priority. If the student is asked as an exercise in another mathematics class to prove proposition B from proposition A, and then A from B, the circle in the proof may be no fallacy. Why not? Because here the program required by the instruction given is to prove each proposition from the other. All it means, in this context, is that the student will have proved that A and B are equivalent. The purpose of the argument is fulfilled by the circular proof. So no requirement of evidential priority is present in the external context of the question in the dialogue.

In both these examples from mathematics the external context of the dialogue offers the evidence of the presence or absence of the requirement of evidential priority. In other cases, the evidence is internal to the dialogue at a local level. In this type of case, if there is a circle in the propositions advanced as answers to a series of questions, one must be careful to examine the wording of the questions as well as the answers. Key indicator-words may be evidence of evidential priority, or the recipient of the argument may indicate doubts about the plausibility of the conclusion.

Each case must be examined carefully. First, one needs to look at the propositions that make up the answers, and, by the process of argument reconstruction, determine whether there is a circle in the argument. But is the circle a basis for criticizing the argument? To answer this question, you must see whether the individual questions ask for propositions that are better established than the proposition queried in the question. For example, if a question takes the form "How can you be sure that A?" or "What previously established evidence do you have for A?", then there is internal evidence that evidential priority is required in the argument.

In short then, there are three steps in evaluating circular arguments. First, you must establish whether or not there is a circle in the argument, by the method of argument reconstruction. But then, the matters of inevitability and evidential priority must be taken up, as the next two steps. Only then can the question of whether the argument is open to criticism on grounds of begging the question be evaluated. Reasons for and against the seriousness of this criticism can then be brought forward and assessed. These reasons are based on internal or external evidence of the context of dialogue.

The question of whether a circle in an argument is open to criticism is partially determined by evidential priority. But we must remember that in some cases, even where the program clearly requires evidential priority, there can be a circle in the argument without the argument's necessarily being a failure. This can occur where there is additional, independent evidence from another source in the argument. The typical example we studied here was the case where A and B are both on a circle, but there is some third proposition, C, that is a premise in an additional convergent argument for B. Here it may be true that B is on a circle, but C can still provide independent, prior evidence for B. So where B is the conclusion to be established by prior evidence, the overall argument for B may be non-fallacious even though there is a circle in it. Much too may depend on whether the argument is linked or convergent. As we saw in section seven, there are various subtleties in interpreting an argument reconstruction that require close attention to the structure of evidential routes in relation to a premise.

In some cases, an argument can be defended against a criticism of circularity, and it should not be ruled out in advance that such a defense may be reasonable. Sometimes, even if it can be shown that there is a circle in an argument, there may also be a possibility of an independent line of argument that could reveal that it is not inevitably circular. In this type of case, the circular argument may have the potential to meet the requirement of evidential priority of the premises, and therefore, possibly it could be reasonably defended as a good argument, in the subsequent context of dialogue. Once again here, the burden of proof is on the critic, if a claim is made that the fallacy of begging the question has been committed.

The detailed case studies 4.9 to 4.14 show that the most difficult practical problem of evaluating a criticism of circularity is the task of argument reconstruction, no trivial job when we confront a realistically controversial argument. Many of the same problems of argument reconstruction are also present when an argument that may be circular, but has not definitely been accused of committing the fallacy of begging the question, is to be evaluated. In fact, the longer and more complex the argument is, the more likely a hidden circle is to go undetected. Therefore, the most interesting, persuasive, and really troublesome instances of circular reasoning, where begging the question is not just a textbook example, but a seriously misleading error, tend to occur in longer, extended sequences of argumentation. As in the case of many of the argument criticisms previously studied, the first job is to pin down exactly what the argument is. Only then can we go on to evaluate alleged criticisms of it, based on the evidence of the corpus of dialogue.

Once we sort out what the argument is, then the criticism of circularity can be dealt with. But sometimes an argument can be modified or improved, as a response to the criticism of circularity. Hence, if the context of argument is left open, as in the cases in this chapter, there may be room for possible continuation of the sequence of dialogue. If, however, such surrounding context of dialogue is not given, any criticism that the argument begs the question must be provisional–the criticism must be treated more as a point of order or request for clarification than as a decisive refutation, or objection that a fallacy has been committed. Such a cautionary evidence-based approach, based on burden of proof, stems from the obligation of a critic to be fair and impartial, especially where the need for judgment arises because the textual or contextual evidence is incomplete.

Cases 4.9 to 4.14 represent an interesting range of arguments that are somewhat complex, and would all be traditionally taken by the textbooks to be instances of the fallacy of begging the question. Yet there is a range of judgments possible here–some of them are clearly more susceptible to this kind of criticism than others. And there seems to be a complex of factors involved in our judgment of whether this criticism can be justified and pinned down.

The remaining cases, the borderline cases 4.15 to 4.18, are even more radically problematic for the analysis of *petitio*. They are test cases for any theory of begging the question as a fallacy.

NOTES

1. Hamblin (1970, p. 32).
2. See chapter two *supra*.
3. See Harary (1969, p. 10).
4. See Walton (1989a, chapter 7).
5. In the exercise manual, *Solutions to Exercises: Introduction to Logic,* Irving M. Copi (New York: Macmillan, and London: Collier Macmillan, 1982, p. 95), the example in question is identified as a case of *petitio principii* (begging the question), with no further comment or explanation offered.

6. Case 4.9 is also the subject of an analysis in Walton (1985a).

7. The sequence of argumentation in this dialogue is similar to an argument on page 4 of an anonymous article, "Universities' Role in Training for Careers," *University of Auckland News,* 15, no. 7 (November 1985): 4-6, 35-40.

8. The story of the moral bees was originally told by Richard Wright in *Black Power* (New York: Harper & Brothers, 1954). As Wright (p. 252) relates the story, the fetish priest describes the bees as his army, sent by God to take care of him. Elaborating on this theme, the priest engages in the following sequence of dialogue with Wright, as quoted by Wright: "Now, that was why I took you to see that box. . . . If you had been an enemy of mine, those bees would have buzzed you out of here. . . . They sting and drive out all of my enemies. Only last week a man came here with evil intentions against me. Those bees drove him out; he ran away, screaming." Wright comments on this dialogue by noting that the priest sincerely thought that the attack by the bees was "proof" of the man's evil intentions. Such a person, he adds, must be "dreaming with [his] eyes wide open."

9. *The National* (CBC Evening News, December 22, 1988).

10. See Mackenzie (1980).

5

Longer Case Studies

The method of argument reconstruction developed in chapter three is still a very crude instrument for its intended purpose, at its present state of development. The method, in a simple form, has proven its utility through its widespread use in recent textbooks in informal logic. Three separate research projects on this subject are yet unpublished but near completion– one by James Freeman, one by Tjark Kruiger, and one by J. Anthony Blair and Robert Pinto. But many elementary theoretical questions about the method as a structure of argument analysis have hardly even been asked yet. It seems as though it is to be a very severe test to try to apply this simple and limited method to genuinely controversial and sophisticated arguments that occur in problematic contexts of scientific or philosophical reasoning.

Even so, it is necessary to attempt this step, because we will never achieve any real understanding of *petitio principii* as a serious fallacy, or shortcoming of argument, unless we get away from the preoccupation that the textbooks have with simplistic examples of outrageously circular arguments, chosen specifically to represent errors that students will willingly accept as fallacious instances of begging the question.

Petitio principii becomes a serious business when it is likely to go undetected, and therefore to succeed as a sophistical tactic to mask successfully an underlying weakness or opening for critical questioning in an argument. At the same time, however, it is just in these seriously interesting types of cases that the method of argument reconstruction runs up against some inherent limitations of its firm applicability.

1. LIMITS OF ARGUMENT RECONSTRUCTION

Argument reconstruction seems to come up against an inherent boundary when it confronts a scientific argument, or any kind of argument based on technical expertise in a specialized domain of knowledge. How can a critic interpret the argument, and correctly perform tasks of reconstruction, like filling in enthymemes, when he is not a specialist in the domain of knowledge in question? In such a case, the context of dialogue has shifted from that of a persuasion dialogue to something more like that of an advice-seeking dialogue between a layperson and an expert in a domain of knowledge or technical expertise.

On the other hand, questioning, interviewing, or seeking advice from experts should not be considered an illegitimate kind of argumentation. It is often necessary for an attorney in court to cross-examine an expert, for example in ballistics or medicine, even though the attorney is not himself an expert in either field.[1] What the attorney must do is to learn a little about the subject on which he must question the expert, and also learn to be skilled in techniques of questioning, cross-examination, and argumentation so that he can pick out the points in the expert's line of reasoning that should be subject to legitimate critical questions.[2]

The situation of the context of dialogue, in such a case, is complex. Each attorney, on either side, is competing against the other to persuade a jury or judge. But then each of them is also interacting in dialogue with a third party, an expert in a particular domain. In this context, there are four main participants, rather than the usual two participants we have previously been familiar with in persuasion dialogue, and other types of dialogue.

But this type of argumentative, complex situation is not confined to the legal context. It is very common in persuasion dialogue on controversial topics, on all matters of values and subjects of public interest, to use the citation of expert opinions to back up one's side of an argument. The appeal to expertise is such a common and effectively used technique of argumentation that it is incumbent upon us all to be able to deal critically with appeals to expert say-so in argument.[3] So while there may be limits to the use of argument reconstruction in this type of context, it should not be concluded or advised that techniques of argument analysis are inherently inapplicable to the argument of an expert, even if the critic is not an expert in that same field.

When studying expert argumentation, the best a critic can hope for is to raise critical questions concerning the weak points in an expert's argumentation where it is open to challenge. If two legitimate experts disagree, for example, a critic can ask some important critical questions about the apparent inconsistency of their conclusions. There is a burden of proof on an expert to resolve the point if his conclusion strongly appears to be inconsistent with common sense, inconsistent with the conclusion of another expert, or even inconsistent with his own statements.

Thus argument reconstruction is especially useful when scientific findings are solicited as expert opinions in persuasion dialogue on matters of public controversy that relate to science. If a scientific argument appears to beg the question, that is generally perceived as quite a serious criticism of it.

Criticisms of circular reasoning can be very worrisome to scientists, who are prone to portraying scientific research as a cumulative process of logical reasoning based on solid foundations. On the other hand, as David

Hull (1967) has shown, the very core of experimental methodology in science involves a feedback process of conjecture, collection of evidence, and refinement of the hypothesis, which may itself be a circular process of reasoning. Of course, this process of "groping" need not involve a fallacy of begging the question. It may be a sequence of successive refinement that is inherently circular without involving any error or fallacy. All this may mean is that feedback is involved in any process of trial and error where assimilation of new evidence requires changes and improvements in scientific hypotheses and terminology.

Hull's suggestion that methods of inductive confirmation in scientific reasoning involve a circle would have disquieted John Stuart Mill, who argued that deductive reasoning is circular, and that therefore inductive reasoning is preferable.[4] It would also disquiet many scientists who think of scientific investigation as a cumulative inquiry that is highly incompatible with circular reasoning.

The first longer case study concerns a controversy that has arisen among specialists in stratigraphy, a field related to geology and paleontology, concerning a type of argumentation central to research methodology in stratigraphy that appears to be a kind of circular reasoning.[5] The remaining two case studies are famous philosophical arguments.

The techniques of argument reconstruction could be applied to the shorter case studies in chapter four with some degree of usefulness because the context of dialogue in these cases relate to practical matters of everyday life familiar to most educated speakers of English who would be expected to deal with these cases. What background context they require can presumably be furnished through the common sense knowledge we all share.

When we try to apply these same techniques of argument reconstruction to philosophical argumentation, however, the exercise can be initially useful, but then it seems to reach a limit. There are two basic reasons for this boundary. One is that meta-philosophical criticisms of a philosophical text tend to expand into context, and typically the limit of that context tends to comprise everything that can be included in the position of the exponent of the argument in the original text. For example, if the argument chosen for evaluation is a version attributed to a particular author, say Descartes, then it quickly becomes fair game for the entire collection of Descartes' writings to be considered as comprising legitimate context of dialogue for the argument. Given a textual base this large, the evaluation of the original argument quickly becomes a controversy open only to a select group of specialists who have become experts in the Cartesian texts. At this point the original persuasion dialogue may have shifted into another type of dialogue–a kind of technical discussion among a group of experts.

The second reason for this boundary in the usefulness of argument reconstruction as applied to philosophical argumentation is that in an explicitly philosophical discussion, standards of strictness in applying rules of dialogue are tightened up. Participants pay more attention to the exact

186 Begging the Question

wording of a sentence in which a commitment was expressed. Participants may be called on to define their key terms in the argument more precisely than they would in a non-philosophical conversation. This tightening is not only characteristic of philosophical argumentation–it also occurs in legal argumentation, for example, in writing a contract, or in a criminal court-room proceeding.

When an argument tightens up like this, the technique of argument reconstruction can still be usefully applied. But because such an argument typically becomes more subtle in various ways, applying the method of argument reconstruction becomes less straightforward and demands greater skills of interpretation.

Although the more significant and interesting cases of *petitio principii* as a fallacy that is a serious threat to good reasoning seem likely to occur in scientific and philosophical argumentation of a complex sort, analysis of these cases faces inherent difficulties. The main difficulty is posed by the inherent limitations of the method of argument reconstruction in dealing with argument in these contexts. Even so, it is necessary to attempt to confront some cases of these types, as an experimental test of the limits of the method of argument reconstruction that will throw light on the analysis of *petitio principii* as a fallacy.

2. A GEOLOGICAL CASE STUDY

Stratigraphy is the study of layers of rock strata as they occur in different levels of the terrain. The study of the order of the rock strata is aided by the study of the fossil remains of organisms contained in the strata. On the other hand, the scientists who are trying to date the fossil remains tend to rely partly on their finding of the order in which the fossils are found as determined by the order of layers of the rock strata. Because of this apparent mutual dependence of these two types of investigation, several scientists have questioned whether there could be a circle implicit in scientific methodology here. The worry is that if there is a circle, could it be a vicious circle, or an indication of fallacious reasoning?

It is easy for any intelligent layperson or student of geology to suspect circular reasoning. After all, the geologists use the rocks to date fossils, and they use the fossils to date rocks. Rastall in the *Encyclopedia Brittanica* has given a clear statement of this criticism.

Case 5.0:   It cannot be denied that from a strictly philosophical standpoint geologists are here arguing in a circle. The succession of organisms has been determined by a study of their remains embedded in the rocks, and the relative ages of the rocks are determined by the remains of organisms that they contain.

If Rastall's remarks are a reasonable interpretation of the way geologists have argued, then it seems justifiable to conclude that this reasoning is circular. However, as we have previously seen, circular reasoning can sometimes be successfully defended against the criticism that it constitutes a *petitio principii* fallacy.

In fact, Rastall himself offers a defense against the charge of vicious circularity.

Case 5.1:   It is possible to a very large extent to determine the order of superposition and succession of the strata without any reference at all to their fossils. When the fossils in their turn are correlated with this succession they are found to occur in a certain definite order, and no other. Consequently, when the purely physical evidence of superposition cannot be applied, as for example to the strata of two widely separated regions, it is safe to take the fossils as a guide; this follows from the fact that when both kinds of evidence are available there is never any contradiction between them; consequently, in the limited number of cases where only one line of evidence is available, it alone may be taken as proof.

How do Rastall's remarks in case 5.1 offer a defense against the charge of circularity? He starts out by claiming that scientists can determine the order of the strata, to a large extent, without reference to the order of the fossils. In other words, Rastall is denying that there is a necessary dependency on knowing the order of the fossils when scientists determine the order of the rocks. So then scientists must have some other evidence for determining the order of the rock strata, other than by appealing to the order of the fossils. What is this other evidence?

According to Rastall's statement, in many cases there is "purely physical evidence of superposition" that enables the stratigrapher to tell which layer of rock is earlier and which is later. It is only in the special case, for example in trying to date two strata from widely separated regions, that the fossil evidence needs to be brought to bear.

So let us take the normal case first. In the normal, or non-special case, Rastall is telling us, there is no circle. First, the stratigrapher starts from ①: the physical evidence of superposition of the rock strata. Then reasoning from that evidence he establishes ②: the order of the succession of the strata. Then finally, from this he can make an inference, if he wants, to ③: the order of succession of the fossils. He can correlate ③ with ②, and he thereby finds a certain definite order in ③ (figure 5.0).

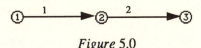

Figure 5.0

There is no circle in the geologist's reasoning so far; ③ is based on ②; and ② in turn is based on ①. Here the context of argument is that of evidential priority.

However, according to Rastall, the situation is different when the two rock strata that need to be comparatively dated come from two widely separated regions. In this type of case, there is no physical evidence of superposition. One rock layer is not found on top of the other. What can the geologist do in this type of case?

According to Rastall's statement, when ② and ③ are determined in their order of dating in the inference modelled in the diagram immediately above, ② and ③ are always found to occur in a certain definite order. Many studies have shown, he is claiming, that the order of the rocks and the order of the fossils in different sequences of layers always correlate in a certain definite order.

How does this finding help the geologist in the special case where there is no physical evidence of superposition, ①, to be found? Well, the problem is that it is in this special case where the circle occurs. In this type of case, the stratigrapher has no direct physical evidence to determine ②. So what does he do? He uses the order of the fossils, ③, as his evidence (figure 5.1).

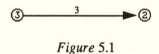

Figure 5.1

But the problem is, as we already saw in the normal case, that ② is used as the evidential basis for ③. So here we have the circle, representing the correlation between the strata and the fossils (figure 5.2).

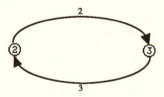

Figure 5.2

Rastall is admitting then, that in this special case, the geologist does argue in a circle. But if so, how can the geologist's reasoning be defended against the suspicion of committing the fallacy of arguing in a circle?

Rastall's answer is that in this special type of case, it is safe to take the fossil evidence, ③, as a guide for ②, the rock order. Why is it safe? His answer is because ② and ③ are always found to correlate, and there is never any contradiction between them. In other words, there is a fourth line of evidence, ④: many studies have shown generally that there is a positive correlation, a certain definite order between ② and ③. Consequently when the geographer argues from ③ to ②, he is also using the additional premise ④ in order to establish ②. This is shown in figure 5.3.

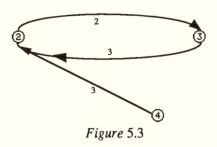

Figure 5.3

In other words, there is a circle in the geologist's argument, but according to Rastall, it is not a vicious circle. For if you look over the argument as a whole, you see that when the geologist argues from ② to ③, he uses the physical evidence of superposition, ①, to establish ②, as we first saw. But then as we observed next, following Rastall's account, when he argues from ③ to ②, he also uses ④ as a basis for ②, in a linked argument. Putting these two single inferences together, we reconstruct the whole argument in figure 5.4.

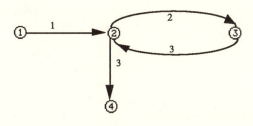

Figure 5.4

According to Rastall's interpretation then, there is a circle, but no fallacy of begging the question, because ② does not depend exclusively on ③ as its sole premise. There is also a linkage with ④, but even more significantly, there is an independent line of evidence from ① to support ② as a premise.

One problem in this case is that most of us who, as critics, approach this argument to assess whether the circle Rastall indicates is any evidence of begging the question, are not experts in geology or paleontology, much less specialists in stratigraphy. We do not want to have to take the position of being judges on how stratigraphers should solve their methodological problems, even though the kind of reasoning they are using does appear to be controversial, from a point of view of informal logic. Thus there is a kind of dilemma. Can any critical comment be ventured or not?

Even the argument reconstruction above seems tentative and conjectural. On one interpretation, it does seem that Rastall is saying that, although there is a circle in the argument, it is not an inevitable circle. Yet he also seems to be saying that if you separate the global argument into two phases, there is no real circle. At the first phase, when physical evidence of superposition is available, then you can argue from the strata to the fossils. But then in the limited number of cases where physical evidence is not available, you can argue from the fossils to the strata of rocks. So, we could interpret him as saying, as long as you keep these two phases separate, there is no circle. It is only when you put them together that a circular sequence of reasoning results.

We seem to be left in some doubt then, whether there is really a circle in the sequence of reasoning, according to Rastall, or not. And if there is a circle, the exact reasons why it is not supposed to be an instance of the fallacy of begging the question are not entirely clear. Although we do have good indications of these reasons, the fact that Rastall speaks from an expert position (and we, as critics do not) poses limits on further argument reconstruction. These limits turn out to be important in devising useful textbook methods for analysis and evaluation of particular cases of the fallacy of begging the question–the subject of chapter seven.

Another problem is that the criticism levelled in case 5.0 by Rastall would not appear to be a claim that geologists have been using a sophistical tactic to try to deceive the non-scientific community (or anyone else) into thinking that their arguments are acceptable, when in fact they are just tricks. Rastall's charge would not appear to be this strong. If he is putting forward a charge that the fallacy of begging the question has been committed, it would appear to be more of a claim that the geologists have unwittingly committed an error of reasoning. Hence this case raises some interesting questions about the distinction between an error of reasoning type of fallacy and a sophistical tactic type of fallacy which will be taken up in chapter six.

Specifically, one might ask here, if the geologists referred to in case 5.0 have committed only an error of reasoning without using a sophistical tactic to try to get the best of some opponents in argument, why is there a *prima facie* inclination to presume that they have committed the fallacy of begging the question at all? The answer to this question will come out in chapter eight, section nine, where it is shown that circular argumentation is an especially serious kind of error in an inquiry. For compilation of stratigraphic evidence in the science of geology is a kind of inquiry, and not a kind of persuasion dialogue or critical discussion.

3. THE STRATIGRAPHIC ARGUMENT REINTERPRETED

A different defense was advanced by Harper (1980), a paleontologist who felt that anyone who concedes Rastall's allegations of circularity could still be left with the misleading impression that the time correlation of strata using fossils could still be flawed or unreliable. Harper argued that if you look at the process of how paleontologists actually use fossils to date strata, no circularity exists. His argument is quoted as case 5.2.

Case 5.2:   If we examine allegations of circularity in the light of how paleontologists actually do use fossils to date strata, it becomes clear that no circularity exists. A physical property of strata, namely superposition, is used to infer relative ages of fossils, but only relative ages at each individual *local* section. Taken by itself, the latter is not even a basis for inferring succession in time of *fossils,* let alone strata (p. 246).

Harper went on to add that, at the local level, the fossils are only given relative dates–relative to the strata that were found to contain them. Any more general conclusions about the dates of the fossils will be determined by regional patterns of many other findings. Harper did not find this process of confirmation circular in any fallacious way.

Consider how the stratigrapher paleontologist uses fossils to correlate strata. He works out local successions of fossil taxa and looks for orderly successions of fossils, i.e. for homotaxial patterns over a region. If and only if regular non-random patterns are found, then he uses these patterns to simultaneously infer relative ages for fossils and, *ipso facto,* the local strata which contain them (p. 246).

According to Harper, the paleontologist's reasoning does not use a premise that is equivalent to the conclusion. Hence the reasoning is not an equivalence circularity. Nor do we have to know the conclusion in order to infer a premise. So it is not a dependency circularity. Harper concludes that there is no circle in the argument. To resolve the problem, we need only to distinguish more sharply between the inference made at the local level, at the spot of a particular site, and the inference made on the basis of homotaxial patterns over a region. Two fossils are said to be *homotaxial* if they both belong to the same classification of types of fossils. Let us now reconstruct Harper's argument.

First, at the local level, superposition of the order of strata found, ①, is used to infer ②, a relative age for both the local fossil and the local strata that contain it (figure 5.5).

Figure 5.5

But Harper's point is that the fossils are not dated apart from the strata. We simultaneously infer the same age for both. In other words, both local fossil ages and local strata ages go together in the one proposition, ②, and cannot be separated, at least at the local level. They can't be separated because, according to Harper, what the paleontologist actually infers, or should properly infer, is the relative ages of strata and fossils at the local level–the age of the one as compared to the age of the other.

But then, at a second step of inference, according to Harper's account, the additional evidence furnished by ③, many observations of homotaxial patterns over a whole region, comes into play. Here a judgment is made not just at the local level, but the evidence found over a larger region is brought in. In other words, at this second stage, ① and ③ are used as linked premises to infer ② (figure 5.6).

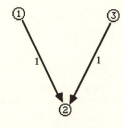

Figure 5.6

Thus according to Harper's reconstruction of the paleontologist's inferences, there is no circle. At the local level, only relative age is concluded. So at that level, it is not really accurate to say that the rocks are used to date the fossils and the fossils are used to date the rocks. Instead, the order in which both are found together only allows the stratigrapher to make a finding of the relative age of both the fossils and rocks, as they occur together in each layer. So there is no circle at that point.

But then at the regional level, if there have been found to be general patterns of findings based on many observations of local successions over the whole region, then this evidence can be brought to bear on the particular case of the findings at one local site being investigated. But once again there is no circularity, because the inference is from the general to the particular. The general patterns of both rocks and fossils are being used as evidence to make conclusions about a particular sequence of relative ages of rocks and fossils.

To summarize then, Harper's interpretation of the methodology of stratigraphy is different from that given by Rastall, even though each of them provides a defense against the charge of *petitio principii*. According to Rastall, there may be a circle in the paleontologist's process of reasoning, but the circle is not vicious, nor evidence of a fallacy. According to

Harper, there is no circle, and hence no fallacious *petitio principii*. Each of these responses represents a reasonable way of handling the criticism of circular reasoning. Rastall's defense involves admission of the circle, but then rejection of its fallaciousness on the grounds that it is not an inevitable circle. Harper's defense involves denial of the circle. According to Harper, if you look at the larger picture, there is no real circularity, only the surface appearance of it.

Both these defenses against the charge of begging the question are, in principle, reasonable. Which one rests on a more accurate or faithful account of how paleontologists do, or should, argue is a question that remains to be settled by the paleontologists themselves. Whichever way they choose to go, two avenues have been opened to them by the defenses of Rastall and Harper. It will be interesting to see how the paleontologists respond in the future sequences of reasonable dialogue now opened for discussion. Certainly, the criticism is a serious one, especially now that it has been formulated by the specialists themselves. However, the two responses so far considered are both reasonable as defenses in practical logic.

This case study shows that evaluating criticisms of controversial cases of circular argumentation can be a serious matter for scientists who aim to present results in their field in the form of an inquiry. Cases of *petitio* relate to ongoing controversies in the hard sciences. Such criticisms can be worth study. This case also shows that before any criticism of circularity can be finally resolved, and the dialogue ended, there must be a clear and agreed-upon account of what the argument is, or should be taken to be, that is alleged to be open to criticism. But in some cases, serious scientific controversies have not yet been finally resolved, and may be open to further dialogue.

However, the basic, limiting problem with this real argument, as we have now seen, is that a critic must use interpretation, judgment, and (in this case) even expert knowledge, in order to reconstruct fairly what the argument is. For premises may be tacitly rather than explicitly stated, and fairly pinning down those premises can only be done on an intelligent understanding of the arguer's position. However, in this case, understanding the arguer's position entails some understanding of stratigraphy as a methodology used in scientific research. Thus there are severe limits on how far the layperson can go in bringing argument reconstruction to bear in order to evaluate whether there really is a *petitio principii* in the argument or not. The best the critic can do is to collaborate with the experts to arrive at a reconstruction that fairly represents how the experts reason when they apply their scientific methods of research. In this type of case then, we are on the borderline between the study of *petitio principii* and the study of expert reasoning, characteristically related in the study of fallacies to the *argumentum ad verecundiam*. The question "What is the line of reasoning?" needs to be resolved before we can begin to test the criticism that such reasoning is embedded in argumentation that begs the question.

4. THE CARTESIAN CIRCLE

The famous Cartesian circle has been the subject of a good deal of philosophical controversy. The objection of *petitio principii* was a particularly serious criticism for Descartes, because he based his *Meditations* on a foundationalist program of trying to base philosophical inquiry on first principles that could not be subject to doubt. Descartes' model of inquiry was Euclidean geometry. He sought basic propositions in philosophy parallel to axioms in geometry, that could be clearly and distinctly known to be true. After these basic propositions were secured as free from the possibility of doubt, the plan was then to build up a scientific philosophy by logical inferences from the basic propositions.[6]

Descartes did not think of philosophy as a persuasion dialogue, based on presumptions that can be proved or refuted according to a burden of proof less than perfect certainty. He saw philosophy as being like scientific argumentation, a context of inquiry that, ideally, is cumulative and based on firmly established premises.[7]

The program of Descartes' *Meditations* adopted the criterion of evidence that the only kind of proposition that cannot be subject to reasonable doubt is one that can clearly and distinctly be perceived as true. By a process of elimination, he found only one proposition, the famous "I think, therefore I am" as a candidate to meet the criterion. Then his program proceeded, by a sequence of reasoning supposedly composed of logical inferences, to draw other conclusions from this single, basic proposition. Ultimately in the *Meditations,* Descartes drew the conclusion that God exists.

However, even Descartes' early critics voiced the objection that his line of argumentation involves a circular sequence of reasoning. In the Fourth Set of Objections *(Objections and Replies,* 4, 214), Antoine Arnauld makes the following objection.

I have one further worry, namely how the author avoids reasoning in a circle when he says that we are sure that what we clearly and distinctly perceive is true only because God exists.

But we can be sure that God exists only because we clearly and distinctly perceive this. Hence, before we can be sure that God exists, we ought to be able to be sure that whatever we perceive clearly and evidently is true.[8]

Arnauld is objecting that Descartes has involved his argument in a criterion of evidence type of circularity by adopting the "clear and distinct perception" criterion of secure acceptance. For Descartes has used this criterion in his proof of the existence of God. But according to Arnauld, Descartes also says that we are sure the criterion is true only because God exists. Arnauld's use of the terms "only because" (repeated) and "before we can be sure" strongly suggest inevitable circularity and evidential priority, indicators that the circle is a case of the fallacy of begging the question.

In his Reply to the Fourth Set of Objections *(Objections and Replies,* 4, 246), Descartes addresses himself to Arnauld's criticism, claiming that he is "not guilty of circularity." Descartes replies by alluding to a distinction he had already made in the *Meditations* between perceiving something clearly and remembering having perceived something clearly on a previous occasion.

> To begin with, we are sure that God exists because we attend to the arguments which prove this; but subsequently it is enough for us to remember that we perceived something clearly in order for us to be certain that it is true. This would not be sufficient if we did not know that God exists and is not a deceiver.[9]

How does this reply meet Arnauld's objection? The answer seems to relate to the basic thrust of the objection, which is this: the "clear and distinct perception" criterion of evidence that Descartes uses is acceptable as true, as Descartes admits, only on the basis of the presumption that God exists. If God did not exist, in other words, this criterion could be shaky. And this is what closes the circle, because the proof of the existence of God depended on the application of the "clear and distinct perception" criterion of evidence.

Descartes' reply is that the criterion does depend on the existence of God, but only indirectly. That is, Descartes replies that the criterion does not *always* or *necessarily* have to depend on the assurance of the existence of a non-deceiving and trustworthy God, in every case. The dependency, on this interpretation, is only partial, and therefore his argument, he maintains, is not an inevitable circle. Hence, he is "not guilty," he maintains, of committing a faulty circular reasoning.[10]

But to go deeper into the reasoning behind Descartes' defense against the objection of *petitio,* it seems that we have to go more deeply into his philosophy concerning the process of philosophical inquiry as he sees it. Descartes seems to be appealing to a distinction between two criteria of evidential acceptability. The first is the type of reasoning where a person is in a calm and reflective state of mind, and clearly and distinctly perceives some proposition to be true. For example, attending to a sound argument for the existence of God, a person knows that this argument proves that God exists, and he cannot have any doubt of this. But the second is the type of reasoning where that person remembered he had proved the existence of God, because at that time in the past when he attended to the proof, he perceived clearly and distinctly that the proof was correct and reliable, beyond doubt. Subsequently, he can take this conclusion as proved, even though it is dependent on memory, because he can remember that, at the time, he perceived it clearly and distinctly.

But memory is fallible. And if a trustworthy God did not exist, something ostensibly remembered as true could possibly turn out to be false. Accepting as true something proved in the past, therefore, depends on the existence of God and on the presumption that God is not a deceiver.

But accepting as true something proved as a conclusion of argument based exclusively on clear and distinct perception does not depend on any prior acceptance of the proposition that God exists, at the time one is attending to the argument in a properly attentive frame of mind.

Descartes' reply could be interpreted as revealing a subtle ambiguity in the structure of his argumentation in the *Meditations*. Three propositions are involved.

①: A non-deceptive God exists.

②: What is clearly and distinctly perceived is known to be true.
③: Memory is reliable as a source of knowledge.

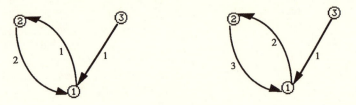

Figure 5.7

In the argument on the left in figure 5.7, the existence of God, ①, is dependent on both the clear and distinct perception, ③, and memory, ②, in a linked argument. Hence the circle, in this case, is worrisome, and could be evidence of a *petitio principii* fault of the argument, because ② also depends on ①. This dependency is worrisome, because ② is a required premise for ①.

But in the argument on the right, the structure is that of a convergent type of argumentation. In this case, ③ can stand by itself as a premise, without a required reliance on ②. In this case, memory is not required, and the clear and distinct perception is, by itself, sufficient proof of the existence of God.

As with the previous geological cases (5.0 to 5.2), the question of whether the argument may rightly be charged with begging the question depends crucially on what the reasoning in the argument is supposed to be. In other words, the basic question is how the reasoning may be reconstructed in the argument diagram. In the Descartes case, in particular, the key question is whether the argument is linked or convergent in structure.

This case clearly shows that there are important differences between the question of whether an argument is circular and the question of whether the argument begs the question. These key differences are overlooked by many of the textbooks, as we will see in chapter seven. And they must be taken carefully into account in the new theory of the fallacy of begging the question present in chapter eight. The new theory must be sensitive to these subtle but important differences.

5. CASE STUDY OF THE ONTOLOGICAL ARGUMENT

The following case is a version of a famous philosophical argument, the ontological argument for the existence of God. Those familiar with St. Anselm's version of the ontological argument will readily appreciate the similarity of its thrust as an argument with the argument for the existence of God in case 5.3. However, the exercise will be to analyze the case on its own merits (or demerits) as an argument designed to convince a non-believer of the existence of God. No reliance on St. Anselm's version of the argument, or any other of the many known versions of this argument, should be presumed, or taken into account, for the purposes of argument reconstruction below.

Briefly put, the ontological argument presupposes a context of dialogue wherein a proponent, who is a believer, has the burden of proving the conclusion "God exists" to a non-believer. The ontological argument proceeds from a premise that postulates the perfection of God to a conclusion that infers the existence of God. In St. Anselm's version, the non-believer is (somewhat prejudicially) called "the fool." The proponent of the argument begins by asking the believer to concede that God is that than which nothing greater can be thought. The argument then proceeds to take the line that to postulate a non-existent God would be to postulate a God than which a greater can be thought, namely one that exists. The conclusion is that a non-existent God is a contradiction, and that therefore, God must exist.

This argument has often been thought to be circular by its critics. In recent times, for example, Rowe (1975) has argued that the ontological argument commits the fallacy of begging the question. Walton (1978) surveys some interpretation of St. Anselm's argument and assesses various criticisms, including those of Rowe, to the effect that the argument commits the *petitio principii* fallacy.

Of course, there are many versions of the ontological argument, and whether or not a criticism of begging the question can be justified will depend on the reconstruction of the argument. This, in turn, as we have seen, will depend on the original text and context of the argument. Even if case 5.3 turns out to commit the fallacy of begging the question, it does not follow that the famous versions of the ontological argument, constructed by the great philosophers, commit the fallacy of begging the question.

Even so, it will turn out that case 5.3 is quite a severe test of our methods of argument reconstruction developed so far, and it will pose some new problems about begging the question that are of interest in their own right.

In the following discussion, a believer and a non-believer are discussing the existence of God. The believer, or theist, is an individual who is committed to the thesis that God exists. The non-believer, or skeptic, does not have to be an atheist (someone who rejects the thesis that God exists). He only needs to be a skeptic—someone who is not committed to the thesis that God exists. The believer advances the following argument.

Case 5.3:   ① [God is the greatest conceivable being.] ② [For if you could imagine a greater conceivable being than God, then this greater being would be God.] ③ [So God could not be God.] ① [So God is the greatest conceivable being.] ④ [Therefore, God is all-powerful.] ⑤ [God is all-knowing.] ⑥ [God is infinitely good.] ⑦ [It follows that God must exist.] Why? ① [God is the greatest conceivable being.] ⑧ [Any being that did not exist would lack the property of existence.] ⑨ [You could always think of a being greater than it by conceiving of one with the same properties, but also with the additional property of existence.] ⑩ [Hence any being that does not exist could not be God.] ⑦ [Therefore, God exists.]

The ultimate conclusion of this extended argument is ⑦, the theist's thesis that God exists. But how does the theist arrive at this conclusion?

The theist starts out by advancing ①, which seems to be a premise. However, we can see that ① is repeated below and that there ① is a conclusion, arrived at through premises ② and ③. Could that be evidence of arguing in a circle, looping back to the same proposition? Is ① being stated twice, first as a premise and then as a conclusion? If you look over the argument, the most reasonable and charitable interpretation is that ① is being used as a premise in the part of the argument that follows the second occurrence of ①. But ② and ③ are being used to back up ①. Therefore ① is functioning first as a conclusion, but then as a premise for the part of the argument that follows. But this repetition need not, it seems, be interpreted as a circular argument. There need be nothing wrong, or viciously circular, about ① being used as a conclusion and then later on repeated, and used as a premise for further argument.

While there is repetition of ①, which suggests a circle, the argument is simply a serial argument where ① is the link that joins one stage of the argument to another. The first part of the argument is the use of ② and ③ as premises to back up ① (figure 5.8).

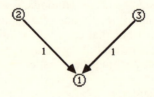

Figure 5.8

But how are ② and ③ being used as premises to support ①? The argument is as follows.

② :   If you could imagine a greater conceivable being than God,
        then this greater being would be God.
③ :   God would not be God.

Now when ③ occurs in the original argument, it is prefaced by the word
"so," indicating that ③ is a conclusion, from ② it would appear. But ③
does not follow from ②, at least not just from ② by itself. What is the
connection between ② and ③?

The proposition ② asks us to see if we could imagine a greater con-
ceivable being than God. If so, let us call this greater conceivable being
God+. But then, as the consequent of ② states, God+ would really be God.
Why? Well, God+ is a greater conceivable being than God. Well then,
why must God+ be God, so that now God would not be God, as ③ states?
Well, the best available reason would seem to reside in ①, the proposition
that God is the greatest conceivable being. For if God+ is the greater, then
God would be the lesser conceivable being. So if, according to ①, God has
to be the greatest conceivable being, then God would not be God.

In other words then, ② as a premise depends on ①. And ③ is a
conclusion from ② because ② and ① function together as premises
required to enable us to deduce ③ (figure 5.9).

Figure 5.9

But if this is the right reconstruction of the argument, there would seem to
be a problem. For remember the reconstruction of the previous part of
the argument above, which showed a convergent structure where ① is a
conclusion based on premises ② and ③. If we put these two parts of the
argument reconstruction together now, we come up with the overall structure shown in figure 5.10.

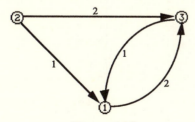

Figure 5.10

But this representation of the structure of the argument clearly reveals a circle, where ③ is used as a premise for ①, but ① is also used as a premise for ③. The diagram shows the circular dependence between ① and ③ as a dicycle.

So far as this stage of the argument has progressed in our consideration of it, ① is the conclusion; ① is repeated as the fourth sentence of the argument, indicating that it is a provisional conclusion that is supposed to have been reached at this first stage.

Premises ② and ③, taken together in a linked argument, go to support ①. The problem is that there is a directed arc going from ① to ③. So ③ is not only a required premise in the linked argument, but the only source of support given for ③ comes from ① (the conclusion to be supported). Clearly then, the circle in this part of the argument is a worrisome kind of one, an inevitable circle that could be an important indicator that the argument, even at this stage, begs the question.

But before reaching any conclusions that the argument commits the fallacy of begging the question, we should carry on with the argument reconstruction to see how the ultimate conclusion is to be reached. Then fuller evaluation of the evidence on both sides of this charge may be possible.

Now even the fact that there is a circle in the argument may suggest that there is suspicion of mischief and the argument is open to criticism. But before we criticize even this first stage of the argument as circular, we might want to retrace our steps a bit, and check to see whether we have reconstructed the line of argument in the best possible light. Does the interpretation above do justice to the original argument?

6. REEVALUATION OF THE FIRST STAGE

We observed that the conclusion ③ does seem to be based on the use of propositions ② and ① as premises. But exactly how do ② and ① work together to generate ③? Let us look back to the statements of ② and ① above. First, ① tells us that God is the greatest conceivable being. Once ① is accepted, ② follows as a consequence. Because if ① is true, then if you have two conceivable beings, God and God+, it must follow that of the two, only God+ could be God.

Figure 5.11

Hence, it follows that God would not be God, as stated by ③. So that is how ③ follows from ②, and ② follows from ①. So a better reconstruction of the argument than the previous one would seem to be that of the diagram in figure 5.11.

This reconstruction does seem more faithful to the context of the original argument. However, curiously enough, it too leads to a problem. For ① is the conclusion of the first stage of the argument when ① is repeated in the original text of the argument. In other words, the argument should more properly be reconstructed as in figure 5.12.

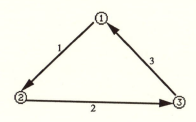

Figure 5.12

But, by this reconstruction, the argument is circular. So either way we reconstruct it, the argument is circular. Does this mean that the argument is open to the criticism of having committed the fallacy of begging the question? Or does it mean that we should reconsider whether our reconstructions of it are fair and reasonable? Certainly, before an argument is rejected as fallacious, some burden of proof should be on the critic to show that his interpretation of the argument is fair and reasonable. Let us look once again at the original text of the argument. What is the arguer really trying to prove?

Put yourself in the place of the arguer who presents the original text of the argument. What is he asking you to do, as the recipient of the argument? Clearly his first statement indicates that he is setting out to prove ① to you. But then examine ② closely; it says, "What if you could imagine a greater conceivable being than God?" But ① just told us that God is the greatest conceivable being. In other words, it follows from ① that there is no conceivable being greater than God. Is the arguer contradicting himself here? No, not at all, because the request to you to try to imagine a greater conceivable being than God is the antecedent of the conditional proposition ②. The arguer is saying, in effect, "Now, my conclusion to be proven is ①. But now imagine for the sake of argument that ① is false. Let's see what follows from this assumption. If a contradiction follows from it, then the antecedent of ② must be false. Hence my original conclusion ① must be true."

The strategy of the arguer here is what was called a *reductio ad absurdum* argument in chapter five. The basic principle behind a *reductio ad absurdum* argument is that if you can deduce a contradiction by valid argument from an assumption, then the proposition stated by the assumption must be false. Therefore, the negation (opposite) of the assumption must be true. The basic principle behind *reductio ad absurdum* proof is one we are already familiar with–if a set of propositions is collectively inconsistent, then all of the propositions in that set cannot be true.

With this in mind, the original case 5.3 can be reconstructed as follows. We want to prove ①, that God is the greatest conceivable being. We start by assuming the negation of ①. That is, we assume we can imagine a greater conceivable being than God. Let's call this assumption ②ⓐ. But ① and ②ⓐ, as joint assumptions, allow us to deduce the consequent of ②, namely ②ⓒ: this greater conceivable being (God+) would be God. This is represented in figure 5.13.

Now ②ⓒ states that God+ would be God. But that is contrary to an enthymematic premise of the argument that seems uncontroversial. We have presumed that God+ is a separate and distinct conceivable being from God. It is not like the case where Samuel Clemens and Mark Twain are the same being with two different names. If you have a greater conceivable being (God+) and a lesser conceivable being (God-), only one can be God. Why? Perhaps the further enthymematic premise is the presumption of monotheism–there can be at most one God. At any rate, whatever the further reasoning here, the proposition ③, that God would not be God, is meant by the arguer to be a contradiction.

Figure 5.13

According to this interpretation, the structure of the argument, as a valid argument, involves the following steps of reasoning. The conclusion is ①.

1.   If ②ⓐ then ②ⓒ [Premise ②; an assumption].
2.   If ②ⓒ then ③ [Enthymematic premise. Label it ④].
3.   ③ is a contradiction [Call this proposition ③ⓕ. It is also a premise].
4.   Therefore ②ⓒ is false [From 2 and 3, by *reductio ad absurdum*].
5.   Therefore ②ⓐ is false [From 1 and 4, by *modus tollens*].
6.   Therefore the negation of ②ⓐ is true [From 5, by double negation].
7.   Therefore ① is true [From 6].

In other words, the whole structure of this much of the argument can be set out as follows, in seven steps. Let us call this reconstruction the seven-step sequence.

The Seven-Step Sequence

1. If you could imagine a greater conceivable being than God, then this greater being would be God.
2. If this greater being would be God, then God would not be God.
3. But the statement "God would not be God" is a contradiction.
4. Therefore, it is false that this greater being would be God.
5. Therefore, it is false that you could imagine a greater conceivable being than God.
6. Therefore, you couldn't imagine a greater conceivable being than God.
7. Therefore, God is the greatest conceivable being.

To see the structure of this sequence of argument, label the propositions as follows. Let ④ be the proposition that ③ is false. Let ㉔ be the proposition that ㉔ is false. And let ㉒ be the proposition that the negation of ㉔ is true. Then the overall structure of these seven steps can be reconstructed according to the diagram in figure 5.14.

Reconstruction A

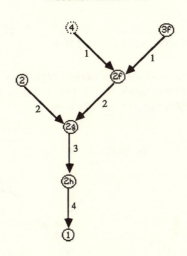

Figure 5.14

According to this reconstruction, the first stage of the argument is not circular.

This case reveals a very important lesson. Even if there appears to be a circle in an argument, a critic must look at the argument very carefully, to be sure that the method of argument reconstruction has been applied in a way that does justice to the argument.

The problem is that, at its present state of development, the method of argument reconstruction cannot be simply applied, in a literal, straight-forward, or mechanical manner, to the given text of discourse. A good deal of interpretation is involved, both of the text and context of the given argument.

In this case, the problem was one of recognizing the underlying subtlety of the argumentation tactic that revealed the real intent and thrust of the line of proof. The strategy was that of the *reductio ad absurdum* argument, a powerful kind of argument technique, but one that depends on the use of an assumption that leads, by logical reasoning, to a contradiction. It was not until this technique was made plain that it was possible to produce a reconstruction that could do justice to the argument.

Not only, then, should there be a burden of proof to show evidential priority, but a critic should also have some burden of proof to show that his argument reconstruction does justice to an argument, before he can be said to have made a good case for the contention that the argument begs the question (or is even circular). There should be a meta-argument "principle of charity" at work to leave open a presumption that a proposed argument reconstruction may not be adequate in a particular case. This consideration adds another requirement in the evidence for backing up any criticism that an argument begs the question.

7. AN ALTERNATIVE RECONSTRUCTION

Before leaving this first stage of the argument, one more possible objection to it needs to be considered. If you ask how ② could be proved, it seems natural to suggest that ② follows from ①.

Reconstruction B

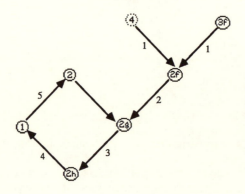

Figure 5.15

The problem is that ② seems to follow naturally from ①. And no other alternative premise or basis in argument for ② has been advanced by the text of the argument. Consequently, it may seem reasonable to add one further arrow, resulting in Reconstruction B, presented in figure 5.15.

On this reconstruction, the argument is circular. Could this be an indication of circular reasoning? If you look back at case 5.3, you see that the premise ①, which says that God is the greatest conceivable being, has been repeated in the argument. Is this an indication that it functions both as a premise and as a conclusion in the argument, as indicated by the circle in Reconstruction B?

Let us look at the circle ①, ②, ②ₐ, ②ₕ, ① in Reconstruction B. Is this circle an indication of begging the question? The reason that the circle was produced is that according to this reconstruction of the argument ② is taken as evidentially dependent on ①. To see this dependency, ask yourself the question: How could ② be proven? Remember that ② is the proposition that if you could imagine a greater conceivable being than God, then this greater being would be God. How could you prove that? Well, the most plausible presumption would seem to be that however you would go about proving it, you would have to presume that ① is true, namely that God is the greatest conceivable being. But is this prior presumption absolutely necessary? If it is, then Reconstruction B is the best analysis of the original argument structure. If not, then Reconstruction A may also be acceptable as an analysis.

The defender of the argument in case 5.3 might argue for the second interpretation of his argument as follows. Imagine in your mind two conceivable beings, a greater being God+, and a lesser being God-. Now ask yourself. Which being would be God? Suppose you answer that given a choice between the two, you would have to select God+. But why? You might answer, "Because God is greater." Now does this answer commit you to the prior proposition that God is the greatest conceivable being? You might answer, "No, not necessarily, because 'greater' does not necessarily imply 'greatest'." If that is a reasonable answer, it follows that ② is not necessarily evidentially dependent upon ① in the argument. In the absence of evidence that ② has to be dependent on ① as a premise, the presumption should be then that Reconstruction A does more justice to the argument. For while it is possible that ② could be inferred from ①, it is also quite possible that there could be other lines of argument for ② open, resting on premises that are not dependent on ①.

Indicators in the textual evidence show that ② is meant to be taken as a premise for the conclusion ①. In the text, the indicator-word "for" prefaces ②. However, there is no comparable indication that ① is meant to be taken as a premise. The presumption we should take as doing justice to the argument, therefore, is that ② is the premise for ①, and not the other way around. This means that Reconstruction A is to be preferred over Reconstruction B, according to the available evidence, interpreted in the balance of what a critic should fairly be required to prove.

Reconstruction B, then, is not without value. It expresses a direction the argument might take, or might be susceptible to. And it remains to be seen whether it would turn out to be an instance of the fallacy of begging the question. But in all fairness, it is not the only legitimate interpretation that is possible. And the available textual and contextual evidence should swing more heavily toward Interpretation A. And part of the reason for this swing is that A is less open to a potentially damaging criticism of question-begging, a factor sure to be important to the believer who is the proponent of the argument.

Hence burden of proof plays a role, even at the level of argument reconstruction itself, prior to any formal charges of *petitio principii* being made by a critic.

8.   THE COMPLETED RECONSTRUCTION

Let us go on to evaluate the next stage of the argument. The next step is that ④, ⑤, and ⑥ are divergent conclusions from ① (figure 5.16).

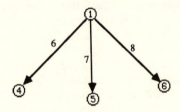

Figure 5.16

In the rest of the argument, ④, ⑤, and ⑥ are not used as premises, but ① is. To reconstruct the rest of the argument, then, we carry on from ① as in figure 5.17.

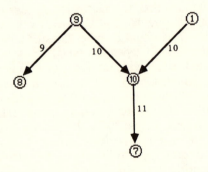

Figure 5.17

Putting the whole sequence of argumentation together by adding these last two parts to Reconstruction A yields the diagram shown in figure 5.18.

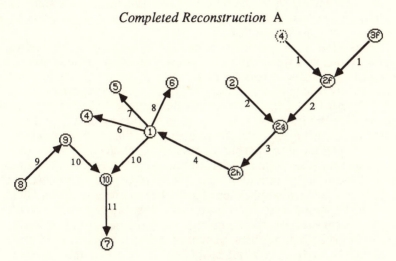

Completed Reconstruction A

Figure 5.18

This argument diagram has no circle in it. But does that mean that the original argument does not commit the fallacy of begging the question?

The answer has to be in the negative. While the reconstruction in figure 5.18 does provide a defense against certain kinds of charges that the argument begs the question–as we have seen–it does not follow that the argument can therefore be certified as free from *all* charges of begging the question that might be made.

And indeed, there still remains at least one notable charge of this kind that should be brought to the reader's attention. This is the charge, made, for example, by Rowe (1975), that even by using the term "God" as a conceivable being, as in premises ① and ②, the proponent of the argument is already defining the term "God" in such a way that what it refers to is a being or entity that could not fail to exist.

This kind of objection is a variant of the point of view that might be called the *existentialist article of faith* that you can never define a thing into existence. The idea is that you can define some term "T" as having such-and-such properties, but existence cannot be one of these properties. For the question of whether something exists cannot be determined by definition. For example, according to Rowe, to define a *magician* as an existing magician is by itself all right, as a definition. But then to infer from this that magicians exist is to beg the question, to presume what is to be proved.

A critic like Rowe is here questioning the conclusion, by claiming all the argument shows is that any being that does not exist could not be God.

In other words, it shows that if we define God as perfect, and therefore as an existing being, it follows that no non-existing being could be God. But does it follow that some actually existing being must exemplify this concept of God? The feeling of the skeptic is that the proposition that some existing thing is God can only be proven by the argument of case 5.3, if we make the prior presumption that God exists.

This kind of objection is related to the concept of the question-begging epithet as a type of fallacy. To pack an argumentative conclusion (without proper support) into the meaning or definition of a term in a premise is widely held to be a species of the fallacy of begging the question.

Whether in fact case 5.3 commits this kind of fallacy of begging the question is still hard to say. Suffice it to say here that it would tax the method of argument reconstruction beyond the limits of the rudimentary state of its present developments in the preceding chapters, if we tried to bring it to bear in any kind of decisive way on this problem of interpretation. Instead, let us turn to another charge of begging the question that has directly significant implications for the further analysis of this fallacy.

The important lesson of this section is that just because a completed argument reconstruction can be given, in a particular case, that shows no dicycle on the digraph of the argument, it does not necessarily follow that the argument is free from all suspicion or criticism that it begs the question. The method of argument reconstruction is, by itself, no final test of this. It only functions as part of the evidence in a larger evidential picture behind the issue of whether an argument commits the fallacy of begging the question. This larger picture remains to be filled in, using the argument diagram as the first stage of analysis.

9. MID-ARGUMENT CIRCLES

An interesting problem arises if we consider, for the sake of argument, what would happen if we were to complete Reconstruction B in the same way that Reconstruction A was completed above. This completion results in an interesting kind of argument, from a point of view of the general question of analyzing circular reasoning in relation to the fallacy of begging the question. We would have a situation where there is a circle in the middle part of the sequence of argumentation, but where the ultimate conclusion, or thesis to be proved, is not on that circle, or on any circle in the argument reconstruction.

This is an interesting kind of case. In fact, we have already encountered a similar situation in case 2.2, where there was a localized circle in the middle of the dialogue on tipping. But in that case, the ultimate conclusion of the whole argument was not on that circle. The problem is that even when the fuller argument is reconstructed, and the context filled in, it still may be hard to know what to conclude in relation to whether the circle is an indication that the argument should be said to beg the question.

To get a better idea of the kind of structure involved in this type of situation, take a look at figure 5.19, where an arc is drawn in from ① to ②, completing a circle. The result is the Completed Reconstruction B, differing only from Completed Reconstruction A in that the additional arc from ① to ② is drawn in.

Completed Reconstruction B

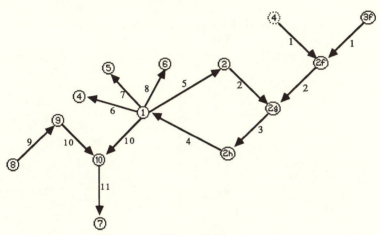

Figure 5.19

When you look over this reconstruction, the problem posed is to know what to infer from the existence of the dicycle ①, ②, ⓘ, ⓗ, ①. Is it some evidence of the argument's having committed the fallacy of begging the question?

One's first inclination may be to think that the circle is not really harmful, because you can get from the initial premises ④, ③f, and ⑧ without having to go around the circle. In fact, for practical purposes of supporting the conclusion on the basis of the premises, it would seem that you can eliminate the circle if you wish. If so, it would not seem to be a harmful circle.

Indeed, if we don't need it, why not simply knock out arc 5, with the result that you get Completed Reconstruction A, with no circle?

The phenomenon that is evident in this case is that while the circle may have appeared to be a serious failing at the first stage of argument reconstruction, looked at in a full reconstruction of the whole sequence of argumentation in which it occurs, the circle appears to be much less serious as a fallacy, or threat to the functioning of the argument as an effective tool of persuasion. The fact is that if ④, ③f, and ⑧ have high initial plausibility values for convincing the non-believer, and ⑦ has a lower initial plausibility value, then the whole argument will still be successful in raising the resultant plausibility value of ⑦, even if it contains the circle in figure 5.19. Whether you use Reconstruction A or B doesn't seem to matter at all in this regard. Both arguments are equally convincing for the purpose of a persuasion dialogue.

The general lesson here is that mid-argument circles may not be harmful, provided that the ultimate conclusion is not on the circle. The situation to watch for in this type of case is that represented by figure 5.20.

MID-ARGUMENT CIRCLE

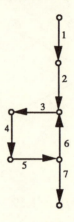

Figure 5.20

In the type of case represented in figure 5.20, part of the argument that produces the circle can be retracted, and the resulting (non-circular) argument can perform the same effective function in the dialogue. In this case, arc 6 can be eliminated, and the resulting argument is linear. In this type of case, the circle appears serious at the local level, but can be seen to be not serious at the global level, where it can even be eliminated.

But the problem is that this elimination may not always be trivial. Consider Completed Reconstruction B once again where ② is linked together with ②₈, and is therefore needed to support ①, and in turn ⑦. If we knocked out ②, then ②f would not be useful as a premise, and therefore the whole argument to ⑦ could fail to meet its ultimate purpose. So then the question is whether ② can stand on its own, without the support of ①. On the diagram for Completed Reconstruction B, ② is the only premise given to support ①. So perhaps you can't just knock out arc 5 between ① and ②.

Much then depends on the weight of presumption that premise ② can carry. If ②, in itself, has a high enough plausibility value to allow the other premises to function together with ② and meet the burden of proof required to prove ⑦, then arc 5 can be removed without unduly weakening the argument. But otherwise, the removal of arc 5 could constitute a significant weakening of the argument as a whole.

Thus the seriousness of a mid-argument dicycle, in relation to a criticism that the argument begs the question, may depend directly on the initial plausibility values of the premises. This subtlety shows once again the vital importance of looking at a localized circle in light of the fuller context of argument of which it is a part.

Case 5.3 turned out to be a subtle and complex argument, testing the method of argument reconstruction in unexpected ways. This method requires a good deal of creative interpretation and skills of sensitivity to the context in its application to any philosophical argument that occurs in the context of a serious controversy.

10. CONCLUSIONS

When is an argument reconstruction complete? That is the big question. In the Descartes case, the text of dialogue was a brief critical question by Arnauld matched with a reply given by Descartes. By its nature, however, such a case tends to lead to textual controversies, and in fact there is a large and growing literature on the controversy of the Cartesian circle. Several interesting interpretations of Descartes' reply to Arnauld's objection are proposed and evaluated by Williams (1978, p. 190). Williams uses textual evidence from Descartes' other writings–particularly the *Regulae*–as a basis for interpreting Descartes' reply. Other papers studying the problem are to be found in the collection of Doney (1987). The project of these scholarly papers is to look at Descartes' reply in the context of his philosophical writings as a whole body of work.

One can see the inevitability of placing Descartes' reply in this larger context of his philosophical position as a whole when, in the sentence just prior to the reply quoted, Descartes himself cited the previous text of his reply to a prior set of objections: "I have already given an adequate explanation of this point in my reply to the Second Objections, under the headings *Thirdly* and *Fourthly*, where I made a distinction between what we in fact perceive clearly and what we remember having perceived clearly on a previous occasion" *(Fourth Set of Replies,* 246). This extension of the context to take into account the whole body of Descartes' philosophical writings is perfectly natural and proper in the history of philosophy as a discipline in its own right. Descartes' reply, as an expression of his philosophical position, should be judged in relation to his body of work as a whole corpus.

But, at the same time, such an expansion of context poses a severe practical problem for the job of evaluating, from a point of view of informal logic, whether Descartes' argument of the *Meditations* commits the fallacy of *petitio principii* or not. The best we have been able to conclude, using the method of argument reconstruction, is that Descartes does have the basis of a point for replying to Arnauld's objection that his argument is that he cannot avoid reasoning in a circle. Whether Arnauld could come back with further support of his objection, or whether Descartes' reply can be deepened or confirmed by his larger viewpoint as a whole, remains unanswered.

Case 5.3 seems to be on a better footing in this regard, because it has been explicitly limited to a fixed text of argument. It is not identified with St. Anselm's version of the ontological argument, Descartes' version, or any other version that can be tied in to a known or documented philosophical corpus of writings. Otherwise, it might become much more open to extended textual disputation, like the case of the Cartesian circle.

Even so, case 5.3 exhibited a kind of expansion of complexity of interest in its own right. First there was Reconstruction A, and then the more complex and subtle Reconstruction B arose from the same initial argument. In principle, we appear to have no way of ruling out an even more subtle Interpretation C, and so forth. When an argument reconstruction can be declared *complete* or *fully adequate* remains an open question.

Since this chapter has shown that an argument reconstruction cannot be declared complete, by the methods available so far, the judgment of the criticism of begging the question is best treated as a matter of burden of proof. It helps a lot if, when such a charge is made, both the text and the context of the argument can be reasonably fixed or limited so they do not run out of control, in relation to the intended scope of the evaluation. But even given firm control in this regard, there are inherent reasons why some arguments cannot be given a complete and binding analysis by the method of argument reconstruction.

Hence the judgment of whether an argument commits the fallacy of begging the question is subject to the limitations of the method of argument reconstruction. This method works most easily in the simpler types of cases, studied in chapter four, where the argument is not too intimately involved with scientific or technical reasoning in a specialized domain of knowledge, or hardnosed philosophical argumentation on a highly contentious passage attributed to an author of a body of philosophical works. The method is still useful in these more difficult cases, but the conclusion it results in should not be expected to be a definitive and final ruling that a fallacy of *petitio* has, or has not, been committed.

Instead, in these contexts, the charge of *petitio* functions more like a procedural objection in the dialogue, a critical questioning of a point in the argument that is open to challenge.

NOTES

1. Bates (1983).
2. See Hoffman (1979).
3. Walton (1987a, chapter 7).

4. See chapter one, section five *supra*.

5. This case is also discussed in Walton (1985b) and Walton (1987a, p. 305).

6. See Williams (1978, chapter two).

7. Ibid.

8. Descartes, 1984.

9. Ibid., p. 171.

10. A similar case study is discussed in Walton (1984, chapter four, section eight), but the argument is not identified with that of Descartes.

6

Fallacies, Faults, Blunders, and Errors

In chapter eight a theory of the fallacy of begging the question will be set out. Before undertaking that task, however, it is necessary to come to a general understanding of the concept of a fallacy. This will be the function of chapter six. In this chapter, systematic care will be taken to distinguish between fallacies and other kinds of faults, blunders, and errors of argumentation that are often confused with fallacies.

In this chapter, a pragmatic definition of the concept of fallacy will be proposed. Van Eemeren and Grootendorst (1984), (1987), and (1989) define a fallacy as a violation of a code of conduct for rational discussants. The same kind of definition of a fallacy as a violation of a game of dialogue was also put forward in Walton (1984), except that fallacies are analyzed as strategic sequences of moves in a game dialogue where one participant tries to get the best of the other. However, here it will be proposed that we must go even beyond this way of defining fallacy in order to see how each fallacy functions specifically as a way of getting the best of an opponent in argumentative dialogue.[1] Accordingly, we will distinguish two types of fallacy, the sophistical tactic type and the error of reasoning type. The sophistical tactic type of fallacy will be defined as a deceptive tactic used by a participant in argumentative dialogue to block or frustrate the legitimate goals of the dialogue by breaking or subverting the rules. The error of reasoning type of fallacy, by contrast, involves no essential reference to a context of dialogue. It will be shown in chapter seven why begging the question is a sophistical tactic type of fallacy.

To apply these definitions to circular reasoning and begging the question, and prepare the way for the theory of begging the question in chapter eight, we must come to see how this fallacy essentially involves a different argumentation tactic than that of the fallacy of many questions. These two fallacies are often confused.[2] At the same time, understanding begging the question as a fallacy will help us to distinguish it from other errors, tactics, and phenomena of argumentation that are often confused with begging the question.

1. THE NATURE OF FALLACY

As Hamblin (1970, p. 12) noted, almost every account since Aristotle tells us that a fallacy is an argument that seems to be valid, but is not. But some cases cited as fallacies, such as *ad baculum* fallacies and other appeals to emotion, are not arguments. They are speech acts used in argumentation, often to distract a respondent from the real issue. They are tricks or tactics used in arguments, but may not actually themselves be arguments, instead being imperatives, threats, or other speech acts.[3]

Even where a fallacy is an argument, it does not have to be one that seems valid to the person to whom it was directed, or to any particular person. Its intended recipient may not be fooled by it at all. It may not seem valid to him, but it may be a fallacy nonetheless. It may be a fallacy if it is the kind of argumentation tactic that could be used to contribute to some legitimate goal of an argumentative discussion, but is not so used in the context of discussion in which it is advanced.

But there is another reason why it is not right to characterize a fallacy as an argument that seems valid, but is not. The fallacy of begging the question is a case in point. A circular argument, like "Snow is white, therefore snow is white," may be an instance of the fallacy of begging the question, even though it is a valid argument.[4] Such an argument may be deductively valid, yet be a fallacy because it is useless to persuade anyone rationally to accept its conclusion (assuming he doesn't accept that conclusion) on the basis of premises he does accept.

What kind of faults or failures then are fallacies, if they are not simply or exclusively arguments that fail to be semantically valid? The standard treatment of fallacies does not give enough context of dialogue in the short, one-line examples that have traditionally been cited. Hence the textbook explanations of why such examples are fallacies have been inadequate. Many of the so-called fallacies, on closer inspection, turn out to be instances of argumentation that are defeasible, or opinion-based cases of presumptive reasoning, but inherently reasonable. Other cases are weak or incomplete arguments that are open to criticism, but are not so bad that they merit the term "fallacious," implying, as it does, a serious and systematic error that makes an argument subject to strong refutation.[5] In any event, the problem with the examples given is that they leave too much room open for interpretation and controversy about what the argument is supposed to be.

When you begin to take a serious look at the examples offered of these so-called fallacies, it becomes apparent that the failures are typically not those of deductive validity. The faults evidently intended to be criticized may be failure to state or stick to an issue in argumentation; failure to document sources of expert opinions cited; failure to ask reasonable and appropriate questions in a discussion; use of emotional appeal to avoid argument, or to try to close off argument prematurely; prejudicial use of unclear terms that may be vague or ambiguous, and so forth.[6] Whatever rules of reasoned argumentation these failures violate, they rarely appear to be rules of deductive validity.   In fact, they most often appear to be violations of rules of reasonable dialogue appropriate to a given social context of argumentative discussion.[7]

Accordingly, van Eemeren and Grootendorst have proposed the following definition of *fallacy* (1984, p. 189): "[a]ny violation of any of the rules of the code of conduct for rational discussants (by whichever party at whichever stage of the discussion) is a fallacy." This definition is a pragmatic conception of fallacy, meaning that a fallacy is conceived of as a violation of a normative rule of dialogue that applies to a context of argumentative discussion that is understood by the participants, and by the critic who proposes to cite one of their arguments as fallacious. Note also that, by this definition, a fallacy does not have to be a fallacious argument.

So a critic's job in advancing the contention that someone's argument is fallacious involves the analysis and interpretation of this person's argument as it was stated in a particular case. This means considering the individual text and context of the arguments on their own merits. Although formal structures are involved, to be sure, the job is more one of practical, or informal, logic in evaluating each case on its individual merits.[8]   To build methods useful for the proper tasks of practical logic, we need to go back to the Aristotelian framework of argument as a sequence of orderly exchanges between two participants in regulated dialogue.[9]

Defining a fallacy as a violation of a rule of reasonable dialogue was the first big step in making serious research on the fallacies possible. But in order to analyze a fallacy like begging the question, it is necessary to go beyond this step. The reason is that a fallacy is not just a violation of a rule of reasonable dialogue. Such violations can be blunders, or other sorts of errors, that are not necessarily such bad or serious errors that we can properly call them fallacies.

It is quite a serious criticism to allege that someone in an argument has committed a fallacy, or that his argument is fallacious. In English, this form of speech is a serious kind of censure that borders on the impolite. It suggests that the arguer criticized has based his argument on some serious, vitiating, underlying, systematic confusion or error. It may even be suggested that this person is ignorant of scientific knowledge, or of enlightened, logical forms of reasoning. This is an extremely strong criticism to advance. It is much more usual, and in most cases more appropriate, to criticize someone else's argument by raising questions about whether the argument may be incomplete, or may be based on assumptions that have not been well enough supported to sustain their conclusion. To say that somebody has committed a fallacy, by contrast, implies that the person so criticized must attack the charge with considerable vigor if he is to retain credibility as a serious advocate.

In many cases, then, it is more appropriate to speak of arguments that are flawed, weak, inadequately supported, or that suffer from specific shortcomings that can be corrected in subsequent dialogue. These arguments may violate rules of reasonable dialogue, or at least not live up to these rules adequately, without being badly enough off to merit the term "fallacies."

A move, or sequence of moves, in an argumentative discussion may rightly be identified as a fallacy if it breaks some rule of dialogue to the advantage of its proponent, evidently as part of a larger strategy to get the best of the opponent (unfairly). However, if such a rule violation is not to the advantage of the proponent, or is even to his disadvantage in mounting a strong case for his conclusion, we rightly perceive the move as more of an error of reasoning type of fallacy, or even a blunder that is not a fallacy.

For example, an obviously circular argument may be a harmless blunder, rather than a fallacious case of begging the question, if it is not advanced by its proponent as a way of persuading his opponent to accept the conclusion on the basis of premises the opponent is supposed to accept. The proponent may even say with embarrassment, once he sees the circle in his reasoning, "Sorry, I appear to be going in circles here. Obviously this is not proving anything. Let me start again." Of course, such a blunder can be serious. But it might not exhibit enough of a systematic strategy of deception, as an attempt to persuade another party of a conclusion, to justify calling it a "fallacy." It could be a flawed argument without being fallacious. Or if it is a fallacy, it could be an error of reasoning on the part of the proponent, as opposed to a sophistical tactic used to try to get the best of the opponent in dialogue.

What then is a fallacy, over and above being a violation of a rule of reasonable dialogue? Some would say that it must involve an intent to deceive. But this psychological requirement is at once too strong and also inappropriate, even though it goes in the right direction.

2. FALLACIES AND ARGUMENTATION TACTICS

A fallacy is more than a faulty argument. Originally, the term meant a deceptive tactic, or trick of argumentation, used by one person in an argument to try to get the best of another. According to the *Latin Dictionary* of Lewis and Short (1969, p. 721), the Latin word *fallacia* (from which the English word "fallacy" comes) means "deceit, trick, artifice, stratagem, craft, or intrigue." The Latin word *fallacia,* in turn, comes from the Greek word *sphal,* meaning "cause to fall." This word was used by Homer to describe wrestling contests. But it can also be used in classical Greek in a more abstract sense referring to verbal tactics used to defeat an opponent in argumentation, that is, to cause someone to fall by argument.

This idea of verbal trickery in contestive argumentation was a familiar idea to the Greeks. Aristotle, in the *De Sophisticis Elenchis* (171 b 22), compares contentious reasoning to unfair fighting in an athletic contest. Both contestants, according to Aristotle, can be bent on victory at all costs, and may therefore fight unfairly. This conception of fallacy as an unfair verbal tactic of defeat in contestive argumentation is consistent with Aristotle's treatment of sophistical refutations in the *De Sophisticis Elenchis.* Aristotle treats the negative use of argumentation tactics as fallacies or sophistical refutations used to get the best of an opponent in eristic discussion. Yet he also indicates how such tactics and refutations represent kinds of moves that can play a positive role in constructive dialectic, or dialogue reasoning used constructively to resolve a disputed case or throw light on a disputed issue.

Although Aristotle's discipline of dialectic has fallen into obscurity and disuse in the modern era, it is well worth rescuing as a methodology underlying the humanities as a serious area of systematic research. Making this step, however, involves a reevaluation of the concept of reasoning, allowing for the existence of interactive reasoning, or reasoning together by two parties to a discussion.

As the term "fallacy" has evolved through the history of logic, it has always had two meanings. During some periods one meaning has been dominant, while at other periods the other meaning has dominated.

One meaning of fallacy is an *error of reasoning,* referring to the failure of a conclusion to be inferred correctly from a set of premises by the appropriate rules of inference or standards of good reasoning. The other meaning of fallacy is a *sophistical tactic,* referring to the use of a trick or deceit used in argument by one party in a dialogue unfairly to get the best of, or defeat the other party. The error of reasoning type of fallacy is a species of monolectical fault–it is a kind of error made by a solitary reasoner who draws a wrong inference. The sophistical tactic type of fallacy is a dialectical fault–it requires an interactive exchange where one participant leads the other participant to draw a wrong conclusion in order to take advantage of this error to gain a victory in the exchange.

As Hamblin (1970, p. 50) notes, Aristotle makes it clear early in the *De Sophisticis Elenchis* (165 a 19) that he is writing about deliberate sophistry, and not just about errors or mistakes–the professional sophists are described by Aristotle as those who make money from an apparent but unreal wisdom through studying and exploiting the types of arguments in which sophistical tactics can be used. Aristotle's approach to fallacies makes it clear that he depends heavily, even centrally, on the concept of fallacy, or "sophistical refutation" as the use of sophistical tactics in dialogue argumentation.

In modern times, especially since the rise of mathematical logic, the concept of fallacy as error of reasoning has become dominant. The *Oxford English Dictionary* (1970, vol. 4, p. 45) lists as the current technical meaning of "fallacy" in logic: "In Logic, *esp.* a flaw, material or formal, which vitiates a syllogism." The OED adds, however, that according to a different concept of "fallacy" used in Wilson's *Logic* (1552), deceit was included as part of the concept. However, the tendency in modern times has been to expunge this "deceit" idea by portraying a fallacy as an invalid argument, that is, an error that is wrong because of a failure to meet a standard of formal validity. This approach makes a fallacy a semantic error–a failure of a set of propositions to meet a standard of validity. However, to concede a little beyond formal validity, the psychological idea that a fallacy is an argument that seems valid is often added.

The German language has two separate words to refer to the kinds of failures covered by the English word "fallacy." According to *Harrap's Standard German and English Dictionary* (Jones, 1967, p. 25), a *Fehlschlusz* is an incorrect, wrong conclusion or a "wrong inference." Outside logic, fehlschlusz means "bad shot," but within logic, it refers to an incorrect or bad argument where no intentional deceit by a second party is necessarily involved.

According to *Duden* (1981, p. 2637), *Trugschlusz* is used in logic to refer to the use of deceit *(Täuschung)* or trickery *(Überlistung)* by one partner in dialogue *(Gesprächpartner)* to make the other draw the wrong conclusion. The aspect of intentional deceit involved in a trugschlusz is made explicit in the *Brockhaus* entry (1974, p. 49), where the word intentional *(absichtlich)* deceit is used. According to this entry a trugschlusz is a type of fehlschlusz where the wrong conclusion is made to be drawn by one partner in dialogue, through the use of trickery or deceit.

In adapting the term "fallacy" to the needs of argumentation theory, it is useful to preserve the notion that there are two types of fallacies. But it is important to avoid extremes in defining these two types. The first thing we need to avoid is accepting the idea that committing a sophistical tactic type of fallacy requires intentional deceit on the part of the perpetrator. This approach entails a psychologistic requirement that you have to show, in a given case, that the proponent of an argument had an intent to deceive, in order to show that his argument is fallacious.

In emphasizing that a commitment is not necessarily a belief of a participant in dialogue, Hamblin (1970, p. 264) warned against this form of psychologism. According to Hamblin, it should be what you say rather than what you believe that defines your commitments in a dialogue. Hence the evidence concerning a charge of fallacy should be looked for in the text of discourse of an exchange in dialogue, not in the motives or intentions of the arguer.

Van Eemeren and Grootendorst confirmed the wisdom of Hamblin's approach to the concept of fallacy when they warned (1984, p. 6) that it is necessary to guard against the "internalization" of the subject of critical argumentation by avoiding "psychologizing." A key feature stressed by their approach is *externalization,* the concentration on the expressed opinions of a participant in a discussion, and on the statements made by that participant in the discussion, as opposed to the "thoughts, ideas and motives which may underlie them." In the spirit of Hamblin's theory, the approach of van Eemeren and Grootendorst also points away from thinking of a fallacy as an intentional deceit. A finding of a deceitful motive on the part of a perpetrator should not be regarded as an essential part of the concept of fallacy.

Thus the trugschlusz notion of fallacy as an intentional deception is too extreme to be valuable, as it stands, for fallacy theory. Fallacies are tricky because they are based on the use of argumentation tactics that are powerful and effective means of carrying out goals of dialogue when two people argue together. Such tactics can be used correctly as ways of implementing argument strategies. A fallacious case occurs where an arguer *misuses* one of these tactics unfairly to try to get the best of his opponent in a way that blocks or hinders the legitimate goals of dialogue.

However, it does not follow that every instance of a fallacy is based on the perpetrator's intent to deceive his opponent in that particular case. It is enough that the arguer has used this tactic in a way that goes against the goals of dialogue, as the textual evidence of the moves made in the sequence of dialogue show. The critic who claims that this arguer committed a fallacy has a burden of proof to show that he used an argumentation tactic in a way that goes contrary to the goals of the dialogue. Such a finding should not necessarily require, however, the determination that the arguer had some particular intention or guilty motive to deceive by trickery.

A similar point needs to be made about the error of reasoning type of fallacy. An error of reasoning is not just any invalid or incorrect inference, but one that is tricky because it tends to seem reasonable to the uncritical evaluator. It does not follow, however, that a fallacious argument of this sort *must* seem valid to the particular audience or respondent to whom it was actually addressed. This psychologistic notion of seeming validity is a severe obstacle to the mature development of fallacy theory as a pragmatic logic for the normative evaluation of conversational discourse.

The difference between the two types of fallacy is that error of reasoning is primarily a matter of whether some propositions follow from others in a chain of reasoning, whereas the sophistical tactic type of fallacy requires essential reference to a normative model of dialogue. The distinction is fundamental but subtle. The evaluator of fallacies must resist the temptation to identify the sophistical tactic type of fallacy with the intentional sophism (trugschlusz), requiring the existence of a motive to deceive by the proponent. The evaluator must also resist the temptation to equate the error of reasoning type of fallacy with the argument that seems valid to the respondent, but is not.

The sophistical tactic category of fallacy includes the *ad verecundiam, ad hominem, ad ignorantiam,* many questions, *ad baculum, ad populum, ad misericordiam,* and slippery slope fallacies. It notably includes all the *"ad"* fallacies. It also includes equivocation. The error of reasoning type of fallacy includes deductive fallacies, like affirming the consequent, and inductive fallacies, like biased and insufficient statistics. It also includes *post hoc* and causal fallacies, and fallacies like *secundum quid* that have to do with presumptive reasoning. Analysis of all of these fallacies involves essential reference to the use of argumentation tactics in dialogue.

In games of persuasion dialogue, there is a contestive or adversarial element, because each player is trying to use his strongest, or most effective, arguments to persuade the other party. The problem of strategy is posed in such games because neither player will commit to any propositions he thinks will directly imply the thesis of the other player. Making such a commitment, in effect, means losing the game to the opposing side. Therefore, each player must devise strategies to gain premises in a piecemeal fashion, then put these premises to use at some later point in the discussion, where the dialogue will (he hopes) come to a close in favor of his own side of the disputed issue.

How such strategies of logical persuasion work were illustrated in the formal dialogue game CB of Walton (1984, pp. 131-37). A formal game of persuasion dialogue like CB has four kinds of procedural rules–locution rules, commitment rules, dialogue rules, and win-loss rules. It was also shown in Walton (p. 152) how strategies can be used by a player to achieve his objective of winning a round of play fairly, according to the win-loss rules. Strategies involve the co-ordination of longer sequences of argumentation so that a proponent can see where his argument is leading, without his opponent's being able to foresee or control the direction the line of argument will take.

The basic problem for the proponent of an argument in persuasion dialogue is to get his opponent to make enough of the right kinds of concessions to be used as premises by the proponent in his attempts to prove his thesis. This involves utilizing premises that one's opponent is explicitly and clearly committed to, as part of his known position on the issue. The more sophisticated games of persuasion dialogue also involve a player's *dark-side commitments*–these are propositions that a player is committed to, but he does not–at any rate, not clearly or explicitly–realize that his position commits him to them. The formal games ABV and CBV in Walton (1987a, pp. 125-31) utilize dark-side commitment sets. These games have a *dark-side rule* to the effect that if a player replies "No commitment" to a query, but he is really committed to the proposition queried, then this proposition is inserted explicitly into his set of commitments (his light-side commitment set) anyway. The presumption is that any arguer's commitments can be divided into two sets–the light-side set of commitments that he is aware of being explicitly committed to, and the dark-side set that he is not clearly aware of.

The concept of the dark-side commitment set is based on the Socratic idea of the maieutic function of reasoned dialogue whereby the elenchtic questioner can assist–like a midwife–in the birth of new self-knowledge of one's deeper commitments on an issue. The function is also well represented by Plato's myth of the cave–the function of elenchtic dialogue is to make a dark or murky commitment become clearer and better articulated.

Reasoned dialogue need not be totally eristic or adversarial, according to this conception. But the adversarial aspect of it can have a positive result. By being forced to articulate and clarify his own deeply held but unclear and vague convictions, through the test of argument, a participant in dialogue can gain insight into his own position at a deeper level.

What are argumentation tactics, in this framework? Tactical rules are different from strategic rules. Tactical rules are more localized. They are suited to particular situations of common types that arise in junctures of play during various points in the sequence of a game of dialogue. Tactical rules are like coaching strategies that can be used to train a student in the art of reasoned discourse to react effectively to types of moves that will be made by an opponent in argumentation. Tactical rules are heuristic tips or pieces of advice that can help the less experienced arguer to attack his opponent's views or defend his own views more effectively during a critical juncture in an argumentative discussion. Unlike win-loss rules, tactical rules don't define what constitutes a winning or losing sequence of argumentation in a context of dialogue. Instead, their function is to help you to achieve a winning argument in tricky situations where you could easily lose to your opponent's last move. Attacking tactics tell you how to attack the other person's arguments. Defending tactics tell you how to defend your own arguments in the face of criticisms.

Argumentation tactics can have a constructive function of supporting the maieutic aspect of persuasion dialogue, but they can also go wrong, or be wrongly used in a discussion where they are deployed in an all-out attempt to win, even by violating or subverting the dialogue rules. Correspondingly, this duality also applies to the kinds of argumentation identified with the traditional informal fallacies.

In Walton (1985a), it is shown, for example, how the *argumentum ad hominem* has this dual nature. Properly used, it can be an effective tactic for shifting a burden of proof in a persuasion dialogue by questioning an arguer's personal commitment to his position, as expressed by his previous concessions, actions, and personal circumstances. Such a tactic is often misused, however, as a powerful weapon of attack in the sophist's arsenal when a persuasion dialogue begins to degenerate into a personal quarrel (eristic dialogue).

The first tactical rule is always to be sure that the kind of argumentation tactic you propose to use is appropriate for the context of dialogue. In the case of the *argumentum ad hominem,* for example, this may mean asking whether questions of character, like personal integrity or veracity, are relevant to the issue of a dialogue. For example, in a political debate such questions may be highly relevant, whereas in the context of a scientific investigation they may be completely irrelevant.

In relation to circular argumentation, and the fallacy of begging the question, the first tactical rule is also very important in judging whether a particular argument is fallacious or not. In a scientific inquiry, with its cumulative direction toward the increment of established knowledge in an area of investigation, circular argumentation could be intolerable, in any form. By contrast, the same pattern of circular argumentation might be less offensive (because it is not so clearly inappropriate) in a persuasion dialogue. In an explanation, particularly where feedback relationships among the entities in the subject matter of the discussion are involved, a circular sequence of argumentation might be quite acceptable and revealing–not a fallacy of begging the question, in this context, or even a faulty kind of argumentation.

Generally then, a fallacy is a violation of a rule of reasonable dialogue. But beyond that, in order to study the documentation of allegations that a fallacy has occurred in a particular case, and to see more deeply how the fallacies function as deceptive and dangerous subversions of reasonable dialogue, we need to define fallacies like begging the question as deceptive and unfair argumentation tactics deployed in a context of dialogue. This reevaluation involves a conceptual shift from a semantic to a pragmatic view of fallacies, or at least a much greater willingness to take pragmatic factors into account. It is a question of how the argument is used in a context of dialogue.

3. FALLACIES AND POINTS OF ORDER

What then is the characteristic argumentation tactic of begging the question that makes it a fallacy? This is a good question–it is a question that will not be fully answered until chapter eight, but the case studies of chapters four and five have already pointed toward an answer. Evidently the fallacy of begging the question relates to a requirement of evidential priority in a context of dialogue. The fallacy seems to reside in the attempt to *make it seem* that a burden of proof has been fulfilled, when in reality it has not been.

But clearly this is not the whole story. Lots of arguments are weak and inadequate, where the proponent aggressively pushes forward his argument to make it seem as though it really meets its burden of proof, when it does not. Lots of arguments of this sort, however, do not commit the fallacy of begging the question, even though they may suffer from various faults, or even commit other kinds of fallacies. The job evidently remains, then, of distinguishing *petitio principii* from these other failings of argumentation, by identifying the particular tactic that is characteristic of *petitio*.

A second problem is posed by the evident fact, which came out of chapters four and five as well, that circular reasoning is not always a fallacy. Consider a case where there is a circle in an argument, and there is a requirement of evidential priority in the context of dialogue, which has not been fulfilled by the argument. Suppose the persuasion dialogue is still under way, and that neither participant has yet succeeded in fulfilling his burden of proof in the argument. The problem is that if the circle is not an inevitable one, then there could still potentially be a line of support open to the offending premise. The proponent could still have a chance of supporting all the premises of his argument that would be required in order to meet his burden of proof successfully, and convince his opponent.

In this type of case, it would be premature to convict the proponent of having committed the fallacy of begging the question. He may have more to say in the dialogue. And, as a result, his argument may come to be vindicated as a successful and useful argument that has fulfilled its function in the dialogue.[10]   In such a case, therefore, it would be incorrect to classify the argument as an instance of the fallacy of begging the question. It cannot be a useful and effective argument that fulfills its goal in the persuasion dialogue, and at the same time be an argument that commits the fallacy of begging the question.

In this type of case, the most serious criticism that the opponent may fairly advance, at the mid point where the issue of the argument is still open to contention, is to say to the proponent: "Your argument is open to a charge of begging the question, unless you can reply by showing how the way is open, and shows promise of leading toward fulfillment of your burden of proof."   The most the critic can say here, then, is to challenge with a point of order, asking the proponent of the potentially question-begging argument to get on with the job of working toward meeting his burden of proof in the argument.[11]

A *point of order* is a kind of midstream objection during the course of an incomplete dialogue where the party can question the other party concerning the possible infringement of some procedural rule of the dialogue, or can question the other party on the direction his line of argument is taking.   One point of order of this second type is the charge made that a line of argument is not relevant.   Another charge of this type is that of the possibility of question-begging in an argument that is circular.

In this connection, it is important to make a distinction between two kinds of charges, on grounds of order of severity.   The charge that an argument commits a *fallacy* is a strong or very severe type of charge, meaning that the argument contains an underlying systematic or structural error which, once revealed, means the argument is refuted.[12]   This conception of fallacy has its roots in the Aristotelian concept of the *sophistical refutation,* a systematic tactic of deception which is deeply incorrect and erroneous.   A fallacious argument, by these standards, is one that ought always to be rejected, once it is revealed as fallacious.

By contrast, to challenge an argument with a point of order does not necessarily require complete abandonment or rejection of the argument *per se*.   It only means that the argument shows signs of going wrong, or of not being happily constructed–in accord with the rules and goals of the dialogue–and therefore the argument must either be corrected (reformulated) or abandoned.

More subtly speaking, there is a distinction to be appealed to here, between strong refutation and weak refutation of the argument.   To say that an argument is *strongly refuted* is to say that the argument is incorrect or erroneous, and therefore cannot fulfill its burden of proof, and must be wholly rejected.   To say that an argument is *weakly refuted* is to say that there is a legitimate question about the acceptability or correctness of the argument as it stands, and to say therefore that the argument cannot be accepted (in the absence of additional evidence or reformulations).[13]   This is an important distinction, and indeed the confusion between strong and weak refutation is itself the basis of an informal fallacy, namely the *argumentum ad ignorantiam* described in chapter two, section eight, and Walton (1989a, pp. 43-48). The fallacy here is the uncritical use of the argument from the premise that a proposition is weakly refuted to the conclusion that this same proposition is strongly refuted.

So a point of order is characteristically an instance of weak refutation of an argument, whereas claiming that an argument is fallacious is a strong refutation.

It should be concluded then that an argument that is still potentially open to continuation in a context of persuasion dialogue should not be accused of committing the fallacy of begging the question, unless there is evidence that the circle in the argument is an inevitable circle. In other words, the third component of inevitability should, like the other two components, properly be regarded as a necessary requirement of the success of a criticism that an argument commits the fallacy of begging the question. The reason for making this generalization subject to some qualification, however, concerns the kind of case where a weak refutation of an argument is advanced in the form of a point of order to the effect that the argument is open to the potential of leading toward begging the question, unless the proponent can reply by showing that the way is open towards his ultimate fulfillment of the burden of proof. In this kind of case, however, it would be misleading and incorrect to say that the argument in question commits a fallacy, or has been shown to have committed a fallacy.

What this means is that begging the question is a more complex kind of criticism of argumentation than has been recognized by the textbooks, where it is treated as a fallacy. Sometimes it is not a fallacy but a weaker kind of criticism–a point of order.

Two other important consequences of this more subtle appreciation of begging the question as a kind of criticism are the following. First, there should be a burden of proof on a critic who brings forward a criticism that someone's argument begs the question. The critic should have to present appropriate textual and contextual evidence to back up this claim. But second, the nature of this burden should very much depend on whether the criticism of begging the question was a point of order or an allegation of fallaciousness.

A point of order is a challenge that questions whether an opponent's argument begs the question. If this challenge is based on good evidence of a circle in the opponent's argument, it successfully shifts the burden of proof onto the opponent to reply to the charge. However, if the opponent's argument is claimed to commit the fallacy of begging the question, that is a much stronger charge. It is a strong claim that needs solid evidence to back it up. Hence, in order to be successful in its objective of shifting the burden onto the opponent's side, this strong charge itself incurs a burden of proof. Not only must the claimant show that his opponent's argument is circular, he must show that in the given context of dialogue, circular argumentation is fallacious. To meet this burden, he should have to present adequate evidence from the text and context of his opponent's argument.

To show satisfactorily that an opponent's argument commits the fallacy of begging the question, a critic should have to show clearly why, in the particular case at issue, his opponent's argumentation tactics fall clearly into the category of sophistical tactics characteristic of *petitio principii* as a fallacy. But this is a bigger job than the textbooks typically make it out to be, as we will see in chapter seven. Not only is it too easy to promote cases begging the question illicitly from the category of point of order to the category of fallacy, even worse, it is common to confuse many other kinds of points of order in argumentation with that of begging the question.

This kind of problem in the textbooks was already noted in chapter one, section eight, where texts cite the use of loaded expressions like "screwball radical" and "cowardly pacifist" as question-begging. However, as noted, there is no serious attempt to show why the use of these terms constitutes illicit or fallacious deployment of circular argumentation. Instead, the main objection seems to be the complex nature of the expression itself. It seems that the texts are "running wild" in labelling all kinds of faults of arguments as instances of the fallacy of begging the question. This problem of restraining and revising the textbooks is taken up in chapter seven.

4. TEN FAULTS OFTEN CONFUSED WITH BEGGING THE QUESTION

As noted in chapter one (sections two and nine), there is an unfortunate tendency, which often prevails, to stretch the criticism of "begging the question" so thin that this label comes to refer to virtually any argument that appears objectionable. One aspect of this is the tendency to attack an opponent's use of terminology, if that terminology seems to go against one's own side of an issue, by declaring that the use of such terminology "begs the question" or commits the fallacy of "question-begging epithet." Too often, no evidence that the offending argument is circular is either offered or expected. Often, in such cases, the objection is not to the supposed circularity of the argument at all, but merely to the aggressiveness of the argument, or to the failure of its proponent to give adequate support for it.

Consider the following case, where an objection of this sort has been advanced, evidently with justification.

Case 6.0:   A psychologist, commenting on the case in which parents encourage their little girl to play with dolls and their little boy to play with a model construction set, describes the parents' behavior as "gender-prejudiced." He concludes that the parents should try harder to make their behavior gender-neutral. The parents object to this term being applied to them because they say that

> they feel there are genuine and important differences
> between boys and girls and, according to their view,
> respecting these differences may be justifiable rather
> than "prejudiced" behavior (Walton, 1989a, p. 244).

In this case, the parents object because the psychologist's use of the loaded term "gender-prejudiced" unfairly occupies the high moral ground, making their own point of view appear illegitimate and unreasonable. They do not see their behavior as "prejudiced." It seems to them that such a term would be reasonably applicable only if it were shown that their behavior was wrong. And evidently, they do not feel that this has been shown, to their satisfaction, by the psychologist.

Of course, there is an *ad verecundiam* argument also involved, for the psychologist, we may presume, speaks as an expert. But perhaps the parents do not feel that the experts should have the last word in this instance—at any rate, without justifying their conclusions.

In this type of case, many would say that the psychologist's use of the phrase "gender-prejudiced behavior" begs the question against the parents' side of the case. But is this right? If it is, then according to the analysis of begging the question advocated in this book, there should be a circle in the psychologist's argument. Where is the circle?

It is at this point that things get sticky, because it simply is not clear— from the text and context given in case 6.0—what the ultimate thesis of each of the parties to the dispute is supposed to be. The only indication from the text is that the psychologist "concludes" that "the parents should try harder to make their behavior more gender-neutral." If this is indeed the main conclusion that is the focus of the dispute between the two parties to the dialogue, then which premise either depends on, or is equivalent to that conclusion, in a way that makes the argument beg the question? Perhaps the offending premise is the assertion by the psychologist that the parents' behavior is "gender-prejudiced." This proposition, however, is clearly not equivalent to, or dependent on, the conclusion, in the required sense.

The real problem with the psychologist's argument—and the basis for the parents' objection to it—is much simpler. Terms in an argument can be defined or used in positive (laudatory) or negative (vituperative) ways, as noted in chapter one. But the whole issue of how a term should properly be defined, or applied in a specific instance, may itself be subject to legitimate disputation in an argument. To define or deploy a term or phrase in a one-sided, or aggressively argumentative, can be highly objectionable.

Now the objection in such a case need not involve the claim that the offending argument is circular. The objection may simply be that the argumentative use of a disputed term has not been supported by the strength of backing that is required to sustain it. The objector is saying, in such a case, "Either defend your use of that argumentative term better, or drop it from your argument." The request here is for the proponent to use a more neutral term. This kind of objection is very common in argumentation, and it need not involve the claim that the offending argument begs the question. Instead, the challenge is more elementary. The objection is simply that the argument contains loaded terminology.

Too often, the charge of *petitio principii* is a heavy-handed way of trying to make an opponent's argument seem much worse than it really is, when the genuine fault of the argument is something else altogether. Ten kinds of faults that are not *petitio principii,* but are often confused with *petitio,* are summarized below.

1. *Overly aggressive use of loaded terms.* The fallacy often identified in these cases is that of *question-begging epithet*–see chapter one, section two. The discussion of case 6.0 shows the usual problem–the alleged circle is not identified, but only vaguely suggested (at best).

2. *Repetition in an argument (without circularity).* Of course, repetition of a premise or conclusion can be a fault, but it is not necessarily the fault of begging the question. For example, Spellman (1968, p. 79) cites as a common error of direct examination of a witness by an attorney in court the tactic of trying to emphasize the witness' satisfactory answer by "virtual repetition," for example, "In other words, . . . " This tactic may be an error in trying to convince a jury, but of course the error is not necessarily that of *petitio principii.* For although the same proposition may be repeated (or an equivalent one), there is not necessarily an interdependency of premise and conclusion that makes the attorney's argumentation circular.

3. *Arguments with inadequately supported premises.* It may often be right to criticize an argument because one of the premises is no more plausible than the conclusion to be proved. It does not necessarily follow, however, that such an argument begs the question. Not all weak or inadequately supported arguments are faulty because they beg the question. For the latter criticism to be appropriate, the argumentation must be circular.

4. *The complaint that an argument is so strong (or clearly valid) that if established, it would disprove the respondent's thesis.* DeMorgan (1847, p. 255) warned of the erroneous "habit of many to treat an advanced proposition as a begging of the question the moment they see that, if established, it would establish the question." This type of counter-attack will be more fully discussed in chapter seven. But it is clear that this kind of defensive tactic, while it can be a fault in reasoned argumentation, is not the same fault as that of begging the question. For as noted in chapter one, section five, not all deductively valid arguments commit the fallacy of begging the question. What must be shown is that one of the premises depends

on, or is equivalent to, the conclusion in a way that makes the argument circular.

5. *The fallacy of many questions.* The classical instance of this fallacy is the famous spouse-beating question, "Have you stopped beating your spouse?" This use of aggressive tactics of questioning has often been confused with the fallacy of begging the question. But what is the essential difference between the two fallacies? This turns out to be a tough question to answer with precision—we will turn to it as the main problem to be addressed in the rest of this chapter.

6. *Paradoxes and problems of self-reference.* The term "sophism" is often used as a synonym for the term "paradox." Many of the paradoxes appear to be problems of self-reference, having to do with reflexivity or circularity of argumentation. Moreover, the terms "sophistical refutation" and "sophism" are often used as synonyms for "fallacy." Taken together, these customary usages, as we say in chapter one, section ten, make it easy to confuse the fallacy of begging the question with paradoxes that evidently involve vicious circles of various kinds. But important distinctions need to be made here. A paradox is a valid argument that appears to have true premises and a false conclusion—an apparent contradiction. A fallacy is a systematic tactic of deception used in an argumentative context of dialogue to try (illicitly, in contravention of the rules of dialogue) to get the best of an opponent. Thus, while a paradox characteristically involves faulty reasoning of some sort, and also a kind of deceptiveness or illusion, it is quite a different sort of entity from a fallacy in argumentation.

7. *Overly aggressive questions (with unacceptable presuppositions).* Often wrongly cited as instances of *petitio principii* are questions with a presupposition that goes against, or aggressively tends to foreclose on or defeat, the respondent's point of view. In many cases, these questions are not cases of the fallacy of many questions or cases of the fallacy of begging the question. They are not circular arguments, but only questions containing a "loaded" or "unfriendly" presupposition that the respondent should reject.

8. *Circular arguments that do not beg the question.* These are arguments, like cases 4.7, 4.8, and 4.9, where there is a feedback relationship involved, but no evidence from the context of dialogue that the argument begs the question.

9. *Cases where the textual and contextual evidence is insufficient to pin down a charge of question-begging.* We saw a range of cases in chapter six. In some of these cases, like case 4.12 (the case of the advertisement for the motorists), there was circular argumentation that was open to challenge on the grounds of potential question-

begging. Yet there was still room for the proponent of the argument to defend himself against this charge. In a case like this, there is some legitimate evidence of begging the question, but there remains legitimate room for doubt whether the argument begs the question or not.

10. *Circular explanations, definitions, or other speech acts that are not arguments.* These may contain faults or errors, but they need not be errors of circular argumentation. These kinds of circular sequences may be related to the fallacy of begging the question, yet they must be carefully distinguished from it. A circular explanation, for example, could be a faulty or erroneous explanation, but an explanation is not necessarily an argument. Note, however, that there can be interesting borderline cases, because why-questions can frequently be ambiguous. Sometimes a why-question is a request for proof or argument. In other instances a why-question is a request for an explanation. For example, in case 4.10, possibly the why-questions posed by City Hall, concerning the improvement of the bus services, could be interpreted either way. In case 4.11, by contrast, the use of the expressions "How can you determine . . .?" and "How can you be sure . . .?" make it evident that argument, not explanation, is being sought.

The remainder of chapter six is devoted to item 5, the fallacy of many questions. However, the remaining items will be further discussed in chapters seven and eight.

5. THE FALLACY OF MANY QUESTIONS

The fallacy of begging the question should be carefully distinguished from the fallacy of many questions, said to be instantiated in the following question.

Case 6.1:   Have you stopped beating your spouse?

This question, the famous spouse-beating question, has several elements that, taken together, combine to make asking it fallacious.

One important element is that the question has the syntactical form of a *safe* question, a question that has a harmless or tautological presupposition. According to the semantics and syntax of questions–see Belnap (1963)–all yes-no questions are safe. Another element is that the question is loaded. The concept of a loaded question is a pragmatic concept–see Walton (1989b)–a *loaded question* is a question where, in a context of dialogue, the respondent is not committed to the presupposition of the question. A *presupposition of a question,* according to Walton (1989b, chapter one), is a proposition that a respondent in dialogue becomes committed to by virtue of his giving any direct answer to the question. Thus the spouse-beating question has an important presupposition because a respondent becomes committed to the proposition that he (she) has a spouse whom he (she) has beaten, as soon as that respondent replies either "yes" or "no" in answer to the question. And the spouse-beating question is loaded with respect to any respondent, in a context of dialogue, who is not committed to the proposition that he (she) has a spouse whom he (she) has beaten.

The fallacy of many questions has important similarities and connections to the fallacy of begging the question. Both fallacies are species of overly aggressive tactics in argumentative dialogue to try to give an opponent no option but to accept a proposition he is (or should be) opposed to, in lieu of providing proper evidence to support this conclusion. Both are failures of evidential priority that try to mask the failure by pushing a respondent to grant something too easily.

Indeed, there is a temptation here to think that both of these sophistical tactics of argument are, at bottom, variants of the same fallacy. Both appear to involve a "begging" of a respondent to accept some conclusion right away, instead of offering proper evidence for that conclusion by a good argument using premises open to independent support.

In some textbooks, complex questions are treated as species of begging the question. Waller (1988, p. 196) takes this approach.

> As a final sort of begging the question, consider *complex questions.* "Are you still drinking too heavily?" Whether you answer yes or no, you seem to be admitting that at one time you *did* drink excessively. And that is how complex questions *beg* the question: They embed an assumption within a question. By answering the question you seem to grant the embedded assumption.

Admittedly, an important similarity is brought out here. In the fallacy of many questions, an assumption or presupposition is embedded within the question asked in such a manner that any direct answer attempted by the respondent will concede the assumption. Similarly, in the fallacy of begging the question, a conclusion is asked to be granted in lieu of being properly argued for.

Creighton (1917, p. 181) classifies the fallacy of *complex question* as "an interrogative form of *petitio.* " Creighton diagnoses the problem of questions like, "Have you given up your drinking habits?" (p. 182) as a fallacy of presumption, resulting from the failure of parties in a discussion to be clear and definite about the principles they accept as true.

Robinson (1936) provides another instance of a traditional logic textbook that defines the fallacy of complex question (a term usually taken to be equivalent to the fallacy of many questions) as a species of the *petitio principii* fallacy. According to Robinson (p. 196), *complex question* is *"petitio principii* in the form of a question which takes something for granted." Robinson uses the spouse-beating question as an example of a question that commits this fallacy.

The majority of the logic texts, however, see the fallacy of many questions and the fallacy of begging the question as distinct logical errors–see Hamblin (1970, chapter 1). So we have here a difference of treatment worth exploring. If they are different, what is the essential difference? This question turns out to be harder to answer than you might think. To answer it properly, we have to understand how each of these fallacies works as a systematic kind of tactic of deception in argumentation.

The problem is made more difficult by the possibility that a question could be said to beg the question. Typically, so far we have thought of question-begging as a failure of arguments, where one premise depends on, or is equivalent to, the conclusion. But if questions as well as arguments can be fallacious, other possibilities are opened up.

6. CAN A QUESTION BEG THE QUESTION?

Can a question beg the question? Or is it only an affirmative premise in an argument that can properly be said to commit the fallacy of begging the question? The answer is that it does seem quite possible for a question to beg the question in a context of dialogue. The reasons are that questions have presuppositions, and questions can be argumentative. Therefore, a presupposition in an argumentative question can act like a premise. And such a presupposition can depend on, or be equivalent to, the thesis to be proved in the discussion by the asker of the question.

It will help to consider an example. Suppose that, in the context of the dialogue on tipping in chapter three, Helen puts the following questions to Bob.

Case 6.2:   What about employers who encourage tipping? What should we say about them? They are making money from this practice, but is that fair? Are these employers, who, after all, are encouraging a practice that ought to have been stopped long ago, really being good citizens and fair-minded people? Or are they just acquiescing in the repression of the rights of their employees in order to line their own pockets?

Here Helen has asked Bob five questions. But look closely at her third question. Clearly it presupposes that tipping should be discontinued. It describes tipping as a practice that ought to have been stopped long ago. In other words, the ultimate thesis that Helen is supposed to prove in the dialogue is a presupposition of her question posed to Bob. It is a yes-no question. No matter which way Bob answers the question–"yes" or "no"–

he automatically incurs commitment to the proposition that tipping is a practice that ought to be discontinued. No matter how Bob answers this question then–if he gives a direct answer, one way or the other–he concedes defeat in the dialogue as a whole.

Therefore, in this case, it seems to be quite correct to say that, in the context of the dialogue, Helen's question begs the question.

Where then is the circle in Helen's question? The answer is that it lies in the equivalence between Helen's thesis to be proved and a presupposition of her question. This answer rests on a kind of analogy, however. It rests on the presumption that a question can be, in some cases, like an argument, a device that has the purpose of extracting a commitment from a respondent in dialogue. In other words, some questions are argumentative. They are not simply requests for information, but ways of trying to get a respondent to make concessions that can be used as premises in a persuasion dialogue.

In principle, case 6.2 does not seem to be too different, as an instance of the fallacy of *petitio principii,* from the type of case where a premise in one of Helen's arguments is dependent on, or equivalent to, her thesis to be proved. The type of problem, or tactical move, in the two kinds of cases seems to be comparable.

To test this hypothesis, let us consider a case that is fairly similar to case 6.2 in the kind of tactic employed, but where the speech acts are assertions instead of questions. Suppose then that in the context of the dialogue on tipping, Helen were to advance the following argumentation.

Case 6.3:   Employers who encourage tipping in their businesses are being greedy and immoral, because they are encouraging a practice that ought to have been stopped long ago by any reasonable and fair-minded civilization. These employers are just repressing the rights of their employees in order to line their own pockets.

As far as question-begging goes, case 6.3 appears to be comparable to case 6.2. The main critical point of both cases is that Helen's thesis that tipping ought to be discontinued is presupposed. In order to accept the assertions contained in Helen's first statement, the hearer must already be prepared to accept the premise that tipping is a practice that ought to be discontinued. Helen's argument is a classical *petitio.* But, in effect, the fault in case 6.2 seems virtually the same. Both speech acts are infelicitous because they beg the question at issue, even though one is a question and the other is an assertion, or positive speech act in the form of a statement made.

All this said, however, there is a significant difference between the two cases. In case 6.2, the offending speech act takes the form of a question. This means that it is open to Bob to choose a reply. But is it really? In this case, the question is really kind of a trap, because no matter which answer Bob gives–of the two direct answers that are open–he commits to Helen's thesis in the dialogue.

So it would seem that a question that begs the question has an additional dimension of unfairness or tactical trickery over a (non-interrogative) argument that begs the question. The argument has a premise that begs the question by being a (closed) assertion. But the question appears to be open. Essentially, a question is a less strong form of speech act than a positive assertion, because it has an open quality. A question opens up a range of possible commitments for its respondent to choose from, whereas an assertion, as a premise in an argument, simply functions as a request for commitment, thereby incurring a burden of proof for its proponent. A question normally, however, does not bring with it a burden of proof for the asker, even though there may be a burden to defend the reasonableness or appropriateness of the question in a context of dialogue.

However, not all questions are as innocent as they may appear to be. For questions do have presuppositions, and therefore do (in effect) make some positive assertions. In fact, some questions can be very aggressive and argumentative, in effect calling for a respondent's commitment to propositions in much the same way that arguments do.

And of course Helen's question in case 6.2 is one of these "loaded" questions. No matter which way Bob answers, he commits himself to a proposition that goes heavily against his side of the argument.

It seems then that the fallacy of begging the question and the fallacy of many questions are more closely related to each other than one might have initially thought. Both appear to involve the same kind of overly aggressive tactic of trying to trap an answerer by structuring an attack in such a way that, no matter how he tries to reply, he commits himself to a proposition that goes heavily against his side of the argument.

7. CAN AN ANSWER TO A QUESTION BEG THE QUESTION?

In case 4.17, we found a borderline case where it seemed that an answer to a question might have committed the fallacy of begging the question. But this case was borderline–it was not clear that there was a circle in the response. It could have been interpreted as merely an inflexible or dogmatic reply, rather than a fallacy of begging the question. Still, case 4.17 seemed to open up the possibility that a reply to a question could be said to be an instance of the fallacy of begging the question.

If this possibility exists in reality, it might suggest that committing the fallacy of begging the question does not always require circular argumentation, with a premise depending on a conclusion. Perhaps the fallacy is that the answer begs the question that it was supposed to be a reply to. If this is possible, it might indicate further affinities between begging the question and question-oriented fallacies and the fallacy of begging the question. It would not be the usual case of circular argumentation principally involving relationships between propositions or assertions as premises or conclusions of an argument. Instead, the problem centrally involves a question, at the local level of the argument.

Questions and assertions are, in principle, different types of speech acts. Hence question-related cases of begging the question are interestingly distinctive and unusual.

The following classical example cited by Engel (1976, p. 75) provides a case in point.

Case 6.4:   When a reporter asked Mayor Richard Daley of Chicago why Senator Hubert Humphrey had failed to carry Illinois in an election, Daley is said to have replied: "Because he didn't get enough votes."

According to Engel (p. 74), Mayor Daley may be said to have employed the fallacy of begging the question–for humor–because the question really was: "Why did Senator Humphrey not get enough votes?" By Engel's account, Mayor Daley begged the question because he answered the question merely by repeating the very same assertion that is the presupposition of the why-question.

However, there is some uncertainty about the context of dialogue in this case, and about the interpretation of Mayor Daley's speech act. It seems likely that Mayor Daley was attempting to give an explanation of Senator Humphrey's failure to carry Illinois. But this case is not altogether free from ambiguity. It is possible, depending on the context of the discussion, that Mayor Daley was trying to prove to the reporter that Humphrey did not carry Illinois, by giving a reason why Humphrey did not carry Illinois.

Let's consider the explanation interpretation first. It is possible for an (attempted) explanation to be circular. Could a circular explanation be an instance of the fallacy of begging the question? This appears to be possible. One might be asked to explain a proposition A, in the sense of showing why A should be accepted as true, by deducing or inferring A from another set of propositions that are independent of A. A circular explanation that already presumes what it is supposed to explain could, according to these requirements, be rejected as spurious.

Presumably, the kind of structures needed to analyze circular explanation would be parallel, in many respects, to the structures we are developing for the analysis of circular argumentation in persuasion dialogues, and other contexts of argumentative dialogue.

Without pursuing the topic of circular explanation further, however, let us ask whether a fallacy of begging the question is to be found in case 6.4 if we interpret the why-question as a request for persuasion-directed argumentation, to give a reason for the respondent to accept Humphrey's failure to carry Illinois.

Is this a genuine case of begging the question under this second interpretation? Yes, it appears to be, because the equivalence implies an inevitable circle, and the failure of the answer to be informative could be construed as a kind of failure of evidential priority (although one of an unusual sort). This case is related to the criteria of evidence type of circularity analyzed in chapter four, section three, because both the questioner and respondent are presumed to know that the customary criterion for failing to carry a riding in an election is not getting enough votes to win it. Hence simply to reply by stating this criterion does not introduce any of the new evidence or informative explanation that the why-question asks for.

This case is not as simple as it looks, however. In the right context, the reply below might not be an instance of the fallacy of begging the question.

Case 6.5:   **Q:**   How can you prove he did not carry Illinois?
              A: He did not get enough votes, and I can prove it.

Here the circle would not appear to be an inevitable one, because the respondent gives an indication that he can offer further (presumably independent) premises to back up his contention. Perhaps he is alluding to a count of the votes, as reported in a reliable source, for example. Here the reply is not complete, but it points the way to a further sequence of open dialogue that could lead to fulfillment of the burden of proof. Hence it should not be judged to be an instance of the fallacy of begging the question, despite its evident similarity to case 6.4.

Thus it is not as easy to distinguish begging the question from other question-related fallacies, like the fallacy of complex question, as we might have thought at the outset. Begging the question is a pragmatic fallacy that occurs in relation to a context of dialogue. Begging the question is always closely related to the asking and answering of questions in dialogue.

8. PRAGMATIC BASIS OF THE FALLACY OF MANY QUESTIONS

Despite the affinities and relationships discovered so far between the two fallacies as they have traditionally been conceived, still it seems there is a basic difference between begging the question and complex questions. The former, unlike the latter, requires a circular argument to be present as the basis of the fallacy.

Even this difference, however, may not be the decisive distinguishing feature that it seems to be. For there is a new subtlety to be considered.

This subtlety is that it seems possible, in principle, for the spouse-beating question (or questions like it that are taken to be paradigm cases of the fallacy of many questions) to beg the question. Consider a context of dialogue where Marcia is trying to prove that Herb has beaten his spouse in the past, and where Herb denies it. This, let us say, is the issue to be settled by the dialogue. In this context, suppose Marcia asks Herb: "Have you stopped beating your spouse?" Now in this particular context of dialogue, no matter which way Herb replies–"yes" or "no"–it will be presumed that Marcia's thesis has been proved and Herb's thesis has been disproved. As soon as Herb gives an answer, he loses the game of dialogue and Marcia wins. In such a context, therefore, the premise that Marcia is asking Herb to concede, by posing this question, is in fact identical to the conclusion she is required to prove to fulfill her burden of proof in the dialogue. So there is indeed a circle here, and Marcia's use of the spouse-beating question can rightly be said to commit the fallacy of begging the question.

This hypothetical case seems to open a frightening Pandora's box for anyone trying to analyze or distinguish between these two fallacies. It seems that in the right dialectical circumstances, even the very paradigm example of the fallacy of many questions could be an instance of the fallacy of begging the question.

Hence our basic question is sharpened. What really is the essential difference between the two fallacies?

The essential difference is to be sought in the difference in the kinds of tactics used by an arguer. But to determine this difference is a pragmatic matter of the context of dialogue in a particular case. The key, then, is that each case must be examined on its own merits, as exemplifying characteristic types of tactics.

In evaluating a particular case, the distinction between the two fallacies rests on requirements of burden of proof to be placed on the critic who makes the charge that one of these fallacies has been committed. If the charge is one of *petitio,* the critic must give clear textual and contextual evidence from the case that establishes decisively that there exists circular argumentation.

However, in some cases, this evidence can be hard to document. In some cases, as we have seen in chapter six, the best finding is that the evidence is incomplete, or inadequate to back up the claim that a fallacy is there to be found. It has been too easy for the textbooks to simply suggest– by a process of "hand-waving"–that such an argument commits the fallacy of begging the question.

The best way to get to the bottom of identifying the argumentation tactic that is characteristic of the fallacy of many questions is to see how this tactic is practically deployed.

To study the relationship between the fallacy of begging the question and the fallacy of many questions in a practical perspective, political debates are a good source of case studies. Questions in political debates are often both complex and aggressive, suggesting that some sort of fallacy or sophism of questioning should be cited for criticism. But pinning down a criticism of fallaciousness is often harder than it may seem, on the surface.

The exchange in case 6.6 took place during the Question Period session of the *House of Commons Debates of Canada (Hansard,* June 10, 1982, p. 18034).

Case 6.6:   **Hon. Flora MacDonald (Kingston and the Islands):** Madam Speaker, my question is also directed to the Minister of Finance. I would like to say to him that his policies are directly responsible for the fact that 1,185 more Canadians are without jobs every single day, 1,185 more Canadians with families to feed and mortgages to pay. How long is the minister prepared to condemn 1,200 more Canadians every day to job loss and insecurity because he is too stubborn and too uncaring to change his policies?

Hon. Allan J. MacEachen (Deputy Prime Minister and Minister of Finance): Madam Speaker, I do not accept for one moment the statement in the hon. member's question that the policies of the government are responsible for the recession which is taking place, not only in Canada but also in every industrialized country in the world. I am surprised that the hon. member, considering her experience, would make such a foolish statement in the House of Commons.

Miss MacDonald: The Minister's answer is appalling.

This question looks a lot like the spouse-beating question. It is complex and has multiple presuppositions. It presumes that the respondent (or his party) is condemning 1,200 Canadians every day to job loss and insecurity. It presumes that this unemployment is due to the minister's policies. And finally, it presumes that the minister is "too stubborn and too uncaring" to change these policies. Some might even say, therefore, that this loaded question begs the question against the responding minister by presupposing that his whole approach to unemployment is misguided and harmful.

But does Ms. MacDonald's question commit either of these fallacies? To evaluate such claims, we have to look to the context of dialogue.

Question Period is a session in the Canadian House of Commons in which the purpose is to allow the opposition party members to ask brief questions to solicit information from government members on issues of the day, or to press members of the government for action on an issue. According to the parliamentary rules for Question Period (recorded in *Beauchesne),* questions asked should not be too long or too argumentative. The questioner is not supposed to be making a speech, for there are other kinds of sessions in parliament where this function is appropriate. For his part, the respondent must give an answer to the question–again, an answer that is relatively brief–or if the information is not available, at least give some indication of when it might become available. .

As one might expect, the questions in Question Period are often quite argumentative. The debates are televised, and the more dramatic exchanges are often featured in media reports. It is difficult for the participants to resist grandstanding.

The Speaker of the House is responsible for enforcing the rules of parliamentary order in Question Period. However, it is clear that the speakers are generally very tolerant of argumentative questions and replies. They tend to intervene only if a participant starts to "speechify" at excessive length, or if name-calling or other serious excesses violate rules of propriety and threaten order in the House.

Nevertheless, the purposes of Question Period as an institution are relatively clear, and often it seems reasonable to suspect that questions like the one in case 6.6 are at odds with these goals of dialogue. To presuppose in your question that your respondent's "stubborn" and "uncaring" policies are responsible for job loss and insecurity is clearly intolerable to a respondent in this sort of forum. To pack such a presupposition into a complex question that asks how long your respondent is going to persist in this intolerable behavior seems to go over the edge of fair questioning practices. Even if the speaker allows such questions, still from a normative point of view of critical argumentation, shouldn't this sort of question be condemned?

But does this question commit either of the two fallacies we are concerned with here?

The question in case 6.6 certainly has the characteristic *modus operandi* of the fallacy of many questions. This complex question, as we noted, contains several damaging presuppositions, even using loaded language like "stubborn" and "uncaring" that verges on the *ad hominem* attack.

The respondent is forced to reply with a strong counter-attack that shifts the burden of presumption away from him. It would not be fair to compel him to give a direct answer to this trick question, for it would lead directly to his political defeat and undoing. Quite rightly, he is allowed to rebut aggressively the harmful presumptions of the question, in his reply.

But some might be inclined to go further than this, and claim that Ms. MacDonald's attack in case 6.6 begs the question against Mr. Mac-Eachen. However, following our previously laid out guidelines for evaluating allegations of this fallacy, we have to determine what Ms. Mac-Donald's thesis is, in the dialogue. Here, however, a severe difficulty poses itself. The dialogue is not a persuasion dialogue. Ms. MacDonald does not even have a well-defined thesis to be established by her argument. Indeed, she is not supposed to be arguing at all. She is supposed to be soliciting information, or pressing for action.

The problem is that although her question is clearly directed to serving both these goals to some extent, it is also highly argumentative.

Just as clearly, it has a purpose of attempting to attack the respondent, and the government generally, by condemning their actions and policies as contrary to the interests of the electorate. But does this mean that Ms. MacDonald's question commits the fallacy of begging the question?

The answer is that there is no question (thesis) to be begged. Ms. MacDonald is not supposed to be proving some conclusion, or thesis, as her burden of proof in the dialogue. To presume that such is the case involves an illicit dialectical shift. For the relevant context for case 6.6 is not that of persuasion dialogue. It is that of a dialogue with the dual purpose of soliciting information and pressing for action.

Now it is possible that there could be circular reasoning, and with it *petitio principii* in either information-soliciting or action-pressing contexts of dialogue. But how the *petitio* might work as a fallacy in these contexts has never been determined.

So it is far from evident that Ms. MacDonald's questioning in case 6.6 can legitimately be criticized as an instance of the fallacy of begging the question. Her question can be criticized as overly aggressive, through using the tactic of packing in loaded presumptions characteristic of the spouse-beating question. But it is another thing to take the step of saying that her question begs the question. Given the context of dialogue, and the nature of Ms. MacDonald's question, this type of criticism is not appropriate.

Thus the real fault of Ms. MacDonald's question is not that it begs the question. The fault lies in the use of a complex question that is aggressively loaded to try to force her respondent to concede prior presumptions that he is offered, with no chance to rebut or refuse to accept.

9. TACTICAL USES OF PRAGMATICALLY COMPLEX QUESTIONING TECHNIQUES

One thing to notice is that complex questions, with multiple presuppositions, should not be judged fallacious in every case. There need be nothing wrong or fallacious in asking a complex question like the following one.

Case 6.7:   Who is the man in the black hat who shot the sheriff and rode out of town?

This is a complex question, but in the proper context, it could be a reasonable question–not a question that should be judged fallacious simply because it is semantically or syntactically complex.

Thus the fact that the spouse-beating question is complex is an important element that plays a role in its fallacious use in dialogue, but we should not attribute the fallaciousness of this question just to its complexity.

It is the use of this complexity to defeat an opponent in an argumentative dialogue that characterizes the fallacy.

How it is used is found in the coercive nature of the spouse-beating question. No matter which way the respondent answers it–"yes" or "no"– he becomes committed to having a spouse whom he has beaten. Thus this sort of question is designed as a trap for the unwary. When it is fallacious, it is primarily because it is used as an unduly aggressive tactic designed to force an answerer to concede something that will entrap him, and can then be used to defeat him in the subsequent line of argument.[14] Thus the fallacy of many questions, like the fallacy of begging the question, should properly be classified as a sophistical tactic type of fallacy.

The best line of defense against such a question is to reply to it with another question: "Do I have a spouse whom I have beaten?" But in some contexts–like school examinations and legal cross-examinations–replying to a question with another question is not permitted. Moreover, in ordinary conversations, there is a Gricean expectation that an answerer will give a direct answer to a question if it is possible and co-operative for the respondent to do so. Hence the strategic use of a question like the spouse-beating question can be that of an instrument to defeat the respondent by aggressively pre-empting his ability to carry on with the normal sequence of question-reply dialogue in a case. When so used, unfairly, such a question can be called fallacious because it is an unfairly aggressive tactic used in dialogue–the use of the loaded presupposition in the question functions as a sophistical tactic to try to force the dialogue to close prematurely in favor of the questioner, and with defeat for the answerer.

But this same tactic of coerciveness is also found in the fallacy of begging the question. The difference is that in the fallacy of many questions, it is the complexity of the question that is used. But it is a pragmatic complexity that is essentially involved.

PRAGMATIC CONTEXT OF DIALOGUE FOR A QUESTION

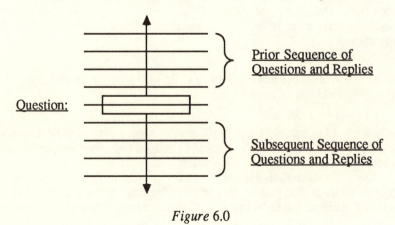

Figure 6.0

It is important to realize that the spouse-beating question could be legitimately and non-fallaciously used in some contexts of dialogue. As Woodbury (1984, p. 220) points out, this question could be quite appropriate and proper to be asked by an attorney who is cross-examining a witness who has already freely conceded his past practice of beating his wife, for the record. It is not the question itself, then, that is fallacious. It is the use of this question in a particular context of dialogue.

In evaluating any question as a possible instance of the fallacy of many questions, one must presuppose a pragmatic context–a profile of reasonable dialogue extending into the past history of the discussion leading up to the question, and into the future sequence of dialogue that can be projected to follow the answering of the question (figure 6.0).

Whether a given question is to be judged fallacious or not depends on both the prior and subsequent sequences of questions and replies in a given context of dialogue. This actual sequence (as far as it is known) must then be compared to a normative model of what we can take to be a reasonable pragmatic sequence for that context.

SEQUENCE OF DIALOGUE FOR THE SPOUSE-BEATING QUESTION

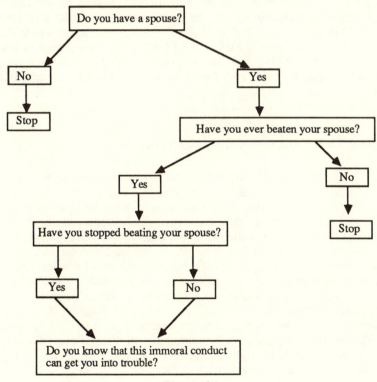

Figure 6.1

Consider the sample sequence for the spouse-beating question in figure 6.1. When the spouse-beating question is used fallaciously, it is because the questioner unjustifiably presupposes prior affirmative answers to one or more of the first two questions in the directed sequence portrayed in figure 6.1. Instead of asking these prior questions first, and giving the respondent a chance to make his position apparent, the questioner starts right in by asking the third question. In effect, he presupposes affirmative answers to the two prior questions. This is the essence of the fallacy of many questions. The questioner is "balling up" a pragmatically complex sequence of questions and replies in one single question, without permitting his respondent to deal with these prior questions in a suitable manner.

Thus the fallacy is a kind of sophistical tactic of attempted forcing of a respondent into an untenable position, no matter how the respondent tries to answer a question. However, the sophistical tactic is even more complex than this. By getting the respondent to answer the question, the questioner puts that respondent in a vulnerable position in relation to the subsequent discussion. The strategy is to entrap the respondent into some damaging admission that can subsequently be used to defeat the respondent and cause him to lose the argument. The *modus operandi* is to use the damaging admission to follow up with further attacks to discredit the respondent, or put him in such a damaging situation that he will lose all credibility in upholding his side of the argument. For example, in figure 6.1, a follow-up question is indicated. This question is intended to lead to further damaging admissions. The respondent gets in deeper and deeper, ultimately losing his case entirely, if he follows the line of questioning without resisting.

10. THE TWO FALLACIES DIFFERENTIATED

At first, classifying the fallacy of complex question as a species of the fallacy of begging the question seems like an outrageous error. The two kinds of fallacies have traditionally been held to be different errors, and on the surface, they do seem to be different kinds of faults— one relating to complex questions and the other to circular arguments.

But on serious reflection, it becomes a lot harder to define accurately and pin down the precise difference between the two fallacies. For one thing, we saw in section six that a question could actually be said to beg the question. And even an answer to a question, as noted in section seven, could justifiably be said to commit the fallacy of begging the question. Perhaps even more worrisome in this connection, we saw that the spouse-beating question, supposedly the paradigm of the fallacy of complex question, could itself be rightly said to be an instance of the fallacy of begging the question in some cases.

To begin to get to the bottom of the real difference between these two fallacies, we have to provide analyses of the fundamental sophistical tactic that defines each of them as a deceptive mechanism of argumentation used to violate rules of reasonable dialogue. The key to understanding the nature of the fallacy of many questions was shown to lie in the pragmatic complexity of this type of questioning. The tactic is to use this complexity to ball up many questions into one, in order to entrap the respondent into damaging admissions that can then be used to undermine his side of the argument.

But of course, this tactic is, in some respects, similar to what appears to be the underlying tactic of the fallacy of begging the question. Both kinds of fallacies are used to try to force a respondent to concede a disputed proposition without properly backing it up, or arguing for it as a legitimate concession.

But in addition to these similarities, there are essential differences between the two fallacies. The fallacy of begging the question essentially involves a circular argument, as exhibited by the argument reconstruction in a given case. The fallacy of many questions does not essentially require or involve circular argumentation. It involves the packing of a presupposition into a question in a manner that is not consistent with a sequence of good dialogue (one that contributes to the goal of dialogue in a useful and proper manner) either prior to, or subsequent to, the asking of the question.

The next step must be to identify the argumentation tactic that is characteristic of the fallacy of begging the question. To do this will be to see not only what rules of reasonable dialogue are violated by this fallacy, but how an opponent in dialogue can be cheated or defeated by using a clever trick to make such an illicit move persuasive. This task, which remains to be done in the last chapter, involves more carefully defining the dependency and equivalence relationships that are the essence of circular argumentation. Having done this, we will then be in a much better position to distinguish more exactly between begging the question and complex question as fallacies. At the same time, we will be able to distinguish more clearly and decisively between the fallacy of begging the question and the other nine kinds of failures of argumentation that are so often confused with this fallacy.

These distinctions require careful and fundamental analysis of the nature of their respective fallacies or faults, if they are to be defended and retained as separate categories of significant logical errors. For it is quite clear, as we will see further in chapter seven, that some theoreticians and textbooks are not just accidentally confusing these categories, but see them as systematically identical.

Evidently in Waller's case, the conclusion that complex questions are subspecies of begging the question derives from a more general thesis that not all question-begging arguments are circular. According to Waller (1988, p. 191), the fallacy of begging the question can be divided into two subcategories–circular begging the question and non-circular begging the question. But can there be a category of fallacy identified with non-circular begging the question? To venture this hypothesis would be to deny that the fallacy of begging the question is separate from some of the other faults and failures identified in our list of ten (section four, chapter six). To the contrary, it has been our hypothesis all along that circularity is a requirement of the fallacy of begging the question. From this hypothesis it would follow that the idea of non-circular begging the question is absurd.

But should it turn out to be the case that there could be a legitimate fallacy of non-circular begging the question, it would follow that there would cease to be any watertight compartmentalization between the fallacy of begging the question and the fallacy of many questions. Should this turn out to be the case, it would entail a radical revision of the conventional wisdom on these two fallacies.

What has been shown in this chapter is that the important, essential difference between the fallacy of begging the question and the fallacy of many questions is that the former, but not the latter, requires that the argument under criticism be circular. By these lights, the reason that a complex question commits the fallacy of many questions lies in its use of the multiple presupposition built into the question, within the structure of the question and the dialogue context, in such a way as to systematically disallow the respondent the option of avoiding conceding that harmful (loaded) presupposition. This structure is essentially different from that of a circular sequence of argumentation.

According to this point of view, the two fallacies are essentially distinct, and the idea of a fallacy of non-circular begging the question is a contradiction. But to back up this point of view convincingly, it needs to be based on a theory of begging the question as a fallacy that is in turn based on an analysis of the argumentation tactic behind this fallacy. This will be the project carried out in chapter eight.

NOTES

1. In Walton (1984) different kinds of argumentation tactics in formalized games of persuasion dialogue are identified and analyzed, and fallacies are equated with violations of procedural rules of these games. However, now the further step will be taken of defining particular fallacies as kinds of argumentation tactics used to violate rules of reasonable dialogue.

2. Sometimes they are even systematically identified, as opposed to being thoughtlessly confused–see section five.

3. Woods (1987).

4. Woods and Walton (1975a).

5. Walton (1987a).

6. See Walton (1987a) and van Eemeren and Grootendorst (1989).

7. Van Eemeren and Grootendorst (1984) and (1987).

8. Walton (1989a).

9. Hamblin (1970) and (1971).

10. Or he may decide to retract a proposition in such a way that it becomes unclear whether there is a circle in his argument any longer.

11. Mackenzie (1979), (1980), and (1981) has been a leading exponent of the concept of a challenge in a game of dialogue.

12. Walton (1986) and (1987a).

13. Woods and Walton (1982b, p. 120).

14. See Walton (1987a, pp. 110-13).

7

Revising the Textbooks

In chapter six, section four, ten faults of argument often confused with the fallacy of begging the question were identified and described. A glance at the treatments of begging the question in the logic textbooks will reveal a confusing multiplicity of different classifications, terminologies, and descriptions of this fallacy. At present, the treatments given by the various textbooks are inconsistent with each other, superficial, and problematic. Such problems are not the fault of the textbook authors (who have often been very creative)–a coherent, systematic theory of begging the question to guide them is simply lacking.

Among the most prominent dubious assumptions accepted by many textbooks are the following: (1) that circular reasoning is inherently fallacious; (2) that arguments with one or more unproven assumptions as premises are fallaciously question-begging; and (3) that as soon as an argument is shown to be circular, or even to have an unproven assumption as a premise, there is no further need to study it or gather evidence in order to show that it begs the question.

All these assumptions were shown to be serious obstacles in the way of evaluating cases of begging the question in chapters five and six. Now we must turn to bringing some order to the kaleidoscopic treatments of begging the question in the textbooks, in order to set out reasonable requirements for a theory of begging the question that could make a unified and adequate theory of this fallacy possible.

In undertaking this task, we will put to use the case study techniques developed in the previous chapters in making some recommendations on how the texts should (or should not) treat *petitio principii*. The most general of these recommendations is that there should be a burden of proof on any critic (notably including criticisms made in logic textbooks) who would charge that an argument is question-begging, to back up the charge with specified kinds of textual and contextual evidence. Two rules for burden of proof on a critic are formulated.

Several pseudo-fallacies are identified–these are phenomena of argumentation that are commonly but wrongly identified with the fallacy of begging the question.

1. ASSUMPTIO NON PROBATA

Among the faults most often confused with begging the question, we noted the fault of arguments with inadequately supported premises–this was item three in the list of such faults in chapter six, section four. Confusing the more general fault of an unproven premise in an argument with the specific fault of the fallacy of begging the question seems to be a long-standing and commonly recurring failing of logic textbooks. Hamblin (1970, p. 34) quotes Abraham Fraunce, *The Lawiers Logike* (London, William How, 1588, p. 28):

Petitio principii, then, is eyther when the same thing is prooved by it selfe, as, *The soule is immortall, because it never dyeth:* Or when a doubtful thing is confirmed by that which is as doubtfull, as
>   *The earth mooveth*
>   *Because the heaven standeth still.*

Confirming a doubtful thing by appealing to something as doubtful is (precisely) the failure to meet the requirement of evidential priority. This failing, however, as we have seen repeatedly, is not the same as the fallacy of begging the question. It is a failure that–along with other factors like circularity and inevitability–is one ingredient in explaining why an argument commits the fallacy of begging the question. Fraunce's example about the earth moving, then, is not a circular argument, so far as the given evidence of the text indicates. It is simply a weak or inadequately supported argument–until some evidence is brought forward to support the premise in such a manner that the premise is shown to be more plausible than the conclusion.

Although it is perhaps less clear, the same kind of conflation appears to be evident in William of Sherwood's *Introduction to Logic* (Kretzmann, 1966, p. 159): "Begging the Original Issue, then, is assuming it [or] what is equally or less well known while proving the conclusion, and for that reason it is called Begging the Original Issue rather than 'begging the conclusion'."

Here, however, it is unclear when William wrote "while proving the conclusion" whether he meant to require that what is assumed be included in the proving, that is, dependent on the conclusion. In other words, was he requiring circularity as a requirement of begging the original issue, or not? One interpretation of his remark that seems possible is that he did not. On this interpretation, assuming "what is equally or less well known" is being said to be equivalent to committing the fallacy of begging the question, or begging the original issue.

More recent texts have carried on this tradition of making what is, from the viewpoint of the fallacy of begging the question presented in previous chapters, a fundamental confusion. This has led to some peculiar terminology and questionable classifications. Hyslop (1899, p. 168) defined *petitio principii* as follows: *"Petitio Principii.–* The common name for this is Begging the Question, but it is here called Assumption of the Principle or general truth which is used for proof. It means that the proposition to be proved is in some way simply assumed without proof." Hyslop went on to divide this fallacy into two forms, *ignoratio elenchi,* or evading the issue, and *petitio argumenti,* or begging the question, defined as: *"Petitio Argumenti.–* This is here technically called Begging the Question, and means that the proof of any proposition is so assumed as to include the proposition under dispute. This assumption may be of a proposition more general than the conclusion, or really identical with it." This definition appears to involve another kind of misidentification, treated below (section three) under the heading of DeMorgan's Opponent Fallacy. Roughly the confusion here stems from mistakenly equating begging the question with the type of case where a premise is more general than the conclusion and would prove the conclusion, if it (the premise) itself were to be proved. This kind of situation does not represent a fallacy. At worst, it is a case of an inadequately proven premise.

Even more remarkably, however, Hyslop went on to distinguish two forms of *petitio argumenti.* One he called *circulus in probando* (p. 171), a species of begging the question "which consists of what is called 'arguing in a circle,' or assuming as proof of a proposition that proposition itself." The other species of begging the question Hyslop (p. 169) called *assumptio non probata.* "The *assumptio non probata* occurs when the proposition or propositions assumed to prove a given assertion can be questioned by those whom we may be endeavoring to convince." This fault is none other than the simple failure to back up a premise with evidence adequate to deal with the questioning of the respondent that the argument has been designed to convince. In short, it is broadly what could be called a weak argument.

Here, then, is where the major confusion of this bizarre system of classifications stands out. The failing of *assumptio non probata* or unproven assumption has been boldly put forward as a subspecies of the fallacy of begging the question. The overly broad characterization of *petitio principii* sponsored by William of Sherwood, and Abraham Fraunce even more explicitly, has now emerged into a system of classification of different subspecies of the fallacy of begging the question that specifically includes *assumptio non probata* as one of these subspecies.

According to the treatment of the cases of the fallacy of begging the question in chapters four, five, and six, this system of classification is intolerable, being based on the worst sort of confusion. *Assumptio non probata* is not a fallacy (in itself), much less a fallacy of begging the question. To say an argument is a case of *assumptio non probata* is simply to say that it is a weak argument, or unduly weak to satisfy its requirement of burden of proof. That in itself is not a fallacy, nor should it be identified with a specific fallacy like begging the question. Most fallacies, failures, and blunders of argumentation have to do with arguments that are unduly weak, in one way or another. But a weak argument *(per se)* need not commit a specific fallacy. Indeed, *assumptio non probata* can be classified as a pseudo-fallacy, especially where it is identified with the fallacy of begging the question.

Evidently it is this mistake of defining begging the question too broadly, by including *assumptio non probata* as a species of question-begging, that lies behind the error of classifying the fallacy of many questions also as a species of begging the question. It was noted in chapter six, section five, that many textbooks classify the fallacy of many questions as an interrogative form of the fallacy of begging the question. These texts include Creighton (1917), Robinson (1936) and Waller (1988). Such a classification seems absurd initially (and even more so, in light of chapter six), but the reasoning behind it starts to make some sense when we realize that these authors are evidently defining the fallacy of begging the question so broadly that it can include cases of *assumptio non probata* as well as cases of circular reasoning. It is not too surprising that, defined this broadly, begging the question can be held to include the fallacy of many (complex) questions, or even any question that contains an objectionable or inadequately justified presupposition.

The connection between these two mistaken classifications is perhaps most explicit in the treatment of Robinson (p. 195), who characterizes begging the question as follows.

Begging the Question. The usual interpretation of this fallacy defines it as the taking of something for granted which is just as uncertain or unproved as the proposition it is used to establish. In a controversy, using as a premise what your opponent will not admit, or has not been forced to admit, is considered a commission of this fallacy.

Having adopted this sort of definition, which in effect allows *assumptio non probata* as a species of begging the question, Robinson unsurprisingly goes on to state that "argument in a circle" *(circulus in probando)* is only a "special form of *petitio principii.*" And it is not too surprising that complex question is defined as *"petitio principii* in the form of a question which takes something for granted" (p. 196).

It is a very common proclivity in textbooks (noted in chapter six, section four) to treat all kinds of arguments that are unduly aggressive or poorly supported as instances of the fallacy of begging the question. For example, in case 1.6, the question "Do you favor the give-away of the Panama Canal?" was cited by a textbook as an instance of question-begging epithet. However, if the analysis of the fallacy of begging the question in chapter six is correct, then this type of case should not properly be said to commit the fallacy of begging the question at all. The questioner in case 1.6 may be trying to lead his respondents to a particular conclusion on the issue of the Panama treaties, but that in itself should not be thought sufficient to warrant the claim that this questioner has committed the fallacy of begging the question.

Failure of evidential priority in persuasion dialogue is not enough, *in itself,* to convict an argument of having committed the fallacy of begging the question. Using overly aggressive language should not be enough, *in itself,* to convict an argument of the fallacy of begging the question. Asking leading or loaded questions (even questions that commit the fallacy of many questions) is not enough, *in itself,* to convict an argument of the fallacy of begging the question. All of these things are, or can be, failures of a sort in different contexts of dialogue. But they are not (exactly) instances of the fallacy of *petitio principii* (begging the question).

2. CIRCULAR REASONING AS A PSEUDO-FALLACY

It is one kind of error to deny that circular reasoning is a necessary condition of committing the fallacy of begging the question. A second kind of error is to presume that circular reasoning is sufficient for committing the fallacy of begging the question.

The first error has already been dealt with in section one. The second kind of error is also, however, widespread in the logic textbooks and other sources on the fallacy of begging the question. The second kind of error is committed by those sources that see circular reasoning as itself a fallacy, or else see the supposed fallacy of circular reasoning as equivalent to the fallacy of begging the question.

For example, Chase (1956, chapter 14) does not use the phrases "begging the question" or *petitio principii* at all. Instead, he writes about "the logical fallacy, *circulus in probando,* or arguing in a circle" (p. 115). The evaluations of the case studies in chapters five and six pointed very clearly to the wisdom of adopting the working hypothesis that there is nothing inherently wrong with arguing in a circle, unless the argument has a probative function and violates a requirement of evidential priority in a context of dialogue. And then, in such a case, it becomes an instance of the fallacy of begging the question (depending on the kind of dialogue, and the tactics used to advance the argument in that context).

One can see, of course, why Chase would prefer to avoid the use of the problematic term "begging the question" and stick to the less confusing language of "arguing in a circle." Even though the problematic phrase "begging the question" has been replaced, reform calls for making a more careful use of these terms. In particular, any approach that implies or suggests that arguing in a circle is inherently fallacious (in any context of reasonable argumentation) should be avoided.

Other texts, like Toulmin, Rieke, and Janik (1979, p. 168), Damer (1980, p. 25), and Copi (1986, p. 107), that use circular reasoning and begging the question as equivalent names for the same fallacy, should also be subject to revision. A more subtle treatment, requiring that a careful distinction be made between these two categories, should be put in place. What should be stressed here is that there can be loops in a sequence of reasoning that do not necessarily indicate the existence of a fallacy, or even an error. Argumentation can exist without there being a probative function of argument, or a requirement of evidential priority in the discussion.

Causal argumentation is a good case in point. We can have loops or circles that indicate mutual causal relationships (feedback) among a set of variables. Our reasoning could proceed from one variable, through others, and back to the same variable. But such a circular sequence of reasoning is not necessarily a fallacious argument, provided it is clear what the program is.

   An excellent example of a mutual causal process of this sort has been presented by Bramer (1984, p. 311), which concerns sanitation in urban areas. Figure 7.0 illustrates the relationships among several variables. The point to be made is that one could have an argument, or sequence of reasoning (not just an explanation or other form of non-argumentative discourse) that proceeds in a circular fashion from one of these variables to another, without any fallacy being committed. For example, in the cycle PMCP, it might be argued that an increase in population in a city causes an increase in modernization, which in turn increases migration to the city, which results in an increase in the number of people in the city. This reasoning is circular, but if it reflects a real situation where mutual causal influences are at work, it should not be condemned as a fallacious sequence of reasoning.

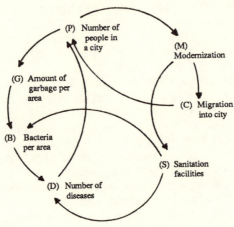

Figure 7.0

Another relevant example to be considered here is case 1.22 of circular reasoning in an expert system cited by Bramer (1984, p. 10). In this kind of reasoning in a knowledge base by an expert system, circularity is a problem, because the program goes into an infinite loop. But does this represent the fallacy of begging the question? Not necessarily, for it depends on what the program is designed to do. The circularity could, in many cases, be harmless enough, provided it is clear what is going on. The circularity may even reveal something valuable about the information in the knowledge base. Circular reasoning is one thing, and the fallacy of begging the question is something else again, in this context of reasoning.

   The textbooks, therefore, should be revised to acknowledge the existence of these kinds of cases of non-fallacious circular reasoning. More serious and systematic attempts should be made at least to differentiate between circular reasoning and begging the question.

It should be noted that the scholarly literature, as well as the textbooks, often portrays circular reasoning as fallacious. Palmer (1981, p. 393) starts out from what is (from the point of view of our theory) quite a suitable pair of premises. One is that circularity is a matter of proof. The other is that question-begging is a misdemeanor of debate. But from these suitable premises, Palmer draws the unsuitable conclusion that there are two separate fallacies–the "fallacy of circularity" is a "defect of reasoning" and the fallacy of begging the question is an error of debate.

This multiplication of fallacies is based on Palmer's DeMorgan-style presumption that a circular argument can be defined in a purely formal way. However, as we have seen, such a formalistic approach does not do justice to the subtlety needed in interpreting an argument in a context of dialogue in order to apply the method of argument diagramming to a particular case. While it is true that circular reasoning can be erroneous or useless if a probative function is required, pinning down begging the question as a fallacy should also involve levels two and three of analysis. Hence there is only one fallacy–that of begging the question–when a circular argument is used fallaciously, not two fallacies. Thus corrections in terminology need to be made by sources like van Eemeren and Grootendorst (1989, p. 33), who write that the fallacy of circular reasoning is also known as *petitio principii* or begging the question. That may be accepted, or even standard terminology, but if the theory of chapter eight turns out to be right, the standard terms need to be revised. Circular reasoning should be treated as a pseudo-fallacy, a kind of argumentation that may (or may not) commit the fallacy of begging the question.

If an argument is discovered to be circular, or even if there is some feeling that the argument may be circular, immediately strong suspicions about the argument are evoked. This may be because, in the most highly regarded type of argument, the cumulative scientific inquiry, no circularity would be allowed. Therefore, the feeling may be that any argument that even shows a *prima facie* appearance of possibly being circular is suspect, because it falls short of the highest standards of argument.

Such an immediate leap to declare an argument untrustworthy may be an error, however, for in some cases a circular argument can perform a legitimate function in a context of reasoned dialogue. What needs to be shown is that the circle, if there is one, somehow interferes with the function of the argument, in its proper context, of using the evidences of the premises to support the conclusion. Essentially, this means showing that the structure of the argument systematically interferes with the operation of the principle of evidential priority in that context. Hence the finding of circularity in an argument should not, in itself, be regarded as sufficient evidence to declare that the argument must commit the fallacy of begging the question.

At present the textbooks–and writings on begging the question generally–fail to make a distinction we have now shown to be necessary and important, between arguing in a circle (circular reasoning, circular argument, *circulus probandi,* etc.) on the one hand, and begging the question *(petitio principii,* question-begging argument, etc.), on the other hand. In general, these two categories are often treated as equivalent or inter-changeable. Or, if a distinction is made, it is made in a less than fortunate manner. The former category should be treated as a classification of argumentation that does not necessarily (in itself) render an argument fallacious. The latter category should be treated as a type of fallacy that is a serious charge to make against an argument (and its proponent), and that requires proper documentation of the evidence described in this chapter to substantiate it. Moreover, the charge draws a burden of proof onto the critic who has made it to document his charge properly.

This recommendation, in particular, is quite sweeping and would affect the current textbook treatments of the fallacy of begging the question radically and comprehensively. Nevertheless, it is a corollary of the analysis of the concept of fallacy worked out in chapter six. And if the analysis is right, then the textbooks should be revised accordingly, or they are basing their teachings on a very serious and fundamental error.

3. OPPONENT FALLACIES

DeMorgan (1847) makes the interesting observation that *petitio prin-cipii* is a double-edged sword that can sometimes be turned back onto the attacker who wields it. DeMorgan (p. 255) cites two types of cases where an overly aggressive criticism of *petitio principii* itself commits a fallacy of *petitio principii*. One is where a chain of inferences that is really an expla-nation is accused of being a demonstration that begs the question. The key distinction is between two different uses of the same inference. What is involved is a dialectical shift from one pragmatic context of use to another. An example is case 3.0, cited by DeMorgan as a type of case where begging the question has been unjustly imputed as a criticism. As DeMorgan notes, it could be said in such a case that it is the critic, and not the person attacked by the *petitio principii* criticism, who really commits the fallacy of begging the question. DeMorgan calls this type of case one where there is an *opponent fallacy* to the original fallacy.

The concept of an opponent fallacy is important to the study of *petitio principii* as an informal fallacy. For it suggests that the fallacy must be judged against a pragmatic background of a two-person dialectical exchange where a criticism is advanced, and may then be responded to, successfully or unsuccessfully. It is not always the critic who is in the right. A premature or inadequate criticism of fallaciousness may itself, in some cases, be said to have committed a fallacy. Hence the study of begging the question as a fallacy should take this dialectical framework into account, with the result that the *petitio principii* fallacy may be more complex than it has initially seemed. There may be several kinds of falla-cies involved.

DeMorgan (1847, p. 255) also cites and identifies another kind of opponent fallacy of begging the question.

Case 7.0:   There is an opponent fallacy to the *petitio principii* which, I suspect, is of the more frequent occurrence: it is the habit of many to treat an advanced proposition as a begging of the question the moment they see that, if established, it would establish the question. Before the advancer has more than stated his thesis, and before he has time to add that he proposes to prove it, he is treated as a sophist on his opponent's perception of the relevancy (if proved) of his first step. Are there not persons who think that to prove any previous propositions, which necessarily leads to the conclusion adverse to them, is taking an unfair advantage?

What DeMorgan cites here as an opponent fallacy is a special case of something that is a basic problem in two-person argumentation having the form of question-reply exchanges. It may happen that one party constantly refuses to make commitments, answering every question, "I don't know," or "I really couldn't say."[1]

What DeMorgan is suggesting is that the fault of prematurely attacking an argument as an instance of the fallacy of begging the question–when the real evidence does not merit this charge–is itself a kind of fallacy. Just as the fallacy of *petitio principii* is a fault (at least partly) because a proponent of an argument is too aggressive in trying to push his argument ahead, the opponent fallacy is a fault of being too defensive by refusing to make any concession at all that might possibly be used by the other side.

Of course, neither aggressiveness nor defensiveness are, in themselves, fallacious in persuasion dialogue. But DeMorgan has a point, that the systematic use of an unjustified and improper imputation of *petitio* could be the sort of systematic error or deceptive tactic that might merit being called a fallacy of sorts.

The premature allegation that an argument begs the question just because the argument is deductively valid is based on an erroneous conception of the fallacy of begging the question. In a deductively valid argument, it is true to say that if the premises were to be established, then the conclusion would be established too. From the point of view of anyone who opposes the conclusion, such an argument will be objectionable. But, of course, it does not follow that the argument is fallacious or, in particular, that it commits the fallacy of begging the question. Generally speaking, equating the fallacy of begging the question with any argument where the premises deductively imply the conclusion is a kind of pseudofallacy itself.

This particular pseudo-fallacy is closely connected to the Sextus-Mill argument (chapter one, section five) to the effect that all deductive reasoning is inherently circular. But, as shown in chapter one, the Sextus-Mill thesis is based on a failure to allow for, or to appreciate the pragmatic context in which a deductive argument is used for purposes of proving or persuading in reasoned dialogue.

Let us reconsider the syllogistic argument used by Mill (1843, p. 120) as his classic case of *petitio principii*.

Case 7.1:   All men are mortal.
Socrates is a man.
Therefore, Socrates is mortal.

Mill claims that this argument has to be circular because the first premise depends on the conclusion. The conclusion has to be part of the proof that is required to establish the first premise, according to Mill (and earlier, Sextus).

But need this be the case? The answer, as we saw in chapter one, is negative. A biologist, for example, might have presented an argument for the mortality of all men that does not depend on the mortality of Socrates, in particular, for the argument to go through. Whether the argument in case 7.1 is circular or question-begging therefore depends on the context of dialogue. It depends on the line of reasoning, or lack thereof, advanced by the proponent in the context of the dispute of which this argument is a part.

Hence to identify circularity with deductive validity is an oversimplification. It is to make begging the question into a pseudo-fallacy. It is surprising how often the logic textbooks support this pseudo-fallacy by claiming that an argument begs the question only because the premises are more general than the conclusion, and that the argument assumes the truth of the conclusion. For example, Creighton (1917, p. 180) defines *petitio principii* or begging the question as "a form of argument which assumes the conclusion to be proved." An example used by Creighton (pp. 180-81) can be compared with case 7.0.

Case 7.2:   The question may be begged by making a general assumption covering the particular point in dispute. Thus, if the advisability of legislation regulating the hours of labour in a mine or factory were under discussion, the question-begging proposition, "all legislation which interferes with the right of free contract is bad," might be propounded as a settlement of the whole question.

Now, in fairness to Creighton, this argument could be circular. But the problem is that not enough context of the dialogue is given for us to say fairly whether it is or not. The error is to claim that the argument does beg the question just because the universal premise (taken together with the appropriate enthymematic premise) deductively implies the conclusion at issue. By itself, this is not good enough.

DeMorgan's point is that the (anonymous) person who is being accused of committing a fallacy, in a case like 7.1, is not being dealt with fairly. Just because his premise (with suitable additions) implies the conclusion at issue, that should not be regarded as a sufficient basis for rejecting his argument peremptorily as inevitably question-begging. So to proceed is to commit an opponent fallacy.

Bertrand Russell was once put in the position of having to defend himself against exactly this sort of attack by a critic who claimed that Russell had assumed the existence of the infinite in his proof of the existence of the infinite in the *Principles of Mathematics*. Russell defended himself (1973, pp. 256-259) by claiming that although his proof assumed premises that are not mathematically demonstrable, it should not, simply on that basis, be rejected as circular or fallacious. Russell conceded that his premises together implied the actual infinite, but he denied that they presupposed the actual infinite.

Pushed to defend himself against this criticism of begging the question, Russell made the general point that presupposition is different from implication.   According to Russell, although these two things are commonly confounded in philosophical argumentation, they should be distinguished, or otherwise all deduction is circular:

Case 7.3:   In all correct deductions, if the conclusion is false, so is at least one of the premises. The falsehood of the premises presupposes the falsehood of the conclusion, but it by no means follows that the truth of the premises presupposes the truth of the conclusion. The root of the error seems to be that, where a deduction is very easily drawn, it comes to be viewed as actually part of the premises; and thus very elementary arguments acquire the appearance, quite falsely, of *petitiones principii.*

This case is interesting, because it shows the point of view of a participant in philosophical argumentation (a very able one, at that) who has to defend himself against the charge that he has committed the fallacy of begging the question. In effect, Russell throws the burden of proof back onto his critic by showing why the charge is unfounded, and even by revealing the pseudo-fallacy upon which the charge was based.

The problem with too many of the examples of allegedly question-begging arguments used by the textbooks is that they don't take the step of looking at the argument from the point of view of the one who is criticized. And therefore they don't do a proper job of presenting enough evidence from the context of argumentation properly to back up a charge of *petitio principii*. In the case of the Cartesian circle (chapter five, section four), Descartes was actually able to defend his own argument against a charge of committing the fallacy of begging the question by revealing a subtle ambiguity in the text of the *Meditations*. Too often, the author is not present to defend himself in cases of this sort.

4. BURDEN OF PROOF ON THE CRITIC

One lesson that has come out of the detailed analysis of case studies of criticisms of begging the question is the difficulty of adequately pinning this type of criticism down. Sidgwick (1910, p. 206) showed an exceptionally deep insight into this important problem when he wrote that although we dream of being able to "nail" a fallacy of this sort "definitely to the counter" with all the authority of logic, in fact the charge of begging the question is a "peculiarly difficult one to substantiate."[2] One inherent problem is that the task of substantiation depends on our capability as critics to work up a good argument reconstruction of the original text of the argument in question. And as chapter five showed, the method of argument reconstruction has inherent limitations, especially where the argument is a serious and subtle scientific or philosophical argument. Another problem, demonstrated by the shorter case studies in chapter four, is that the context of dialogue, in many cases, may not be completely given or known. And, in such a case, the criticism must be conditional on where a line of argument could possibly go from the point known, according to the given information.

It is because of these inherent difficulties in pinning down a criticism that an argument has committed the fallacy of begging the question that burden of proof should be involved at the meta-level of criticism. Because of these same difficulties, as well, the error of having committed a fallacy may fall more onto the critic than on the one initially criticized. Sometimes criticisms of *petitio* are so poorly documented that one could be justified in concluding that it is the critic who has committed the fallacy.

These conclusions lead to a meta-argumentation problem of allocation of burden of proof. Who has the burden of proof–the critic who alleges that an argument begs the question, or the defender who alleges that it does not? This question has no easy answer, straightforwardly applicable to all cases. But, in general, the burden of proof should fall more strongly upon the critic who has alleged that someone's argument commits the fallacy of begging the question to (1) show by argument reconstruction that there is a circle in the argument, and (2) show indications from the text or context of dialogue that evidential priority is applicable as a requirement of the argument. Certainly these conditions apply to persuasion dialogue. Let us therefore deal with the case of persuasion dialogue first, and then go on to discuss the inquiry in the next section.

Any ruling on burden of proof, of course, should be sensitive to the distinction between the fallacy of begging the question–meaning that the argument so criticized is to be strongly refuted–and the procedural objection that an argument is open to a charge of begging the question as a point of order. This weaker type of objection to an argument can be legitimate, but it should not be confused with the stronger type of objection claiming that an argument commits the fallacy of begging the question. Let us formulate the weaker burden of proof rule first–the rule that applies to the point of order. Then we will formulate a stronger rule for the claim of fallaciousness.

Generally, the burden of proof is on a critic of an argument who alleges that an argument is open to criticism, on the grounds that it begs the question, to show that the context of argument is appropriate for the requirement of evidential priority to be obligatory. This is stated in the following *burden of proof rule for criticisms based on a requirement of evidential priority (Burden EP-Rule).*

BURDEN EP-RULE: If a criticism has been advanced that an argument is faulty, not useful, or open to criticism as an instance of begging the question, the burden of proof is on the critic, not on the proponent of the argument, to show that the text and context of dialogue indicate that evidential priority is an appropriate requirement for the argument in question.

By the Burden EP-Rule, the critic is obliged to give evidence of one of the three forms indicated below, in order to back up his criticism as a reasonable one.

1. Internal evidence within the dialogue may be given by the recipient. The recipient will likely have indicated doubts or nonacceptance of the plausibility of the conclusion of the argument, and it should be clear what burden of proof is required to overcome these doubts.

2. External evidence is given by what we know of the context of dialogue. The context of the dialogue may be that of a dispute, like the dispute on tipping in chapter one, where the issue to be contended is clear.

3. Most importantly, internal evidence may be given by key indicator-words. There are indicator-words in the corpus of dialogue that indicate a requirement of evidential priority.

For example, an arguer might state his argument in the following terms: "Now we have established such-and-such [a set of premises], we can conclude on this basis that such-and-such other proposition [the conclusion] is also established." This type of internal evidence is often the best available indication of a requirement of evidential priority.

Clearly, in persuasion dialogue the Burden EP-Rule applies only to the first two levels of analysis. But if an allegation is made that the *fallacy* of begging the question has occurred, tactical considerations at level three must be taken into account. In this type of case, the critic must meet even stronger requirements of burden of proof in order to make his criticism stick. Here he must show (again by the appropriate textual and contextual evidence) that the proponent of the argument has adopted a systematic tactic of exclusion of all other lines of reasonable argumentation to support the premise in question, other than those that include, or are dependent on, the conclusion to be proved in the discussion. This leads to the formulation of a stronger burden of proof rule to cover this type of case.

BURDEN TACTICAL RULE: If a criticism has been advanced that an argument is a case of the fallacy of begging the question (petitio principii), the burden of proof is on the critic, not on the proponent of the argument, to show (1) that the text and context of dialogue indicate that evidential priority is an appropriate requirement for the argument in question and, (2) that the text and context of dialogue show that the proponent has adopted a systematic tactic of excluding all lines of argumentation that support the premises, other than ones that include, or depend on, the conclusion to be proved in the dialogue.

The evidence required to meet the Burden Tactical Rule requires utilization of an argument diagram in conjunction with evidence from the text and context of dialogue pertaining to the proponent's tactics used to support his argument.

Applying these burden of proof rules, in order to rule on whether a criticism of *petitio* is justified or not, requires judgment, especially in the kinds of briefly presented cases that are so prevalent in logic textbooks. In many of these cases, the critic (the textbook author) has not backed up his criticism strongly enough.

Some of the most problematic kinds of cases are those where little indication of the type of dialogue is given, and little context of an isolated argument is given. According to the graph method of Walton and Batten (1984), once the premises and relevant rules of inference are given, the graph displays all possible ways of proving the conclusion from the given premises. Hence theoretically, according to this method, an argument is either inevitably circular or it is not. But a practical problem inherent in applying this method to cases is that in fact all the premises (or even the ultimate conclusion) may not be given. Thus practically speaking, any judgment of begging the question in an argument must be relative to what is known about the argument.

5. Critical Burden in the Inquiry

Another problem is that the Burden EP-Rule and the Burden Tactical Rule don't seem to apply to the inquiry in the same way they applied to judging cases of *petitio principii* in the persuasion dialogue. From previous discussions of the inquiry, it would appear that the Burden Tactical Rule is not needed, and that the Burden EP-Rule, by itself, is enough to certify an argument as a case of the fallacy of begging the question. Why is this so? It seems it is so because the inquiry is cumulative.

The goal of cumulative reasoning is to work from premises based on solid highly confirmed evidence so that one's conclusions will be highly reliable, and not subject to continued controversy and questioning.[3] In this context, any circular argument violating evidential priority seems like such a bad or questionable kind of argument that it can be refuted as fallacious purely by means of the Burden EP-Rule. No stronger rule appears to be needed.

Euclidean geometry is a good example of the attempt to achieve cumulative reasoning in science. The theorems are deduced from propositions called *axioms,* which are supposed to be premises that can be accepted as highly plausible, or even clearly self-evident.[4] Then from these well-established premises, conclusions called *theorems* can be deduced using logical inferences. The sequence of reasoning in this context of argument is supposed to have a certain direction or flow. The theorems are numbered, and they have higher numbers than the axioms. As Mackenzie (1980) has shown, circular reasoning is simply not tolerated in this context of argument.

Take, for example, the Pythagorean theorem that the square on the hypotenuse of a right-angled triangle is equal to the sum of the squares on the other two sides. If asked to prove this theorem, a student would be expected to deduce it from the axioms, or from some previous theorems deduced from the axioms at an earlier stage. It would not do to argue, "The Pythagorean theorem is true, therefore the Pythagorean theorem is true." This circular argument would violate the more plausible premises rule, applicable in this cumulative context of argument.

In this kind of context, the requirement of evidential priority is so clearly applicable that a critic scarcely needs to argue to meet the burden of showing that it is a requirement. It would be stating the obvious. So in this type of case, the burden seems to fall more onto the defender to deny that evidential priority is applicable to his argument. However, in a cumulative inquiry, as Euclidean geometry is intended to be, any chance of this defense succeeding is virtually non-existent, and clearly so from the outset. Hence even in this type of case, it seems that the burden may still be on the critic's side, but it is such an easy burden to meet that tactical considerations appear to be irrelevant.

However, if Basu (1986) is right, tactical considerations may not be so irrelevant as they seem in judging *petitio principii* in the inquiry. According to Basu (p. 20), Aristotle's theory of demonstration was not intended as a model of how scientific research should proceed. Basu thinks that, instead, it was intended to be interpreted as a model of didactic dialogue, a model of how a teacher should present knowledge to a student. According to this interpretation, the scientific tutor begins a particular case of demonstration with a particular proposition to be demonstrated. Then he goes on to search for some premises to use for this purpose. However, ultimately he has to use some basic premises from which he works his way to other premises from which the conclusion follows. According to the interpretation of demonstration suggested by Basu, the scientific tutor gets these basic premises from the field scientist–they represent established propositions that represent the state of knowledge in a particular scientific discipline.

On this interpretation of the Aristotelian concept of a demonstration–which could apply, as well, to its modern counterpart, the inquiry–the demonstration (inquiry) is not a model of how scientific hypotheses were originally discovered or confirmed by working scientists. Rather, it is an account of how these propositions are organized and presented as knowledge, once these results have been consolidated and are ready to be presented (perhaps in a scientific research paper, a textbook, or in teaching the state of the art).

This interpretation fits Euclidean geometry very well. For the numbering of theorems in Euclidean geometry does not necessarily represent an order of discovery of the various propositions. Instead, it represents a careful tidying up and presentation of the results, for the purposes of instructing others on how the theorems can be deduced from the given axioms.

It seems then that the inquiry is somewhat more complex than it may have initially appeared to be. As a species of reasoned dialogue, it may have a strong didactic element. And if careful presentation is one of the goals, it is no longer so obvious that tactical considerations are to be excluded. Of course, the argumentation tactics in the inquiry may be quite different than those appropriate for persuasion dialogue.

Galen *(circa* 129-199), a leading theorist of scientific demonstration in antiquity, saw demonstration as a way of trying to defend scientific knowledge from the attacks of skeptics. Galen's short treatise "On the Best Teaching" argued against the skeptic Favorinus, who taught his students to argue for both sides of a disputed point.[5] Galen argued that this freewheeling approach would destroy confidence in the common starting points of human knowledge and instead advocated the "linear" proof *(grammatike apodeixis)* of geometry as the best pattern of scientific proof to be taught to students.

Unfortunately, Galen's major work on demonstration *De Demonstratione (Peri Apodeixeos)* was lost some time after the sixth century.[6] However, we can get some ideas of Galen's views from other writings that survived. His *Institutio Logica* (Introduction to Logic) concentrated less on questions of the foundations of logical theory, like syllogistic, and more on practical questions of what he calls "usefulness for demonstration" *(Inst. Log.,* ch. XIV, 8). According to Kieffer (Introduction to Galen, *Inst. Log.,* p. 6), the aim of Galen's textbook was to introduce students to a life devoted to scientific investigation. According to Kieffer, demonstration had a double role in science in Galen's view of it. First, demonstration is useful for establishing facts in scientific investigation. And second, demonstration is useful to refute errors, or to argue against the adherents of erroneous theories.

These philosophical views suggest the very plausible hypothesis that the inquiry could be a single model of argumentation that can be used for different purposes, or play different roles in scientific reasoning. First, in a scientific investigation, the researchers in a field may work forward by basing their investigations on assumptions that are already held to be well-established results–by virtue of prior investigations. This way of proceeding is a kind of forward-moving process that would be inimical to circular reasoning generally.

But second, the model of the inquiry could also be used once again when these results are presented in an organized fashion to one's colleagues or students as findings. Yet even in this second use, the cumulative forward-directed kind of argumentation typical of the inquiry can be observed. One begins with established results that can be accepted as assumptions or premises, and then works forward to new findings or conclusions, presented for acceptance. An axiomatic systematization like Euclidean geometry would be the leading case of this second use of the inquiry as a model of argumentation.

These ambiguities and uncertainties about the inquiry as a model of reasoned argumentation suggest that it is an interesting problem for further research to determine what burden of proof rules are for the inquiry and how they should be used in evaluating circular reasoning in the inquiry. Certainly what we can say is that the burden of proof on a reasonable critic needs to be set out and applied somewhat differently in the inquiry than in the case of the persuasion dialogue. In the inquiry, generally the presumption is that any kind of circularity is inappropriate or erroneous. The meta-burden of proof in an inquiry should be placed in the opposite way to that of the persuasion dialogue. That is, in the inquiry, the burden of proof should be on the proponent of any argument that has been shown to be circular by a critic. The proponent should have to show, by the appropriate textual or contextual evidence, either (1) that his argument is not circular, or (2) that his argument does not beg the question even though it is circular. Usually, it would seem that (1) is the better option for a proponent who wants to defend his argument instead of retracting it, because circularity is generally regarded as highly suspicious in any inquiry. This, as we will see in chapter eight, section nine, is because of the linear or tree-structure sequence of reasoning in the inquiry. In principle, circularity is not allowed within the forward-moving probative function characteristic of reasoning in the inquiry.

Whatever the final word on *petitio principii* in the inquiry turns out to be, the textbooks that deal with this fallacy should at least warn the reader that it can occur in contexts of reasoned argumentation other than the persuasion dialogue. And it should be made clear that, in these other contexts, the conditions for setting burden of proof on a critic to make a case for an allegation that the fallacy has been committed may be different from those appropriate for persuasion dialogue. Of course, the vast majority of cases of *petitio principii* we have studied have been instances where the argument has evidently been advanced in the context of a persuasion dialogue. But it is not always so, and the texts should warn of the possibility of dialectical shift in the context of argumentation.

6. CRITICIZING WITHOUT A TEXT OF ARGUMENT

A difficulty with judging many alleged instances of *petitio principii* arises when the critic describes the content of the argument he is criticizing in his own words, instead of giving the exact wording of the text of the argument. In some cases, a particular proponent of the argument in question is not even named. Instead the argument is postulated as representing the point of view of some school of thought or some type of proponent. Clearly this kind of case poses severe problems for applying the Burden EP-Rule and Burden Tactical Rule to the critic's allegations. For these rules require a critic to give evidence from the exact wording of the text he proposes to criticizes.

A good example of this type of case concerns an argument said to beg the question by McTaggart (1918, pp. 134-35). This discussion is on the topic of punishment, and McTaggart expounds Hegel's theory of punishment, but at the same time presents his own views on punishment. According to McTaggart, Hegel "hated nothing more bitterly than sentimental humanitarianism." Following this remark, McTaggart goes on to outline a particular point of view, a school of thought on the philosophy of punishment. Evidently this school of thought is supposed to be that of "sentimental humanitarianism," but McTaggart does not cite any names of proponents of this viewpoint. Nor does he quote any text of argument that is supposed to represent the speeches or writings of this school of thought. Instead, he gives his own thumbnail sketch of what he takes to be the gist of this argumentation on punishment:

Case 7.4:   There are certain people who look on all punishment as essentially degrading. They do not, in their saner moods, deny that there may be cases in which it is necessary. But they think that, if any one requires punishment, he proves himself to be uninfluenced by moral motives, and only to be governed by fear. (It is curious, by the way, that this school generally accepts the idea that government by rewards is legitimate. It does not appear why it is less degrading to be bribed into virtue than to be frightened away from vice.) They look on all punishment as implying deep degradation in some one,— if it is justified, the offender must be little better than a brute; if it is not justified, the brutality is in the person who inflicts it.

Clearly McTaggart is describing the argument of this school in a way that indicates he rejects it, or finds it implausible. And indeed, the criticism he faults it for is that it begs the question:

> This reasoning appears to travel in a circle. Punishment, they say, is degrading, there-fore it can work no moral improvement. But this begs the question. For if punishment could work a moral improvement, it would not degrade but elevate. The humanitarian argument alternately proves that punishment can only intimidate because it is brutalizing, and that it is brutalizing because it can only intimidate.

This appears, at least initially, to be an interesting case of *petitio principii* for analysis. One might well be tempted to work up an argument diagram of the reasoning to see whether McTaggart's allegation of begging the question is justified. But if you try to carry this project out, you will quickly run up against a severe problem.

The problem is that once you start looking for the premises used in the argument to support the conclusion that all punishment is essentially degrading, once questions of unexpressed premises begin to arise, you find no specific text of the argument given. Thus there is no really firm evidence whether something is a premise or not.

This problem becomes acute when McTaggart–who is, remember, a hostile or opposed critic–rephrases and interprets the argument in different wording, in order to bring out the circle he perceives in its reasoning. Certainly McTaggart has shown that a dependency circularity exists, but does the circle fairly represent the argument of the "sentimental humani-tarian"? Having no original text of argument to go on, we are blocked from giving an answer to this question without opening it to the live possi-bility of committing the straw man fallacy, that is, the error of unfairly and unsympathetically representing an opposed party's position in an argument.

The basic problem is that without a specific text to give the exact wording of an argument to be criticized, the process of argument diagramming becomes unstuck in a sea of possible (but unverifiable) alter-native interpretations.

Of course, we could make the argument diagram relative to the assumption that McTaggart's reconstruction of the sentimental humani-tarianism point of view fairly expresses the thrust of the argument. This assumption may or may not be true, but to the extent that McTaggart's statement of this argument does seem like a worthwhile and interesting variant of the argument to examine, it may be a useful exercise to carry out the argument reconstruction based on it.

The extent, then, to which it is a worthwhile project to undertake an argument reconstruction of case 7.4 depends on how accurate and revealing is McTaggart's capturing of the basic argument of sentimental humanitarianism on punishment. If McTaggart has captured the gist of this argument, then the work of reconstructing his version of it, in order to evaluate the *petitio principii* allegation, would be a worthwhile and genuinely interesting project. But if not, or if we have no reason to think so, then McTaggart's criticism of the argument tends to be academic or pointless. For any reconstruction, no matter how subtle or careful, is too susceptible to the straw man fallacy to be of use or interest.

It is in this kind of case where an arguer's dark-side commitments become important. Lacking a specific text of argumentation, a critic can not pin down an explicit commitment of the proponent of the argument by saying: "There it is, in black and white. That's exactly what you said. Do you want to change your mind, or are you going to stick with what you said?" Instead, the critic has to convince his audience that the version or paraphrase he has put forward as the argument at issue really does represent the underlying commitments of the school of thought it is supposed to represent. In principle, he could bring forward evidence to back up this sort of claim. But needless to say, it is harder to back up a claim of this sort than it is in the case of light-side commitments. Dark-side commitments, by their nature, are not fully known until explicitly stated or conceded in an argument, and then they become light-side commitments.

In a case where a charge of *petitio principii* has been made without the exact wording of the text cited, the value or interest of the criticism has to depend on the extent to which the critic's portrayal of the argument criticized represents an important position as a strong enough argument to be worth refuting. In case 7.4, sentimental humanitarianism is not presented as a precise enough argument, or as a position that is compelling enough to command much serious commitment, in order to make McTaggart's *petitio* against it much of a success. However, not all cases of this type are such failures.

The context of the following case is a speech by William Lee Wilbanks (1988) that criticizes a popular point of view, a philosophical position to the effect that whenever anyone does something bad, it is because he "couldn't help doing it." According to this position, as sketched out by Wilbanks, it is becoming a "common myth" of popular belief that human beings are acted on by external forces over which they have no control, and so they should not be held responsible for giving into irresistible temptations. For example (p. 660), smokers are said to be "addicted" to cigarettes, so that they have lost control and cannot help themselves. Alcoholism is said to be a disease, and so it is said that it is impossible for anyone to cure his own alcoholism. Drug addiction is said to be such a powerful force that people who use drugs lose control and can't help themselves. Even groups devoted to helping those "addicted" to extra-marital affairs have been formed to help these people stop their "addictive behavior." Wilbanks sees this popular point of view as being very powerful and influential in current moral thinking, and he makes out a very compelling case for his contention.

In this context, Wilbanks considers yet another phase in the "medicalization of deviance" whereby gambling is said to be a form of "compulsive disease" (p. 663). The position Wilbanks finds to be gaining popular acceptance is that people who gamble are suffering from an uncontrollable craving or compulsion to gamble that can only be cured when the sufferer states in public that he has lost control and seeks help from a Gamblers Anonymous support group.

Investigating the logic of this position further, Wilbanks asks how it distinguishes between a gambling habit and a gambling addiction.

Case 7.5:   How do we distinguish between uncontrolled gambling and uncontrollable gambling? The "professionals" in this field have an easy answer. If someone reaches a point where the gambling appears to be uncontrolled the assumption is made that the gambler has lost control. If there was ever a case of circular reasoning or tautology, surely this is it. The observer tries to explain deviant behavior ("excessive" gambling) by inferring that the cause of the deviance is an uncontrollable compulsion to gamble but the only evidence we have of this uncontrollable compulsion is the excessive gambling. There is no independent evidence of the alleged "addiction" other than the behavior itself.

Now in contrast to McTaggart's argument, this criticism of *petitio* is relatively successful and revealing, primarily for two reasons. One is that Wilbanks gives quite a good account of why the circular reasoning he cites is an inevitable circle, because "no independent evidence" is given by the argument he criticizes, other than the circular reasoning. Another reason is that Wilbanks does such a good job of sketching out the position he criticizes that the reader can see that it is a point of view that hangs together and commands a wide and growing popular support. It is a target worth attacking.

Of course, Wilbanks does not directly quote specific texts of argumentation that represent the views of the "professionals" on gambling that he purports to refute by *petitio principii*. So his argument is inherently open to rejoinder by the straw man criticism. But even so, his article has entered into the dialectic on the issue in an engaging way that takes pains to express the underlying philosophical basis of the position he has criticized. Thus despite its inherent weakness, his use of the *petitio principii* criticism is not entirely worthless as an exercise in argumentation. It is curiously revealing, and if nothing else, it shifts a burden of proof onto those who are inclined to accept the addiction-disease position to defend their point of view against the charge of circularity. Because this position is a viewpoint that appears to be very prevalent as a dark-side commitment in current trends of popular opinion, Wilbanks' exposure and criticism of it in case 7.5 carries weight as a social criticism. By contrast, the criticism of begging the question by McTaggart in case 7.4 carries less weight because it is not clear what sentimental humanitarianism represents as a prevalent or compelling dark-side commitment that is further in need of explicit formulation.

7. WORKING FROM A PARAPHRASE

A criticism that a particular argument begs the question, where the specific text of the argument is not supplied, may not be worthless, provided that the critic has given a plausible paraphrase that fairly represents the underlying thrust of the argument he has set out to criticize. But, even so, such a criticism tends to be inherently weaker, because the arguer so criticized can always say in reply, "That doesn't really represent my position on the issue," especially once he sees that the criticism is effective in refuting the paraphrased position. So it is always better to give an exact quotation of the argument you propose to criticize as question-begging.

On the other hand, some arguments are subtle and complex. Producing a paraphrase can be a valuable part of the procedure of argument diagramming. If the paraphrase is sympathetic and really enters into the dialectic, representing the dark-side commitments of its proponent in a convincing and revealing manner, even the resulting "second-hand" version of the argument may be well worth discussing and evaluating.

The classic instance of this is case 4.14, where a version of the argument to justify induction is criticized by Rosenberg (1978) as an instance of the fallacy of begging the question.

Of course, the danger of any secondary paraphrase of an argument, like Rosenberg's, that does not cite the exact wording of the original text to be criticized, is the straw man fallacy. The criticism can always be repelled as a misrepresentation. The proponent of the argument to justify induction that Rosenberg is engaged in criticizing is really a hypothetical construct of Rosenberg's. Let us call this hypothetical proponent the *h-proponent*.

Who is to say, then, whether Rosenberg's way of structuring the argument is, or should be, acceptable to the h-proponent? The h-proponent does not actually exist, so he cannot be consulted. And we do not have the text of his argumentation to act as a guide in reconstructing his views. This raises some interesting questions about the burden of proof on a critic.

There is an ambiguity in Rosenberg's representation of what is supposed to be the thesis to be proved by the h-proponent. In case 4.14, Rosenberg is quoted as writing, "The issue in dispute . . . is whether *any* expectation about the future is reasonable." But in the quotation cited just below case 4.14, Rosenberg cites the issue in different terms: "The question is whether any of our expectations is reasonable." According to this (quite different) interpretation of the issue, the h-proponent's thesis to be proved is that any of our expectations (and not exclusively our expectations about the future) is reasonable. The second interpretation is a much more broad construal of the h-proponent's thesis than the first.

Following the argument reconstruction in figure 4.21, let's take the first interpretation as representing the h-proponent's conclusion. Even granting this presumption, several other questions of interpretation remain.

There are two ways of interpreting the justification of induction as an argument—a stronger and a weaker way. According to the weaker interpretation, the argument claims that it is reasonable to expect the future more or less to resemble the past, in the way it has done in the past. This version of the argument takes it to be a kind of plausible reasoning about normal expectations, which by their nature are subject to exceptions. This argument can perspicaciously be viewed as an *argumentum ad ignorantiam,* to the effect that (in the absence of evidence to the contrary) there is no justification for expecting anything different from the way things have generally happened in the past. This version of the argument claims that if there is no good reason to think that the future will *not* resemble the past in a particular instance–like one's waking up as a cockroach, or something of the sort–then it is a reasonable (but defeasible) presumption that the future will be similar to the past. On this interpretation, the argument is not a knowledge claim, but only a claim about what it is reasonable to presume in normal circumstances.

A second and stronger interpretation is that the proponent who is trying to justify induction is making the claim that expectations are verified as knowable because they work. When Russell, as quoted by Rosenberg, puts the justifier's claim as the argument "that we have reason to know that the future will resemble the past," he is evidently interpreting the argument in this stronger way. Rosenberg's own phraseology, however, in terms of "reasonable expectations," consistently suggests the weaker interpretation (despite the quote from Russell).

In judging whether the circle in the argument revealed in figure 4.21 is an instance of the fallacy of begging the question, it is a matter of applying the rules for burden of proof on a critic. Should there be a requirement of evidential priority placed on the h-proponent's argument? In trying to answer this question, there is no original text to go by. But it is also important to notice that there are no key indicator-words like "now we can establish" or "on this basis, it can be proved" in Rosenberg's paraphrase of the argument.

Of course, the stronger interpretation of the argument, suggested by Russell's use of the term "know," might be used as a basis for requiring evidential priority. But is the h-respondent claiming to *know* that the future will resemble the past? On Rosenberg's paraphrase of the h-proponent's argument (apart from the Russell quote), there appears to be no evidence to support this stronger interpretation. It follows that, even though the argument is circular, as figure 4.21 shows, it should be judged questionable whether the requirement of evidential priority is applicable, and whether the argument begs the question.

On the other hand, as noted in chapter four, section eight, the whole project of *justifying* induction seems to imply a need for evidential priority. How could you satisfactorily justify induction by an argument that already presupposes that at least some instances of inductive reasoning are justified or reasonable, as trustworthy arguments? The nature of the dispute itself seems to put at least some measure of burden of proof on the side of the h-proponent to vindicate the circle in his reasoning, when reconstructed along the lines indicated by Rosenberg's paraphrase of it.

Given all the open questions about the exact wording of the h-proponent's argument, and the strong evidence of the appropriateness of the weaker interpretation of the argument as being expressed by Rosenberg's paraphrase of it, this burden of proof should be judged a light one.

How could the h-proponent shift this light burden of proof back onto his critic, Rosenberg? He could do this quite effectively and reasonably by bringing out the essentially defeasible nature of his claim, as follows. He could begin by emphasizing that it will have to remain a matter of conjecture whether the future will in fact resemble the past. Conjectures can never be proven or established beyond reasonable doubt. They are fallible. Even so, we have to make plans about the (uncertain) future. In doing so, it is reasonable to expect that the future will resemble the past in many cases (with exceptions), and to base this presumption on the conclusion that some expectations about the future are reasonable.

Of course, this latter proposition cannot be established as knowledge, or anything we can ever be highly assured of as reliable and solid fact. But that need not prevent us from facing the future, basing our planning on the presumption that things will remain relatively stable except where there are indications to the contrary. True, this is a shaky assumption, which turns out in many cases to have been unjustified. But *(ad ignorantiam),* it is a reasonable, general presumption to make in trying practically to carry out one's goals in the face of an uncertain and changeable (but fairly stable) future, which does tend to resemble the past in ways that are often predictable.

True, in planning, one is continually incorporating feedback into modifying one's plans and actions as the future becomes the past. And this is a circular process. But is the circularity fallacious? Does it beg the question to be proved by the h-proponent? It is open to him to deny the charge, on the grounds that his proof is based on plausible reasoning rather than well-established knowledge, because that is the best one can ever hope for in making assumptions about the future anyway.

Provided that the h-proponent recognizes the circle in his argument, and that he recognizes that his argument is not a proof in the sense of a conclusion established by an inquiry, or other sort of argument that requires evidential priority, he can shift the burden of proof back onto his critic. This would imply that the burden of proof is on the critic to show why our expectations about the future are not reasonable, or to show why we should expect something in the future that is different from what has happened in the past. If it is possible to be skeptical about induction, it is likewise possible to be skeptical about the point of view that the future is so unlike the past that induction, or assuming that any of our expectations about the future are reasonable, is an inherently worthless or useless kind of argumentation.

Looking more carefully, then, to the explicit rules for burden of proof on a critic (given in chapter seven, section four), we see that the weaknesses in the allegation of question-begging put forward by Rosenberg in case 4.17 have become more apparent.

For someone who requires a justification of induction that does not itself depend on the presumption that induction is, at least in some cases, a reasonable kind of argumentation, the argument paraphrased by Rosenberg will not be useful. This argument does not try to base induction on some more reliable kind of argumentation, other than induction. Hence it is circular. But this circular argument can only rightly, and with justification, be said to beg the question once the requirement of evidential priority is shown to be clearly part of the program of the justification of induction.

Thus the argument considered by Rosenberg poses a question. What is to count as a *justification* for the purposes of the problem of justifying induction? The argument paraphrased by Rosenberg does offer a practical vindication of induction as a fallible, but by no means worthless, method of dealing with an uncertain future. But it does not succeed in justifying induction by basing it on some less fallible or more reliable method of argumentation than induction.

But whether this failure is a fallacy, or means that the argument begs the question it is supposed to resolve, depends on how you construe it as a program of justification. The circle is an inevitable one in figure 4.21, at least in the sense that no evidential route to ① is given that does not depend on a premise that depends on ①. But this circle is not an error unless it can be shown that it violates a requirement of evidential priority. This is a claim that is far from conclusively warranted by the textual and contextual evidence available in Rosenberg's paraphrase of the argument.

So despite the ingenuity of Rosenberg's argument, it has turned out to be quite a bit harder than we initially thought for it to be used successfully to pin down a criticism of begging the question against the justifier of induction. Not that Rosenberg's attempted refutation is uninteresting or a complete failure; far from it. In fact, his criticism is so revealing precisely because he has entered into the spirit of the dialectic in an engaging and sympathetic way. But the inherent limitations of working exclusively from a paraphrase pose difficulties in meeting the proper requirements of burden of proof on a critic, in order to use the criticism of question-begging as a decisive tool of refutation.

8. RETHINKING QUESTION-BEGGING EPITHET

One area of the textbooks that needs radical rethinking is the fallacy of question-begging epithets. The vast majority of alleged examples of this fallacy cited by the textbooks are cases where it has not been shown, nor does the textual or contextual given evidence clearly indicate, that the reasoning is circular. Many of the alleged examples of this fallacy cited by the text are one-liners or short examples that could possibly be circular arguments (if we found out more about them). But as they stand, they are instances of *assumptio non probata,* DeMorgan's opponent fallacy, or other kinds of argumentation that may look superficially like cases of begging the question, but are not.

One classic case of this type is case 1.4: "This doctrine is heresy; therefore it should be condemned." The use of the loaded (vituperative) term "heresy" in the premise makes the argument an instance of DeMorgan's opponent fallacy. Presumably, heresy being bad, the premise, if established, would establish the conclusion. It is also a case of *assumptio non probata* if the premise has been merely advanced, without any support being given for it. But neither of these things makes the argument fallacious. And indeed, the argument has not been shown to be circular, unless it is shown that the premise depends on, or is equivalent to the conclusion, according to a reconstruction of the reasoning in the argument.

Of course, the argument in case 1.4 might be circular. But then again, it might not be. In the absence of the critic's having presented the evidence required to meet the Burden Tactical Rule or the Burden EP-Rule, no text should cite case 1.4, or a similar case, as an instance of begging the question. That is, however, exactly what the majority of texts currently do. For it is precisely this sort of case that is the paradigm of what is taken to be the fallacy of question-begging epithet. Here, then, is a tradition worth correcting.

Consider the following possible context of dialogue of case 1.4. Herman and Rodney are members of a church that has a list of heresies, formulated in the Holy Writ, and both of them are committed to the sanctity of the Holy Writ as the authoritative word on what is heretical or not. Rodney and Herman agree, in their common starting points, that any doctrine that is heresy (according to the list) should be condemned. Suppose further that Herman cites a particular doctrine, showing to Rodney how it is an instance of one of the items on the list in the Holy Writ. And suppose then that Herman advances the argument of case 1.4 to Rodney. Is Herman's argument an instance of begging the question?

The answer is that, as things stand, Herman's argument should not be judged to beg the question. According to Herman, this doctrine should be condemned because it is on the list, and all items on the list are heresies. Since any heresy should be condemned by both Herman and Rodney, it follows that this doctrine should be condemned by them. This argument is a kind of appeal to authority, and it also has a deductively valid form, but it does not follow that it is circular. The items on the list could (quite possibly) be defended as heretical by the arguments put forward by the doctrines of the church that Herman and Rodney belong to, without depending on the prior presumption of the conclusion that this particular doctrine is to be condemned by Herman and Rodney. In such a context, the argument in case 1.4 need not be circular.

Similarly, in case 1.5, the use of an emotionally loaded phrase like "the most vicious crime known to man" in making a murder charge could certainly be objectionable. But, in itself, the deployment of loaded or emotional terminology does not amount to committing the fallacy of begging the question. To call this use of language "question-begging" is to stretch the concept of begging the question far beyond any reasonable limits that the analysis of chapter eight could bear.

Another case of this sort we have already examined at some length is case 6.0. Here the use of the term "gender-prejudiced" by the psychologist to describe the parents' behavior could well be described in the current idiom of the texts as a question-begging epithet. True, the use of this phrase (perhaps quite unfairly) goes strongly against the parents' point of view. But that is not enough to entitle a critic to conclude that the psychologist's use of this loaded term is part of a circular sequence of reasoning that depends on his conclusion to be proved. It might be, of course. But then again, it might not be. Not all use of prejudicial language is circular reasoning.

Other kinds of cases cited as question-begging epithets, like the use of phrases such as "screwball radical" or "cowardly pacifist" cited under this heading by Copi (1986, p. 103) and Toulmin, Rieke and Janik (1979, p. 167), are closer to the fallacy of complex question, if any fallacy at all is involved. To call these kinds of cases "question-begging epithet," it must be shown that the argument is circular, and the circular reasoning must be identified in an argument diagram.

One might, at this point, begin to wonder whether the whole category of question-begging epithet is really a pseudo-fallacy. Does it always reduce to some non-fallacious objection like *assumptio non probata,* or to some other fallacy like complex question or one of DeMorgan's opponent fallacies? The answer would appear to be "no." For it does appear to be possible that an argument could beg the question because of the kind of loaded terminology used in a premise.

To see why, consider case 1.4 once again. It could well be that in case 1.4, the dialogue might continue as follows. The respondent might ask the proponent how he can prove that the doctrine in question is heresy. Suppose the proponent replies: "Because it is fully deserving of the strongest possible condemnation." Now it is not difficult to show that this new premise, in turn, is dependent on the conclusion of the argument in case 1.4, namely the proposition that the doctrine in question should be condemned (in a linked argument structure). This shown, it is shown that the argument is circular.

At any rate, given the right sort of profile of dialogue, the argument in case 1.4 could be set in a context where the evidence exists to identify it as an instance of begging the question. In such a case, the circularity stems from the usage of a particular term in the premise, namely "heresy," which is argumentative, or slanted. In this kind of case, it seems reasonable enough to call the fault one of question-begging epithet, or question-begging language.

Along these lines then, it seems reasonable to acknowledge the existence of a category of criticism called "question-begging epithet" that can be a fallacy or a point of order of question-begging. The only difference between begging the question generally and the special case of question-begging epithet is that in the latter instance, the problem is inherently linguistic in origin–due to an argumentative or loaded term or phrase used in a premise.

But if cases of question-begging epithet are supposed to be classified as cases of begging the question (as they should be), then the same requirements of burden of proof on a critic must apply here too. And the overwhelming problem with the current treatment of the examples put forward in the texts is that they come nowhere near meeting the proper requirements of critical burden of proof.

Another problem with cases often cited as instances of question-begging epithet is that they are easily confused with circular definitions. A typical case illustrating this kind of problem is discussed in Walton (1989a, p. 247). In this case, two parties are arguing about whether murder is always wrong, or whether there are exceptions to this general rule. Taking the first point of view, one party argues: "Murder is always wrong, because *murder* is defined as unjustified killing." The problem here is that this way of defining "murder," once accepted, leaves the other party no room to argue. It settles the issue, and this aspect of inevitability about it appears to make the argument a case of question-begging.

But is this argument question-begging? For the other party is free to dispute, or even to reject the proposed definition. If established, the definition would establish the thesis of the one side (in a parallel to DeMorgan's opponent fallacy). But does that make it an instance of the fallacy of begging the question? There seems to be good reason to doubt this, as we will see further in discussing a similar kind of case (case 7.7).

9. CIRCULAR DEFINITIONS AND EXPLANATIONS

The fallacy of question-begging epithet has to do with the use of language in an argument. Therefore, like question-begging arguments generally, the fault is the failure of the probative function of reasoning to be fulfilled. In cases of circular definitions and explanations, also often cited by the textbooks as kinds of fallacies, the fault is not probative failure. Evidently then, if there are faults to be found here, it is because explanation and definition have functions that are parallel to the probative function of reasoning that fail to be fulfilled.

Let us consider explanation first. Evidently an explanation that is circular somehow fails to be useful or informative. Where the *explanans* depends on the *explanandum,* the explanation somehow fails to fulfill its function of explaining the thing to be explained (the explanandum). But are circular explanations always worthless? Perhaps not, in feedback situations where the explanandum is inherently circular. If not, then, precisely what requirement of a good or successful explanation is violated by a circular explanation, when it is wrong or unsuccessful? This question is open, and poses a good research project for a pragmatic study of the concept of explanation, which might parallel to some extent the foregoing work on *petitio principii* in the pragmatics of argumentation.

Another excellent question is whether circular explanations should properly be called "fallacious" when they are unsuccessful, wrong, or erroneous because of circularity. Should fallacies be (only) incorrect arguments, or is it possible to have fallacious explanations as well? This is a trickier question than you might think, once Govier's (1987, p. 160) point is taken that the distinction between explanation and argument, normally taken for granted as a clear and straightforward dichotomy, becomes more subtle once we start to take a pragmatic view of argument. It appears that there are some explanations that are not arguments, and some arguments that are not explanations, but there are other cases where the same case can rightly be said to be both an explanation and an argument.

If this is right, an explanation could be fallacious because it is also an argument, and because the argument in it is circular and begs the question in a context of dialogue. Given this possibility, an explanation could be fallacious not because it is a circular explanation–or not entirely because of that–but because it contains a fallacious argument.

However, it is not feasible to explore the concept of circular explanations further here, even though this would be an excellent project for further research. It is enough to comment that the textbooks could cite the distinction between circularity in arguments and circularity in explanations, if only to indicate that the "fallacy" that could be committed by a circularity–if "fallacy" is the right word–is likely to be a different kind of failure than the kinds of errors of argumentation that come under the heading of begging the question.

This is not to say that there will not turn out to be parallels in these two kinds of cases. Mackie (1967, p. 178) draws the parallel quite well.

Case 7.6: Just as a circular argument fails to give support, so a circular explanation fails to explain. There are concealed circularities of explanation; for example, some mental performance is explained by reference to a faculty, but further inquiry shows either that to say that this faculty exists is only to say that such performances occur or that, although more may be meant, there is, apart from such performances, no evidence for the existence of the faculty. Words like "tendency," "power," "disposition," and "capacity" lend themselves to circularities of this sort.

Still, some caution is needed, and whether Mackie is justified in calling these kinds of fault "fallacies in explanation" remains to be seen. If an explanation, for example, that tries to explain the efficacy of a sleep remedy by referring to its "dormative power" is a bad or useless explanation because of its circularity, it may remain unclear in what sense the explanation is an instance of the fallacy of begging the question. To investigate this kind of claim, we need to know what corresponds in explanation to the tactical level of argumentation analysis. This finding awaits a pragmatic analysis of the concept of explanation.

The issue of whether circular definitions can properly be said to be fallacious, at first sight, appears to be parallel to the issue of circular explanations. To investigate the issue, you would presumably have to look into the different functions in a discussion, and then specify when and how the use of a circular definition fails to fulfill a particular function.

But this parallel breaks down, in many cases, it seems, because the kind of fallacy of begging the question often cited in the texts is more the use of a definition in an argument that has a probative function. The *petitio principii* in these cases is not a problem of a circular definition *per se,* but rather it is a circular argument where a definition is advanced as part of the proponent's tactic of inevitability.

A good case in point is the following example cited by Damer (1980, p. 32) as an instance of the fallacy of "question-begging definition."

Case 7.7:   Suppose that Paul maintains the empirical claim that *true* love never ends in separation or divorce. When he is presented with examples of true love followed by divorce, he insists that such cases were not *genuine* cases of true love. His "evidence" that they were not cases of true love is that they ended in divorce. Paul is hereby settling the issue by definition, for his judgment is that any marriage that ends in divorce could not have been a case of true love. No evidence is allowed to count against his claim. If Paul wishes to define *true love* as love that would not end in separation, that is his prerogative, although such a definition is a questionable one from the perspective of ordinary language.

According to Damer, the fallacy here stems from Paul's tactic of presenting his claim as an empirical one, when in his argument he treats it more like a definitional claim. This could be a kind of confusion, or perhaps illusion.

Nevertheless, Paul has a right to introduce a proposed definition of one of the key terms in his argument. If Paul's respondent in the argument thinks that Paul's definition is objectionable, then he (the respondent) has a right to object to it. No fallacy is committed by either side at this point.

If Paul clings too strongly to his proposed definition, however, in the face of reasonable objections to it, this refusal to deal with objections could be subject to reasonable criticism.

In the description of case 7.7, Paul is proposing a definition that would win the argument in favor of his own side. Moreover, he is "insisting" that his definition has to be accepted, and he allows no evidence "to count against his claim."

One can see an aspect of inevitability here. Paul clings dogmatically to his own way of defining "love," thereby excluding any possibility for his critic to bring forward the apparently relevant evidence that would cast his argument into doubt, or even refute it, given a more standard interpretation of the word "love."

As already noted in chapter seven, section one, however, the usual problem with this type of case is not circularity, but more simply the use of a premise that has not been adequately justified. Such cases, for example, are often instances of *assumptio non probata* or of DeMorgan's opponent fallacy. But in case 7.7, a circle is involved, for if Paul insists on defining "true love" as love that would not end in separation, and his conclusion to be proved is that true love never ends in separation (or divorce, a form of separation), then his reasoning is circular. His premise, even though it is only a definition (ostensibly) and not an empirical proposition, has to depend on the truth of the conclusion for it to make sense as an acceptable definition.

One difference between this case, and the "murder is always wrong" case discussed in section eight, is that according to Damer's description of case 7.7, Paul is "settling the issue by definition" and "[n]o evidence is allowed to count against his claim." Another difference is that in case 7.7, as we have shown, there is definite textual evidence that a circular sequence of reasoning is expressed in the argument.

Of course, in the murder case, these two additional elements could be present as well in the context of dialogue. But until the right evidence is brought forward to establish this by a would-be critic, it should not be classified as a case of question-begging epithet.

Both these cases are extremely interesting, however, because they show how many cases, of the kind so often cited by the texts, teeter on the borderline between two fundamentally distinct categories of critical failure: (1) cases of overly aggressive or pre-emptive use of language, or deployment of argumentative definitions; and (2) genuine, certifiable cases of an argument that begs the question in a discussion. Many of these cases clearly fall into category (1) and teeter on the brink of falling into category (2), if only more evidence from the context of dialogue could be brought forward. Yet in the absence of such evidence, placing this kind of argument in category (2) is itself a kind of error.

Much depends on exactly how the definition in question is put forward by its proponent. If our interpretation of case 7.7 is right, it does seem that Paul's way of putting forward his definition of true love involves an inevitable circle.

What we seem to have here, then, is a classical case of a dependency *petitio* that begs the question through failure of its probative function to meet the requirement of evidential priority in its context of persuasion dialogue. The only twist is that the offending premise is really a proposition that is supposed to be true by definition of the key word that occurs in it, even though some attempt is made by the proponent to make the proposition play the role of an empirical proposition in the argument.

It would seem that, in general, circular explanation and circular definition are more closely connected than you might initially think, in regard to why both can be thought useless or incorrect. This is so because the purpose of offering a definition is often to *explain* the meaning of the term to be defined. Presuming that the term may be unclear to any respondent who is supposed to make use of the definition, using that same term again in the definition would defeat the purpose of offering the definition. Hence a circular definition is a kind of useless explanation of the meaning of a term. It is useless in a way parallel to the way a circular argument is useless to fulfill a probative function of argument.

Along these lines, the suggestion may be put forward that a definition or an explanation can have a clarifying function–it is supposed to make something clear that was previously unclear. To fulfill this function in a context of explanation or definition, a kind of conceptual priority requirement must be met–the explanation or definition must appeal only to concepts that are clearer than the concept to be explained or defined, according to the understanding of the audience to whom the explanation or definition is supposed to be useful for purposes of clarification.

Copi (1982, p. 166) expresses the connection between circular definition and explanation succinctly in his discussion of the rule, "A definition must not be circular" in his chapter on definition: "It is obvious that if the definiendum itself appears in the definiens, the definition can explain the meaning of the term being defined only to those who already understand it. In other words, if a definition is circular, it will fail in its purpose, which is to explain the meaning of its definiendum." It is interesting to note that, at least in some cases, a circular definition fails in its purpose because it is an inadequate explanation.

An excellent research project would be to inquire into what is wrong with circular definitions and circular explanations, based on what we already know about circular arguments and what is wrong with them (when they are open to criticism).

10. WHAT THE TEXTS SHOULD AIM FOR

A leading recommendation for revising the textbooks calls for getting away from the current practice of treating examples of *petitio principii* as one-step arguments that seem like such obvious blunders they can peremptorily be dismissed without much real analysis of the specific error allegedly committed. This means moving toward a policy of treating an example of a fallacious argument as a case that requires enough context of argument to be filled in to permit an adequate analysis of the alleged failure, utilizing evidence from the text and context of the argument.

To properly analyze any purported case of the fallacy of begging the question, the textbooks should adopt a case study approach that begins by identifying the argument. The very first question to be asked is: what is the conclusion? The next question is: what are the premises? Moreover, what is critical to *petitio* is to identify the proponent's ultimate conclusion (thesis, point of view) in the global context of dialogue.

This first stage of evaluating for *petitio* should begin with a reconstruction of the sequence of reasoning by means of an argument diagram. Another important recommendation for revising the textbooks is that the fallacy of begging the question should be studied either alongside or after the technique of argument diagramming has been taught. The two topics should not be treated as though they were unrelated to each other—as is now almost universally the case in both current and traditional texts. The two techniques should be taught and used so that they fit together, each one supporting the other.

Another important recommendation is for textbooks to show a greater sensitivity to the possibility that there can be different contexts of dialogue. This means that the job of showing that an argument commits the fallacy of begging the question must involve essential reference to the goals of dialogue of a particular type, and show why the alleged fallacy involves a failure to meet a legitimate goal, or a strategy of frustrating or trying to block the fulfillment of a goal of dialogue. Where the context is that of persuasion dialogue, much more attention should be given to analysis of reasonable standards of burden of proof appropriate to a case. The evaluation should also take rules of plausible reasoning into account, in evaluating these standards.

The Burden-EP Rule and the Burden Tactical Rule require that a burden be on the critic, that is, in this instance, the textbook author, to show convincingly how the allegedly fallacious argument that is said to beg the question fails to meet evidential priority as an appropriate requirement for the context of dialogue. Use of the Burden Tactical Rule requires the critic to cite some sort of relevant evidence.

The remaining component of a circular argument that makes it a fallacy of *petitio principii* is that the offending argument must be used by its proponent to try to convince its respondent that it is a good (effective) argument that meets its requirement of burden of proof successfully. In other words, there is an element of deception or duplicity involved in the fallacy of *petitio*. It is not that the proponent of the fallacious *petitio* must literally intend to deceive the respondent to whom his argument is directed. Rather, the fallacious *petitio* must be part of a systematic type of argumentation tactic designed to persuade the respondent that the burden of proof has been met, when in fact the circular argument in question is not one that can meet the required burden of proof in the context.

When evaluating a case to investigate or mount a charge of question-begging, generally the textbooks should take a more methodical and comprehensive approach that addresses each of the following seven questions.

1. *What is the reasoning?* First, identify the conclusion and premises of the argument that is alleged to be circular. Then ask what the function of the argument is. Is there a probative function? Be careful here to

consider whether what you are dealing with may be an explanation, or something other than an argument with a probative function.

2. *Is the reasoning circular?* Do an argument diagram. Identify any unexpressed premises. Identify all circles in the digraph of the reasoning.

3. *What is the context of dialogue?* Identify the goal of the dialogue. Identify the proponent and the respondent.

4. *Is there a requirement of evidential priority?* Identify the role of each party to the discussion. In particular, identify the proponent's burden of proof. State the requirements of evidential priority.

5. *What are the proponent's tactics?* Identify whether the circles in the argument are inevitable circles or not. Identify any false assumptions of common starting points. If there is circular reasoning in the argument, show how (by the evidence of the text and context) the proponent is using the circular reasoning to fulfill the probative function (or to appear to do so).

6. *How does the use of circular reasoning interfere (if at all) with the realization of the goal of the dialogue?* Identify whether the circular reasoning is (1) acceptable, (2) grounds for a point of order that the argument begs the question, or (3) grounds for the criticism that the argument is an instance of the fallacy of begging the question. Cite the textual or contextual evidence to support your choice, meeting the requirements for burden of proof on a critic if (2) or (3) is chosen.

7. *How could the proponent of the argument reply most strongly to your criticism of his argument?* Examine further lines of argumentation that may remain open to the proponent. Check to see whether he could reply that your charge involves a pseudo-fallacy like *assumptio non probata,* non-fallacious circularity, or DeMorgan's opponent fallacy.

What the textbooks mainly need to worry about is showing more sensitivity and care in the way the word "fallacy" is thrown about in making charges of *petitio principii*. To make this charge is to enter into a critical dialectic with the position of the proponent of the argument criticized. This means taking care to interpret the textual and contextual evidence in a judicious and balanced analysis that takes all relevant considerations into account. Very often, it is better to construe such criticisms as points of order rather than as allegations that a fallacy of *petitio principii* has been committed. For a carefully documented and supported point of order is very often quite a strong enough criticism to cause an argument to fall down.

NOTES

1. See Walton (1989a).
2. This passage from Sidgwick's *The Application of Logic* (1910) was quoted more fully in chapter one, section seven, where Sidgwick's analysis of *petitio* was outlined.
3. See chapter eight, section nine.
4. Ibid.
5. Gilbert (1967, p. 262).
6. Ibid., pp. 261-62.

8

A Theory of Begging
the Question

In chapter eight, an analytical survey is made of the leading elements, theories, and interpretations that have been used (as expounded already by previous chapters) to try to explain begging the question as a fallacy. These components are put into a broader perspective, which reveals that they are really not so much competing hypotheses or theories as partial explanations of different aspects of begging the question. Out of this wider perspective, a new theory of begging the question is constructed (and advocated) in this chapter.

According to this new theory, an argument will be said to commit the fallacy of begging the question if, and only if, it is an instance of circular reasoning advanced by its proponent as a systematic kind of tactical maneuver designed to frustrate its respondent from raising critical questions about the premises, or the evidential basis of the premises. A circular argument, where a premise depends on or is equivalent to the conclusion, is useless to fulfill its probative function of properly working toward meeting its burden of proof according to the requirements of evidential priority appropriate for the context of dialogue. But worse than this, an argument that commits the fallacy of begging the question uses coercive and deceptive tactics to try to get a respondent to accept something as a legitimate premise that is really not, and to slur over the omission, to disguise the failure of any genuine proof.

Begging the question should primarily and most importantly be regarded as a sophistical tactic type of fallacy that requires a context of dialogue (and within that context, a requirement of evidential priority). This is not to deny that circular reasoning could be a blunder (that is not a fallacy), or an error of reasoning type of fallacy. But it is to deny that begging the question is just an error of reasoning or a blunder. The fallacy of begging the question is inherently pragmatic in nature–it requires essential reference to a context of dialogue. According to the new theory proposed here, the expression, "He accidentally begged the question against himself," makes no sense–see case 4.18–unless the individual's reasoning could be placed in a context of dialogue where he is "arguing with himself" in a kind of internal dialogue where the same person plays two dialectical roles. To beg the question is to beg the question against your opponent in dialogue. Intent to deceive is not necessarily required–see chapter six–but the use of a sophistical tactic in dialogue must be essentially involved. The other requirements will be stated in the summary in section ten.

Compared to what many of the logic textbooks require, this is a relatively strong theory of *petitio* as a fallacy that implies that various other kinds of faulty arguments and argument tactics that are often cited as question-begging–like loaded questions, complex questions, arguments that use overly aggressive language, or arguments that demand concessions that are not properly justified–do not necessarily commit the fallacy of begging the question.[1]

1. THE EPISTEMIC AND DIALECTICAL INTERPRETATIONS

As we look over the conventional wisdom on begging the question, there are two main streams of thought, representing the two basic explanations of begging the question as a fallacy given by the various theoreticians and textbook writers.[2] One is the *epistemic interpretation,* which sees the *petitio* as a failure of knowledge, that is, a violation of a requirement that the premises should be better known than the conclusion of an argument. The other is the *dialectical interpretation,* which sees circular argument as useless to persuade a respondent in dialogue who already doubts the conclusion of the argument.

This duality of interpretations of *petitio* is, of course, characteristic of Aristotle's account of the fallacy, as we saw in chapter one, section four.[3] In the *Topics* and the *De Sophisticis Elenchis,* Aristotle saw the fallacy as a participant's failure to prove his thesis in a contestive (elenchtic) game of dialogue when such a participant asks for his thesis to be granted (begs for it) without proving it. In the *Prior Analytics* account, begging the question is seen as a different kind of failure. Here the fallacy occurs when an argument that purports to be a demonstration is not genuine because it violates the requirement that the premises be "more certain" or "prior" in relation to the conclusion. Clearly this variant of the fallacy is meant by Aristotle as an epistemic rather than a dialectical failure. Here, circular reasoning is fallacious (when it is fallacious) because it violates an epistemic pecking-order of propositions– the less well known conclusion must be proved only by deriving it from premises that are better known.

The epistemic interpretation was clearly stated by William of Sherwood (thirteenth century), who followed Aristotle's account of this fallacy (or paralogism, as William calls it) fairly closely. In the translation quoted below (Kretzmann, 1966, p. 158) from William's *Introduction to Logic,* Aristotle's concept of "prior and better known premises" is in the forefront of the explanation.

The acceptability of an inference *(veritas argumentationis)* lies not merely in the necessity of the consequence *(consequentie)* but is inseparable from its producing belief regarding a doubtful matter *(sed est simul cum hoc, ut faciat fidem rei dubie)*. That cannot be accomplished, however, except on the basis of [premisses] that are prior and better known.

However, the idea that a circular argument fails to be acceptable because it does not "produce belief regarding a doubtful matter" could equally well apply to the dialectical as to the epistemic interpretation of begging the question.

The epistemic interpretation is also clearly visible in the account of begging the question given by Antoine Arnauld in his *L'Art de Penser* (1662) in the translation (Dickoff and James, 1964, p. 247): "Since what serves as proof must be clearer and better known than what we seek to prove, we see easily enough that begging the question is altogether opposed to genuine reasoning." Certainly the phrase "better known" indicates the epistemic interpretation even if, like William's account, the addition of "clearer" and "seek to prove" could possibly allow other interpretations as well.

As noted in chapter one, section eight, a leading twentieth-century advocate of the epistemic interpretation is John Biro, who explains the fallacy of begging the question as a violation of a requirement of epistemic seriousness. According to Biro (1984, p. 239), an *epistemically serious argument* is one where the premises are more knowable than the conclusion. By this account, an argument that begs the question is one that violates this epistemic requirement.

There are two subspecies of the epistemic interpretation of begging the question. According to the *static theory,* the premises should be better known (better established) than the conclusion. According to the *dynamic theory,* it should be possible to come to know the premises better than the conclusion is presently known. Or to put the requirement another way (following Biro), the premises should be more knowable than the conclusion.

William of Sherwood's explanation, that begging the question is a fallacy because it fails to produce belief regarding a doubtful matter, could equally well be applied to a dialectical context of persuasion dialogue where one party doubts a conclusion the other party is obliged to prove. This dialectical interpretation of begging the question has been included by other writers as well. For example, Whately (1859, p. 220) applied it to the kind of situation where a person addressed in argument is "not likely to know, or to admit" a premise of the argument, "except as an inference" from the conclusion.[4] Here the phrase "likely to know" may suggest an epistemic interpretation, but the inclusion of the phrase "to admit" clearly allows for the dialectical interpretation.

In modern times, John Barker has been a notable advocate of the dialectical interpretation of begging the question. As we noted in chapter one, section eight, Barker (1976, p. 242) claims that the fallacy of begging the question always presupposes a context of disputation. Barker takes this to mean that the fallacy only exists in a context of dialogue where one party doubts a conclusion that another party is trying to prove by means of argument.

A somewhat similar point of view has been put forward and expressed very clearly, by Rosenberg (1978, p. 41), who also sees the fallacy of begging the question as presupposing a dialectical context. According to Rosenberg, there must be two parties to a debate. One is a critic who disputes a conclusion at issue. The other is an arguer who accepts the conclusion as true. The critic who wishes to challenge the thesis must do so, according to the understood rules of the dialectical game, by addressing his challenge "to the structure of reasoning which supposedly supports the arguer's view [conclusion]." To challenge the conclusion directly, instead of challenging the premises it is based on, is to opt out of the game, by not playing according to the understood rules. Hence the fallacy of begging the question is given a dialectical interpretation by Rosenberg that is somewhat different from Barker's explanation.

Similarly, however, according to Barker, the fallacy of begging the question occurs where one person in a disputation asks the other to grant the question at issue that he (the first person) is supposed to prove. According to this approach, the fallacy is committed against one party (the respondent in the disputation) by the other party, who might be called the "perpetrator."

There are two subspecies of the dialectical interpretation of begging the question. According to the *respondent's concession theory,* a circular argument advanced by its proponent is faulty because it asks the respondent to grant or concede some proposition as a premise, when this proposition is the very conclusion that should be proved by the proponent. According to the *common starting point theory (CSP theory),* a circular argument is faulty because it has a premise that is not included in the common store of propositions that both participants (the proponent and the respondent) have agreed not to disagree about.

Most commentators and textbooks have pretty well taken it for granted that the respondent's concession theory is the only explanation of begging the question that makes sense, and most have attributed this theory to Aristotle. Hamblin (1970, p. 33) described begging the question, following Aristotle, as occurring in a context of disputation "on the Greek pattern" where one party sets out to "argue a case to another" and asks that other to grant certain premises on which he may build his case. The fallacy of begging the question then, according to Hamblin, is "asking to be granted the question-at-issue, which one has set out to prove." This description of the fallacy expresses the respondent's concession theory, because the fallacy is described as a transgression of the proponent against the respondent–the respondent is asked to grant a concession that would be improper for him to grant. The respondent should not freely grant this particular kind of proposition because, in the context of the disputation, the proponent must fulfill a burden of proof to this respondent before the respondent should grant the proposition. Thus, on this account, the failure turns essentially on the failure of the proponent's burden of proof, and on the respondent's gratuitous concession of something he should not concede without proper proof.

The non-standard approaches to *petitio* advocated by Johnson (1967) and DeMorgan (1847)–described in chapter one, section three–would seem most likely to come under the common starting point theory. Recently too, there has been a very interesting advocacy of the common starting point theory by van Eemeren and Grootendorst (1984), (1987), and (1989).

2. THE COMMON STARTING POINT THEORY

An alternative theory of begging the question as a fallacy arises from the etymological interpretations of Aristotle by DeMorgan outlined in chapter one, section three. According to this theory, a disputant begs the question if he tries to prove a proposition by deducing it from a principle other than one of the selected general propositions (principles) accepted by both parties as generally received truths–see the quotation from DeMorgan (1847, p. 298) in chapter one, section three. This theory locates begging the question as a special type of failure of burden of proof.

The same general type of theory was suggested by the remarks of Johnson (1967, p. 137), who saw the fallacy of begging the question as the use of a general principle by a disputant to back up his argument, in a case where he cannot (or refuses to) prove the principle. Here too the fault seems to be a failure of burden of proof where the failure applies to the lack of proof for a "general principle" in an argument.

This theory does seem to reveal an aspect of the way the phrase "begging the question" is currently used. Moreover, this theoretical conception of begging the question could be cited as a justification for the widespread tendency in the textbooks to treat arguments that fail to meet burden of proof, or arguments or questions that are inappropriately strong or aggressive in presentation, as instances of the fallacy of begging the question–even if these arguments are not circular. The theory does seem to express a possible meaning of begging the question whereby one party might be said to "beg the question" against another disputant by utilizing a general proposition that the second disputant could not be convinced to accept, because of the prior agreements made by both parties when they agreed to enter into dialogue together.

According to van Eemeren and Grootendorst (1987, p. 288), begging the question or *petitio principii* is one of a group of failures that are violations of the following rule of dialogue for a reasonable critical discussion.

> *Rule VI:*   A standpoint must be regarded as conclusively defended if the defence takes place by means of arguments belonging to the common starting point.

A *common starting point* in a discussion is a set of propositions that both participants agree on at the outset as commitments that they will not cast doubt on. Hence propositions in a common starting point can be presumed by the protagonist of an argument as premises. They do not need to be proved. However, according to van Eemeren and Grootendorst, falsely trying to raise the status of a proposition, as though it were in the common starting point of a discussion, is a common attempt to evade the burden of proof in argument.

Now, of course, the initial point of view (thesis) to be proven by a proponent is not included within the common starting point of a critical discussion. This thesis is subject to doubt by the respondent or antagonist in the discussion. Therefore, by the very nature of a critical discussion, this particular proposition must be excluded from the common starting point, according to van Eemeren and Grootendorst (1984, p. 190). For if it were not excluded, there would be no dispute.

The fallacy of begging the question, according to van Eemeren and Grootendorst (1984, p. 190; 1987, pp. 288-89; 1989, pp. 333-35), arises in two ways. The first way corresponds to the equivalence conception. The second way corresponds to the dependency conception. The fallacy arises in the first way when the protagonist "wrongly assumes that a proposition is one of the common starting points . . . when he defends his standpoint [thesis] by advancing a premise that amounts to the same thing as that standpoint" (1989, p. 33). Such a protagonist turns around in circles because, "like Baron Münchausen," he is trying to "pull himself out of the morass by his own hair." This is an error because the proposition used as premise is the very point at issue in the dispute.

The second way of begging the question cited (1989, p. 334) concerns arguments where the offending premise is not identical with the conclusion, but where the two propositions are interdependent. Citing the God and the Bible example (case 1.3), van Eemeren and Grootendorst (p. 334) diagnose the problem as being that the premise, "The Bible is the word of God" depends on the truth of the proposition "God exists," which is the point at issue. The error here too, then, is a violation of Rule VI, because the protagonist should know that this proposition, "God exists," does not appear in the set of propositions in the common starting point of the dialogue.

This diagnosis of the problem posed by the God and the Bible example is interesting and insightful, because the real problem in this kind of discussion is that the parties tend to lack much common ground to serve as premises or common starting points in their arguments, in order to persuade the other party. Thus it often seems, in such debates, that neither party can make a move that does not beg the question against the other side.

However, there are grounds for doubting whether the CSP theory applies to all instances of begging the question. Consider case 4.13, for example, the case of equality of opportunity at the universities. If you look back to this case again, and in particular at figure 4.18, you will recall the problem. Each time George questioned Karl to give reasons for his premises, Karl was driven back to advocating further premises as reasons.

At one point, in order to support ③, Karl advanced premise ⑤. But then in order to support ⑤, Karl used ⑦ as a premise. But the problem was that it appeared that ⑦ had to rest on ③, since no other reasons for accepting ③ were given by Karl. This was a localized case of a circle within an argument. And it seemed that it was a legitimate case of begging the question. But what is unclear is how such an evaluation could be justified by giving evidence that the circle was due to a failure of one of the propositions to be in the common starting point of both the arguers. This is a problem generally for mid-argument circles that constitute cases of the fallacy of begging the question.

It is possible then that the CSP theory applies to some cases only, and is not a generally applicable theory that conflicts with the respondent's concession theory. For there are some special cases where begging the question does appear to stem specifically from a failure to have common starting points in an argument.

The idea of common starting points is interesting because it points out the relationship that clearly obtains, in some cases particularly, between the circular argument and prior conditions set in the earlier stages of an argument, that is, the opening and confrontation stages. For generally, it is in these earlier stages that matters of burden of proof are (or should be) established.

In some extreme cases, however, it seems that the initial requirements and parameters of success of the argument are set, at these early stages, in such a way that neither participant has any common starting points available that can be effectively used as premises in his arguments without begging the question. The outstanding cases of this sort were the cases of criteria of evidence circularity studied in chapter four, section three, and the argument that no arguments are plausible (case 3.21), studied in chapter three, section eight. The problem with these kinds of cases seemed to be that no matter how hard the proponent seemed to struggle, the prior structure of the argument never allowed his arguments to get a "grip," and they always begged the question.

The following case can be used to illustrate this sort of problem. The difficulty appears to be a result of the way that the two participants try to structure the rules and criteria of success of the discussion (importunately) within the conduct of the discussion itself. While they do have some common starting points, it seems that they do not have enough of the right sort of common starting points to enable them to settle their dispute without inevitably begging the question. It seems to be a failure of their initial agreements that is the cause of all the trouble.

Case 8.0: Plato and Aristotle are arguing about who should fill the vacant position as Head of the Academy. Both agree that they themselves are the two best qualified candidates for the position. They decide that the best arguer should be Head of the Academy, and agree that this should be

determined by whichever one of them turns out to have
the stronger argument on who should be Head. They go
on arguing about the brilliance of their arguments, and
so forth, but cannot come to any conclusion, in the end,
on who has the stronger argument. Despairing of the
inconclusiveness of the dispute, they decide to take it to
a third party referee. But they both agree that the only
person wise enough to act as a referee would be the
person best suited to fill the position of Head of the
Academy.

In this situation, Plato and Aristotle seem to be doomed to beg the question
against each other. Suppose Plato, for example, argued to Aristotle: "I
declare myself to be the official referee, and in my judgment, my argument
has been stronger than yours. It follows that I am the one who should fill
the vacant position." But when Aristotle asks him, "Why do you think you
are the only person wise enough to settle the dispute?" it appears that the
only answer Plato has available that will be convincing is that he (Plato) is
the person best suited to fill the position of Head of the Academy. And of
course, Aristotle could equally well declare himself referee, using the same
circular argument in reply. It seems that they are both doomed to beg the
question against each other, no matter how each one tries to prove his contention. It seems to be a failure of the two participants to establish enough
of a basis, at the beginning of their argument, for them to have the right
sort of common starting points.

The CSP fits case 8.0 very well, because the problem is that the two
participants cannot agree on any common ground. But this type of case is a
special one. The problem with the majority of the cases studied in chapters
four and five was not the failure of a common ground, specifically. The
problem was posed in these cases by a circle in the argument that was used
by one participant in a dialogue to try to convince deceptively the other
participant that the requirement of evidential priority had been met by his
argumentation, when in fact it had not. In these cases, one participant
begged the question *against the other,* by using premises that the other
participant should not accept, given the other participant's doubts about the
conclusion to be proved by the first participant.

Thus the CSP theory works well for some cases, but it does not seem
to be the theory to do justice to the fallacy of begging the question in the
vast majority of important cases. To remedy this gap, we turn to a different theory, which is a version of the respondent's concession type of
theory.

In the case studies in chapters four and five, the fallacy of begging
the question was always associated with a failure of evidential priority to be
met—essentially, one party had an obligation or function of carrying
forward a burden of proof that he failed to perform. The key factor was
the probative function of argument in dialogue.

3. THE PROBATIVE FUNCTION OF ARGUMENT

A more general approach to begging the question emphasizes the common element of the epistemic and dialectical interpretations. The epistemic interpretation emphasizes the requirement that the premises of an argument should be better known than the conclusion. But there is a parallel here with the dialectical interpretation, which sees an argument as useless to persuade if the premises are equally as doubtful as the conclusion. In both cases, the fault that is alleged to be the basis of the fallacy is a failing of the premises to have evidential priority over the conclusion. In both cases, the failure is one of a probative function of arguments whereby the premises are supposed to have a greater proving value, of some sort, than the conclusion, which can then be transferred forward to the conclusion. This forward movement whereby the premises are used to prove the conclusion of an argument could be called the *probative function* of argument.

To my knowledge, the first to show an awareness of this probative function of argument was Sextus Empiricus.[5] Sextus' discussion of it was generally negative and critical, for he was skeptical about the conceptions of proof that were advocated by the various schools of thought on the subject in Greek philosophy. According to Sextus *(Outlines of Pyrrhonism,* II, 143-44), these philosophers were in the habit of explaining proof as "an argument which by means of agreed [pre-evident] premises discovers by way of deduction a non-evident inference" (Bury translation, 1933, p. 243). Sextus discussed many variants of this conception (rejecting all of them), but a general pattern can be seen in his discussions. An argument, aside from any structural properties it might have (like being a valid deduction), can also have a probative function, meaning (in the terms favored by Sextus), it can be used to make evident a non-evident conclusion, by means of pre-evident premises. Sextus discussed different uses of argument, but common to them can be discerned a probative function, which reflects the general idea that the premises are (or should be) used to increase the evidentiary value of the conclusion. It seems then that the Greek philosophers did discuss this aspect of arguments, and did accept the idea that arguments could be evaluated in relation to having this pragmatic property of a probative function or use, in addition to structural properties like deductive (syllogistic) validity.

The next place in the history of logic this idea surfaced once again was in the *Summulae Logicales* (1245?) of Peter of Spain (later Pope John XXI). Peter wrote that the fallacy of begging the question does not prevent an inferring syllogism *(syllogismum inferentem),* but does prevent a probative syllogism *(syllogismum probantem).*[6] The same, or a similar idea, seems to be reflected in the treatment of begging the question in many of the modern logic textbooks. Beardsley (1950, p. 385) describes the fault of circular arguments as being useless for proving a conclusion, even if valid. Manicas and Kruger (1976, p. 288) describe the fallacy of begging the question as a kind of argument that only appears to prove something when, in fact, it does not. Toulmin, Rieke, and Janik (1979, p. 169) write that question-begging "amounts to a failure to advance substantial evidence in support of a claim."

Copi (1986, p. 108) describes the fault of a question-begging argument by noting that even though such an argument may be valid, it is "useless for the purpose of *proving* or *establishing* the conclusion." All these accounts seem to rest on the idea of some sort of probative function of an argument that makes the argument useful to prove its conclusion, apart from the question of the deductive validity or invalidity of the argument.

In recent times, this third school of thought, which seems to indicate that begging the question should not be specifically tied to either an epistemic or dialectical interpretation, is represented by David Sanford's viewpoint. According to Sanford (1977), the central purpose of argument is to show that something is worthy of belief. According to Sanford's view, this purpose can be accomplished without requiring the doubt of a respondent (contrary to Barker's view). Sanford's explanation of the fallacy of begging the question is that it is a failure to increase the degree of confidence one has in the conclusion of an argument. According to Sanford (1972, p. 198), "An argument formulated for Smith's benefit, whether by Smith himself or by another, begs the question either if Smith believes one of the premises only because he already believes the conclusion or if Smith would believe one of the premises only if he already believed the conclusion." The problem with this kind of account is to know how rational Smith is, for, as Sanford admits, an argument that begs the question for one person (Smith) might not beg the question for another person (Jones).

Whately (1859, p. 220) recognized the danger of subjectivity in this type of analysis when he defined a question-begging argument as one where the person to whom the argument was addressed would not be "likely to know, or admit" a premise "except as an inference" from the conclusion. For by this kind of criterion, an argument that begs the question against one person, in virtue of what he is likely to know or admit, may not beg the question against another person, whose reluctance to admit the same proposition may be greater. Biro (1977, p. 263) criticized Sanford's analysis for its "audience-relativity," which he, Biro, thinks is a "psychologizing" of begging the question that goes in a wrong direction.

However, there is another way of interpreting the probative function of argument that makes begging the question a matter of how a reasonable critic should respond to an argument rather than a psychological matter of how any particular individual would or did respond to it. There are hints of such an interpretation in some remarks of Rosenberg (1978, p. 41). Rosenberg made these remarks specifically in connection with philosophical arguments, but in fact they can be applied more generally to any kind of argument that is supposed to have a probative function as it is meant to be used.

In general, any argument meant to have a probative function is put forward so that reasons are given or, according to a burden of proof, should be given by the premises to support the conclusion. By the same token, however, any appropriate criticism of such an argument must answer to these reasons given. In other words, as Rosenberg puts it, a reasonable criticism of any argument "supporting a conclusion must differ from a mere disagreement with the conclusion." This means that, in general, there are two kinds of challenges that can be given, in response to an argument: (1) the conclusion can be challenged directly (disagreed with), or (2) the argument can be challenged, by challenging one or more of the premises on which it is allegedly based.

Quite generally then, for any argument that is supposed to have a probative function in using premises to support a conclusion, a correct challenge to the argument must meet, or at least be directed toward, the premises. To attack the conclusion (directly) instead is not an appropriate or genuine criticism of the argument. In particular, if the proponent uses a circular argument, by using or presupposing the conclusion within the premises, he is not confronting any appropriate kind of criticism of his argument in a proper way. A question-begging argument of this sort is incorrect or faulty because it is not directed toward meeting any proper challenge by any fair or reasonable critic. Such an argument can never fulfill its proper or real probative function.

This account of probative function is independent of the actual beliefs (psychology) of the particular respondent in a discussion. Rather, it pertains to the proper functions or obligations in dialogue of any reasonable proponent and respondent who are using premises to support a conclusion in a probative argument, or who are responding to such an argument with reasoned and appropriate criticisms. The failure to fulfill one's probative function in an argument is broader than the failure to argue from common starting points. It could also be a failure to argue from premises that you accept but your opponent does not.

It seems to be quite generally true that, in all kinds of arguments, there is an important distinction between the function of the premises and that of the conclusion. If so, the probative function can exist independently of any particular context of argument or dialogue. This suggestion might well lead us to recall Aristotle's definition of reasoning. This critical probative function identified with reasoning by Aristotle depends on a distinction between the different roles of premises and conclusion in various special contexts of reasoning.

Aristotle, at the beginning of the *Topics* (100 a 25), set out to say generally what reasoning is, and proposed the following definition: "Now reasoning is an argument in which, certain things being laid down, something other than these necessarily comes about through them." Four kinds or special contexts of reasoning are identified. Reasoning is a *demonstration (apodeixis)* when its premises (from which the reasoning starts), are "true" and "primary" (100 a 28). By contrast, reasoning is *dialectical (dialektikos)* when it starts from opinions that are generally accepted (100 a 31). Reasoning is *contentious (eristikos)* where it starts from opinions that appear to be generally accepted, but are not really (100 b 24). Reasoning is *misreasoning (paralogismos)* where it starts from assumptions in a special science that are neither true nor primary (101 a 10).

Aristotle's conception of reasoning places key importance on where the premises of reasoning have come from. For Aristotle, premises are not any arbitrary assumptions or "designated" propositions. Demonstration and dialectical reasoning are the two primary kinds of reasoning. What distinguishes them as species of reasoning is the type of premises that each starts from. Dialectical reasoning is opinion-based reasoning. Demonstration appears to correspond fairly closely to how we in the twentieth century think of scientific investigation or inquiry. It starts only from premises that can be established as "true" or "known to be true" by the sciences–that is, by the different, established fields of scientific knowledge.

Contentious reasoning, or *eristic* as it is sometimes called, is the degeneration of reasoned dialectic into a purely adversarial struggle, the quarrel or verbal combat. The area of contentious reasoning is that of sophistical refutations and fallacies. But similarly, Aristotle thought that demonstrative reasoning also had a negative counterpart, "misreasoning" *(paralogismos)*. It seems hard to know what this might amount to in modern terms. The closest thing that comes to mind is Martin Gardner's *Fads and Fallacies in the Name of Science* (1952).

Following Aristotle, it seems useful to distinguish between reasoning generally, and the various different contexts in which reasoning can take place. Two contexts are primary. Reasoning can take place in dialectical argumentation, or it can take place in inquiry (investigation of a question or problem). But reasoning need not be tied exclusively to these two contexts. It could occur in a context of the deliberations that lead up to an action, for example. It could even take place in a context of interest-based bargaining (negotiation). And in each different context, the appropriateness and correctness of the reasoning have to be judged by different standards and rules.

However, common to a whole class of contexts of reasoning, there are certain general principles that apply. And when these principles are violated, misreasoning or contentious reasoning of various kinds can be the result. One result of this sort, of course, could be a fallacy.

Following this line, let us say that the probative function characterizes any kind of reasoning where there is argument such that premises are laid down, and a conclusion is supposed to be *proven,* or *argued for,* on the basis of these premises. Consequently, in any reasoning of this type, whatever specific context of dialogue it occurs within, the way in which a rational critic is supposed to oppose or attack the conclusion (correctly) is by means of questioning the premises that provide its basis. In other words, it is a kind of failure to engage in reasoning (which could be misreasoning or unduly contentious reasoning in different contexts), if someone who doubts a conclusion attacks that conclusion directly, instead of directing his doubts or counter-arguments against the premises upon which that conclusion is supposedly based.

According to this approach, begging the question is misreasoning, but the reasoning is fallacious because of how it has been used in the given type of dialogue that the participants are supposed to be engaged in. The problem is not one of common starting points but one of the different

kinds of starting points imposed by the different obligations of the participants according to their roles in a dialogue. The one participant is obliged
to doubt a particular proposition (thesis) that the other one is supposed to
prove. Various ways of failing to fulfill these obligations in dialogue are
possible. One is the failure to argue from common starting points.

Begging the question is a failure of reasoning of a different, but
related, sort. The proponent of reasoning must match his reasoning to a
critic's reasonable doubts or objections that might possibly be directed
against his reasoning. He can accomplish this through the probative function of his premises, which are his grounds put forward as the basis to
support his conclusion. Including the conclusion within the premises, or
presuming it in order to provide a basis for these premises, defeats the
probative function of reasoning. The conclusion is supposed to be something other than the premises, in probative reasoning, and the premises are
propositions that are laid down in order to provide a probative basis for
the conclusion (not the other way around).

An argument that begs the question is therefore a transgression
against the proper role of any rational critic of the arguer's reasoning,
because it prevents such a critic from expressing his doubts or rebuttals in
a proper way. It puts the critic in the inappropriate role of having to
attack the conclusion in order to direct his doubts against the premises.
And that is the very thing he is not supposed to do. It leaves the critic
no way out, other than acquiescing in misreasoning or objecting to the
proponent's argument as question-begging. This problematic juncture is
the kind of situation that should be unacceptable to both parties, but arises
when a question-begging argument is put forward by one of them.

This failure of proof to move forward in a constructive manner is
unsatisfactory in persuasion dialogue, because it prevents both parties from
going ahead and fulfilling their legitimate obligations in the discussion. It
is also unfortunate in an inquiry, because it prevents the inquiry from
going ahead to establish new knowledge, or to prove the conclusion that
is properly supposed to be proved by the inquiry, using the premises as
established evidence.

The failure of the probative function, however, in either of these
contexts of argumentative discussion, does not yet represent a full-fledged
instance of the fallacy of begging the question. It does represent a failure
of an attempted proof to be useful, which could certainly be open to
criticism as a point of order. And this is a key ingredient in the fallacy of
begging the question.

4. THE PRAGMATIC PROBATIVE THEORY

To do justice to the heterogeneous aspects of the fallacy of begging the
question, we need to recognize that several tiers of analysis are involved in
evaluating any particular charge that this fallacy has been committed. If
Sanford is right, there seems to be some common element to both the

epistemic and dialectical interpretations. Also, it seems important to have a theory that is pragmatically sensitive to different contexts, but is not open to the criticism of subjectivity suggested by Whately, and made overtly by Biro.

To accommodate these intuitions, a pragmatic probative theory of begging the question will now be constructed. According to this theory, there should be three levels of analysis of any claim that an argument commits the fallacy of begging the question.

The pragmatic probative theory is hard to express in the traditional language of logic, because this tradition has been so distorted by the supremacy of the semantic conception of argument. Consequently, the best way to express the theory is to introduce what appear to be some radical new definitions of the concepts of reasoning and argument.

According to these new definitions, reasoning is an abstract yet dynamic structure, which can be exhibited in argument. Argument is a much more richly pragmatic concept, which provides different goal-directed contexts in which reasoning is used. While reasoning can occur as a solitary act, argument always occurs in a context of dialogue (dialectical context). Whether circular reasoning begs the question depends essentially on the context of argument in which it is used.

Reasoning is a sequence of steps from some propositions to others, linked by a thread, rule, or warrant. Reasoning is a dynamic process that can go "forward" or "backward." Forward reasoning is identified with the probative function of reasoning. It is characterized by advancing by a step, or series of steps, from premises to a conclusion, where a link or rule binds one step to the next step. Reasoning is sequential, and hence its essential structure is naturally represented by an argument diagram.

Reasoning is normally directed to some goal, but it need not be. There can be "aimless reasoning." Indeed, one form of criticism of circular reasoning is that it is due to aimlessness. However, this kind of criticism is not the basis of the fallacy of begging the question stressed by the case studies in chapters five and six.

For example, in case 4.8, the man who forged the Hitler diaries was accusing the academics of committing the fallacy of begging the question. If they were committing a fallacy through their use of circular reasoning, it was an error of reasoning type of fallacy. Or it may have been simply a blunder, if it was not really a fallacy.

Reasoning can be solitary or interactive, that is, when two or more parties "reason together." Reasoning characteristically occurs in a context of argument. For example, in case 4.7, the fallacy jointly or collectively committed by the flying-saucer writers is an error of reasoning, and not a sophistical tactic type of fallacy. The circular appeal to authority is unconvincing, because it exhibits a lack of external support for the claim made. It is a bad argument, and an error in the use of circular reasoning. But it should not properly be called an instance of the fallacy of begging the question.

Argument is a social and verbal means of trying to resolve or deal with a conflict or instability that has arisen between two parties.[7] It always involves a claim advanced by at least one of the parties. This claim is often an opinion, but it need not be. It could be another sort of claim, like a claim to ownership of goods, or a claim to financial remuneration, as in the kind of argument characteristic of negotiations.

The conflict or instability could be a conflict of opinions, an unsolved problem, an unanswered question, an unproved conjecture, or even a situation where both parties are blocked from further action because there is a scarcity of facilities or resources they both lay claim to or need.

An argument can often be reasoned or reasonable, but not all arguments consist of reasoning. Sometimes one party just insists, "Yes, I will," and the other claims, "No, you won't." This is not reasoning (at least properly), but it certainly could constitute an argument. One kind of argument, called the quarrel, seems aimless but is not.[8] In the quarrel, called "eristic reasoning" by Aristotle, the purpose of each party is to defeat the other by any means. Thus the quarrel is unregulated, but not aimless.

Argument is always goal-directed, because it is an attempt to deal with instability. It can't be entirely aimless, even though it may wander and be misguided (as in irrelevant argumentation).

There has also evolved a logician's use of "argument," often found in logic textbooks. This use of "argument" refers to a structure with premises and a conclusion (or propositions so designated). This usage is confusing—it is a kind of distortion and misnomer. What really should be referred to in this kind of situation is reasoning, not argument.

A good argument, from a logical point of view of the sophistical tactics type of fallacies, is one that uses reasoning correctly in dialogue. Since arguments can have different purposes, in different contexts of dialogue, whether an argument is good or not (or used correctly or not) depends on the purpose it is supposedly being used for.

The probative function of argument is referred to as the property of "groundedness" in Woods and Walton (1978a, pp. 85-88). According to this account, to say that one proposition is *grounded on* another is to say that one is accepted on the basis of the other in a line of reasoning in a context of argument (like a Hamblin game or a Kripke model).[9] What is really referred to here is the probative function of reasoning, especially forward-moving reasoning, where a conclusion is a derived step from premises that are laid down initially.

If reasoning is circular, that in itself is not necessarily bad. But if reasoning has a probative function, as it does when deployed in certain kinds of arguments, circular argumentation may be useless to fulfill this probative function. This can lead to criticisms of begging the question, especially in certain types of argumentative dialogue.

The probative function is an abstract property of reasoning—it is a particular kind or function of reasoning that applies to different contexts of argument in different ways. When it is applied to the two contexts of argument called the persuasion dialogue and the inquiry, it produces the principle of evidential priority. In the inquiry, the requirement that the premises must be prior to the conclusion means that the premises have to be better known or more knowable than the conclusion. In the persuasion dialogue, priority means that the premises must be more plausible than the conclusion.

As we look over the various interpretations and theories of begging the question, a general pattern falls into place. The epistemic and dialectical interpretations have a common element in the probative function of reasoning. The probative function applies to many different contexts of argument, but as it applies to the inquiry and to persuasion dialogue (and possibly other contexts as well), it expresses a general principle or requirement of evidential priority. This principle explains why a particular circular argument is not useful, in a particular context of argument, to fulfill the probative function of reasoning in that context.

However, this level of explanation does not explain, nor can it be used (by itself) to justify why a particular argument commits the fallacy of begging the question. To get to a justification, you have to go to a deeper explanation of the fallacy, and ask what exactly is wrong with a given failure to meet the requirement of evidential priority. This means looking at the tactical situation, which can be reconstructed from the text and context of dialogue. Has there been a tactic of trying to force the issue, an attempt to slur over or mask the failure to meet evidential priority, or a failure of communication through lack of common starting points?

The key distinction at issue in this third stage is that between a fallacy of begging the question and a criticism that is a point of order or challenge weaker than a charge of fallaciousness. An argument may be open to questioning or challenge if it fails to meet evidential priority, but that does not in itself make it a fallacious argument.

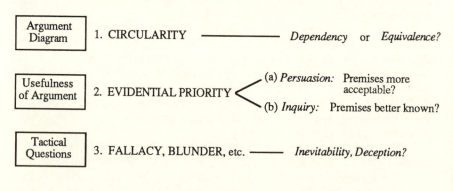

Figure 8.0

According to the theory advocated here, there should be three levels of analysis of begging the question. The first level is that of the argument diagram, and the question of circularity should be raised here. The second level has to do with the context of argument. In persuasion dialogue and inquiry, this level raises the question of evidential priority. The third level has to do with the diagnosis of the error of begging the question. At this level tactical questions of argument should be raised. These three levels are briefly summarized in figure 8.0, and even more fully and explicitly summarized in section ten of this chapter.

It is at this third and deepest level that the distinction between begging the question as a fallacy and as a point of order should be evaluated. The case studies of chapters four and five showed that failure of evidential priority may be good grounds for raising a point of order on begging the question, but it does not necessarily mean that the fallacy of begging the question has been committed.

5. THE THIRD LEVEL OF ANALYSIS

The two elements of circularity and failure of evidential priority are each necessary to begging the question as a fallacy. But taken together, they are not sufficient to make us conclude that an argument commits the fallacy of begging the question. The reason for this failure to be sufficient are that not every fault or shortcoming of an argument is a fallacy, and that begging the question involves the committing of a sophistical tactic type of fallacy. A sophistical tactic type of fallacy involves the use of a systematic technique of argumentation that is employed as a tactic by one party in a dialogue to defeat, undermine, or attack the argument of another (opposed) party in the dialogue.[10] But a circular argument that fails to meet its burden of proof may, in many instances, be not so much a fallacy in this sense as simply an instance of bad or ineffective strategy. In such a case, the faulty argument could better be classified as a blunder, or weak (failed, ineffective) argument, rather than as a fallacy. Or if it is a fallacy of the error of reasoning type, it is not an instance of the fallacy of begging the question.

Despite these important distinctions between fallacies, and between fallacies and other kinds of faults of arguments, as outlined in chapter six, many of the textbook accounts of the fallacy of begging the question have been content to stay at level two. However, failure to meet burden of proof is not necessarily to commit a fallacy. And chapter seven has shown that the confusion between these two things has led many sources to classify as fallacies what are really only pseudo-fallacies, even if they are faults of argument (of some sort).

Of course, various kinds of procedural objections, as noted in chapter six, can be made to an argument on grounds of its circularity without the argument being an instance of the fallacy of begging the question, as we noted in the analysis of case 4.7 in chapter four, section three. In this case of the flying saucers, Chase (1956) rightly evaluated the fault as "arguing in circles," but it was not an instance of the fallacy of begging the question. To say an argument commits a fallacy is a strong form of criticism that implies that the argument is based on a systematic, underlying error or flaw that makes it subject to strong refutation. The charge of "Fallacy!" brings with it an obligation of strong repudiation of the offending argument, and with that the necessity of strong evidence to back up the charge.

In some accounts of begging the question, there have been deeper attempts to give an explanation of the fallacy by asking what's wrong with failure of evidential priority. These attempts fall into four categories. The first explanation sees circular argument as useless to persuade in an argument, and therefore sees any use of circular arguments as an attempt to engender the illusion of proof. The second explanation sees circular argumentation as fallacious when it is used as a tactic of coercion to try to suppress or unfairly dismiss the respondent's reasonable doubts about the conclusion. The third explanation cites the inevitability of an argument that commits the fallacy of begging the question–no way is left open for the respondent to come to accept the conclusion, other than ways that must require or depend on the conclusion of the argument. The fourth explanation sees circular argumentation as a kind of uncooperative failure to engage properly in argumentation that is the result of an initial failure for there to be enough common ground between two participants in a discussion. The problem perceived here is that the argument can't even get properly started because there is not enough of a basis for agreement.

The first kind of explanation, which refers to an illusion, is reminiscent of the psychological criterion of seeming validity, which we have already rejected in chapter six as a satisfactory account of what constitutes a fallacy. But perhaps the concept of illusion refers to some kind of deception or deceit in argument. But what does this mean? Does it just mean that it looks like the burden of proof has been met, when it has not really been met?

Some accounts of begging the question appeal to the idea of an illusion, but still fasten on the failure at level two, and try to account for the fallacy in these terms. This attempt to explain the fallacy sees circular argument as useless to persuade in an argument (quite rightly), but then wrongly concludes that any use of circular argument must be a fallacious attempt to engender the illusion of proof. This inference is wrong, however. For the idea that a fallacy has occurred involves the additional idea that some arguer has tried to make it appear that proof has been given when, in reality, it has not. A useless argument is not necessarily a fallacious argument.

Moreover, just to say that there is an illusion of correctness is not very helpful. We need to know exactly how the illusion works, how the mechanism of the deception functions when one arguer perpetrates a fallacy of begging the question against another.

This brings us to the second explanation, that of coercion. We recall from chapter one, section seven, that Sidgwick (1910, p. 205) described the fallacy of begging the question as a dialectical failure of openness of an assumption in an argument. According to Sidgwick's insightful account, the fallacy consists of the proponent's trying to force the respondent to accept a conclusion by suppressing the respondent's questions or doubts. This very useful suggestion, however, by itself cannot be the complete analysis of the fallacy of begging the question, because it fails to distinguish between this fallacy and other fallacies that also have an aspect of forcing of a respondent's options. The most notable case in point is the fallacy of many questions, which was analyzed in chapter six as a fallacy of this sort.

The third explanation, which cited the factor of inevitability, that played a major role in many of the case studies in chapters four and five, seems more characteristic of begging the question. For it is a kind of circularity that evidently can be modelled in the argument diagram of a case. Not all circles in argument are fallacious, but it most often seemed in our case studies that the inevitable circles turned out to be the fallacious ones.

But why did inevitable circles seem to indicate the existence of a fallacy of begging the question? The answer seemed to be that an inevitable circle leaves the proponent no room for justifying his premises without having to be locked in to presuming the conclusion. By the same token, an inevitable circle leaves the respondent no room for questioning the premises without first requiring the acceptance of the conclusion.

But note that this problem sounds very much like forcing or coercion. Neither party is left room to argue without foreclosing the argument by requiring the acceptance of the proponent's conclusion. Perhaps then, the two elements of forcing and inevitability could be combined into a single explanation of what is wrong with fallacious cases of begging the question.

According to this new explanation, what is wrong, when this fallacy is committed, is that the proponent has adopted a sophistical tactic of trying to seal off the respondent's legitimate questioning by advancing an inevitably circular argument that leaves the respondent no way of utilizing the premises to prove the conclusion that does not already require the assumption of the conclusion as true. Thus inevitability is defined, by this new explanation, as a kind of forcing tactic on the part of the proponent.

In the rest of this chapter, we will support this new explanation of the third level of analysis of the fallacy of begging the question. There are several problems with it that need to be resolved. But in the end, we will argue that this explanation is the deepest and most satisfactory account of the fallacy at the third level of analysis.

Before this, however, let us turn to the fourth explanation, which sees the fallacy of begging the question as stemming from a lack of a sufficient initial basis for agreement between two participants in an argument. This explanation is related to the common starting points theory outlined in section two of this chapter.

There is a kind of inevitability involved in this explanation as well. If two arguers lack common starting points, they seem to be doomed to beg the question against each other, whenever they try to argue. But this account of the fallacy is different and distinctive, because the fault is to argue from premises not held in common by both parties to a dispute.

6. TACTICS AND RULES OF DIALOGUE

According to the respondent's concession theory, which has been advocated here, a circular argument is fallacious because one of the premises is not a commitment of the person whom the argument is supposed to convince. By contrast, according to the CSP theory, a circular argument is fallacious because one of the premises is not a commitment of either party to the argument, the proponent or the respondent whom the argument is supposed to convince. In a word, it is not in their CSP.

The essential difference between the two theories, then, is simply this. According to the first theory, the question-begging argument begs the question against the position of the respondent (the person to whom the argument was directed, in order to convince that person to accept the conclusion). According to the second theory, the question-begging argument begs the question against the shared position of both parties to the argument–namely, their CSP.

Both theories seem initially plausible, but presumably only one can be right. What, really, is the difference between the two theories, in practical terms? To see this, let us examine a particular case.

Consider case 4.1, the theological dispute between Sue, the atheist, and Penny, the fervent Christian, concerning the benevolence of God. If the reader will recall, Penny advanced this argument in order to convince Sue.

Case 4.1:   God has all the virtues.
         Benevolence is a virtue.
         Therefore, God is benevolent.

The reader will recall, from the discussion of this case in section 4.2, that the question-begging problem with the argument arose from the first premise. The problem is that Sue, being a non-believer, does not accept the first premise. Not only does Sue not accept the premise as a whole, but she does not even accept the existence of God, a proposition that is evidently presupposed by the first premise.

We could say, then, that from the point of view of Sue's position, the argument in case 4.1 begs the question. Given Sue's rejection of the conclusion, and her acceptance of the second premise, she can hardly accept the first premise. Given her position as a non-believer, and consequent rejection of the conclusion of the argument in case 4.1, she can hardly accept the first premise of this argument, unless Penny can give some further line of argument for this premise that Sue could accept independently of her position, which goes so directly (as things are) against that premise.

This analysis of the fallacy to be found in case 4.1 appears to support the respondent's concession theory of the fallacy of begging the question.

Or, at any rate, the analysis so far has been carried out by appealing to that theory. But how would the fallacy be analyzed using the CSP theory?

According to the CSP theory, the argument in case 4.1 would be held to commit the fallacy of begging the question on the ground that Penny has wrongly portrayed the first premise as being in the CSP for the argument. In other words, given that the dispute is about the existence of God, the first premise certainly cannot be taken for granted, as being part of the CSP for the argument, because this premise presupposes the existence of God. The problem is not just, or specifically, that Sue fails to accept this premise. The problem is that it fails to be in the CSP. What makes the argument beg the question, additionally, is that Helen is trying (presumably) to act as though this premise is, or should be, in the CSP.

But what is the difference between the two theories here? Or is there any difference? For Penny is, of course, inclined to accept the first premise. After all, she is using it as part of her argument designed to convince Sue. So Penny is not going to disagree with it. For all practical intents and purposes, then, it would seem, this proposition is going to fail to be in the CSP, if and only if it fails to be in Sue's stock of accepted premises (her commitment-set). At the first two levels of analysis, then, there seems to be little, if any, real difference between how the two theories judge arguments as question-begging. If there is a failure of probative function or a failure of evidential priority in an argument, it seems to matter very little, or not at all, from a point of view of begging the question, whether the offending premise is objectionable because it is not in the CSP, or more specifically, whether it is not in the respondent's commitment-set.

Perhaps, however, this difference could make a significant difference at level three of analysis. Of the two kinds of fault, perhaps the first one could be the more serious kind of error, because the CSP represents a special kind of set of commitments for the respondent of an argument in a reasonable discussion. Presumably, the CSP commitments in a discussion are prior agreements on which the possibility of meaningful communication is premised. To try falsely or deceptively to get a respondent to accept a concession as though it were in this set, when it is really not, is a special and serious kind of transgression in an argument.

It would be far too narrow an approach to suggest, however, that all cases of the fallacy of begging the question can be fully explained and evaluated by citing a violation of Rule VI, stating that an argument is conclusively defended by means of premises belonging to the CSP in a discussion. For the fallacy of begging the question involves the violation of not just one rule of reasonable dialogue, but several, most notably including the rule that stipulates the burden of proof in a dialogue. And moreover, the fallacy (at the third and deepest level) cannot be determined by simply citing the violation of a rule of reasoned dialogue. You have to go into more specific details of how the rule was violated. In particular, you have to go into consideration of the arguer's tactics, in order to determine whether the violation is of the kind that can be identified with a specific fallacy.

Much depends, then, on what is meant by the term "fallacy" in this connection, and this general issue, although it has been a main theme of the foregoing chapters, deserves some final consideration.

First, a fallacy has been characterized in chapter six as a violation of a rule of dialogue, where the pragmatic concept of a dialogue as an organized two-person (or many-person) exchange provides the context in which any argument is to be criticized. This conception fits very well into the research program on fallacies in pragma-dialectical perspective outlined by van Eemeren and Grootendorst (1987). According to their program, incorrect moves in a critical discussion (persuasion dialogue) are violations of a set of rules for the critical discussion. And accordingly (p. 284), "[t]hese incorrect moves correspond roughly to the various kinds of defects traditionally referred to as *fallacies.*" A fallacy then is a violation of a rule of dialogue.

This program fits in well with the theoretical approach of Hintikka (1987), who interprets the so-called fallacies in Aristotle not as mistaken or incorrect inferences, but as breaches of rules in games of questioning, like those practiced in the Academy and the Lyceum in ancient times. Unlike Robinson (1971a), who rejected the Aristotelian game of *elenchus* as old-fashioned and irrelevant to the serious search for truth, Hintikka, like van Eemeren and Grootendorst, sees games of question-reply dialogue as the essential theoretical backbone of the study of fallacies as a branch of logic.

One important class of mistake in a critical discussion identified by van Eemeren and Grootendorst into which *petitio principii* could fit as a fallacy, is the tactic of *evading the burden of proof.* This mistake is a violation of the following rule, postulated in van Eemeren and Grootendorst (1987, p. 285).

Rule II: Whoever advances a standpoint [thesis in a critical discussion] is obliged to defend it if asked to do so.

This rule postulates a proponent's obligation to defend any proposition he has advocated or advanced in the context of a persuasion dialogue.

The analysis of begging the question as a procedural point of order (at levels one and two) could nicely be described in relation to Rule II as follows. An argument, or sequence of moves in a critical discussion, commits the fallacy of begging the question if, and only if, it is a circular argument that violates Rule II. According to this approach to *petitio principii* the fault consists of the use of a circular argument that fails to meet the burden of proof required by the context of dialogue.

The (in my opinion, overwhelming) objection to this approach at the third level is that while it does capture begging the question as a species of point of order in a dialogue, it does not do justice to the idea of begging the question as a fallacy. According to the preferred theory, the two other elements of inevitability and self-sealing (closure) should also be included in any claim that an argument commits the *fallacy* of begging the question.

These elements could be taken into account, however, by relating *petitio principii* to another important rule of critical discussion postulated by van Eemeren and Grootendorst (1987, p. 284).

Rule I: Parties must not prevent each other from advancing or casting doubt on standpoints.

This rule bans the practice of a proponent's trying to impose restrictions on the ability of a respondent to ask the proper critical questions regarding the standpoint or argument that this proponent has advanced. The violation of this rule is a restriction of the fundamental right of a respondent to ask questions or cast doubts in relation to an argument he wishes to criticize or query. To try to restrict this right, in violation of Rule II, is in effect to try to make your argument immune to criticism–a form of dogmatic or pre-emptive tactic in dialogue.

According to this stronger (preferred) theory of begging the question, a circular argument commits this type of fallacy not just in virtue of its being a violation of Rule I, but also because, at the same time, and within the same systematic tactic as a sequence of moves in dialogue, it is also a tactical maneuver to violate Rule II. According to this approach, more needs to be involved than just the attempt to evade burden of proof. It must also be a self-sealing kind of evasion that, through circular argument, tries to pre-empt critical questioning, in order to qualify fully as a *petitio principii* fallacy. At least, this is true for persuasion dialogue, even if standards may be somewhat different in the inquiry, or in other contexts of dialogue.

However, there is evidence that van Eemeren and Grootendorst might support this stronger conception of fallaciousness needed to back up the preferred theory of begging the question as a fallacy. In certain remarks (1987), they do appear to suggest that the concept of a fallacy should include not just a violation of a rule of dialogue, but a systematic type of sequence of moves which, in violating a rule, is designed to block or frustrate the further progress of discussion in a dialogue. They put it by writing that, in their conception, "committing a fallacy . . . is wrong in the sense that it frustrates efforts to arrive at the resolution of a dispute." Accordingly, it could be proposed that a fallacy as a type of sophistical refutation or tactic of wrong argumentation in dialogue has two requirements: it is a violation of a rule of the dialogue, but also an overly aggressive tactic designed to cut off or block the asking of legitimate critical questions by a respondent in a dialogue.

According to this fuller conception of fallacy, begging the question should only properly be considered to be an informal, logical fallacy in a particular case, where both requirements above are fulfilled. And this in turn implies, according to the point of view expressed here, that only this stronger new theory of *petitio principii* can capture the most fully adequate, correct, and useful idea of begging the question as a logical fallacy.

The usefulness of the new theory presented here depends directly on the application of the method of argument reconstruction with its associated use of digraphs as a technique of argument diagramming to the case studies evaluated in chapters four and five. The development of this method is a topic of research within the larger framework of research on the analysis and evaluation of argumentative discourse. The application of the method of digraphs clearly presupposes the application of skills of interpreting a text of argumentative discourse by transforming it from a basic text into a reconstructed text to which normative models of dialogue consisting of sets of rules for successful argumentation can be applied. These case studies point to the usefulness of the new theory.

The practical problem of evaluating begging the question typically posed by the case studies of chapters four and five is the following kind of situation. On initial analysis of a text of an argumentative discussion, we find some sort of circular reasoning sequence that appears in the argument diagram. But it is not too clear, on the surface, whether this circle indicates that the argument is an instance of the fallacy of begging the question. Figure 8.1 represents the typical case.

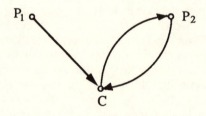

P_1 P_2

C

Figure 8.1

The conclusion of the argument is C, and there are two premises that have been advanced by the proponent to support C.

In a case of this kind, we confront the question, "Does this argument beg the question?" The best answer has sometimes turned out to be: "We don't know, or can't say, until we have more information." One thing we need to know is whether it is a linked or convergent argument. If it is a linked argument, then P_1 and P_2 are both required to support C. So the circle seems like a serious impediment to fulfillment of a requirement of evidential priority. For in order to support C by the given reasoning, you have to rely on P_2. And no other evidential route to P_2 has been given by the proponent (according to the diagram) other than the one that comes from C. On the other hand, if it is a convergent argument, the circle does not seem so serious. For, after all, if it is a convergent argument, both P_1 and P_2 are independent lines of reasoning that can be used to support C. So even though P_2 and C are on the same circle, P_1 is still available as an independent line of argument that can be used to support C. In principle, the burden of proof for C could be fulfilled through the evidential route of P_1 alone. And P_1 is not on any circle.

But suppose the argument is shown to be a linked argument, in the particular case under consideration. How could we show that the circle is evidence that the fallacy of begging the question has been committed?

In evaluating case studies of this sort, we were typically required to ask whether the circle was "inevitable" or not. That is, did the proponent have some alternative route available to support the premise? Or was this route sealed off, so that the circle was inevitable?

The problem of pinning down the fallacy in these kinds of cases was that inevitability was not (at least completely) defined or determined by the graph of the argument reconstruction. We had to look at evidence from the text and context of the argument, in the particular case under study, to see if we could interpret the circle as being inevitable or not. Inevitability was partly determined by the tactics used by the proponent, as judged by the language he used in the given text and context of dialogue.

7. INTERPRETING INEVITABILITY AS A TACTICAL ELEMENT

Interpreting inevitability is done by applying the method of argument reconstruction to a particular text of an argument, resulting in an argument diagram taking the form of a digraph. If a dicycle appears on the digraph, then the question arises–is it an inevitable circle? This question can be rephrased equivalently as follows: Is there a possible line of argument leading into the premise in question that does not include the conclusion in question as one point on the line? But this question, in turn, is relative to the given evidence of the argument represented by the digraph. And it can still be asked whether the argument is closed, or in other words, whether the argument reconstruction represented by the digraph is complete.

For a criticism of *petitio,* as an allegation that a fallacy has been committed, is relative to all possible lines of evidence that can be given by the proponent, during the course of an argument. *Petitio,* in other words, is a global question involving a whole context of dialogue, in any particular case.

But we already know, from the case studies of chapters four and five in particular, that the question of whether an argument reconstruction is complete is not answered internally on the digraph of the argument. It is an external question, depending on textual or contextual evidence concerning whether or not the closing stage of the dialogue has been reached. Thus, to interpret inevitability adequately to found a charge of *petitio* as fallacy, we have to take other evidence into account, external to the argument diagram. Moreover, chapters four and five have shown that there are important aspects of an argument that are not determined by the argument diagram. The diagram indicates the sequence of reasoning from premises to conclusion used by the proponent in the dialogue.

Consider case 4.12 and its associated argument diagram in figure 4.16. There is a circle in figure 4.16, but to judge properly whether the argument was an instance of the fallacy of begging the question, a close look had to be taken at the textual evidence of the editor's sequence of questions in the dialogue. Was the writer's reliance on the presumption that many motorists had read the ad backed up by the writer strongly enough to meet the requirement of burden of proof? We judged not, given the doubts the editor raised by asking the questions he did. Hence the editor would be justified in raising a charge of question-begging on the part of the author. But the evidence of misuse of circular reasoning as a tactic to mask failure to fulfill the probative function was not strong enough, in this case, to conclude that the author had committed a fallacy of begging the question.

The evidence of whether an argument has properly reached the closing stage is not pictured on the digraph of the reasoning in the argument in a given case. So we must often look to tactical factors indicating how tight the circle is to evaluate the evidence that the fallacy of begging the question has been committed in a particular case. This was the key difference between case 4.12 and case 4.13. In the latter case, the equality of opportunity in the university case, the circle seemed tight because one premise in the circle seemed very definitely to include the other, according to the textual evidence.

One should expect a fallacy to have "dodgy" borderline cases that are on the knife edge of committing the fallacy or not. It is just these dodgy cases that clever exploiters of the fallacy will take advantage of. As we become wiser in our analysis of a fallacy, sophistical arguers can be expected to become more clever in exploiting it. It is similar to the development of "smarter" weapons and defenses against these new weapons.

In the moral bees case (4.15), there was not enough evidence to definitively convict the priest of committing the fallacy of begging the question. But the vagueness of the language and the use of subtleties of implicature in the priest's arguments did offer some textual evidence of all the ingredients of the committing of this fallacy.

Cases like 4.16 indicate that we may even have to propose more than one possible interpretation of the text of discourse in a case, and then make any claim of fallacy conditional to an interpretation.

Even tricky cases like these can be manageable, however, once we have a clear normative analysis of begging the question as a fallacy. As noted in chapter seven, the problem of dealing with the uncertainties of particular cases can be solved by setting good requirements for burden of proof on a critic.

The fallacy of *petitio principii* occurs where the proponent of an argument is using a tactic of trying to close off the argument prematurely by making it seem as though he has fulfilled his burden of proof. The inevitability involved in this kind of move is tactical. The proponent, in such a case, is adopting a stance of making it clear that no further argument is needed to established his conclusion or persuade his opponent. The argument may not really be closed, but the proponent is trying to make it seem as though it should be closed.

Petitio principii is a fallacy because it is a systematic type of tactic designed to frustrate or prevent the raising of further critical questions by an opponent in relation to one's argument in persuasion dialogue. This becomes a particularly offensive (and effective) tactic when the proponent of the circular argument uses it as part of a strategy of sealing off any possible further objections by appearing to bring the argument to a close. Evidence of the use of this tactic is to be sought in indicator words like "certainly," which attempt to show that the argument has been brought to a close and that no further doubts can be entertained.

In this respect, it was Alfred Sidgwick who most deeply understood the real nature of begging the question as a logical fallacy when he characterized the fallacy–see chapter one, section seven–as an attempt of a disputant to prevent question-raising by a wrong way of putting forward an assumption in an argument. Sidgwick (1910, p. 213) went to the heart of the matter when he advanced a conception of the fallacy of *petitio principii* as a tactic designed to "slur over, in a dispute, any doubts which an opponent may be asking us to consider." So conceived, the fallacy is the pragmatic failure of using an argumentation scheme, in a context of dialogue, which has the function of shifting the burden of proof while leaving open critical questions, while at the same time presenting the argument in such a way as systematically to close off the possibility of the respondent's asking these critical questions. It is a kind of argument strategy that runs contrary to itself–it appears to be open, yet at the same time shuts off the openings it purports to offer to a respondent. The function of any argument during a persuasion dialogue is to remain partly open to reply, even while shifting a burden of proof toward a respondent. But an argument that begs the question destroys this function by sealing off these legitimate openings improperly.

Once the tactical element is recognized as a proper part of the fallacy of begging the question, it can be seen how this fallacy comes under the general heading of evading the burden of proof in critical discussion. The fallacy is a failure on the part of the proponent to fulfill his probative function properly. Begging the question arises as a fallacy because there are various ways of trying to disguise this failure. One method used is to play down the aspect that the argument is part of a persuasion dialogue, an argument that stands in need of proof. Another method is to "immunize" the argument by trying to suggest that it is so obvious or clearly beyond doubt that the need for evidence to back it up appears to be obviated (van Eemeren and Grootendorst, 1987, p. 285). When circular reasoning is used as part of such a method of disguising failure to fulfill the probative function, the fallacy is that of begging the question.

What is important, therefore, in diagnosing this tactical element in a particular case is the kind of language used to express the conclusion of the proponent's argument. Any language suggesting that the argument is beyond doubt, and stands in no need of proof, should be suspect. Alternatively, aggressive forms of language demanding that the respondent accept the proponent's conclusion, suggesting that otherwise the respondent is a fool, or something of the sort, are important indicators of the fourth element.

The third level of analysis consists partly of the rule violation of evading the burden of proof in a persuasion dialogue, found at the second level of analysis. There is also a tactical element of trying to immunize one's argument from all possible criticisms by presenting it in a manner that makes it self-sealing. This means that no lines of argument are left open for the respondent except ones that absolutely require that he accept the conclusion as true, in order to accept a necessary premise.

According to the pragmatically probative theory of begging the question we advocate, the determination of whether an argument is open to a charge of begging the question is made at the second level of analysis. At this second level, the question of whether an argument violates a rule of reasonable dialogue (and in particular, a requirement of evidential priority) is raised. But it is at the third level of analysis that it is decided whether this circular argument can rightly be said to commit the fallacy of *petitio principii* or not.

In beginning to study *petitio principii,* it is natural to think that inevitability can be defined at the first level or the second level of analysis. In Walton and Batten (1984, p. 150), a conclusion is said to be *inevitably circular* in an argument if every available evidential route to that conclusion, according to the digraph of the argument, lies on a dicycle. It is tempting to think that inevitable circularity can be defined purely in terms of the argument diagram, as this definition seems to indicate. However, even in Walton and Batten, there were doubts expressed about whether this kind of inevitability defines the fallacy of begging the question. A *fallaciously circular argument* was there defined as an argument that "seems" to justify an argument that is inevitably circular. The quotes around "seems" expressed these doubts.

Now however, it appears much better to say that even though the argument diagram is a necessary and important means of helping to determine inevitability in a particular case, levels two and three must be taken into account as well. Therefore, the best approach is to define inevitability as a tactical concept of argument, at level three, even though findings from the other two levels are crucial for any determination of inevitability, in addition to the findings of level three.

When it comes to defining the key dependency relation at level two, it is once again very tempting to build inevitability into the definition. According to such an approach, a premise in an argument would be said to *depend on* the conclusion if, and only if, *every* directed path in the argument diagram going into that premise is on a cycle that also contains the conclusion. Essentially, this approach means that the *only* way you can prove this premise is by presuming the conclusion. Or to follow Biro

(1984, p. 239), for example, non-dependency means that there should be at least one way we can learn the truth of the premises so that we can use that knowledge to argue to the truth of the conclusion. In effect, the dependency condition then amounts to the condition called (CM) in Woods and Walton (1975a, p. 109): there is some premise that can be known to be true only by inference from the conclusion.

Now, however, after the developments of research on this subject since 1984, it seems better not to build the requirement of inevitability so tightly into the second level by offering this type of definition of the dependency condition. But how exactly should dependency be defined? We now turn to a resolution of this problem.

8. THE DEPENDENCY RELATION REVEALED

The dependency conception that is the basic idea behind many of the intuitions in the textbook accounts and historical sources of *petitio principii* as a fallacy has always remained obscure. It emerged through the discussions in chapter one of the views of Sextus, Mill, and DeMorgan, however, that the dependency relationship is not a purely semantic relation of deductive logic, but a pragmatic concept pertaining to the dialectical context of an argument. As noted in section five of chapter one, evidently the existence of dependency in a particular argument means that in the absence of the premises, the conclusion would be subject to doubt, so that the premises are instrumentally required to remove this doubt and secure acceptance of the conclusion.

Now we can see what dependency amounts to, in pragmatic terms. In persuasion dialogue, the function of an argument is to secure the acceptance of the respondent so that, through the argument, he will become committed to the conclusion. In this type of dialogue, by its nature, the context presupposes that initially, at the beginning of the dialogue, the respondent did not accept the conclusion. Thus there are two stages in the working of an effective argument. Initially, the premises will not be more plausible than the conclusion for the respondent, but then as an effective argument gets built up by the proponent, a set of premises is collected that are, as a group, of a favorable distribution of plausibility values so that they are collectively greater than the value of the conclusion.

Then, at the second stage, these premises are put into place and presented by the proponent in such a manner that, according to the rules of plausibility adjustment, they shift the value of the conclusion upward for the respondent. The argument is successful, in persuasion dialogue, when it persuades the respondent to become committed to the conclusion on the grounds that it is a plausible proposition, according to the rules for judging plausibility values of propositions.

The effective argument removes the respondent's doubt, even though the proponent's conclusion was originally subject to the respondent's doubt.

And the basic thing that is wrong with an argument that begs the question is that it is systematically useless to perform this function of argument.

But when we say that the conclusion *depends on* the premises in such an argument, or that a premise may *depend on* the conclusion, we do not mean that the one proposition implies the other (by deductive logic), we mean that without the one, the other would be subject to doubt (by a respondent in a context of dialogue). Dependency, in other words, should be seen as a fundamentally pragmatic conception in relation to the logic of begging the question as a fallacy.

When it is said that a proposition A *depends on* a set of propositions, $B_1, B_2, \ldots, B_i$, it means that (1) for a respondent in a context of dialogue, A is subject to reasonable doubt as an acceptable proposition, suitable for that respondent's commitment as a plausible proposition, in the absence of the securing of $B_1, B_2, \ldots, B_i$ as relatively plausible propositions for the respondent by the proponent of the argument with $B_1, B_2, \ldots, B_i$ as premises and A as conclusion; and (2) once these premises are secured as relatively plausible then a burden of proof will be shifted onto the respondent such that A must reasonably be accepted by him as plausible unless he immediately asks certain critical questions. The basic idea of dependency, so defined, allows for a certain characteristic openness. The respondent is not forced to accept the conclusion unconditionally or uncritically. Rather, a burden of proof is placed on him either to concede the conclusion or to show it is still subject to reasonable doubt by posing relevant critical questions. The tactic of attempting to force a respondent to accept such a conclusion in persuasion dialogue by forestalling or preventing the asking of critical questions is, in fact, a feature of an argument that can lead to its being declared fallacious, and then this is what needs to be considered at level three in weighing whether it is a case of *petitio principii* as a fallacy.

Whether a dependency relationship can be said to exist in the case of a particular argument is a question to be settled by the argument reconstruction, showing the structure of the argument as a linked argument in certain parts, as a convergent argument in other parts, and so forth. Utilizing the argument reconstruction technique in a particular case, a critic can then reach an informed evaluation of whether the premises can potentially be backed up by further argumentation in order to fulfill the burden of proof required to prove the conclusion. This judgment depends on the overall structure shown by the argument diagram, taking into account which premises are linked or convergent, and how convergent and serial arguments are put together in that structure.

This analysis of the dependency relation, taken along with the pragmatic analysis of the equivalence relation given in chapter four, section two, and with the definition of inevitability as a species of coercive tactic given in chapter eight, section seven, completes our analysis of the fallacy of begging the question in the context of persuasion dialogue. But what about the inquiry? Does it get the same tri-level analysis?

9. CIRCULAR ARGUMENT IN THE INQUIRY

The fallacy of *petitio principii* is a pragmatic error that relates to a context of dialogue. Most of the cases we have examined are cases where the primary context is that of persuasion dialogue. In these cases, *petitio principii* is a failure of the burden of proof to be realized, a failure to meet evidential priority. In this kind of context however, inevitability of the circle turned out to be very important because not all circular argumentation is fallacious, even if it fails to meet evidential priority.

In other contexts, however, circularity appears to be a more severe failure of argument in and of itself. In the cumulative inquiry, a circular argument tends to seem strongly unacceptable as a useful or appropriate kind of argument. The reason is that a circular argument does not contribute to the forward-moving kind of proving in the probative function of the inquiry, which starts from established propositions and moves ahead to prove other propositions as established, on the basis of the prior propositions.

Circularity by itself, without evidence of inevitability or failure of evidential priority, often seems to be enough, in an inquiry, to condemn an argument as inimical to the spirit of the undertaking. In this context, a circular argument could justifiably be said to be inappropriate, and perhaps even fallacious, wherever it occurs. For example, in Euclidean geometry, or in any axiomatic system of proof, or in many other contexts of scientific inquiry, circularity of a sequence of proofs is not tolerated as an acceptable proof.

There need be nothing wrong with circular reasoning in mathematical reasoning generally. An equivalence proof, for example, may be regarded as a kind of circular reasoning. First one proposition, B, is shown to follow from another proposition, A. And then, proving the other side of the equivalence, A is shown to follow from B. As long as it is clear that the program is to reason from A to B, and also from B to A, such a circular sequence is not vicious or fallacious.

However, the situation may be quite different if the program is to prove B from an established premise or assumption A, along with (only) other premises that have been previously assumed, or that follow from the given assumptions. In such a case, to assume B, the conclusion to be proved, might be highly erroneous. The reason is that the problem is to prove B from A, and therefore to assume B along with A would be to defeat the whole purpose of the project intended. The program, in this kind of case, is to prove B from A, without making additional assumptions that would short-circuit the project and make the "proof" pointless.

Euclidean geometry, or an axiomatic presentation of a theory, represents a structuring of proof so that what one is allowed to assume, for the purposes of the project, is tightly controlled. This is the whole purpose of the inquiry–to make the progress of reasoning unidirectional in a careful and controlled sequence from "old knowledge" to "new knowledge."

As the context of dialogue in a particular case shifts from that of the persuasion dialogue to that of the inquiry, there is less tolerance of circularity. As the geological case study of circular argumentation in chapter seven showed, tolerance of this kind of argumentation in scientific reasoning is not high, and any evidence that an argument is circular is greeted with considerable suspicion and worry. The case study of the Cartesian circle[11] was also particularly interesting because Descartes adopted a foundationalist method of philosophical inquiry modelled on Euclidean geometry as a style of proof. Here we have a kind of persuasion dialogue that shows very strong indications of a dialectical shift toward the context of an inquiry. Hence the argument in Descartes' *Meditations* is strongly susceptible to the criticism of *petitio principii,* should any evidence of circularity in his line of reasoning appear as a basis for objections.

In analyzing cases of circular reasoning in the context of an inquiry, the epistemic interpretation of *petitio* comes to predominate. The idea of an inquiry is that during its progress, certain propositions (premises) can be laid down as established by the evidence turned up at that point. Then the inquiry can make progress, or "leap ahead" by drawing further conclusions from these premises. For example, in a public inquiry into an air disaster, the investigators begin by amassing all the physical evidence they can find, and then trying to establish "the facts" on the basis of this evidence. At this stage, they will concentrate on putting together an account of what happened. For example, they may consult witnesses, and look at the physical evidence of the debris. Experts will be consulted on interpreting the evidence provided by the debris at the crash site. Then, typically, at a later stage of the inquiry, those conducting it will try to draw out inferences based on the existing findings at that point, and determine whether some relevant conclusions can be established as confirmed or not. For example, at this point, they may attempt to establish the cause of the crash.

The identifying factor of the inquiry as a context of reasoning is that it is intended to be cumulative. To say that a context of reasoning is *cumulative* means that if a proposition is established as true (or an acceptable commitment) at any point in the sequence of reasoning, then it must always remain true (or an acceptable commitment) at every succeeding point in the same sequence of reasoning. What this means, essentially, is that if a context of reasoning is cumulative, then once a proposition is established as true or acceptable, it can never subsequently be retracted in that context.

This point of difference illustrates the basic distinction between the inquiry and the persuasion dialogue as contexts of reasoning. In most kinds of persuasion dialogue, some form of retraction of commitment is possible. But in the inquiry, at least in theory, retraction is not supposed to be possible. For an inquiry has the goal of *proving* a conclusion beyond reasonable doubt, on the basis of the known evidence. The inquiry is designed to be a relatively permanent establishing of its conclusion.

Of course, in practice, inquiries don't always work that way. For example, the rhetoric of science as a collaborative enterprise paints a picture of scientific investigation as an inquiry that takes the greatest care to establish its conclusion with solemn finality. However, in fact, such scientific conclusions are always in the process of being revised and "improved." Hence, more realistically speaking, scientific reasoning is more often a kind of persuasion dialogue, even if a guarded and careful kind. But the ideal of scientific investigation is that of the cumulative inquiry. This is the model of reasoning that provides the goal, even if, inevitably, actual practices will often have to fall short of the goal.

A technical definition of cumulativeness was given in Woods and Walton (1978a, p. 84), based on the following four elements: (1) a set of points, which represent stages at which commitments are made in a sequence of reasoning; (2) an ordering relation that defines the sequence of points as an orderly thread of reasoning; (3) a set of propositions that are said to be true or false (commitments or not) at various points, and (4) a function that takes a pair composed of a point and a proposition onto a pair of truth-values. Then a system composed of these four elements is said to be *cumulative* if, and only if, for any points, a proposition has a particular truth-value at a given point, it has the same value at every successive point.

Many of the most difficult problems of evaluating whether circular reasoning commits the fallacy of begging the question arise because of retraction of commitments in dialogue. But in an inquiry, this kind of problem is totally eliminated, because retraction is not allowed. This feature makes the inquiry much simpler as a context for *petitio principii*. In fact, circular reasoning generally stands out much more sharply as an error in the inquiry than it does in the persuasion dialogue.

One formal model of the inquiry is the intuitionistic semantics of Kripke (1965), which uses a tree-structure to represent advancing states of knowledge in a sequence of reasoning. In a tree structure, there are no circles.[12] Hence it appears that in this particular formalization of the inquiry, circular reasoning is altogether banned.

The tree model utilized by Kripke represents propositions as being verified or not verified at different "evidential situations" or points of time at which we, the investigators, have information, which may change. For example, let G be the root, or first point in an inquiry. Let us say that a particular proposition, A, is verified at G. From G, let's say, there are two possibilities of advance open. We could "leap ahead" to point H_1, where both propositions A and C are verified. Or, we could go to point H_2, where, instead, propositions A and B are verified. Suppose the inquiry takes the second course. Then we may well gain enough new knowledge to advance to point H_4, where A, B, and C are all established. Or alternatively, we could go to H_3, where we have gained the knowledge to exclude ever verifying proposition C. This particular example of a Kripke tree structure is pictured in figure 8.2 (Woods and Walton, 1978a, p. 81).

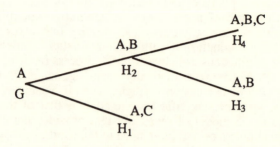

Figure 8.2

As you can see from figure 8.2, the Kripke model does not altogether bar every kind of reasoning that could be called circular. The step from point H_2 to H_3 could perhaps be called repetitive or circular. But it does bar the kind of explicit circularity where you could go from a given point and circle back to that same point. The tree structure never allows this "closed loop" kind of reasoning at all.

The Kripke model is only a very simplified model of the inquiry as a dynamic context of reasoning. But it does model some of the basic features of the inquiry, like cumulativeness and non-circularity of reasoning, very well.

What this means is that if the context of dialogue is that of an inquiry, rather than a persuasion dialogue, then you don't have to worry about the tactical element (level three) in order to pin down begging the question as a fallacy. If there is circular reasoning in an inquiry, and it violates evidential priority, then immediately a good case can be made out that the argument in question begs the question fallaciously.

However, there remains room for caution in these cases. In some cases, the textual and contextual evidence of an argument is clearly meant to be that of an inquiry. In such cases, the textual evidence, particularly indicator-words like "now we can establish" and so forth, are of key importance. It must be made clear, in any case, what conclusion the inquiry is supposed to prove. And it must be shown how the premises that have supposedly been established at any particular point in the inquiry are being used as a basis to leap ahead toward proving the conclusion. All this may not be so easy to do, in a particular case.

Hence, although the question of the fallaciousness of circular reasoning is theoretically simpler in the inquiry (as opposed to the persuasion dialogue), in fact analyzing a particular case of an argument as a purported inquiry can often be replete with as many textual uncertainties and problems of argument reconstruction.

The general point is that any critic who advances a charge of begging the question should be aware of the key differences between the inquiry and the persuasion dialogue.

10. SUMMARY OF THE NEW THEORY AND ITS PREDECESSORS

This chapter began with a review of the various theories and interpretations of the fallacy of begging the question, such as have been gleaned from the various sources on the subject. These viewpoints seemed heterogeneous, and often appeared to contradict each other. The most outstanding initial conflict was the apparent opposition of the epistemic and dialectical interpretations of the fallacy.

However, on deeper inspection, it emerged that these two interpretations could represent the *petitio* as it occurs in two separate, and equally legitimate, contexts of reasoned argument. Moreover, since both refer to ways of using reasoning, they can be portrayed as stemming from a common root notion–the idea that reasoning can be used to perform a probative function.

The probative function relates to the use of the premises to support the conclusion. Therefore criticism of the conclusion of a probative argument is different from criticism of the premises. The goal of the proponent, if he is to meet legitimate criticisms properly and fairly, should be to fulfill the probative function by overcoming, or replying to, reasonable criticisms. This he must not do by trying to proceed as though the conclusion were one of the premises, or as though one of the premises could only be proved by depending on a proof of the conclusion. For that would be to act, inappropriately, as though the legitimate challenge was really to the conclusion itself, rather than to his argument for it, making it impossible for the probative function of the argument to be fulfilled properly.

This probative function may initially appear to be a third theory, opposed to the epistemic and dialectical theories, but chapter eight showed how it can be interpreted as an underlying root notion to the epistemic and dialectical interpretations.

Finally, as summarized in figure 8.3, there were four other kinds of explanations of what is wrong with begging the question, and each of these could be interpreted as a kind of viewpoint, or attempt to explain the basis of the fallacy as a logical error of argumentation. These are the four bottom elements in figure 8.3. At first these explanations seem to contradict each other, and to be opposed to each other. But after analyzing them, we found that they could be portrayed as special ways of showing how the fallacy of begging the question, in a context of dialogue, can be pinned down as a fallacy or systematic tactic of deception in argumentation.

The new theory sees the fallacy of begging the question as a pragmatic failure of the probative function of argument in a context of dialogue. It allows for different contexts of dialogue, and consequently this probative failure can be given an epistemic interpretation in some contexts of dialogue and a dialectical interpretation in other contexts of dialogue.

STRUCTURE OF THEORIES OF BEGGING THE QUESTION

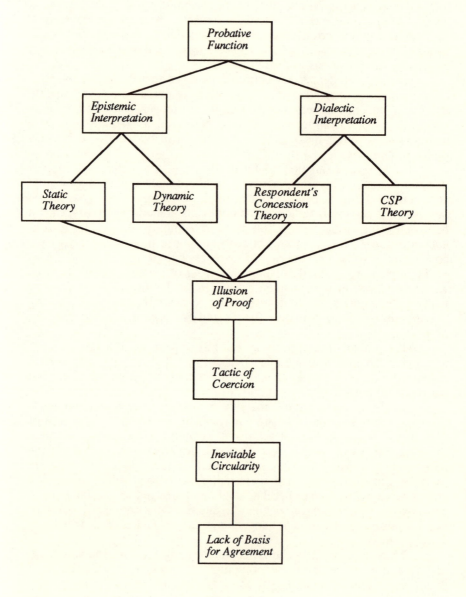

Figure 8.3

The new theory is generally a type of respondent's concession theory, except that it can allow for the CSP theory as a specialized type of explanation of what is fallacious about begging the question in certain special kinds of cases. The new theory is a dynamic theory, but under requirements of closure of dialogue, it can be interpreted in some cases as a static viewpoint as well.

One of the main aspects of the new theory is that it differentiates between begging the question as a fallacy (specifically, a sophistical tactics type of fallacy) and begging the question as a point of order, where no claim of fallacy is advanced. In the former type of case, the new theory requires that the argument be inevitably circular, but it interprets inevitability as an aspect of the tactics used by the proponent in a dialogue. Where the fallacy of begging the question occurs, the proponent has used circular reasoning as part of a tactic to avoid fulfilling the proper requirements of burden of proof in a dialogue, in such a manner as to create an illusion that the burden has been fulfilled. According to this theory, circular reasoning is not always fallacious.

Generalizing from the positive insights afforded by the valuable aspects of these theories and interpretations, chapter eight went on to construct a new theory of the fallacy of begging the question that incorporates these previously disparate elements into a unified analysis. One central focus of the new theory was the explanation of how and why begging the question can be a fallacy in persuasion dialogue.

An argument in persuasion dialogue can be useful to persuade or convince the respondent to whom it is directed only if the premises are already secured as commitments of the respondent so that for him they are more plausible than the conclusion that he doubts or questions. This is the implementation in persuasion dialogue of the probative function of argument, first described by Sextus Empiricus. This function generally means that in probative reasoning, there is a direction or flow of argument from the premises toward the conclusion. Certainly this is true in a persuasion dialogue because the premises must be commitments of the respondent that are, from his point of view, more plausible than the conclusion. They must be, to be useful to prove the conclusion to him successfully. It is true in other contexts of argument as well, where a requirement of evidential priority applies, that question-begging arguments are useless.

One kind of argument that may tend to violate this requirement that the premises be better secured as commitments is the circular argument. The problem posed by circular arguments is that the flow goes both ways– from premises to conclusion and from conclusion to premises. So the circular argument lacks this unity of direction, and that interferes with its ability to fulfill the probative function and meet a requirement of evidential priority.

But every circular argument of the form "A therefore A" is a deductively valid argument. Such an argument must be deductively valid because if A is true, then it is impossible for the same proposition, A, to be false. So if any argument is deductively valid, certainly one of the form

"A therefore A" is. But such a circular argument lacks a singleness of direction, and this may interfere with its being useful to persuade or convince a respondent who is not already convinced of the conclusion.

Whatever is wrong with circular arguments (when they are wrong), it is not failure of deductive validity. It is a pragmatic fault of argument separate from the semantic question of deductive validity. And it pertains to the requirement in persuasion dialogue that the premises be evidentially prior to the conclusion in the order of proof, according to an appropriate configuration in an argument diagram, which shows that the inevitability of the circle functions as a device of presentation of the argument systematically to block legitimate critical questioning of the argument.

Circular reasoning is not, in itself, inherently fallacious or objectionable as a kind of reasoning, in many instances. In fact, feedback as a type of practical reasoning is essential to goal-directed, knowledge-based, action-guiding reasoning. When an agent comes to perceive the consequences of his actions, and then corrects his way of proceeding on the basis that these consequences are not contributing to his goal, thus modifying his course of actions, this agent is reasoning in a circular (reflexive) fashion. But this kind of reasoning is "smart" or intelligent goal-directed (practical) reasoning. It is not inherently erroneous or fallacious *(per se)* as a type of reasoning. It is, in fact, a species of reasoning from consequences, and it can be represented as an instance of a legitimate and correct argumentation scheme.

Case 4.8 concerning the Hitler *Diaries* showed, however, that a circular argument can be wrong because it contains an error of reasoning. The problem here was that there was no evidence that either of the documents was genuine, and so the argument went in a circle. Here the circular argument was useless to convince a rational skeptic.

However, in this case, and also in the previous case of the flying saucers, the fault was not correctly diagnosed as the fallacy of begging the question. The error was one that the perpetrators were making against themselves, so to speak, as opposed to the use of a sophistical tactic to convince others. From the textual evidence, the fairest criticism is more one of incompetence than dishonesty. At any rate, the fault does not have to be one of committing the fallacy of begging the question, even though the use of a circular argument is evidence of an error of reasoning.

The case study of the ontological argument in chapter five shows that much depends on how the argument is reconstructed. One interpretation of it might have a different structure of the circular reasoning in the argument than another equally legitimate interpretation. Thus the first step should always be the argument diagram of the reasoning in the argument. And then the remaining job of evaluation concerns the assessment of the import of that reasoning as used in the dialogue.

To evaluate circular reasoning to determine whether the fallacy of begging the question has been committed or not, it was contended in this chapter that three levels of analysis must be carried through. At a second level, it must be determined whether the circular argument violates a rule of reasonable dialogue. Is it a failure to meet proper requirements of burden of proof? If so, it could be open to criticism as an error of reasoning. But then, at a third level, the question of whether the argument might be an instance of the fallacy of begging the question needs to be evaluated. These three levels are described and summarized as follows.

1. ARGUMENT RECONSTRUCTION: *Circular Reasoning?*
   What is the argument, the premises, the conclusion? The argument diagram shows the sequence of reasoning.

2. CONTEXT OF DIALOGUE: *Requirement of Evidential Priority?*
   Is it a persuasion dialogue, an inquiry, or some other kind of dialogue (according to the textual and contextual evidence)?

3. ARGUMENTATION TACTICS: *Fallacy, Blunder, or OK?*
   Given that the argument is circular, and is open to a procedural objection of begging the question, can it be pinned down as a fallacy of begging the question? Evaluate whether the circle is inevitable, using evidence from levels 1 and 2, and further evidence from the text and context that indicates the kind of tactics being used.

What the fallacy of begging the question consists in then is not circular reasoning *per se,* but the misuse of circular argumentation to block legitimate goals of dialogue. Such misuse involves the systematic violation of rules of dialogue. To be nailed down as an instance of the fallacy of begging the question, instances of such misuse must be properly documented as meeting the relevant theoretical criteria, according to the textual and contextual evidence available in a particular case where a charge of *petitio* is appropriate, or has been advanced by a critic.

According to the new theory of the fallacy of begging the question, both the dependency and the equivalence concepts of *petitio* can be deployed using tactics that try to force a sure-fire or inevitable victory in dialogue, leaving a respondent no option to raise the critical questions he is supposed to ask. In a dependency *petitio* argument, the person to whom the argument is directed in persuasion dialogue is supposed to infer that the conclusion is true or acceptable on the basis that the premises are true or acceptable, but because of the structure of the argument, and the way it is presented, this person may also have to accept the conclusion in order to be able to accept the premises. But this forced mutual dependency is a tactic to destroy or subvert the whole purpose of the argument, which is to present independent evidence that the respondent can accept, reject, or criticize on its merits, conveyed in the reasons given in the premises.

According to the *equivalence conception,* an argument is circular if one of the premises is identical to, or equivalent to, the conclusion of the argument. If you were to ask me to prove that Auckland is in New Zealand, and I replied "Auckland is in New Zealand, therefore Auckland is in New Zealand," then the premise and conclusion of my argument would be identical. Consequently, you would be quite justified in feeling that my argument is not a useful proof that Auckland is in New Zealand. And you would be fully entitled to reply that my argument fails to prove what it was supposed to prove, and is therefore pointless, as well as being inadequate as a convincing argument.

However, equivalence in this connection cannot adequately be defined as semantical equivalence, as we showed in chapter four, section two. What is required is pragmatic equivalence–the two propositions must amount to the same assertion, and both have the identical burden of proof in the context of the dialogue. To prove one is to prove the other, because both must represent the same commitment in the context of dialogue.

If I were to present you with a map and say "Look here. Auckland is in New Zealand. It's on the North Island. There it is on the map." then that would be the sort of evidence you might (with reason) not find objectionable on grounds of circularity. Why not? Because if you accept as a plausible presumption that this map is correct, then the map gives you a basis for argument that could be more plausible as a reason for accepting what you had found dubious or questionable before. Therefore, what is wrong or open to criticism about a circular argument when it begs the question is that it leaves no room open to provide a line of argument to premises that are potentially more acceptable, or less dubious, than the conclusion of the argument at issue, nevertheless sophistically portraying this hopeless argument as one that has fulfilled the probative function it was supposed to serve in the dialogue.

Another context where circularity is fallacious is in the special context of dialogue called the inquiry. This special context is one where it should be required in an argument that the premises be firmly established as better known to be true than the conclusion to be proved. This context, or one very like it, appears to be indicated in the remark of Aristotle (*Prior Analytics* 64 b 30) where it is required of a demonstration that the premises should be better known or established than the conclusion to be proved from them. In other words, Aristotle was saying that a *demonstration* is a special kind of argument where the premises are better known than the conclusion. Therefore, in terms of evidence or knowledge, the premises are prior to the conclusion in a demonstration. Hence it follows that the conclusion cannot at the same time be prior to the premises. The inquiry or demonstration is even more strongly inimical to circular reasoning, and apt to classify it as fallacious, than the persuasion dialogue. In certain structured contexts of scientific reasoning, for example in Euclidean geometry or in other axiomatic systems, or where experimental methods stress cumulative collection of verified results, circular reasoning is properly treated with intense suspicion as a potential source of error, confusion, or misdirection.

NOTES

1. See the list in chapter six, section four. The concrete results of these confusions are spelled out in greater detail in chapter seven.

2. See Woods and Walton (1982b, p. 598).

3. This duality in Aristotle's treatment was brought out very clearly by Hamblin (1970). See also Woods and Walton (1982a).

4. Note that the criterion for the fallacy of begging the question by Whately in the 1836 edition of the *Elements of Logic* (p. 184) is quite different from the version given in the ninth edition (1859).

5. See the outline of the views of Sextus in chapter one, section five.

6. De Rijk (1972, p. 168). See Hamblin (1970, p. 33) and Mackenzie (1984a).

7. Van Eemeren and Grootendorst (1984) would appear to generally support this point of view.

8. See Woods and Walton (1982a, p. 6).

9. The Kripke model is defined in chapter nine, section nine.

10. Walton (1986) and Hintikka (1987).

11. Chapter five, section four.

12. Harary (1969).

Bibliography

Acock, Malcolm. *Informal Logic: Examples and Exercises*. Belmont, Calif.: Wadsworth, 1985.

Aristotle. *The Works of Aristotle Translated into English*. Ed. W. D. Ross. Oxford: Oxford University Press, 1928.

Aristotle. *On Sophistical Refutations*. Trans. E. S. Forster. Loeb Classical Library Edition. Cambridge, Mass.: Harvard University Press; London: William Heinemann Ltd., 1955.

Arnauld, Antoine. *La Logique, ou l'Art de Penser*. 1662. Edition entitled *The Art of Thinking*. Trans. James Dickoff and Patricia James. New York: Bobbs-Merrill, 1964.

Barker, John A. "The Fallacy of Begging the Question." *Dialogue* 15 (1976): 241-55.

Barker, John A. "The Nature of Question-Begging Arguments." *Dialogue* 17 (1978): 490-98.

Barth, E. M. and E.C.W. Krabbe. *From Axiom to Dialogue*. New York: Walter De Gruyter, 1982.

Bartlett, Steven J. "Varieties of Self-Reference." In *Self-Reference: Reflections on Reflexivity*, ed. Steven J. Bartlett and Peter Suber, 5-28. Dordrecht, Holland: Martinus Nijhoff, 1987.

Basu, Dilip K. "A Question of Begging." *Informal Logic* 8 (1986): 19-26.

Bates, Frank. "Expert Evidence: Some Recent Cases." *Criminal Law Journal* 7 (1983): 278-88.

Beardsley, Monroe C. *Practical Logic*. New York: Prentice-Hall, 1950.

Beauchesne's Parliamentary Rules and Forms, 5th ed. Alistair Fraser. G.A. Birch, and W.F. Dawson (eds.), Toronto: The Carswell Co. Ltd., 1978.

Belnap, Nuel D., Jr. *An Analysis of Questions: Preliminary Report*. Santa Monica: Systems Development Corporation, 1963.

Bentham, Jeremy. *The Book of Fallacies*. 1838. In *The Works of Jeremy Bentham*, vol. 2, ed. John Bowring, 375-487. New York: Russell & Russell, 1962.

Biro, John. "Rescuing Begging the Question." *Metaphilosophy* 8 (1977).

Biro, John. "Knowability, Believability and Begging the Question: A Reply to Sanford." *Metaphilosophy* 15 (1984): 239-47.

Black, Max. *Critical Thinking: An Introduction to Logic and Scientific Method.* 2nd ed. Englewood Cliffs, N.J.: Prentice-Hall, 1952 [originally published in 1946].

Blair, J. Anthony. "Comments on Frans van Eemeren." *Text* 6 (1986): 17-24.

Bramer, M. A. "Expert Systems: The Vision and the Reality." *Research and Development in Expert Systems,* ed. M.A. Bramer, 1-12. Cambridge: Cambridge University Press, 1984.

Bratko, Ivan. *Prolog Programming for Artificial Intelligence.* Reading, Mass.: Addison-Wesley, 1986.

Brockhaus Enzyklopädie. Wiesbaden: F.A. Brockhaus, 1974.

Brown, Robert. "The Burden of Proof." *American Philosophical Quarterly* 7 (1970): 74-82.

Canada: House of Commons Debates (Hansard). Ottawa: Queen's Printer.

Cederblom, Jerry, and David W. Paulsen. *Critical Reasoning.* Belmont, Calif.: Wadsworth, 1982.

Chase, Stuart. *Guides to Straight Thinking.* New York: Evanston, Ill.; and London: Harper & Row, 1956.

Clifford, W. K. "The Will to Believe." *Contemporary Review* 30 (1877): 42-54.

Cohen, Morris R., and Ernest Nagel. *An Introduction to Logic and Scientific Method.* New York: Harcourt, Brace & World, 1934.

Colwell, Gary. "God, The Bible and Circularity." *Informal Logic* 11 (1989): 61-73.

Copi, Irving M. *Introduction to Logic.* 6th ed. New York: Macmillan, 1982.

Copi, Irving M. *Informal Logic,* 7th ed. New York: Macmillan, 1986.

Creighton, James Edwin. *An Introductory Logic.* New York: Macmillan, 1917.

Damer, T. Edward. *Attacking Faulty Reasoning.* Belmont, Calif.: Wadsworth, 1980.

DeMorgan, Augustus. *Formal Logic.* London: Taylor and Walton, 1847.

De Rijk, L. M., ed. *Peter of Spain: Tractatus (Sumule Logicales).* Assen, Holland: Van Gorcum, 1972.

Descartes, Rene. *The Philosophical Writings of Descartes.* Trans. John Cottingham, Robert Stoothoff, and Dugald Murdoch. Cambridge: Cambridge University Press, 1984.

Doney, Willis, ed. *Eternal Truths and the Cartesian Circle.* New York and London: Garland Publishing Co., 1987.

Duden: Das Grosse Wörterbuch der Deutschen Sprache. Mannheim: Bibliographisches Institut, 1981.

Encyclopedia Britannica. 10th ed. Article on "Geology" by R.H. Rastall, 168-73.

Encyclopaedia Britannica. 15th ed. Article on "Evidence" by Ronan E. Degnan, 905-16.

Engel, S. Morris. *With Good Reason: An Introduction to Informal Fallacies.* New York: St. Martin's Press, 1976.

Evans, J.D.G. *Aristotle's Concept of Dialectic.* London: Cambridge University Press, 1977.

Fearnside, W. Ward, and William B. Holther. *Fallacy: The Counterfeit of Argument.* Englewood Cliffs: Prentice-Hall, 1959.

Fogelin, Robert J. *Understanding Arguments: An Introduction to Informal Logic.* New York: Harcourt Brace Jovanovich, 1978.

Forsyth, Richard. *Expert Systems.* London: Chapman and Hall, 1984.

Freeman, James. "Dialectical Situations and Argument Analysis." *Informal Logic* 7 (1985): 151-62.

Galen. *Institutio Logica* (second century). Ed. and trans. John Spangler Kieffer. Baltimore: The Johns Hopkins Press, 1964.

Gardner, Martin. *Fads and Fallacies in the Name of Science.* New York: Dover Books, 1952.

Gilbert, Neal W. "Galen." In *The Encyclopedia of Philosophy,* ed. Paul Edwards, vol. 3, 261-62. New York: Macmillan, 1967.

Gough, James, and Christopher Tindale. "Hidden or Missing Premises." *Informal Logic* 7 (1985): 99-106.

Govier, Trudy. *Problems in Argument Analysis and Evaluation.* Dordrecht, Holland; and Providence, R.I.: Foris, 1987.

Hamblin, C. L. *Fallacies.* London: Methuen, 1970 reprinted by Vale Press, Newport News, Va. 1986.

Hamblin, Charles L. "Mathematical Models of Dialogue." *Theoria* 37 (1971): 130-55.

Harary, Frank. *Graph Theory.* Reading, Mass.: Addison-Wesley, 1969.

Harper, C. W., Jr. "Relative Age Inference in Paleontology." *Lethaia* 13 (1980): 239-48.

Harrah, David. "Formal Message Theory." In *Pragmatics of Natural Languages,* ed. Yejoshua Bar-Hillel. Dordrecht, Holland: Reidel, 1971.

Harrah, David. "Formal Message Theory and Non-Formal Discourse." In *Pragmatics of Language and Literature,* ed. Teun A. van Dijk. Amsterdam: North-Holland, 1976.

Hintikka, Jaakko. "The Logic of Information-Seeking Dialogues: A Model." In *Konzepte der Dialektik,* ed. Werner Becker and Wilhelm K. Essler, 212-31. Frankfurt am Main: Vittorio Klostermann, 1981.

Hintikka, Jaakko. "The Fallacy of Fallacies." *Argumentation* 1 (1987): 211-38.

Hoffman, Herbert C. "The Cross-Examination of Expert Witnesses." *Planning, Zoning, and Eminent Domain Institute* 8 (1979): 313-49.

Hoffman, Robert. "On Begging the Question at Any Time." *Analysis* 32 (1971): 51.

Hofstadter, Douglas R. "Metamagical Themas." *Scientific American* 246, no. 6 (June 1982): 16-24.

Hull, David L. "Circularity and Certainty in Evolutionary Taxonomy." *Evolution* 21 (1967): 174-89.

Hyslop, James H. *Logic and Argument.* New York: Charles Scribner's Sons, 1899.

Intelliware. *Experteach.* Software and Manual. Los Angeles: Intelligence Ware, Inc., 1986.

James, William. *The Will to Believe and Other Essays in Popular Philosophy.* London: Longmans Green, 1896.

Johnson, Oliver A. "Begging the Question." *Dialogue* 6 (1967): 135-50.

Johnson, Oliver A. "To Beg a Question: A Reply." *Dialogue* 7 (1968): 461-68.

Johnstone, Henry W., Jr. *Philosophy and Argument.* University Park: Pennsylvania State University Press, 1959.

Jones, Trevor, ed. *Harrap's Standard German and English Dictionary.* London: George G. Harrap & Co. Ltd., 1967.

Joseph, Horace W. B. *An Introduction to Logic.* 2d ed. Oxford: Oxford University Press, 1916.

Kapp, Ernst. *Greek Foundations of Traditional Logic.* New York: Columbia University Press, 1942.

Krabbe, Erik C. W. "Formal Systems of Dialogue Rules." *Synthese* 63 (1985): 295-328.

Kretzmann, Norman, ed. *William of Sherwood's Introduction to Logic* (thirteenth century). Minneapolis: University of Minnesota Press, 1966.

Kripke, Saul. "Semantical Analysis of Intuitionistic Logic I." In *Formal Systems and Recursive Functions,* ed. J. N. Crossley and M. Dummett. Amsterdam: North-Holland, 1965.

Latta, Robert, and Alexander MacBeath. *The Elements of Logic.* London: Macmillan, 1956.

Lewis, Charlton T., and Charles Short. *A Latin Dictionary.* Oxford: Clarendon Press, 1969.

Mackenzie, J. D. "Question-Begging in Non-Cumulative Systems." *Journal of Philosophical Logic* 8 (1979): 117-33.

Mackenzie, J. D. "Why Do We Number Theorems?" *Australasian Journal of Philosophy* 58 (1980): 135-49.

Mackenzie, J. D. "The Dialectics of Logic." *Logique et Analyse* 94 (1981): 159-177.

Mackenzie, J. D. "Confirmation of a Conjecture of Peter of Spain Concerning Question-Begging Arguments." *Journal of Philosophical Logic* 13 (1984a): 35-45.

Mackenzie, J. D. "Begging the Question in Dialogue." *Australasian Journal of Philosophy* 62 (1984b): 174-81.

Mackie, J. L. "Fallacies." In *The Encyclopedia of Philosophy,* vol. 3, ed. Paul Edwards, 169-79. New York: Macmillan, 1967.

McTaggart, John M. E. *Studies in Hegelian Cosmology.* Cambridge: Cambridge University Press, 1918.

Manicas, Peter T., and Arthur N. Kruger. *Logic: The Essentials*. New York: McGraw-Hill, 1976.

Manor, Ruth. "Dialogues and the Logics of Questions and Answers." *Linguistische Berichte* 73 (1981): 1-28.

Manor, Ruth. "Pragmatics and the Logic of Questions and Assertions." *Philosophica* 29 (1982): 45-96.

Maruyama, Magoroh. "The Second Cybernetics: Deviation-Amplifying Mutual Causal Processes." *Modern Systems Research for the Behavioral Scientist,* ed. Walter F. Buckley, 304-13. Chicago: Aldine Publishing Co., 1968.

Massey, Gerald. "The Fallacy Behind Fallacies." *Midwest Studies in Philosophy* 6 (1981): 489-500.

Mill, John Stuart . *A System of Logic*. London: Longmans Green, 1843.

Moore, Christopher W. *The Mediation Process*. San Francisco: Jossey-Bass Publishers, 1986.

Moore, James A., James A. Levin, and William C. Mann. "A Goal-Oriented Model of Human Dialogue." *American Journal of Computational Linguistics* 67 (1977): 1-54.

Noxon, James. "Question-Begging." *Dialogue* 6 (1968): 571-75.

The Oxford English Dictionary, vol. 4. Oxford: Clarendon Press, 1970.

Palmer, Humphrey. "Do Circular Arguments Beg the Question?" *Philosophy* 56 (1981): 387-94.

Perelman, Chaim. *The Realm of Rhetoric*. Notre Dame and London: University of Notre Dame Press, 1982.

R. H. Rastall, 'Geology,' *Encyclopaedia Britannica,* 10, 1956, 168-173.

Rescher, Nicholas. *Plausible Reasoning*. Assen-Amsterdam: Van Gorcum, 1976.

Rescher, Nicholas. *Dialectics*. Albany: State University of New York Press, 1977.

Rescher, Nicholas. "How Serious a Fallacy is Inconsistency?" *Argumentation* 1 (1987): 303-16.

Robinson, Daniel Sommer. *The Principles of Reasoning*. New York: Appleton-Century-Crofts, 1936.

Robinson, Richard. "Begging the Question, 1971." *Analysis* 31 (1971a): 113-17.

Robinson, Richard. "Arguing from Ignorance." *Philosophical Quarterly* 21 (1971b): 97-108.

Rosenberg, Jay F. *The Practice of Philosophy: A Handbook for Beginners*. Englewood Cliffs, N.J.: Prentice-Hall, 1978.

Rowe, William L. "The Ontological Argument." In *Reason and Responsibility,* 3rd ed. Ed. Joel Feinberg, 8-17. Encino, Calif.: Dickenson, 1975.

Russell, Bertrand. *The Problems of Philosophy*. New York: Oxford University Press, 1959.

Russell, Bertrand. "The Axiom of Infinity." In *Essays in Analysis,* ed. Douglas Lackey, 256-59. London: Allen and Unwin, 1973. [Originally published in the *Hibbert Journal* 2, 1904, 809-12].

Sacks, H., E.A. Schlegloff, and G. Jefferson. "A Simplest Systematics for the Organization of Turn Taking for Conversation." *Language* 50 (1974): 696-735.

Salmon, Wesley C. *Logic.* 3rd ed. Englewood Cliffs, N.J.: Prentice-Hall, 1984.

Sanford, David H. "Begging the Question." *Analysis* (1972): 197-99.

Sanford, David H. "The Fallacy of Begging the Question: A Reply to Barker." *Dialogue* 16 (1977): 485-98.

Sanford, David H. "Superfluous Information, Epistemic Conditions of Inference, and Begging the Question." *Metaphilosophy* 12 (1981): 145-58.

Schank, R. G. *Dynamic Memory.* Cambridge: Cambridge University Press, 1982.

Schank, Roger, and Robert Abelson. *Scripts, Plans, Goals and Understanding.* Hillsdale, N.J.: Lawrence Erlbaum Associates, 1977.

Sextus Empiricus. *Outlines of Pyrrhonism* (second-third century). Trans. R. G. Bury. London: Loeb Classical Library, 1933.

Sextus Empiricus. *Against the Logicians.* Trans. R. G. Bury. London: Loeb Classical Library, 1933.

Shoesmith, D. J., and T. J. Smiley. *Multiple-Conclusion Logic.* Cambridge: Cambridge University Press, 1978.

Sidgwick, Alfred. *Fallacies: A View of Logic from the Practical Side.* New York: D. Appleton & Co., 1884.

Sidgwick, Alfred. *The Application of Logic.* London: MacMillan, 1910.

Sidgwick, Alfred. *Elementary Logic.* Cambridge: Cambridge University Press, 1914.

Smith, Michael. "Virtuous Circles." *Southern Journal of Philosophy* 25 (1987): 207-20.

Snoeyenbos, Milton H. "Proofs and Begging the Question." *Informal Logic* 3 (1980): 13.

Sparkes, Alonzo. "Begging the Question." *Journal of the History of Ideas* 27 (1963): 462-63.

Spellman, Howard H. *Direct Examination of Witnesses.* Englewood Cliffs, N.J.: Prentice-Hall, 1968.

Sproule, J. Michael. "The Psychological Burden of Proof." *Communication Monographs* 43 (1976): 115-29.

Suber, Peter. "Logical Rudeness." In *Self-Reference: Reflections on Reflexivity,* ed. Steven J. Bartlett and Peter Suber, 41-67. Dordrecht, Holland: Martinus Nijhoff, 1987.

Toulmin, Stephen, Richard Rieke, and Allan Janik. *An Introduction to Reasoning.* New York: Macmillan, 1979.

Van Eemeren, Frans. "Dialectical Analysis as a Normative Reconstruction of Argumentative Discourse." *Text* 6 (1986): 1-16.

Van Eemeren, Frans H., and Rob Grootendorst. *Speech, Acts in Argumentative Discussions.* Dordrecht, Holland; and Cinnaminson, USA: Foris, 1984.

Van Eemeren, Frans H., and Rob Grootendorst. "Fallacies in Pragma-Dialectical Perspective." *Argumentation* 1 (1987): 283-302.

Van Eemeren, Frans H., and Rob Grootendorst. *Argumentation, Communication and Fallacies.* Unpublished typescript, 1989.

Waller, Bruce N. *Critical Thinking: Consider the Verdict.* Englewood Cliffs, N.J.: Prentice-Hall, 1988.

Walton, Douglas N. "Mill and DeMorgan on Whether the Syllogism is a *Petitio,*" *International Logic Review* 8 (1977): 57-68.

Walton, Douglas N. "The Circle in the Ontological Argument." *International Journal for Philosophy of Religion* 9 (1978): 193-218.

Walton, Douglas N. *"Petitio Principii* and Argument Analysis." In *Informal Logic: The First International Symposium,* ed. J. Anthony Blair and Ralph H. Johnson, 41-54. Inverness, Calif.: Edgepress, 1980.

Walton, Douglas N. *Logical Dialogue-Games and Fallacies.* Lanham, Md.: University Press of America, 1984.

Walton, Douglas N. *Arguer's Position.* Westport, Conn.: Greenwood Press, 1985a.

Walton, Douglas N. "Are Circular Arguments Necessarily Vicious?" *American Philosophical Quarterly* 22 (1985b): 263-74.

Walton, Douglas N. "What is a Fallacy?" In *Argumentation: Across the Lines of Discipline,* ed. Frans H. van Eemeren, Rob Grootendorst, J. Anthony Blair, and Charles A. Willard, 323-30. Dordrecht, Holland; and Providence, R.I.: Foris, 1986.

Walton, Douglas N. *Informal Fallacies: Towards a Theory of Argument Criticisms.* Amsterdam and Philadelphia: John Benjamins, 1987a.

Walton, Douglas N. "The *Ad Hominem* Argument as an Informal Fallacy." *Argumentation* 1 (1987b): 317-32.

Walton, Douglas N. "Burden of Proof." *Argumentation* 2 (1988): 233-54.

Walton, Douglas N. *Informal Logic: A Handbook for Critical Argumentation.* Cambridge: Cambridge University Press, 1989a.

Walton, Douglas N. *Question-Reply Argumentation.* Westport, Conn.: Greenwood Press, 1989b.

Walton, Douglas N., and Lynn M. Batten. "Games, Graphs and Circular Arguments." *Logique et Analyse* 106 (1984): 133-64.

Whately, Richard. *Elements of Logic.* New York: William Jackson, 1836.

Whately, Richard. *Elements of Logic.* 9th ed. New York: Sheldon & Co., 1859.

Whately, Richard. *Elements of Rhetoric.* Ed. Douglas Ehninger, Carbondale and Edwardsville: Southern Illinois University Press, 1963. Reprint of the seventh British edition published by John W. Parker in London, 1846.

Wilbanks, William Lee. "The New Obscenity." *Vital Speeches of the Day,* Aug. 15, 1988, 658-64.

Williams, Bernard. *Descartes: The Project of Pure Enquiry.* Harmondsworth: Penguin Books, 1978.

Williams, M. E. "Begging the Question?" *Dialogue* 6 (1968): 567-70.

Wilson, Thomas. *The Rule of Reason.* London: Grafton, 1552.

Windes, Russel R., and Arthur Hastings. *Argumentation and Advocacy*. New York: Random House, 1965.

Wittgenstein, Ludwig. *Tractatus Logico-Philosophicus*. London: Kegan Paul, 1947.

Woodbury, Hanni. "The Strategic Use of Questions in Court." *Semiotica* 48 (1984): 197-228.

Woods, John. 'Ad Baculum, Self-Interest and Pascal's Wager." In *Argumentation: Across the Lines of Discipline,* ed. Frans H. van Eemeren, Rob Grootendorst, J. Anthony Blair and Charles A. Willard, 343-349. Dordrecht, Holland; and Providence, R.I.: Foris Publications, 1987.

Woods, John, and Douglas Walton. *Petitio Principii," Synthese* 31 (1975a): 107-27.

Woods, John, and Douglas Walton. "Is the Syllogism a *Petitio Principii?" The Mill News Letter* 10 (1975b): 13-15.

Woods, John, and Douglas Walton. "Arresting Circles in Formal Dialogues." *Journal of Philosophical Logic* 7 (1978a): 73-90.

Woods, John, and Douglas Walton. "The Fallacy of *Ad Ignorantiam." Dialectica* 32 (1978b): 87-99.

Woods, John, and Douglas Walton. "Circular Demonstration and von Wright-Geach Entailment." *Notre Dame Journal of Formal Logic* 20 (1979): 768-72.

Woods, John, and Douglas Walton. "The *Petitio:* Aristotle's Five Ways." *Canadian Journal of Philosophy* 12 (1982a): 77-100.

Woods, John, and Douglas Walton. "Question-Begging and Cumulativeness in Dialectical Games." *Noûs* 4 (1982b): 585-605.

Woods, John, and Douglas Walton. *Argument: The Logic of the Fallacies*. Toronto: McGraw-Hill Ryerson, 1982c.

Woods, John, and Douglas Walton. *Fallacies: Selected Papers: 1972-1982*. Dordrecht, Holland: Foris, 1989.

Index

About the Author

DOUGLAS N. WALTON is Professor of Philosophy at the University of Winnipeg and Fellow-in-Residence of the Netherlands Institute of Advanced Study. He is the author of numerous works on informal logic and argumentation, including *Informal Fallacies, Informal Logic, Practical Reasoning,* and *Question-Reply Argumentation* (Greenwood Press, 1989).